GNOSTICISM AND LATER PLATONISM

SOCIETY
OF BIBLICAL
LITERATURE

SBL

SYMPOSIUM SERIES

Christopher R. Matthews, Editor

Number 12
GNOSTICISM AND LATER PLATONISM
edited by
John D. Turner and Ruth Majercik

John D. Turner and Ruth Majercik, editors

GNOSTICISM AND LATER PLATONISM

Themes, Figures, and Texts

Society of Biblical Literature
Atlanta

Gnosticism and Later Platonism

edited by
John D. Turner and Ruth Majercik

Copyright © 2000 by the Society of Biblical Literature

Library of Congress Cataloging-in-Publication Data

Gnosticism and later platonism : themes, figures, and texts / John D. Turner and Ruth Majercik, editors.
  p. cm. — (SBL symposium series ; no. 12)
Includes bibliographical references.
ISBN 0-88414-035-0 (pbk. : alk. paper)
  1. Gnosticism—Congresses. 2. Platonists—Congresses. 3. Neoplatonism—Congresses. I. Turner, John D., 1938– II. Majercik, Ruth Dorothy. III. Symposium series (Society of Biblical Literature) ; no. 12.
B638.G587 2000
186'.4—dc21   00-049244
          08 07 06 05 04 03 02 01 00 5 4 3 2 1

Printed in the United States of America
on acid-free paper

CONTENTS

PREFACE

This volume is a collection of ten papers originally presented at sessions of the Gnosticism and Later Platonism Seminar held from 1993–1998 in connection with Annual Meetings of the Society of Biblical Literature. The idea of a Seminar devoted exclusively to the relation between Gnosticism and later Platonism grew out of earlier discussions, panels, and presentations on this theme in the context of other groups and sections within the Society of Biblical Literature and the American Academy of Religion, notably the SBL Nag Hammadi and Gnosticism Section and the AAR Platonism and Neoplatonism Group. John D. Turner was responsible for organizing the Seminar and bringing together a steering committee that included himself, Robert M. Berchman, Jay Bregman, John P. Kenney, Michael A. Williams, and Ruth Majercik. Ruth Majercik served as Chair of the Seminar during its six-year term.

In organizing the Seminar, a main objective was to bring together a group of well-known scholars with expertise in the areas of Gnosticism and/or later Platonism (i.e., Middle Platonism and Neoplatonism) from a variety of disciplines and methodologies who could bring a diversity of views and approaches to the general problematic of the Seminar. This was accomplished by attracting scholars from within the AAR and SBL as well as reaching out to newcomers who have now become members of these societies. The core group of active participants each year consisted of approximately sixteen members with an average of twenty auditors attending each session. In structuring our sessions, we initially decided that we should have two papers presented each year on a single topic with two respondents. The purpose was to have each presenter analyze a given topic from the perspective of his or her expertise in Gnosticism or Platonism; the respondents would reply in a similar manner. In addition, each presenter was also asked to incorporate the other perspective to the degree that he or she could, with the understanding that we did not expect our participants to be equally knowledgeable in both areas. In some years this routine was varied by having a single presenter and two respondents so that certain issues could be explored in more detail. This method resulted in a great deal of creative thinking and discussion on the part of our participants. During the course of the Seminar, most of the presenters also had an opportunity to act as a respondent. Additional respondents were John

Sieber, Birger Pearson, and Ruth Majercik. Due to the length of the volume and other considerations, we were not able to include the remarks (some quite extensive) of the respondents; however, many of their critical comments have been addressed in the final versions of papers.

The topic for each session was mutually decided upon during our annual business meetings, with the various topics generally reflecting the current research interests of our presenters. The topics include: Platonic and gnostic doctrines of matter (Einar Thomassen and Kevin Corrigan); gnostic ritual and Neoplatonic theurgy (John D. Turner and Gregory Shaw); the case for a pre-Plotinian Middle Platonic setting for the *Anonymous Commentary on the Parmenides* and the Nag Hammadi Sethian treatises *Zostrianos* and *Allogenes* (Kevin Corrigan and John D. Turner); the relationship between the metaphysics of Iamblichus and the Platonizing Sethian treatises, especially *Marsanes* (John Finamore); Platonic and gnostic uses of negative theology (John P. Kenney and Michael A. Williams); and the nature of Providence in Plotinus and Sethian Gnosticism (Frederic M. Schroeder).

In preparing the volume for publication, John D. Turner and Ruth Majercik were responsible for editing the papers in cooperation with the authors. They also compiled the bibliography. An earlier version of Gregory Shaw's paper originally appeared in *The Journal of Neoplatonic Studies,* whose publisher has authorized its appearance here in revised form. The editors wish to thank the Society of Biblical Literature for sponsoring our Seminar and the SBL Symposium Series under the direction of Gail O'Day for accepting our collected papers for publication.

R. M. and J. D. T

ABBREVIATIONS

Primary Sources

1 En.	1 Enoch
2 Clem.	2 Clement
2 En.	2 Enoch
Acts Pet.	Acts of Peter
Acts Phil.	Acts of Philip
Acts Thom.	Acts of Thomas
Alcinous/Alkinoos/Alcinoos (= Albinus)	
Did.	Didaskalikos
Alexander of Aphrodisias	
De An.	De anima
In Metaph.	In Metaphysica
Ap. John	Apocryphon of John
Apoc. Adam	Apocalypse of Adam
Apoc. Mos.	Apocalypse of Moses
Apuleius Metam.	Metamorphoses
Aristotle	
An. post.	Analytica posteriora
De an.	De anima
Eth. nic.	Ethica nicomachea
Gen. an.	De generatione animalium
Gen. corr.	De generatione et corruptione
Metaph.	Metaphysica
Mot. an.	De motu animalium
Phys.	Physica
Athanasius Apol. sec.	Apologia secunda (= Apologia contra Arianos)
Calcidius In Tim.	In Timaeum
Chald. Or.	Chaldean Oracles
Clement of Alexandria	
Exc.	Excerpta ex Theodoto
Strom.	Stromateis
Corp. herm.	Corpus hermeticum
Damascius	
Dub. et Sol.	Dubitationes et Solutiones
Princ.	De Principiis

Did.	*Didache*
Epiphanius *Pan.*	*Panarion (Adverses haereses)*
Eugnostos	*Eugnostos the Blessed*
Exeg. Soul	*Exegesis on the Soul*
Gos. Eg.	*Gospel of the Egyptians*
Gos. Phil.	*Gospel of Philip*
Gos. Thom.	*Gospel of Thomas*
Gos. Truth	*Gospel of Truth*
Hippolytus	
El.	*Elenchos*
Ref.	*Refutatio*
Homer *Il.*	*Iliad*
Hyp. Arch.	*Hypostasis of the Archons*
Iamblichus	
DA	*De anima*
In Nicom. Ar.	*In Nicomachi Arithmeticam*
In Phaedr.	*In Phaedrum*
In Phil.	*In Philebum*
Myst.	*De mysteriis*
Theol. Arith.	*Theologumena Arithmeticae*
John Lydus *Mens.*	*De mensibus*
Justin Martyr	
1 Apol.	*Apologia*
Dial.	*Dialogue with Trypho*
Macrobius *In Somn. Scip.*	*In Somnium Scipionis*
Marius Victorinus *Ar.*	*Adversus Arium*
Nicomachus of Gerasa	
Arith. Intro.	*Arithmetica Introductio*
Odes Sol.	*Odes of Solomon*
Orig. World	*On the Origin of the World*
Origen	
Cant.	*In Canticum canticorum*
Cels.	*Contra Celsum*
Comm. Jo.	*Commentarii in evangelium Joannis*
Philo	
Abr.	*De Abrahamo*
Det.	*Quod deterius potiori insidari soleat*
Fug.	*De fuga et inventione*
QG	*Quaestiones et solutiones in Genesin*
Somn.	*De somniis*
Philostratus *Vit. Apoll.*	*Vita Apollonii*
Plotinus *Enn.*	*Enneads*
Plato	

Phaed.	*Phaedo*
Phaedr.	*Phaedrus*
Pol.	*Politicus*
Rep.	*Republic*
Soph.	*Sophista*
Symp.	*Symposium*
Tim.	*Timaeus*
Plutarch	
An. procr.	*De animae procreatione in Timaeo*
Is. Os.	*De Iside et Osiride*
Gen. Socr.	*De genio Socratis*
Quaest. plat.	*Quaestiones platonicae*
Porphyry	
Abst.	*De Abstinentia*
De regressu an.	*De regressu animae*
Historia Phil.	*Historia Philosophiae*
In Parm.	Anonymous [Porphyrius?] *In Parmenidem commentaria*
Sent.	*Sententiae ad intelligibilia ducentes*
Vit. Pyth.	*Vita Pythagorae*
Priscianus	see Simplicius
Proclus	
Elem. Theol.	*Elements of Theology*
In Tim.	*In Timaeum*
In Parm.	*In Parmenidem*
Plat. Theol.	*Platonic Theology*
Psellus *Hypotyp.*	*Hypotyposis*
Sextus Empiricus	
Math.	*Adversus mathematicos*
Simplicius *In phys.*	*In physica*
[Simplicius] (Priscianus?)	
In. de anima	*In Aristotelis de anima*
Steles Seth	*Three Steles of Seth*
Stobaeus *Anth.*	*Anthologus*
Syrianus *In Metaph.*	*In Metaphysica*
T. Levi	*Testament of Levi*
Tatian *Or. Graec.*	*Oratio ad Graecos*
Tertullian	
Bapt.	*De baptismo*
Herm.	*Adversus Hermogenem*
Res.	*De resurrectione carnis*
Val.	*Adversus Valentinianos*
Theon of Smyrna *Exp.*	*Expositio*

Thund.	*Thunder: Perfect Mind*
Tri. Trac.	*Tripartite Tractate*
Trim. Prot.	*Trimorphic Protennoia*
Val. Exp.	*A Valentinian Exposition*
Zost.	*Zostrianos*

Secondary Sources

ANRW	*Aufstieg und Niedergang der römischen Welt*. Edited by H. Temporini and W. Haase. Berlin: de Gruyter, 1972–.
BCNHE	Bibliothèque copte de Nag Hammadi, Section "Études"
BCNHT	Bibliothèque copte de Nag Hammadi, Section "Textes"
CQ	*Classical Quarterly*
CUA: SCA	Catholic University of America: Studies in Christian Antiquity
EPRO	Études préliminaires aux religions orientales dans l'empire romain
FRLANT	Forschungen zur Religion und Literatur des Alten und Neuen Testaments
HR	*History of Religions*
HSCP	Harvard Studies in Classical Philology
HTR	*Harvard Theological Review*
JHS	*Journal of Hellenic Studies*
JR	*Journal of Religion*
JRH	*Journal of Religious History*
JRS	*Journal of Roman History*
JTS	*Journal of Theological Studies*
LCL	Loeb Classical Library
NHLE	*The Nag Hammadi Library in English*. Edited by J. M. Robinson. 3d rev. ed. Leiden: Brill; San Francisco: Harper & Row, 1988.
NHMS	Nag Hammadi and Manichaean Studies [= NHS]
NHS	Nag Hammadi Studies
NovT	*Novum Testamentum*
PW	*Paulys Realencyclopädie der classischen Altertumswissenschaft*. Edited by G. Wissowa. Stuttgart: J. B. Metzler, 1894-1972.
REG	*Revue des études grecques*
RSPT	*Revue des sciences philosophiques et théologiques*
RTP	*Revue de théologie et de philosophie*
SAC	Studies in Antiquity and Christianity
SBLDS	Society of Biblical Literature Dissertation Series
SBLSP	Society of Biblical Literature Seminar Papers
SC	Sources chrétiennes
SHR	Studies in the History of Religions

SJLA	Studies in Judaism in Late Antiquity
SVF	*Stoicorum veterum fragmenta.* H. von Arnim. 4 vols. Leipzig: Teubner, 1903–1924.
TF	*Theologische Forschung*
ThH	Théologie historique
TLZ	*Theologische Literaturzeitung*
TS	Texts and Studies
TU	Texte und Untersuchungen
TUGAL	Texte und Untersuchungen zur Geschichte der altchristlichen Literatur
TZ	*Theologische Zeitschrift*
VC	*Vigiliae Christianae*
ZNW	*Zeitschrift für die neutestamentliche Wissenschaft*
ZTK	*Zeitschrift für Theologie und Kirche*

The Derivation of Matter in Monistic Gnosticism

Einar Thomassen
University of Bergen

In his article "The Platonism of the *Tripartite Tractate* (NHC I,5)," John Peter Kenney has compared the ontological structure of this Valentinian treatise with various forms of Middle Platonism. He concludes that "the theology of the *Tripartite Tractate* is closest in its philosophical design to the sort of Middle Platonism represented by Albinus (Alkinoos) or Numenius."[1] This conclusion is based on the following elements of comparison:

(1) in *Tripartite Tractate*, the aeons are represented as the thoughts of a self-thinking Father, in the same way that the ideas are the thoughts of a noetic First God in these Platonists;

(2) in both systems this god and the way he generates (i.e., by self-contemplation) are distinct from a second, demiurgic figure who shapes the cosmos;

(3) the Logos, as the fallen aeon, is restored though contemplation in the same way that lower hypostases are united with the higher in Platonism.

The pertinence of these *rapprochements* is, I think, beyond doubt. But once they have been established, further questions arise. Granted that those similarities exist, how are we to account for the no less real *dissimilarities* between these Middle Platonists and the Valentinian system of *Tripartite Tractate?* It is one of these dissimilarities that forms the topic of this paper: the position of Matter. Albinus/Alkinoos treats Matter as a principle (*Did.* 163.11 Hermann; τῆς πρώτης ὕλης 171.43 H.). The same is the case with Numenius, for whom Matter is the same as the Dyad, and is *sine ortu et generatione* (frg. 52.10 des Places = Calcidius, *In Tim.* 295). *Tripartite Tractate*, however, denies explicitly that there can be any ὕλη existing along with the Father from the beginning (53,31–32). Instead, the tractate's protological myth offers a theory that explains Matter as deriving from something that exists prior to it: Matter is brought into existence by the "presumptuous thought" of that aeon that *Tripartite Tractate* calls "the

---

[1] J. P. Kenney, "The Platonism of the *Tripartite Tractate* (NHC I,5)," in *Neoplatonism and Gnosticism* (ed. Richard T. Wallis and Jay Bregman; Albany: SUNY Press, 1992), 200.

Logos." This "thought" gives rise to numerous chaotic powers
(75,17–80,11). Upon seeing this, the Logos repents, and his repentance
produces a new set of powers, superior to the first, which they combat
(80,11–85,15). As a result of the struggle between the two kinds of powers, those of presumption and those of repentance, "matters of various
sorts"[2] (85,10) are produced.

A theory about the origin of Matter forms part of all the attested vari-
ants of the Valentinian system. According to the Valentinian model system
offered by Irenaeus, the material substance from which the world was created originated in the passions of Sophia, specified as sorrow, fear, and
perplexity: ταύτην σύνταξιν καὶ οὐσίαν τῆς ὕλης γεγενῆσθαι λέγουσιν, ἐξ
ἧς ὅδε ὁ κόσμος συνέστηκεν (Irenaeus *Haer.* 1.4.2).[3]

This is not a theory that is specific to Valentinianism. As Hans Jonas
has put it, the theory "that no original world of darkness or of matter is
assumed to oppose the primal being, but that the dualism of existing reality is derived from an inner process within the one divinity itself" is "a distinctive feature of the Syrian and Alexandrian *gnosis* and its major
difference from the Iranian type of gnostic speculation, which starts from
a dualism of pre-existent principles."[4] An explicit assertion of this kind of
theory can be found in NHC II,5 (somewhat misnamed by some modern
editors as *On the Origin of the World*):

> Seeing that everybody, gods of the world and mankind, says that nothing
> existed prior to chaos, I in distinction shall demonstrate that they are all mis-
> taken, because they are not acquainted with the origin of chaos, nor with its
> root. Here is the demonstration. How well it suits all men, on the subject of
> chaos, to say that it is a kind of darkness! But in fact it comes from a shadow,
> which has been called by the name darkness. And the shadow comes from
> a product that has existed since the beginning. It is, moreover, clear that it

---

[2] ϨⲚϨⲨⲖⲎ ⲈⲨϢⲂⲂⲒⲀⲈⲒⲦ, probably < *ποικίλαι ὕλαι; this has Platonist connotations, going back to *Tim.* 50d5 (cf. *Chald. Or.* frg. 34 des Places; Clement of Alexandria *Exc.* 50.1; Irenaeus *Haer.* 1.4.1).

[3] Cf. *Haer.* 1.2.3: ἐντεῦθεν λέγουσι πρώτην ἀρχὴν ἐσχηκέναι τὴν οὐσίαν τῆς ὕλης, ἐκ
τῆς ἀγνοίας καὶ τῆς λύπης καὶ τοῦ φόβου καὶ τῆς ἐκπλήξεως (this is an interpolation
coming from a different source than the one used by Irenaeus for his main account);
1.8.4 (parable of the lost sheep): πλάνην δὲ τὴν ἐκτὸς πληρώματος ἐν τοῖς πάθεσι δια-
τριβὴν, ἐξ ὧν γεγονέναι τὴν ὕλην ὑποτίθενται; Clement of Alexandria *Exc.* 67.4 τῆς
ἄνω θηλείας ... ἧς τὰ πάθη κτίσις γέγονεν, τῆς καὶ τὰς ἀμόρφους οὐσίας προβαλλού-
σης. Irenaeus returns to this doctrine when he seeks to refute the Valentinian theories
in Book 2: *a praedictis passionibus emisit tantam conditionis materiam* (*Haer.* 2.10.3;
cf. the whole of 10.3–4); *materiae emissio et reliquae mundi fabricatio ... ex passione
et ignorantia volunt substantiam habere* (2.13.7; also cf. 2.18.7; 2.19.4; 2.20.5).

[4] H. Jonas, *The Gnostic Religion* (Boston: Beacon, 1963), 105.

(viz., the product) existed before chaos came into being, and that the latter is posterior to the first product. (97,24–98,7; trans. Bethge et al. in *NHLE*)

It is then explained that this first product arose as a likeness resembling the primeval light, out of the volition of Pistis Sophia (98,13–16). NHC II,5 is not Valentinian, and the general theory about the nonoriginality of Matter was not invented by the Valentinians. But we shall argue that it was the Valentinians, more than any other group of gnostics, who made use of a specific set of concepts derived from the philosophical schools to express the theory.

The Valentinian doctrine that Matter, and subsequently the world, originates from the passions of Achamoth struck the polemical mind of Tertullian, who ridiculed the Valentinians for this fantastic innovation. Here indeed, he says, was something new to be learned for both Pythagoreans and Stoics, and even for Plato.[5] Tertullian doubtless assumes that all the schools of philosophy regard Matter as an unoriginate first principle. In this view Tertullian is, generally speaking, correct. The Pythagoreans were traditionally known to propound a dualism between the Monad and the Dyad-ἄπειρον, the Peripatetics opposed Form and Matter, and the Stoa similarly Logos and ἄποιος ὕλη. The Platonists, of course, taught a tripartition of God, the Ideas, and Matter. This is the model to which Albinus/Alkinoos and Numenius adhere as well.

However, Numenius also informs us that certain Pythagoreans take a different view:

> But certain Pythagoreans have not properly grasped the force of this theory. For them, this indeterminate and unlimited Dyad is itself brought forth from the single Monad, when the Monad withdraws from its nature and wanders into the condition of the Dyad [*etiam illam indeterminatam et immensam duitatem ab unica singularitate institutam recedente a natura sua singularitate et in duitatis habitum migrante*]. (frg. 52.15–19 des Places = Calcidius *In Tim.* 295)

Numenius has only scorn for this doctrine, which has the Monad unaccountably disappear and turn into the Dyad, thus transforming God into Matter. Numenius's testimony, however, is only one of several that attest to the existence in Pythagorean circles of monistic theories attempting a derivation of the Dyad-Matter from the Monad.[6] These testimonies begin with

---

[5] *Age nunc discant Pythagorici, agnoscant Stoici, Plato ipse, unde materia, quam innatam uolunt, et originem et sustantiam traxerit in omnem hanc struem mundi; quod nec Mercurius ille Trismegistus, magister omnium physicorum, recogitauit* (Tertullian *Val.* 15.1).

[6] Cf. A.-J. Festugière, *La révélation d'Hermès Trismégiste*, vol. 4: *Le Dieu inconnu et la gnose* (Paris: Librairie Lecoffre, 1954), chs. 2 and 3, in particular pp. 36–40;

the Pythagorean *Hypomnemata* quoted by Alexander Polyhistor around 80 B.C.E.,[7] and further include Eudorus of Alexandria (first cent. B.C.E.),[8] Moderatus of Gades (end of first century C.E.),[9] the report in Sextus Empiricus 10.248ff., and other Neopythagoreans such as Nicomachus of Gerasa. (This dossier is not exhaustive.) This monistic type of Pythagoreanism thus shares with Valentinianism, as well as with Neoplatonism, the view that matter has secondary, or derived, existence.

According to this Neopythagorean theory, matter, in the sense of the material from which the sensible bodies of the cosmos are made, is not derived directly from the first principle (called the Monad, or the One) but from the principle, or idea of matter, the (Indefinite) Dyad, which in turn originates in the first principle. The Indefinite Dyad (ἀόριστος δυάς) is of course the principle of plurality, extension, formlessness, movement, etc., which Plato took over from the old Pythagoreans and developed into a major feature of his oral teaching and which continued to play an important role in the subsequent Platonist tradition. But whereas Plato and the Old Academy considered the Dyad an independent principle, the Neopythagorean trends with which we are dealing here inserted it into a monistic system of derivation.

In Valentinianism as well, cosmogonic matter only comes into being at the end of a process. The main feature of this process is the passion of Sophia. Is it possible, then, that the passion of Sophia here serves to express the same idea as the Dyad in monistic Pythagoreanism? In my view there exists conclusive evidence that these Neopythagorean theories about the derivation of matter were known to the Valentinian theologians and that they formed a source from which Valentinian systems were persistently built. This evidence consists in a series of Neopythagorean technical terms that occur in these systems and that can be shown to express the same ontological notions.[10]

H. J. Krämer, *Der Ursprung der Geistmetaphysik* (Amsterdam: B. R. Grüner, 1967), 320–21, 330–35; J. M. Rist, "Monism: Plotinus and Some Predecessors," *Harvard Studies in Classical Philology* 69 (1965): *passim;* J. M. Dillon, *The Middle Platonists* (Ithaca, N.Y.: Cornell University Press, 1977), 120–21, 126–29, 342–61.

[7] In Diogenes Laertius, 7.25.

[8] In Simplicius *In phys.* 181.10ff. Diels. The One as cause of Matter also figures in Eudorus's emended version of Aristotle's *Metaph.* A 6, 988a10–11, quoted by Alexander of Aphrodisias *In Metaph.* ad loc., 59.1 Hayduck.

[9] Simplicius *In phys.* 230.34ff. Diels.

[10] In what follows I draw on my previously published article "The Philosophical Dimension in Gnosticism," in *Understanding and History in Arts and Sciences* (ed. Roald Skarsten et al.; Acta Humaniora Universitatis Bergensis 1; Oslo: Solum, 1991), 69–79.

1. *"Audacity"* (τόλμη)

This is the one term that has long been recognized as shared by the Valentinians and the Neopythagorean-Platonist tradition. It is well known that τόλμη, which qualifies the passion of Sophia in Irenaeus *Haer.* 1.2.2, also occurs in Plotinus, who uses it generally (in the form τόλμα) to describe the self-positing of a lower hypostasis as distinct from a higher one.[11] Plotinus took over this term from the Neopythagoreans, who employed it as an epithet of the Dyad. It refers to the breaking loose of the Dyad from the Monad.[12] Plotinus used it as a way of expressing that all emanation has a dyadic aspect. In Valentinianism the idea, if not perhaps the term itself, is also found in *Tri. Trac.* 76,19–20, "he acted highmindedly" (ⲁϥⲉⲓⲣⲉ ϩⲛ̄ⲟⲩⲙⲛ̄ⲧⲛⲟϭ ⲙ̄ⲙⲉⲩⲉ), as well as in the references to the ἐνθύμησις or ἔννοια of Sophia in other sources. The Valentinians undoubtedly drew on the same sort of sources as Plotinus in using the term. But, as we shall try to show in what follows, this is not an isolated example nor a case of merely coincidentally shared vocabulary.

2. *"Extension"* (ἔκτασις)

To characterize the Dyad the term "extension" (ἐκτείνειν/ἔκτασις) is used in Sextus Empiricus *Math.* 10.277: The One is always delimiting, whereas the Dyad becomes two and extends the numbers into an unlimited multitude (τοῦ μὲν ἑνὸς ἀεὶ περατοῦντος τῆς δὲ ἀορίστου δυάδος δύο γεννώσης καὶ εἰς ἄπειρον πλῆθος τοὺς ἀριθμοὺς ἐκτεινούσης). The same term occurs in Moderatus of Gades, when he describes the entity he calls "Quantity," which in fact is his name for the Dyad. "Quantity" is characterized by "privation, breaking loose, extension and severance" (στέρησιν καὶ παράλυσιν καὶ ἔκτασιν καὶ διασπασμόν, Simplicius *In phys.* 230.19–20 Diels).[13] In later sources the word occurs not infrequently.[14]

The term ἔκτασις can also be used to describe the movement of the Monad itself from oneness to plurality, as in the Pseudo-Clementine

---

[11] A presentation of the entire philosophy of Plotinus has been built around this concept by N. Baladi, *La pensée de Plotin* (Initiation philosophique 92; Paris: Les presses des universités de France, 1970).

[12] Cf. Krämer, 321 n. 483; Henry's and Schwyzer's note on *Enn.* 5.1 [10].1.4 in P. Henry and H.-R. Schwyzer, eds., *Plotini Opera* (3 vols.; Scriptorum classicorum bibliotheca Oxoniensis; Oxford: Clarendon Press, 1964–1982).

[13] Moderatus makes a distinction between Quantity as such (ποσότης) and Quantity (ποσόν) as the matter (ὕλη) of bodies, the first serving as the paradigm of the latter. It is more precisely to this last Quantity-as-Matter that the description quoted refers, but it is apparently intended to be equally applicable to the more original concept.

[14] Iamblichus *In Nicom. Ar.* 10.12 Pistelli; [Iamblichus], *Theol. Arith.* 13.16–17 de Falco; Proclus *Elem. Theol.* prop. 128 Dodds, τὴν εἰς πλῆθος ἔκτασιν.

Homilies 224.34 (Rehm): κατὰ γὰρ ἔκτασιν καὶ συστολὴν ἡ μονὰς δυὰς εἶναι νομίζεται; cf. ibid., 234.18: ἀπ' αὐτοῦ εἰς ἄπειρον ἔκτασιν. In Christian trinitarian theology the Sabellians and Marcellus of Ancyra took up the term in order to explain how God by extension and spreading out (πλατύνειν) is a Triad as well as a Monad.[15]

It is this precise term, we believe, that is put to use in Irenaeus's Valentinian model system to describe the effect of the passion of Sophia. On account of her unfulfillable desire for the Father, it is said, Sophia "extended herself indefinitely" (ἐκτεινόμενον ἀεὶ ἐπὶ τὸ πρόσθεν, Irenaeus *Haer*. 1.2.2; ἐκτεινομένης αὐτῆς καὶ εἰς ἄπειρον ῥεούσης τῆς οὐσίας, 1.3.3). In the latter passage we note also the presence of two other Pythagorean terms as well: ἄπειρον is of course the traditional Pythagorean word describing the indefiniteness of the Dyad. ῥεῦσις, "flowing," is a word used to express how the dyadic line issues from the monadic point.[16] Thus, by describing the passion of Sophia as producing an extension into indefiniteness the Valentinians cast into the form of a tragic myth the Neopythagorean theory of the derivation of plurality from the Monad through the Indefinite Dyad.

3. "Passion"

An objection that might be raised against this interpretation is that in the Valentinian systems Sophia does not originate directly from the Father and that her generation therefore is not comparable to the way that the Dyad derives from the Monad/One in Neopythagoreanism. Instead, Sophia is only one among a multitude of aeons that have already been projected from the Father. She is not herself the cause of this multiplicity, only one of its products. The initial plurality comes into being with the generation of the Son (= Monogenes, Nous, etc.), according to most sources,[17] and there is nothing negative about this, the primal projective act.[18]

---

[15] Cf. Athanasius *Apol. sec.* 4.13, and Lampe, s.vv. ἐκτείνειν, πλατύνειν. πλατύνειν is found, for instance, in Nicomachus *Arith. Intro.* 2.7.3.

[16] Cf. Krämer, *Der Ursprung der Geistmetaphysik,* 320 n. 481, who cites Sextus Empiricus *Math.* 3.19, 28, 77; 7.99; 9.380, 381; 10.281; Martianus Capella, *De Nuptiis Philologiae et Mercurii* 7.732; also cf. E. Thomassen and L. Painchaud, *Le Traité Tripartite (NH I,5)* (BCNHT 19; Québec: Les Presses de l'Université Laval, 1989), 401.

[17] In several instances the Father is given a female σύζυγος (Sige, Ennoia, etc.), but this is not a genuinely independent entity but rather a hypostatization of the self-reflecting mental activity of the Father that precedes as a precondition the projection of the Son.

[18] This kind of objection is voiced by A. H. Armstrong, who therein sees a fundamental difference between Plotinus and the Valentinians: "In the system of Valentinus the Pleroma ... was fully constituted before there was any question of any sort of *tolma*.... In no Gnostic system is the Pleroma ... the result of *tolma*.

At this point it is important, however, not to be deluded by the mythological form of the Valentinian system. In fact, it can be plausibly argued that the account of the passion of Sophia, in its basic idea in Valentinianism, is just an exposition in mythological form of the general theoretical problem of how plurality can be derived from unity. Her passion is the necessary consequence and epitomization of the difficulties inherent in the notion of projection/emanation as such and is not a mere accident arising in the course of this process.

That this is so is shown by the fact that the same terms that describe the passion of Sophia may also be used for the generation of the Son. In *Tripartite Tractate* it is explained that while the Father remains unaffected in his transcendence (64,28ff.), the Son is "the one who extended himself and spread himself" (ⲡⲁⲉⲓ ⲇⲉ ⲁϥⲥⲁ[ⲩ]ⲧⲛ̄ ⲙ̄ⲙⲁϥ ⲁⲃⲁⲗ ⲙ̄ⲙⲓⲛ ⲙ̄ⲙ[ⲁϥ] ⲁⲩⲱ ⲡⲉⲛⲧⲁϥⲡⲁⲣⲉϣϥ̄ ⲁⲃ[ⲁⲗ], 65,4–6). Behind the Coptic terms ⲥⲁⲩⲧⲛ̄ ⲁⲃⲁⲗ and ⲡⲱⲣϣ̄ ⲁⲃⲁⲗ it is possible to recognize the Greek ἐκτείνειν and πλατύνειν.[19] The use of this terminology for the Son indicates that his function is conceived along the lines of the Neopythagorean Dyad: Through him the All as a plurality comes into being from the Father.

The same terminology can be recognized in Irenaeus *Haer.* 1.4.1, where Christ is said to extend himself beyond the Limit/Cross: διὰ τοῦ σταυροῦ ἐπεκταθέντα. This refers, of course, to an extension into the unlimited. Finally, the term "spreading out" (ⲡⲱⲣϣ [ⲁⲃⲁⲗ] < *πλατύνειν) occurs in *Val. Exp.* 23,27–31: "He brought [him]self forth, and in the second [he] manifested his will, [and] in the fourth he spread himself [out]." Here the term seems to be related to the generation of the Pythagorean *tetraktys*.

If this argument is correct, we should be entitled to expect that even the idea of passion itself, the most characteristic feature of the "fall" of

---

There is always in the Gnostic systems a break in the middle of the procession of all things from the first principle, a radical disorder and discontinuity between the spiritual world and the ignorant and inferior power which makes the material world" (*The Cambridge History of Later Greek and Early Medieval History* [ed. A. H. Armstrong; Cambridge: Cambridge University Press, 1967], 243–44). Similarly, Dillon, *The Middle Platonists,* 386–87: "For Valentinus ... there is nothing evil about Ennoia. She is simply the condition for the generation of everything after the Forefather. Evil only arises at a much lower level, with the most junior of the aeons." Also H. Jonas (*Gnosis und spätantiker Geist,* vol. 1: *Die mythologische Gnosis* [3d ed.; FRLANT NS 33; Göttingen: Vandenhoeck & Ruprecht, 1934], 333–34) sees the passion of Sophia as a willful act of will by a character in a mythological narrative, rather than as the allegorization of a philosophically necessary implication. In my view these scholars have misjudged the philosophical intentions of Valentinian systematic exposition.

[19] The combination of the two terms is in itself significant, of course.

Sophia, would not be restricted to her only, but that passion is implied
even at the point of the first duality when the Father projects and manifests himself as and in the Son. That this is really the case is confirmed
by Irenaeus *Haer.* 1.2.2, where it is explicitly stated that "this (passion)
in fact began among those associated with Nous and Truth, but burst
forth in this erring aeon" (ὃ [sc. πάθος] ἐνήρξατο μὲν ἐν τοῖς περὶ τὸν
Νοῦν καὶ τὴν Ἀλήθειαν, ἀπέσκηψε δὲ εἰς τοῦτον τὸν παρατραπέντα).
Also in Hipp. *El.* 6.31.1 the Pleroma as a whole is strongly affected by
the passion of Sophia. And in Clement of Alexandria *Exc.* 30 it is said
that the rest of the Pleroma "suffered together with" (συνεπάθησεν)
Sophia. In all these passages it is implied that the passion experienced
by Sophia is inherent in the notion of projection itself, in the coming
into being of duality, of that which in the Pythagorean-Platonist tradition
is referred to as the Dyad. The basis for this is the view that the Monad
represents impassibility and rationality, and the Dyad passion. As John
Lydus says, "The rational comes from the Monad, ... the passible and
passion from the Dyad."[20] Thus ὁρμή is frequently referred to as an
attribute of the Dyad.[21] (I have not, however, been able to find πάθος
used in this context.)

The Valentinian notion of projection is fundamentally ambiguous. On
the one hand it has a negative aspect, in so far as duality implies infinite
multiplicity and thus, in line with the nature of the Pythagorean-Platonist
Dyad, inevitably produces passion and Matter. On the other hand, projection also has the positive aspect of divine manifestation; the Father gra-
ciously allows himself to be known by others through his begetting of
aeonic offspring. It is this ambiguity that expresses itself in the fact that
"extension" may be used, as we saw, *both* to describe the fall of Sophia
and the subsequent salvation from the fall, when the Savior is "stretched
upon" the Cross, i.e., he extends himself beyond the Limit in order to
redeem Sophia on the outside.

The same ambiguity applies to the notion of the passion. So as if to
condense it in one expression, the Valentinians used the word "compassion" to describe an act that is at the same time tragic and salvific. After
describing the extension and spreading out of the Son quoted above, *Tripartite Tractate* goes on to state that this was done "because of his endur-
ing suffering for them (sc. the All)" (ⲁⲃⲁⲗ ⲛ̄ⲧⲉϥⲙⲛ̄ⲧϣⲟⲡ ϩⲓⲥⲉ ⲁⲣⲁⲩ
ⲉⲧϣⲟⲟⲡ, 65,11–12). This may be compared with Clement of Alexandria,
who in *Exc.* 30.1 records with indignation that the Valentinians say that the
Father "suffered," because he showed compassion towards Silence who

---

[20] *Mens.* 1.11: τὸ μὲν γὰρ ... λογικὸν ἐκ τῆς μονάδος ... τὸ δὲ θυμικὸν καὶ
ἐπιθυμικὸν ἐκ τῆς δυάδος.

[21] Cf. Krämer, *Der Ursprung der Geistmetaphysik,* 322 n. 488.

desired to know him.[22] Thus the notion of compassion retains an element of passion, while at the same time signifying an act of grace. The systems express this ambiguity by means of horizontal and vertical distinctions: Sophia represents the negative aspect of projection, the Son is positive aspect. Or, the Father remains impassible (*Tri. Trac.* 64,38), while the Son is the one who suffers compassion. But the systems never really solve this initial ambiguity in theoretical terms—only the ritually mediated unification of the *syzygoi* in the Bridal Chamber offers what is, in the final analysis, a religious solution to this ontological dilemma.

4. "Otherness" (ἑτερότης)

This is another term that belongs to the traditional vocabulary of the Dyad.[23] In Valentinian literature this term probably lies behind the description of the generation of the Son in *Val. Exp.* 22,35–36 "he conceived a thought of otherness" (ⲁϥ̄ϫⲓ ⲚⲞⲨⲘⲈⲨⲈ Ⲛ̄Ⲱ̄ⲘⲘⲞ).

On this point there is a very interesting remark in Irenaeus *Haer.* 1.4.1 (end), where the passion of the lower Sophia (Achamoth), who has remained outside the Pleroma, is contrasted with that of the first Sophia, who was brought back to the Pleroma: "Her sufferings did not have the nature of otherness, as was the case with her mother, the first Sophia, who was an aeon, but of contrariness" (καὶ οὐ καθάπερ ἡ μήτηρ αὐτῆς, ἡ πρώτη Σοφία αἰών, ἑτεροίωσιν ἐν τοῖς πάθεσιν εἶχεν, ἀλλὰ ἐναντιότητα). This distinction between otherness and contrariness seems very likely to go back to the system of diaeresis that Plato developed in his oral teaching, reported by Hermodorus and quoted by Simplicius (*In phys.* 247.30ff. Diels). Here, Plato distinguished between the categories of the absolute (καθ' αὐτά) and the relative (πρὸς ἕτερα), and subdivided the latter into the contrary (πρὸς ἐναντία) and the undetermined relative (πρός τι).

A version of this theory appears in Sextus Empiricus's report on Pythagorean doctrine in *Math.* 10.261ff. According to Sextus, the Monad is described as self-identity (αὐτότης) and as creating otherness by being added to itself, and from this ἑτερότης the Indefinite Dyad comes into being. Related to this theory is a system of categories distinguishing between the absolute (κατὰ διαφοράν), the contrary (κατ' ἐναντίωσιν) and the relative (πρός τι). The

---

[22] ἐκλαθόμενοι τῆς δόξης τοῦ θεοῦ παθεῖν αὐτὸν λέγουσιν ἀθέως. ὁ γὰρ συνεπάθη-σεν ὁ Πατήρ, στερεὸς ὢν τῇ φύσει, φησὶν ὁ Θεόδοτος, καὶ ἀνένδοτος, ἐνδόσιμον ἑαυτὸν παρασχών, ἵνα ἡ Σιγὴ τοῦτο καταλάβῃ, πάθος ἐστίν. ἡ γὰρ συμπάθεια, πάθος τινὸς διὰ πάθος ἑτέρου.

[23] Plutarch *An. procr.* 24; Sextus Empiricus 10.261; Theon of Smyrna *Exp.* 27.2 Hiller; Plotinus *Enn.* 5.1.1.4; Porphyry, *Vit. Pyth.* 48; Krämer, *Der Ursprung der Geistmetaphysik,* 322 n. 487.

category of the contrary is related both to the Monad and to the Dyad in so far as it is determined (it contains pairs that mutually exclude one another), as well as relative, whereas the relative proper (where one can speak of more or less) is wholly undetermined and belongs only to the Dyad.

Of course, this is a system of logical classification, and if we try to compare it with the use of the categories of otherness and contrariness in the myth of Sophia, obscurities remain. In what sense can the logical category of the contrary describe passions? And how can a system of logical classification be used in a theory of cosmological derivation, where these passions described as contrariness subsequently give rise to matter? However, the fact that the system of diaeresis does appear in a Neopythagorean context, and that Neopythagoreans were concerned with the derivation of matter from the Dyad, defined as ἑτερότης, suggests that the distinction ἑτεροίωσις/ ἐναντιότης in the Valentinian text does depend on Neopythagorean models making use of Old Academic diaeresis in a physical context.[24]

5. *"Movement"* (κίνησις)

"Movement" is closely associated with the notions of passion and otherness as a description of the Dyad.[25] In Valentinianism movement is a characteristic of the passion of Sophia: τὴν φόβου κίνησιν, Irenaeus *Haer.* 1.5.4.[26] In *Tripartite Tractate* "the Logos which had moved" (ⲡⲗⲟⲅⲟⲥ ⲉⲛⲧⲁϩⲕⲓⲙ) is a fixed expression referring to the fallen aeon (85,16–17, etc.). However, as with "extension" and "passion," "movement" can also be found in connection with the very first projection, that of the Son: According to *Valentinian Exposition* the Father is characterized by silence (22,21.24–26; 23,22) and tranquillity (22,22, ⲡⲥϭⲣⲁϩⲧ < *ἡσυχία), whereas the Son is described as "the God who has gone forth" (22,30–31) and "who has moved" (ⲉⲛⲧⲁϩⲕⲓⲙ, 22,38). Here we discern a distinction between an immovable Monad and a moving Dyad.

6. *"Formlessness"*

Formlessness is of course an essential characteristic of the suffering Sophia as well as of the Dyad and its cosmological specialization, Matter. The common and traditional terminology here is easily recognizable; e.g., οὐσίαν ἄμορφον, Irenaeus *Haer.* 1.2.3; ἄμορφον δὲ καὶ ἀνείδεον, 1.2.4 (cf. 4.1); εἰς ἄπειρον ῥεούσης τῆς οὐσίας, 1.3.3; πολυμεροῦς καὶ πολυποικίλου, 1.4.1; οὐσίαν ἄμορφον καὶ ἀκατασκεύαστος, Hipp. *El.* 6.30.8. To give just

---

[24] Plotinus, too, seems to be alluding to this pair of concepts in *Enn.* 5.1.1.4–7.

[25] Cf. Krämer, *Der Ursprung der Geistmetaphysik,* 322 n. 487.

[26] Also cf. *Gos. Truth* 26,15–19: "All the spaces were moved (ⲕⲓⲙ) and troubled.... Error was anguished."

one example: Moderatus portrays his "Quantity" as ἄμορφον καὶ ἀδιαίρετον καὶ ἀσχημάτιστον (Simplicius *In phys.* 231.10–11 Diels). This terminology is obviously derived from Plato's description of the Receptacle in *Tim.* 51a7 ἀνόρατον εἶδός τι καὶ ἄμορφον.

7. *"Division" and "Separation."*

The notion of "division," or "separation," often occurs in the Pythagorean sources describing the coming into being of the Dyad. Thus the *Theologumena Arithmeticae*, an edition of a work by Iamblichus incorporating materials from Nicomachus of Gerasa, states that "the first Dyad separated itself from the Monad" (πρώτη γὰρ ἡ δυὰς διεχώρισεν αὐτὴν ἐκ τῆς μονάδος, 9.5–6 de Falco).[27] Iamblichus uses the idea in *Myst.* 8.3, where he says that God produced Matter after having cut off the principle of matter from the principle of substance (ὕλην δὲ παρήγαγεν ὁ θεὸς ἀπὸ τῆς οὐσιότητος ὑποσχισθείσης ὑλότητος). It is the same theory which appears in Moderatus, who explains that the "Unitary Logos" separated from itself Quantity by a process of self-privation, depriving it of all its own rational constituents and ideas (ὁ ἑνιαῖος λόγος ... κατὰ στέρησιν αὐτοῦ ἐχώρισε [ἐχώρησε MSS; emended by Zeller, Festugière] τὴν ποσότητα πάντων αὐτὴν στερήσας τῶν αὐτοῦ λόγων καὶ εἰδῶν, Simplicius *In phys.* 231.7–10 Diels). Finally, Numenius exploits the idea of the schismatic nature of the Dyad, though within a dualistic framework, in his description of how the third god is separated from the second: The second god, by coming into contact with Matter, the Dyad, unifies Matter but is itself divided by it because the Dyad has a concupiscent and flowing nature (σχίζεται δὲ ὑπ' αὐτῆς ἐπιθυμητικὸν ἦθος ἐχούσης καὶ ῥεούσης, frg. 11 des Places).

It is this idea that in all probability lies behind the notion of the division or separation of Sophia, which is a constant and characteristic feature of the Valentinian systems. Her unlimited outward movement provokes the appearance of the Limit (ὅρος), who separates from her the irrational part of her passion (χωρισθείσης γὰρ τῆς ἐνθυνήσεως ἀπ' αὐτῆς σὺν τῷ ἐπιγενομένῳ πάθει, Irenaeus *Haer.* 1.2.4; ἀφορισθῆναι, ibid., cf. 1.4.1; διαίρεσις, Hipp. *El.* 6.31.2; ἀποχωρίζειν, ibid., 6.31.4). In *Valentinian Exposition* Sophia is said to be "cut off" (ⲁⲥⲱⲁⲁⲧⲥ̄ ⲁⲃⲁⲗ) from her σύζυγος (34,38), and in *Tripartite Tractate* the Logos "suffered a division and a turning" (ⲟⲩⲡⲱⲱϣⲉ ⲡⲉ ⲛ̄ⲧⲁϥⲛ̄ⲕⲁ2 ⲙ̄[ⲙⲁ]ϥ ⲙ̄ⲛ ⲟⲩⲣⲓⲕⲉ, 77,21–22). The perfect part of the Logos hastens back to the Pleroma (77,37ff., cf. *Val. Exp.* 33,36), whereas the part that remains outside is emptied of masculinity (77,12–13), rationality (λόγος) and light (78,34–35). This is, I believe, essentially the same process as the one described by Moderatus, who lets

---

[27] Cf. also Krämer, *Der Ursprung der Geistmetaphysik,* 320 n. 479.

Quantity come into being from the Unitary Logos through an act of deprivation of rationality (κατὰ στέρησιν). The widespread application of this theory in Valentinianism is further attested by Irenaeus *Haer.* 1.11.1, where Sophia gives birth to Christ "with a certain shadow," which he then cuts off (ἀποκόψαντα) from himself before he ascends to the Pleroma, as well as by Clement of Alexandria *Exc.* 33.4, where the term ἀποτομία applied to the Demiurge serves to indicate his essentially defective origin and nature.

The ambiguity we noted vis-à-vis the first projection also manifests itself with regard to the notion of separation. The purpose of this notion is to safeguard unity while at the same time explaining plurality. On the one hand plurality is cut away from the oneness; on the other hand plurality thereby asserts itself as a separate reality. Through their separation from one another, the two can only be conceived, however, in a mutual relationship. The principle of plurality now exists as pure negativity, a κένωμα (Irenaeus *Haer.* 1.4.1; Clement of Alexandria *Exc.* 31.4), opposite a unity which after the restoration to it of the rational part of the suffering aeon is now also a multiplicity, a πλήρωμα: As a result of the restoration of Sophia the aeons form a perfect unity—each individual, while retaining its individuality, is at the same time all the others—and as an expression of this new phase of harmonious unity Jesus is brought forth, being at the same time one and many (Irenaeus *Haer.* 1.2.5–6; etc.). Thus we here seem to have a model according to which the Father, who is a transcendent oneness on the supreme level, gives rise to an opposition between a unity-in-multiplicity and pure negativity on a second level. This corresponds to what we find in authors such as Eudorus, Moderatus, and Numenius, where there is a first absolutely singular One above a second One, which contains the ideas and exists in opposition to the Dyad. Thus, for instance, the second One of Moderatus is the Unitary Logos, which exists relatively to Quantity in the sense that Quantity comes into being by privation, whereas the Unitary Logos on the contrary contains within itself all the forms (Simplicius *In phys.* 231.16–17 Diels). This στέρησις thus corresponds to the Valentinian κένωμα, just as the ἐνιαῖος λόγος is the counterpart of the πλήρωμα.

It may be added here that this is one point, perhaps the most important one, where the Valentinian system of derivation differs from Plotinus's notion of emanation. For the Valentinians an element of rupture seemed inevitable in their account of the relationship between the primal unity and the world. Plotinus thought he could do without such a notion. Indeed, he insists that there is no break in the flow of emanation. This insistence appears to be deliberately directed against the kind of theories we have been discussing here. On this point, then, the Valentinians are closer to the Neopythagorean sources common to them and Plotinus, than is Plotinus.

8. *"Shadow"*

A brief note may be inserted here on another terminological parallel, which illustrates further the kinship of thought. "Shadow(s)" (σκιά) is a favorite image with the Valentinians (and other gnostics[28]) in their descriptions of the derived, purely negative, and only seemingly real, existence of the material principle that has been cut off from the Pleroma (e.g., Clement of Alexandria *Exc.* 31.4; Irenaeus *Haer.* 1.4.1; 1.11.1; *Tri. Trac.* 77,16–17). Precisely the same image is employed by Moderatus: Matter is "a shadow (σκίασμα) cast by the primary non-being existing in quantity and having descended still further and being derived from it" (Simplicius *In phys.* 231.4–5 Diels).

9. *"Limit"*

From the preceding discussion it should be clear that the Limit (ὅρος) which separates Sophia from the Pleroma fits neatly into the Neopythagorean framework. The Pythagoreans too, of course, spoke of a πέρας delimiting the ἄπειρον of the Dyad. The difference in vocabulary here may not be taken as more than evidence that the Valentinians, as Christian theologians, made creative use of Pythagorean ideas, expressing them partly in terminology invented by themselves. Nevertheless a significant verbal affinity is found in Moderatus, who describes how Matter is being kept in check by the Good and is not permitted to overstep its "boundaries" (καταλαμβάνεται ὑπ' αὐτοῦ καὶ ἐξελθεῖν τῶν ὅρων οὐ συγχωρεῖται, Simplicius *In phys.* 231.21–22 Diels). Also Plotinus often speaks about how the ἀόριστον of the Dyad is delimited by an ὁρισμός.[29] The idea of privation implied in the Limit is expressed, moreover, in *Tri. Trac.* 76,30–34: "For the Father and the All withdrew from him [ⲀⲨⲤⲀⲔⲞⲨ ⲚⲈⲨ ⲤⲀⲂⲞⲖ ⲘⲘⲞϤ], in order that the boundary [ⲠϨⲞⲢⲞⲤ] which the Father had fixed might become firm." This, again, parallels how the Unitary Logos in Moderatus detaches from itself the material principle by depriving it of rational content.

The functions of delimiting the unlimited and giving form to the formless are expressed in various ways in Valentinianism. In *Valentinian Exposition* the Limit is said to have four powers: separation, consolidation, formation, and the giving of substance (26,31ff., 27,30ff.). In Irenaeus *Haer.* 1.3.5 only the first two of these powers are attributed to the Limit. In this system, however, as well as in that of Hipp. *El.* 6.29ff., the function of the Limit is doubled by that of Christ and the Holy Spirit (cf. Irenaeus *Haer.* 1.2.5, Hipp. *El.* 7.31.2). This duplication seems rather redundant and is

---

[28] Cf. *Poimandres* 14; *Hyp. Arch.* 95,5–9; *Orig. World* 98,17–27.

[29] Krämer, *Der Ursprung der Geistmetaphysik,* 312ff.

perhaps to be explained as caused by a combination of different sources. In all these systems, however, the dyadic nature of Sophia is controlled by the operation of one or two distinct power hypostases, the Limit and/or Christ-Holy Spirit.

In the case of *Tripartite Tractate*, however, we find that the Son combines in himself both of these opposite functions. On the one hand the projection of the Son represents, as we have seen, the dyadic function of extension and spreading out. On the other hand it is also the Son who gives the All "firmness and a place and a dwelling-place" (65,7–8); that is, he provides the consolidation that in other texts is attributed to the operation of the Limit and/or Christ-Holy Spirit. The outcome of this double operation is an All, or a Pleroma, which is a multiplicity as well as a unity: The "dwelling-place" of the All is said to be a Name (65,9), which at the same time consists of many names (65,35–67,34). Thus by attributing both functions to the same hypostasis the ontologically ambiguous character of the Pleroma as both plurality and unity is accentuated.

The combination of both functions within one hypostasis is what we find in Plotinus as well, where the dyadic nature of the πρόοδος of Mind from the One is complemented by the limiting act of ἐπιστροφή, when Mind directs its attention to its source. By this process Mind is constituted as a unity-in-multiplicity. It is not inconceivable that Plotinus was influenced by gnostic precursors on this point, but it is *prima facie* more probable that the model of going forth and return as complementary aspects of the process of emanation already existed in the Neopythagorean sources common to both. An indication that this is the case is provided by the remark in the Pseudo-Clementine *Homilies* quoted above, that the Dyad is considered to arise from the Monad by a double process of ἔκτασις and συστολή (224.34 Rehm: κατὰ γὰρ ἔκτασιν καὶ συστολὴν ἡ μονὰς δυὰς εἶναι νομίζεται).

To repeat: The Valentinian structure

Father
↓
Son = νοῦς = Pleroma ↔ Sophia

corresponds to the Neopythagorean one of

First One
↓
Second One = Ideas ↔ Dyad.

Sophia, just like the Dyad, is derived from, but subsequently cut off from its noetic counterpart and deprived of rational content, so as to become the principle of Matter. The inner logic of the connection between the three terms is, however, to give form to the relationship between the first and the second. The dyadic nature of the Son, viz. the Second One, implicit in its being a first alterity is, as it were, removed from it and relegated to the third term. Thus, by the action of the limiting power, the second hypostasis remains a unity, while at the same time representing plurality. But the ambiguously double nature of the first projection may also be expressed (in a way more similar to Plotinus) by placing both the dyadic extension and the limiting consolidation within one and the same hypostasis.

The subsequent phases of derivation in the Valentinian system repeat the pattern of the initial separation—a repetition entailed by the still unsolved ambiguity of that separation: Unity acts on formlessness, producing form through division. The following phases may be distinguished:

9.1. Distinction of Spirit and Soul

This phase contains two subphases: (a) The pure negativity of the separated and formless lower Sophia is first turned into receptivity for formation (this is called the formation according to substance) by Christ, who is sent out from the Pleroma. He extends himself beyond the Cross (= the Limit) (διὰ τοῦ σταυροῦ ἐπεκταθέντα). In physical terms this translates as a movement into the unlimited; in soteriological terms it implies that Christ subjects himself to "suffering" for the sake of Sophia by "extending himself" on the "Cross." Having completed his formative purpose he "withdraws" (ἀναδραμεῖν, συστείλαντα αὐτοῦ τὴν δύναμιν). Here we meet again the same Pythagorean pair of concepts that we discussed above.[30] In *Tripartite Tractate* this point in the process is represented by the intercessory "help" (βοήθεια) given to the abandoned aeon by the aeons in the Pleroma (81,10–82,9). It is connected with the ἐπιστροφή of the fallen aeon—a term which here seems to refer not only to a psychological-religious μετάνοια but also to physical notions akin to the Plotinian term (cf. above).[31] Thus the conversion of Sophia is also described as a phase in the derivation of matter, in terms of a delimitation of the dyadic extension, involving συστολή, or ἐπιστροφή.

---

[30] Already K. Müller, "Beiträge zum Verständnis der valentinianischen Gnosis," in *Nachrichten von der Königlichen: Gesellschaft der Wissenschaften zu Göttingen* (Philologisch-historische Klasse; Göttingen: Dieterichschen Buchhandlung, 1920), 232, related this terminology to the πλατύνεσθαι and συστέλλεσθαι of God in Marcellus of Ancyra. Müller was undoubtedly on the right track here, because, as we have pointed out above, the trinitarian doctrine of Marcellus was inspired by Pythagoreanism.

[31] The conversion, ἐπιστροφή, of the fallen aeon is a constant feature of the systems, cf., e.g., G. C. Stead, "The Valentinian Myth of Sophia," *JTS* NS 20 (1969): 83.

This ἐπιστροφή can also be described as an awakening of a rational element in the fallen aeon, and as becoming receptive of illumination by a turning upwards. This corresponds in fact to the description of the "slumbering World Soul" in such Middle Platonists as Plutarch and Albinus/Alkinoos.[32] This World Soul, which is conceived by these writers according to traditions about the Dyad, is in fact aroused by the noetic God, who turns it towards himself.[33]

(b) In the second subphase the Savior-Jesus is sent out from the Pleroma to the fallen aeon. Unlike Christ, who seems to represent a still unsettled relation of Monad and Dyad, the Savior represents the Pleroma as a mediation of unity and multiplicity (he is accompanied by a retinue of angels). He forms Sophia by separating her from her passions (the formation according to *gnosis*).[34] As a result a division is established between the passionless, rational, and spiritual on the one side, and the passions on the other.

9.2. Distinction of Soul and Matter.

The same process is repeated with the passions: (a) The passions are still incorporeal, and the Savior transforms them into a substance (εἰς οὐσι-ʹαν ἤγαγεν αὐτά, Clement of Alexandria *Exc.* 45.2); that is, he turns them into an incorporeal Matter capable of becoming bodies (καὶ ἐξ ἀσωμάτου πάθους εἰς ἀσώματον ὕλην μεταβαλεῖν αὐτά· εἶθ᾽ οὕτως ἐπιτηδειότητα καὶ φύσιν ἐμπεποιηκέναι αὐτοῖς, ὥστε εἰς συγκρίματα καὶ σώματα ἐλθεῖν, Irenaeus *Haer.* 1.4.5). This preparatory role of the Savior seems to correspond structurally to that of Christ vis-à-vis Sophia.

(b) To an inferior power, the Demiurge, is delegated the task of handling this substance and turning it into actual bodies. (He is, to be sure, invisibly moved by his mother Sophia). He too works essentially through division and limitation, as his primary task is to separate Matter and Soul.[35]

---

32 Cf. Dillon, *The Middle Platonists,* 204–6, 287.

33 "He rouses and turns towards himself its Mind and itself from, as it were, a sort of trancelike sleep, that it may look upon the objects of his intellection and so receive to itself the Forms and shapes, in its striving towards his thoughts" (ἐγείρων καὶ ἐπιστρέφων πρὸς αὐτὸν τόν τε νοῦν αὐτῆς ὥσπερ ἐκ κάρου τινός, ὅπως ἀποβλέπουσα πρὸς τὰ νοητὰ αὐτοῦ δέχηται τὰ εἴδη καὶ τὰς μορφάς, ἐφιεμένη τῶν ἐκείνου νοημάτων, Albinus *Did.* 169.31–35 Hermann). Also cf. 165.1–2 τὴν ψυχὴν τοῦ κόσμου ἐπεγείρας καὶ εἰς ἑαυτὸν ἐπιστρέψας.

34 χωρίσαντα αὐτὰ [sc. τὰ πάθη] αὐτῆς ... ἀποκρίναντα χωρίσει, Irenaeus *Haer.* 1.4.5; ἀποστήσας δὲ τὰ πάθη τῆς πεπονθυίας ... διακρίνας, Clement of Alexandria *Exc.* 45.2; ἐκστῆναι τὰ πάθη ἀπ᾽ αὐτῆς, Hippolytus *Ref.* 6.32.6; ⲡⲱⲣ︤ⲝ︥, *Tri. Trac.* 88,24; 96,11; etc.

35 διακρίναντα γὰρ τὰς δύο οὐσίας, Irenaeus *Haer.* 1.5.2; διακρίνας δὲ ὁ δημιουργός τὰ καθαρὰ ἀπὸ τοῦ ἐμβριθοῦς, Clement of Alexandria *Exc.* 48.1. In *Val. Exp.*

Matter, being coarser and heavier, tends downwards, while the lighter psychic substance moves in the opposite direction. This account of demiurgic division is based on late Hellenistic διάκρισις-cosmogonies,[36] the division between the psychic and the hylic substances being conceived along the lines of the division between the lighter and heavier elements in those cosmogonies. But it also fits excellently into the framework of the Neopythagorean physical theory employed by the Valentinians, as the final stage in the derivation of Matter after a series of successive delimitations of the unlimited Dyad.

Conclusion

We have attempted here to show that Valentinian systematic exposition contains and represents a theory of physics that in its details as well as in its underlying conception is Neopythagorean. This means that the Valentinian theologians have a legitimate place in the history of ancient philosophy—as part of the "paradigm shift" (to use, for once, this hackneyed expression) in late antiquity from two- or three-principles theories to one-principle ones.

Neopythagorean theories of derivation is thus an essential key to the understanding of the Valentinian systems. This does not imply, however, that these systems are just philosophy. They are not. They are also the verbal statements of the hopes and aspirations of a religion of salvation. In this context the tale of the fallen aeon is also an account of the fall of the soul from its divine home. And on the collective level it is the story of the exile of a superior race of people from the divine assembly to which they belong, and about their reintegration into it. The presence of these complementary, and necessary, components, does not, however, reduce the genuine philosophical interests that also lie behind the construction of the Valentinian systems.

35,30–34 it is the Savior himself who acts in the role as dividing demiurge. In *Tri. Trac.* 88,34–35 the two lowest orders are split by the manifestation of the Savior and are kept apart by a certain "power" (97,36ff.).

[36] W. Spoerri, *Späthellenistische Berichte über Welt, Kultur und Götter* (Schweizerische Beiträge zur Altertumswissenschaft 9; Basel: F. Reinhardt, 1959), ch. 1; Thomassen and Painchaud, *Le Traité Tripartite (NH I,5)*, 368–69.

Positive and Negative Matter in Later Platonism: The Uncovering of Plotinus's Dialogue with the Gnostics

Kevin Corrigan
University of Saskatchewan

In this paper, I shall examine four different but related questions about matter, in order to develop a clearer understanding of the attitude of later Platonism (and particularly, of Plotinus) to the gnostics on this and related topics. Most of what I have to say arises out of an attempt to think through some difficult problems in the *Enneads,* and I must confess that until the preparation for this paper I had not really appreciated the importance of gnostic thought either in itself or for an understanding of Neoplatonism. I offer my remarks here, then, as an attempt to work out the importance of Gnosticism for an understanding of what philosophy really was for Plotinus and Porphyry.

My first question is simple, but I think far-reaching. In the context of ancient thought, from Plato to Moderatus, Plutarch, Atticus, and the *Chaldean Oracles* (and even in Aristotle and the Stoics), space, matter, or the ultimate substratum of physical things is invariably described in positive, negative, or neutral (often all three) terms. What then distinguishes Plotinus's doctrine? How are Plotinus's views of matter really "new," and how do we distinguish them from gnostic views? What I shall try to show as part of an answer to these questions is how Plotinus develops an inner, hidden dialogue with Aristotle on the question of matter, and then later how in certain passages there is a further level of dialogue still, and one that clearly addresses the gnostics.

A similar problem is associated with the generation of matter. The derivation of matter from the first principle was quite common Pythagorean doctrine in the second and first centuries B.C.E. It is also found in Moderatus of Gades (first century C.E.) and in the *Chaldean Oracles.*[1] Now if soul's generation of matter as a good, not an evil act, most separates Plotinus from the gnostics,[2] why is Plotinus so thoroughly obscure on this point that

---

[1] See Diogenes Laertius 8.25 and Simplicius *In phys.* 181.33–34 Diels. For Moderatus in Porphyry's account, see Simplicius *In phys.* 231.5–27.

[2] For this view, see D. O'Brien, *Théodicée plotinienne, théodicée gnostique* (Leiden: Brill, 1993), chs. 3–4.

Hans-Rudolph Schwyzer for one believes that there is no such generation in the *Enneads.*[3] This is puzzling, but I think it bears on the very character of philosophy as practiced by the school of Plotinus. An answer to this problem, therefore, will shed some light upon Plotinus's *implicit* attitude to possible gnostic adversaries.

My third question will be to ask how Plotinus's analyses of matter are to be situated in the context of his explicit critique of gnostic thought in 2.9. This is a complex question,[4] but what I propose is simply this. Is 2.9 alone intended to be the critique, or should 3.8; 5.8; and 5.5 be included (which have been shown by Harder to constitute one work, a *Großschrift*)?[5] And if the latter, how does the whole work function as a complex critique? If we can reach a workable conclusion on this part of the question, then we can compare the results with Plotinus's analysis of matter to determine the context and spirit of Plotinus's polemic.

Finally, I want to turn briefly to some of the major texts of Sethian Gnosticism to look at the whole question of influence. Is Plotinus influenced by Gnosticism or Gnosticism by Plotinus, or are both drawing upon

---

3 H.-R. Schwyzer, "Zu Plotins Deutung der sogenannten Platonischen Materie," in *Zetesis: Album amicorum door vrienden en collega's aangeboden aan Prof. Dr. E. de Strycker ter gelegenheid van zijn 65e verjaardag* (Antwerp: De Nederlandsche Boekhandel, 1973), 266–80.

4 While I would not go so far as to argue that Plotinus is closer to Gnosticism than to the Platonic tradition (with Hans Jonas, *Gnosis und spätantiker Geist,* vol. 1 (Göttingen: Vandenhoeck & Ruprecht, 1934), 46; cf. idem, *The Gnostic Religion* (Boston: Beacon, 1958), I share the view of V. Cilento that Plotinus's positive exposition in these treatises is part of the whole critique (*Plotino. Paideia antignostica* [Firenze: F. Le Monnier, 1971]; cf. C. Elsas, *Neuplatonische und Gnostische Weltablehnung in der Schule Plotins* [Berlin and New York: de Gruyter, 1975]; D. J. O'Meara, "Gnosticism and the Making of the World in Plotinus," in *The Rediscovery of Gnosticism: Proceedings of the International Conference on Gnosticism at Yale, New Haven, Connecticut, March 28–31, 1978,* vol. 1: *The School of Valentinus* [ed. B. Layton; SHR 41; Leiden: Brill, 1980], 364–78; A. P. Bos. "Worldviews in Collision: Plotinus, Gnostics, and Christians" in *Plotinus amid Gnostics and Christians* [ed. D. T. Runia; Amsterdam:, VU Uitgeverij/Free University Press, 1984], 11–28; F. García Bazán, *Plotino y la Gnosis* [Buenos-Aires: Fundación para la Educación, la Ciencia y la Cultura, 1981]), but I am particularly sympathetic to O'Meara's view that Plotinus's attempt to develop an account of the making of the world in terms of productive contemplation prepares the ground for an antignostic critique, although the line of interpretation I shall adopt will go somewhat further than this. For an overview of this whole gnostic question in Plotinus, see K. Corrigan and P. O'Cleirigh, "Plotinian Scholarship from 1971 to 1986," *ANRW* 2.36.1:571–623.

5 R. Harder, "Eine neue Schrift Plotins," *Hermes* 71 (1936): 1–10.

some common body of texts?[6] Further, are Plotinus's gnostic adversaries Sethian gnostics, as the *Vita Plotini* would seem to indicate,[7] or Valentinian, perhaps Ptolemaean gnostics, as Igal has argued?[8] I shall propose that while Sethian gnostic texts, among others, are part of the object of Plotinus's polemic, Plotinus *is,* at the same time, influenced by these texts in his description of the fall of soul and of matter but in ways that have perhaps not been fully appreciated.

1. Positive and Negative Matter in Platonism

If we examine the history of the notion of matter starting with Plato's Receptacle, it becomes difficult to see what is so distinctive in Plotinus's theory. On the one hand, Plato's Receptacle, or χώρα, is nurse and principle of becoming, "that in which" things come to be, "of which" and "out of which" they are fashioned (*Tim.* 52d). On the other hand, it is also a principle of precosmic disorder (30a2–6; 53b) and of active resistance to order (48a; 56c; cf. *Pol.* 269c–270a). How the irrational disorders of this substratum are to be related to the soul is a problem not only of the late *Laws* (896e–897d; 904a–c) and *Epinomis* (988d–e), but also of the whole middle Platonic tradition,[9] which results in the evil, demiurgic world soul of Plutarch and Atticus,[10] and by contrast an evil, ungenerated matter in Numenius.[11] Even for Aristotle, although form is contrasted with privation rather than matter with form,[12] the notion of matter itself ranges in meaning from positive

---

[6] For Sethian Gnosticism see H.-M. Schenke, "The Phenomenon of Gnostic Sethianism," in *The Rediscovery of Gnosticism* (ed. B. Layton; Leiden: Brill, 1980), 588–616, and for a convincing comparison see especially the detailed study by J. D. Turner, "Gnosticism and Platonism: The Platonizing Sethian Texts from the Nag Hammadi in Their Relation to Later Platonic Literature," in *Neoplatonism and Gnosticism* (ed. R. T. Wallis and J. Bregman; Albany: SUNY Press, 1992), 425–57 (on this see also note 75).

[7] *Vit. Plot.* 16.1–9.

[8] J. Igal, "The Gnostics and 'The Ancient Philosophy' in Plotinus," in *Neoplatonism and Early Christian Thought: Essays in Honour of A. H. Armstrong* (ed. H. J. Blumenthal and R. A. Markus; London: Variorum, 1981), 138–52.

[9] On this see J. Dillon, *The Middle Platonists* (London: Duckworth, 1977), hereafter *MP.*

[10] Plutarch *Is. Os.* 369E–372E; *An. procr.* 1014–1016E, 1026E–1027A. Atticus apud Proclus *In Tim.* 1.381.26–382.3; 391.6–12.

[11] Numenius frg. 52 des Places. Numenius, however, is reported not only to have held that matter is the principle of all evil (paragraph 296, Calcidius) but also to have identified matter with an evil world-soul, source of random motion (paragraph 297, J. C. M. Van Winden, *Calcidius on Matter* [Leiden: Brill, 1959]).

[12] Aristotle *Phys.* 192a11–25.

potentiality and neutrality to indeterminacy, unknowability, and even resistance to form.[13] The neutral Middle Platonist formula for matter ("neither
body nor incorporeal, but potentially body")[14] tends to follow one strand
of the Aristotelian tradition, whereas the positive-negative view is clearly
related to the interpretation of Plato. Thus, as has long been recognized,[15]
the Plotinian schema of hypostases and two forms of matter are to be found
already in Moderatus of Gades (if not in Plato himself, according to Simplicius). Following upon the three Ones (The One "beyond being," the second One "truly existent," and the third "psychic" One), Simplicius relates,
"the lowest nature … that of the sense-realm, does not even participate, but
receives order by reflection from those others, Matter in the sense-realm
being a shadow cast by Not-Being as it manifests itself primally in Quantity,
and which is of a degree inferior even to that."[16] In this general line of interpretation are also the *Chaldean Oracles* and certain gnostic texts, as well as
Plotinus and Porphyry. In the *Oracles* matter springs from the "Source of
Sources" (frg. 34), is of various kinds, sometimes positive (frgs. 216; 173),
and yet is also evil, even "bitter" (frg. 129).[17] A similar view can be found
in the *Corpus hermeticum*. The "downward bearing elements of nature are
left bereft of reason so as to be matter alone," but at the same time God is
the source of "mind, nature, and matter."[18] In gnostic writings, while the
source of evil is identified with entities of the spiritual world,[19] and while

---

[13] For positive potentiality cf. *Metaph.* 1039b29, 1042a27; for neutrality cf. *De an.*
414a10, *Metaph.* 1029a20; for indeterminacy *Phys.* 209b9, 207a22, *Metaph.* 1037a27;
for unknowability *Metaph.* 1036a9, *Phys.* 207a25–26; and for resistance or privation,
Phys. 192a22 ("accidentally ugly"), *Gen. an.* 769b12, *Phys.* 207b35–208a4.

[14] Albinus *Did.* 8.6–7, p. 163 Hermann.

[15] E. R. Dodds, "The *Parmenides* of Plato and the Origin of the Neoplatonic
One", *CQ* 22 (1928): 129–42. See also Dillon's comments, *MP* (see note 9),
346–49.

[16] Simplicius *In phys.* 230.34–231.27. Trans. J. Dillon, *MP* (note 9).

[17] See especially frgs. 88, 100, 105, 134, 172, 180 Majercik. Cf. frg. 129: "Save also
the mortal covering of bitter matter" (πικρᾶς ὕλης) (Majercik) and *Enn.*
2.3.17.24–25: "matter … a sort of sediment [ὑποστάθμης] of prior realities, bitter and
embittering [πικρᾶς καὶ πικρὰ ποιούσης]." See Dillon's comments on these two passages in "Plotinus and the Chaldaean Oracles," in *Platonism in Late Antiquity* (ed.
S. Gersh and C. Kannengeisser; Notre Dame, Ind: University of Notre Dame Press,
1992), 139–40. The active bitterness of matter in Plotinus (ποιούσης) is surely a
reflection of the *Oracles,* and it might also be a result of Plotinus's dialogues with
the gnostics, as I shall argue here.

[18] Cf. *Corp. herm., Poimandres* 1.10–11a and 3.1a.

[19] Cf. Hans Jonas, *The Gnostic Religion* (see note 4), 179–84; *Tri. Trac.* 80–85;
Orig. World 98–101.

matter is sometimes positive, particularly in the Sethian treatises,[20] the active negativity of darkness or matter becomes more prominent and is seen as a cause of evil in other forms of darkness.[21] This active notion of matter or darkness as evil we find particularly in *Enn.* 1.8 [51] and 2.3 [52].17, and later still in Porphyry. In the *Sententiae,* matter is an active principle of evil,[22] and absolute nonbeing, but in the *Commentary on the Timaeus,* Porphyry seems to adopt a different position, according to which matter is generated from the One. Porphyry distinguishes the Father and the Demiurge. The Father generates "the whole" from himself, and the Demiurge receives matter from the Father. In the later history of Neoplatonism, of course, Plotinus's view that matter is the ultimate source of evil is rejected. For Syrianus, Proclus, and Pseudo-Dionysius, evil springs from privation or nonbeing as an accidental consequence of being.[23] In such a context, therefore, Plotinus's theory looks rather unremarkable, a recognizable interpretative development of some difficult passages in Plato. It seems close to the doctrine of the *Chaldean Oracles* and to certain elements in gnostic thought, particularly the idea of an evil matter or a darkness that "makes" other things dark

---

[20] On this see Hans-Martin Schenke, "The Phenomenon and Significance of Gnostic Sethianism" (note 6), 614–15.

[21] Cf. *Ap. John* 29,26–30: "And the angels changed themselves in their likeness into the likeness of their (the daughters of men) mates, filling them with the spirit of darkness, which they had mixed for them, and with evil." *Zost.* 1,10–17: "After I parted from the somatic darkness in me and the psychic chaos in mind and the feminine desire [that is] in the darkness... After I found the infinite part of matter ["the boundlessness of my material (nature)" JDT], then I reproved the dead creation in me"; cf. 45–46; 5; 9,14–15: "and an origin of matter begotten of lost darkness ["the dark, corrupt product" JDT]." See also 77–78, which seems to envisage an intelligible or precosmic dark other (?), not dissimilar from Plotinus's descriptions of *Penia* in 3.5 [50] and 1.8 [51].14. *Marsanes* 5,9–27; *Trim. Prot.* 39,20–26: "there appeared the great Demon who ... has neither form nor perfection, but on the contrary possesses the form of the glory of those begotten in darkness"; 40–41; *Tri. Trac.* 89 ("the Outer Darkness," "Chaos," "Hades," "the Abyss"); 109 (a very "Plotinian" passage setting out alternative theologies); *Orig. World* 99,19–21: "just so matter came into being out of shadow and was projected apart. And it did not depart from chaos; rather matter was in chaos"; 125,36–127,5: "something that has never been. And the product to which the darkness had been posterior will dissolve. And the deficiency will be plucked out by the root (and thrown) down into the darkness. And the light will withdraw up to its root" (cf. *Marsanes* p. 5).

[22] *Sent.* 30 (Mommert reads κακοὶ ἡ ὕλη), Lambertz (κακόν), 20.

[23] See Proclus, *De Malorum Subsistentia in Procli Opuscula* (ed. H. Boese; Berlin: de Gruyter, 1960), 253.9–256.43. Pseudo-Dionysius *Divine Names* 4.732C–D Migne.

or evil. What then distinguishes Plotinus's view from the *Chaldean Oracles* or from a generally gnostic view?

2. The Ancient Philosophy and the Inner Level of Argumentation in Enn. 2.4 [12]

The beginning of an answer can be found, I believe, in the *Vita Plotini*, chapter 16, where Porphyry tells us that there were at that time in Rome many Christians "as well as sectarians [*haeretikoi*] who had abandoned the ancient philosophy ... and produced revelations by Zoroaster and Zostrianos and Nicotheos and Allogenes and Messos and other people of the kind." Porphyry refers apparently to some of the Sethian texts of the Nag Hammadi library. What is not clear, however, is his attitude to these gnostics. The phrase αἱρετικοὶ δὲ ἐκ τῆς παλαιᾶς φιλοσοφίας ἀνηγμένοι (2–3) has received two mutually exclusive translations: Ficino's *ex antiqua philosophia egressi* (sc. *orti*) and Bouillet's "qui s'écartaient de la philosophie antique" (cf. A. H. Armstrong's translation above).[24] In accord with the first translation, and with Plotinus's reference to the gnostics as "friends" (2.9 [33].10.3–4), H.-C. Puech held that Plotinus regarded the gnostics as belonging to his own group and as devotees of the mysteries of Plato.[25] Igal, on the other hand, taking into account the obvious incompatibility between the claim that the gnostics were devotees of Plato and their disparagement of Plato and subversion of the cosmology of the *Timaeus* (*Vit. Plot.* 16.8–9; 2.9 [33].6ff.), has argued that the force of the criticism should be understood in the following way: while the gnostics derive their thought from "the ancient philosophy" they go on to develop an *idia hairesis* that subverts rather than complements Platonic thought.[26] 2.9 [33].6.10–13 draws a distinction between two groups of gnostics, those whose doctrines have been taken from Plato and those who have "innovated" in order to establish an ἰδία φιλοσοφία. On the basis of this, Igal concludes that with the exception of the un-Greek doctrines that Plotinus attacks at 2.9 [33].6.57–62, Plotinus is "overly eager to trace back the Gnostic doctrines to Plato,"[27] so much so that he oversimplifies and comes dangerously close to treating the gnostics as κλεψιλόγοι. I too favor Ficino's translation of ἀνηγμένοι. Gnostic doctrine is, according to Plotinus, at least, in part, derived from Plato, and one of Plotinus's major criticisms is that the gnostics develop their own

---

24 See J. Igal, "The Gnostics and 'The Ancient Philosophy' in Plotinus" (note 8), 139 and 147 n. 10.

25 H.-C. Puech, "Plotin et les gnostiques," in *Les sources de Plotin* (Vandoeuvres-Genève: Fondation Hardt, 1960), 161–74, discussion 175–90.

26 J. Igal, "The Gnostics and 'The Ancient Philosophy' in Plotinus," 139–41.

27 Ibid., 141.

idiosyncratic version of reality without giving reasons for the things they assert or offering rational support for the revelations they narrate. However, it is plain from Plotinus's remarks in 2.9 [33].6.10–13 and 10.3–4 that many gnostics, if not actually part of the circle of Plotinus, were indeed considered to be friends and fellow philosophers. Thus, the context of Plotinus's critique, I suggest, is not simply a polemic but rather the establishment of a basis for rational discussion and, indeed, philosophical conversation. Hence, I take a broader, more positive view than Igal of what Plotinus is doing in the *Großschrift*. I propose that Plotinus establishes an implicit basis for rational understanding in the earlier treatises (3.8 [30]; 5.8 [31]; and 5.5 [32]) and only then singles out the ἰδία αἵρεσις in 2.9.[28] This is consistent with his normal practice. He rarely cites authorities explicitly (even Plato) but proceeds indirectly either in a hidden dialogue form or by setting up an argument with reference to an implicit subtext. First, then, I shall outline this interpretation in the light of what I take to be the meaning of the phrase "the ancient philosophy" and with the purpose of determining what is distinctive in Plotinus's doctrine of matter-evil. Second, I shall examine the generation of matter and the descent of the soul, and, finally, I shall give a brief analysis of what I take to be the overall context of the *Großschrift*.

What is "the ancient philosophy" for our understanding of the context of Plotinus's writings? Its most conspicuous source is Plato, but in Porphyry's famous estimate, Plotinus's writings are full of hidden Stoic and Peripatetic doctrines. Aristotle's *Metaphysics,* in particular, "is condensed in them" (*Vit. Plot.* 14.6–8), and Middle Platonic (Severus, Gaius, Atticus) as well as Neopythagorean (Cronius and Numenius) and Peripatetic commentaries (Aspasius, Adrastus, Alexander) were read in the school meetings. While these obviously helped to form a context for Plotinus's own writings, Plotinus's thinking itself took "a distinctive personal line" in its contemplative scrutiny (ἴδιος ... καὶ ἐξηλλαγμένος ἐν τῇ θεωρία), Porphyry stresses, and brought "the mind of Ammonius" (about which we know little or nothing)[29] to bear on the investigation at hand.[30] Plotinus's characteristic approach, then, was not to speak directly out of a textbook but to take his own creative line of argumentation derived from the context of ancient philosophy, with Stoic and Aristotelian *dogmata* concentrated in a hidden, implicit way in its subtext. This is, at least, what Porphyry claims, and if true, it may well help to distinguish Plotinian and gnostic writings.

---

[28] See especially 2.9 [33].6.2–12; cf. 9.26–31, 45–51, 74–83.

[29] On Ammonius Saccas, see F. M. Schroeder, "Ammonius Saccas," *ANRW* 2.36.1:493–526.

[30] *Vit. Plot.* 14.14–18. All translations from the *Enneads* will be drawn from the Loeb edition by A. H. Armstrong (though they will sometimes be adapted).

Despite Porphyry's testimony, the precise character of Plotinus's philosophical method has often gone unnoticed, and the presence of genuinely Aristotelian elements in his thought (to give Aristotle the prominence that Porphyry gives him for understanding the *Enneads*) has received scrutiny only from a few scholars.[31] De Gandillac, in fact, has recently rejected Porphyry's claim that the *Metaphysics* is condensed in the *Enneads*.[32] Yet what is most distinctive about all of the treatises that are devoted to the problem of matter is that they contain at their core, not only a reflection upon Platonic doctrines, but an argument with Aristotelian philosophy that is incorporated as a minor key in the much larger picture of ancient thought within which Plotinus develops his own position.[33] Schwyzer has pointed out that Plotinus simply identified the Platonic Receptacle with Aristotelian matter, following such an august authority as Aristotle himself, of course, but hardly in accord with the nature of the evidence before us.[34] Yet Plotinus does not *simply* identify

---

[31] For different viewpoints and approaches compare C. Rutten, *Les catégories du monde sensible dans les Ennéades de Plotin* (Paris: Les Belles Lettres, 1961); K. Wurm, *Substanz und Qualität* (Berlin and New York: de Gruyter, 1973); J. Igal, "Aristoteles y la evolución de la antropología de Plotino" *Pensiamento* 35 (1979): 315–16; T. Szlezák, *Platon und Aristoteles in der Nuslehre Plotins* (Basel: Schwabe, 1979); and for a generally unfavorable assessment of Plotinus's use of Aristotle, A. C. Lloyd, *The Anatomy of Neoplatonism* (Oxford: Oxford University Press, 1990).

[32] M. de Gandillac, "Plotin et la Métaphysique d'Aristote," in *Études sur la Métaphysique d'Aristote: Actes du VIe Symposium Aristotelicum* (ed. P. Aubenque; Paris: J. Vrin, 1979), 247–59.

[33] Because of lack of space, I shall deal here primarily with 2.4 [12] and only briefly with 1.8 [51]. However, 3.6 [26], which is arguably the most Platonic of the three treatises, contains a central argument that stems from Aristotle. If matter is impassible, in what sense is this to be understood? Only formal, specific contraries can produce affections. For example, the hot and the cold work upon each other, and so too the red or not red, or blue, but not the red and the cold. But if matter underlies contraries, then it cannot be affected like compound subjects. Therefore, the affection that matter undergoes requires a different manner of speaking (3.6 [26] chs. 8–10, especially 11.24–25).

[34] On "agreement" between Plato and Aristotle, see A. H. Armstrong, *The Cambridge History of Later-Greek and Early Medieval Philosophy* (Cambridge: Cambridge University Press, 1969), 9, 82–83, 197. On the identification of the Receptacle with matter see H.-R. Schwyzer, "Zu Plotins Deutung der sogenannten Platonischen Materie" (note 3), 266ff.; cf. Calcidius *In Tim.* 308: "(Silvae) nomen dederunt auditores Platonis ipse enim nusquam silvae nomen ascripsit"; F. Solmsen, "Aristotle's Word for Matter" in *Didascaliae: Studies in Honour of A. M. Albareda* (ed. S. Prete; New York: B. M. Rosenthal, 1961), 393–408.

the Receptacle with Aristotelian matter. Rather, in his first work on matter, he starts with a Platonic view of higher or intelligible matter (2.4 [12].1–5) and then proceeds to explore the meaning and limits of the Aristotelian-Peripatetic notion of sensible matter (2.4 [12].6–16). In this latter portion of the work, his starting point is an orthodox statement of Aristotelian-Peripatetic doctrine.[35] Matter plays a positive role in the composition and dissolution of compounds (2.4 [12].6), and Plotinus even takes a chapter to point out the cogency of Aristotelian thought against earlier pre-Socratic views (7). In the following chapters he explores the meaning of the indefiniteness of matter, namely, that it is not quantity, quality, or any of the other categories, and he even provides a compelling view of what it means to say that we experience indefiniteness (10–11). He argues subsequently that while privation does relate to form, it also surely characterizes the very lack of nature in matter too:

> If then it is non-existent because it is not being, but some other existing thing different from being, the definitions are two, one comprising the substrate, and that of privation making clear its relationship to the other existing things. (2.4 [12].14.22–24)

Plotinus is sensitive to Aristotle's insistence that form is opposed to privation, not matter, and therefore that the definitions of matter and privation should differ. However, he thinks that Aristotle does not go nearly far enough:

> Or perhaps the definition of matter shows its relationship to other things and that of the substrate also shows its relationship to other things, but that of privation, if it shows the indefiniteness of matter, might actually touch upon it itself; but in this case they are both one in substratum, but two in rational definition. But if privation, by being indefinite and unlimited and without qualities, is the same thing as matter, how do the definitions still remain two? (10.24–30)

Plotinus starts with a tentative suggestion (τάχα) and concludes with a question! Why does he do this, particularly at such a critical juncture of his argument, namely, the ultimate reference of privation that "might actually touch upon" indefiniteness and matter? The answer, I propose, is that without ever mentioning Aristotle, Alexander, Aspasius, or any Peripatetic by name, Plotinus has constructed an inner dialogue with Peripatetic philosophy on the nature of matter at the level of indefiniteness and this is based

---

[35] See the assessment of E. Bréhier in his Notice to 2.4 [12] in *Les Ennéades de Plotin* (Paris: Les Belles Lettres, 1924–1938), 49–50. 2.4 [12] 6 and 7 are a faithful commentary of *Metaph.* 12.2, in Bréhier's view, probably Peripatetic in origin.

on the text of Aristotle. Thus, the introduction of ἀπείρῳ at line 29 (the meaning of which he will explore in the next chapter) is an implicit appeal to the reader of Aristotle's *Physics:* the "infinite" is not the container, but the contained, and it is a cause as matter whose being is privation (τὸ μὲν εἶναι αὐτῷ στέρησις in 207b35–208a2). Indeed, more than an echo of Aristotle's sophisticated notion of infinity pervades the final chapter (16) of 2.4. According to Aristotle, it is characteristic of the infinite that "one thing is always being taken after another" (*Phys.* 206a27–28). For Plotinus, matter is always "other" (2.4 [12].16.26), not in the sense of Platonic "otherness" from the *Sophist* (16.1–3), for "what it is it becomes still more" (16.15–16).[36] Thus, Plotinus concludes against Aristotle's criticism that the Platonists make matter desire its own extinction (*Phys.* 192a16–25), that on the contrary, matter's desire for form "brings what it is naturally to actuality and perfection, like the unsown field when it is sown" (16.11–16).[37] This remarkable conclusion indicates the hidden, revolutionary nature of his transformation of the notion of matter. Matter's negative, "misformed," evil nature is a direct function of its positive role in generation. When the compound physical thing becomes formed or limited, matter is the recipient of form, and the coming-to-be of the compound would be impossible without that recipient. Hence, in the light of form, matter is positive, for it becomes shaped in compounds and possesses a natural potentiality in this shaping. In its own nature, however, a nature necessarily devoid of all the categories of being, matter is revealed as absence or privation by the very presence of form itself. For Plotinus, therefore, the negative, evil nature of matter is a necessary development of Aristotle's own thought, which stopped short at the name of "indefiniteness" and did not pursue the analysis, as he implicitly thinks it should have done, into the privative nature of the indefinite substratum itself.

2.4 [12], then, provides us with a perfect example of Plotinus's method. First, since the topic is matter, the question of Aristotle's opposition to the Platonic view has to be confronted. The object, I suggest, is not to reconcile

---

[36] Cf. 2.5 [25].5.3–7.

[37] See also the words immediately following this: "and as when the female conceives by the male, and does not lose its femaleness but becomes still more female" (13–15). Most probably this reflects Aristotle *Phys.* 192a22–25. There is no space here for an examination of the role of the feminine in Plotinus's accounts of matter. Any treatment would, however, have to take account of Plotinus's treatment of *Penia* (Plato's *Symposium*) especially in III, 5 [50] and I, 8 [51] 14. For a fascinating account of part of this topic in gnostic thought, see Birger A. Pearson, "The Figure of Norea in Gnostic Literature," in *Proceedings of the International Colloquium on Gnosticism, Stockholm, August 20–25, 1973* (ed. G. Widengren; Stockholm: Almqvist & Wicksell, 1977), 143–52.

Plato and Aristotle, but rather to develop a highly individual line of thought that can show Peripatetics how *on Aristotelian grounds* such a reconciliation between two living forms of thought might take place. Second, if this is "the ancient philosophy," then what Plotinus practices is not the citing of authority (though he sometimes does that too) but the development of an inner conversation (in the reflection of Plato, Aristotle, the Stoics, etc.) that is based upon shared discovery rather than private revelation. All in all, then, it is a mistake to suppose either that Plotinus gets more pessimistic about matter as he gets older or, conversely, that it is only in the earlier writings that he thinks about matter in a dualistic way and that in "combating the Gnostics he came to more optimistic thoughts."[38] Plotinus's mature view is already implicit in 2.4 [12] but, of course, it is not yet fully developed. What we can say at this stage is that if the positive and negative functions of matter are so interrelated, then there has to be a positive view of matter and of the cosmos in the light of form or λόγος. Furthermore, the cause of evil cannot simply be located in the λόγος or in an ignorant demiurge, since whatever privation there might be in the soul, its ultimate cause has to be traced to matter in the sense of final deficiency. On the other hand, to locate evil simply and solely in an apparently independent and ungenerated matter, as Numenius appears to do, is not possible on the terms of Plotinus's theory, because then one leaves the correlative, but predominant, positive function of matter out of account.

3. The Generation of Matter and Some Difficult Passages in the Enneads: A Hidden Dialogue with the Gnostics?

It is at least in part this subtle analysis of matter with its inner level of hidden conversation that, I believe, is responsible for one of the major mysteries of the *Enneads,* namely, the problem of the generation of matter. Schwyzer holds that it is not generated, O'Brien and others (myself included) that it is.[39] But why should Plotinus be so cagey on the issue? O'Brien recently suggested (in an as yet unpublished paper) that this

---

[38] See H.-C. Puech, *Sources* (note 25) 184; J. Zandee, *The Terminology of Plotinus and of Some Gnostic Writings, Mainly the Fourth Treatise of the Jung Codex* (Istanbul: Nederlands Historisch-Archaeologisch Insituut, 1961), 19.

[39] For references and *historia quaestionis,* see R. Schwyzer "Zu Plotins Deutung der sogenannten Platonischen Materie" (note 3); D. O'Brien "Plotinus on Evil: A Study of Matter and the Soul in Plotinus' Conception of Human Evil," in *Le Néoplatonisme* (Paris: Éditions du CNRS, sciences humaines, 1971), 114–46; idem, "Plotinus and the Gnostics on the Generation of Matter," in *Neoplatonism and Early Christian Thought* (ed. H. J. Blumenthal and R. A. Markus; London: Variorum, 1981), 108–23; K. Corrigan, "Is There More Than One Generation of Matter in the *Enneads?*" *Phronesis* 31.2 (1986): 167–81.

doctrine is one of the secret doctrines from the teachings of Ammonius Saccas.[40] But if this is so, then why should it be common Neopythagorean doctrine, to be discovered also in such diverse sources as the *Chaldean Oracles,* Tatian, and even perhaps Plutarch?[41] According to Tertullian, the whole question was virtually a *topos* in Middle Platonist schools of the second century.[42]

3.1. The Critical Background: 3.4 [15].1; 4.8 [6].6; 2.9 [33].3

O'Brien has recently devoted an entire book to the criticism of a small article I published in 1986 on the generation of matter.[43] There I tried to show that certain difficult passages in the *Enneads* constrain us to accept that Plotinus views the generation of matter in several, rather different ways and consequently that a rigid two-tier theory of matter, Intelligible and Sensible matter, is not entirely adequate to the subtlety and richness of all Plotinus's analyses. I argued, in particular, that only one passage in the *Enneads,* 3.4 [15].1, yields conclusive proof (without need of any further "argument") that matter is generated by the partial soul, but that other passages trace this generation to soul in its integrity and that lower matter may even be said to be an implicit consequence of the emergence of Otherness from the One, disclosed only as *lower* matter by its remaining eternally "unlit."[44] I further argued (against O'Brien) that lower matter does participate in the good precisely and only to the degree it is formed, and I also tried to show that when Plotinus talks hypothetically in a later treatise about soul generating matter in undergoing an affection (παθοῦσα, 1.8 [51].14.51), this is a position that he can also assimilate, and I established parallels for this in other treatises.[45]

I still hold to this overall view, and O'Brien's two recent books on this topic fail to persuade me otherwise. In fact, in matters of real substance my

---

[40] In a paper delivered to the MacKenna Society Colloquium at Trinity College, Dublin, in May 1992 (to appear in *Hermathena*).

[41] See note 1 above. Cf. also *Chald. Or.* frg. 34 Majercik, ἔνθεν (= source of sources, frg. 30); cf. Psellus *Hypotyp.* 27, ἡ μὲν ὕλη πατρογενῆς ἐστι; Tatian *Or. Graec.* 5 (matter is generated by the demiurge); 12.1 (matter is produced by god). Plutarch *Quaest. plat.* 1001B–C. On this generally, see P. W. van der Horst and J. Mansfield, *An Alexandrian Platonist against Dualism* (Leiden: Brill, 1974), 15–16.

[42] Tertullian *Herm.* 16.11ff. Waszink.

[43] D. O'Brien, *Plotinus on the Origin of Matter. An Exercise in the Interpretation of the Enneads* (Napoli: Bibliopolis, 1991).

[44] K. Corrigan, "Is There More Than One Generation of Matter in the *Enneads?*" (note 39), 168–72.

[45] Ibid., 172–76.

own position and that of O'Brien are very close. Of course, he rejects my positive view of lower matter, but despite his excessive criticism of my article, he is now prepared to trace the generation of matter to soul in its integrity and to accept the "affection" of soul as Plotinus's own view in his most recent work.[46] As far as I can tell, these were not features of his earlier articles.[47] Let this serve as a preface and context for the approach I shall take here on the generation of matter.

Surely it is remarkable that only one passage in the *Enneads* should yield conclusive proof (without need of any further argument) that matter is generated by the partial, but pure soul (in this case the soul as a power of growth).[48] "What is generated," Plotinus states at 3.4 [15].1.10–12, "is no longer a form of soul, but absolute indefiniteness" (ἀοριστίαν ... παντελῆ). "Absolute indefiniteness" can signify nothing else but matter. Plotinus continues: "When it is perfected it becomes a body, receiving the form appropriate to its potentiality" (14–15). This conspicuous statement should refute the widely held view that matter as such has no positive potentiality for Plotinus. In fact, it echoes the conclusion of 2.4 [12].16: even "misformed" matter or ultimate evil is "preserved in being" and "brought to ἐνέργεια and τελείωσις" by form (11–13). The positive-negative doctrine of matter is, therefore, connected with Plotinus's view of its generation. Unfortunately, however, all other passages relating to its generation are ambiguous (5.2 [11].1.18–27; 5.1 [10].7.46–48; 2.3 [52].18.10–13; 4.3 [27].9.20–26; 3.9 [13].3; 1.8 [51].14.51–54).[49] Plotinus may be referring to body or matter, or the view expressed may be only hypothetical, and so on. Yet Plotinus's position is relatively clear. The partial soul generates matter not by any sinful inclination (as Plotinus makes clear also in his critique of the gnostics in 2.9),[50] but as a function of its being soul.

The situation is, however, much more complex than this initial statement might lead us to believe. What seems characteristic of these and other ambiguous passages is how far Plotinus seems to leave the question open

---

[46] D. O'Brien, *Théodicée plotinienne, théodicée gnostique* (note 2), 41 n. 17, 55–56; 34–35, 66–67, 75–76.

[47] D. O'Brien, "Plotinus on Evil" (note 39).

[48] 3.4.1.4–5: ὅταν δὲ ἐν φυτοῖς γένηται, αὕτη κρατεῖ οἷον μόνη γενομένη.

[49] It is impossible in the circumstances to provide the detailed analyses that these passages merit. For analysis, see the works cited in note 39.

[50] See 2.9 [33].8.39–43: Do souls descend by compulsion or voluntarily? Plotinus asks of the Gnostics. These two alternatives do not exclude one another: the soul's descent is both voluntary (without being chosen) and necessary (without compulsion). Cf. 4.3.13.17–20 and also the fine analysis of O'Brien, *Théodicée plotiniènne, théodicée gnostique* (note 2), 5–18, which points out the (Aristotelian) distinction between "will" and "choice."

or to allow the reader to form his or her own view. Thus in 4.8.6, two possibilities are presented, but on both, Plotinus argues, matter must be taken
to participate in good:

> The nature of matter, then, either existed for ever, and it was impossible
> for it, since it existed, not to participate in that which grants all things as
> much good as each one of them can take; or else its coming into being
> was a necessary consequence of the causes before it, and not even so was
> it required to be separate because that which gave it existence as a kind
> of gracious gift became stationary through lack of power before it came
> to it. (18–23)

But if one adopts the first alternative, there is little reason not to adopt the
second, because if an independent matter participates in some way in the
good, why should one continue to think of it as originally independent? Of
course, to the degree that matter is not a cause, but an accidental nature
(as Aristotle might define this in *Phys.* 2), the viewpoint that it always
existed as independent still perhaps makes some sense as an initial position. O'Brien holds that the first of these alternatives must concern intelligible matter, since sensible matter cannot participate. But surely Plotinus is
arguing with a hidden interlocutor here, quite possibly a gnostic, and he
wants to make the point that whichever point of view one takes—the ultimate abandonment of matter or its consequential connectedness with
being—one is effectively compelled to the same conclusion.

A more direct dialogue and similar alternative theories about matter
are to be found in the explicit critique of the gnostics in 2.9.3, where Plotinus insists on the eternal dependence of the physical world on intelligible
illumination. If "anyone says" (τις … λέγοι) that generated things will be
corrupted into matter, then why, Plotinus argues, "should he not also say"
that the matter will be corrupted? But if "he is going to say"
(φήσει) that, what necessity was there, "we will say" (φήσομεν), for it to
come into being?[51] Plotinus then takes up the two alternatives, the abandonment of matter or its connectedness with being (here recognizably
gnostic), which he had presented in 4.8 [6].6:

> But if they will say [φήσουσι] that it was necessary for it to come into being
> as a consequence of the existence of higher principles [παρακολουθεῖν],
> the necessity is there now as well. But if matter is going to remain alone,
> the divine principles will not be everywhere … they will be, so to speak,
> walled off from matter; but if this is impossible, matter will be illuminated
> by them. (2.9 [33].3.15–21)

---

[51] See also D. O'Brien, *Théodicée plotinienne, théodicée gnostique* (note 2),
36–37.

In both passages, but in 2.9 [33] demonstrably, there is a hidden dialogue, and the object is to have the interlocutor see the apparent truth of the question on the basis of reason itself. This gives us a clear insight into one purpose of ambiguity in the *Enneads*. Ambiguity is a rational means of respecting the presence of an explicit or implicit interlocutor and of providing sufficient openness for an inner dialogue to be effective. Finally, since the "aloneness" of lower matter is a recognizably gnostic viewpoint that Plotinus rejects in 2.9 [33].3, and since there is a precise sense in which "lower" matter may be said to participate (namely, to the degree that matter is formed), then I conclude that both alternatives in 4.8 [6].6 refer to lower matter.

3.2. 2.5 [25].5 and 2.4 [12].5: Lower Matter and Intelligible Matter

Let us take another curious passage about matter from 2.5 [25].5. Although to the best of my knowledge no one has yet proposed this, there are echoes of a gnosticizing mythology in this chapter. Matter is, "so to speak, cast out and utterly separated" from the Intelligible (2.5 [25].11–12), just as the intention or desire of the higher Sophia becomes "cast out into the spaces of the Shadow and the Void" in the form of the lower Sophia in Valentinian Gnosticism.[52] Matter has "walked out of true being" (28), like a gnostic personification of passion giving rise to matter.

> It was not anything actually from the beginning, since it stood apart from all realities, and it did not become anything; it has not been able to take even a touch of colour from the things which wanted to plunge into it, but remaining directed to something else it exists potentially to what comes next; when the realities of the intelligible world had already come to an end it appeared and was caught by the things that came into being after it and took its place as the last after these two. So, being caught [καταλειφθεῖσα] by both, it could belong to neither class of realities; it is only left for it to be potentially a sort of weak and dim phantasm unable to receive a shape. So it is actually a phantasm [εἴδωλον] ... a falsity. (12–23)

The negative side is emphasized here, but the positive function is implicit, if puzzling, for matter has come out of the Intelligible and therefore must be traced back to the first outpouring of otherness from the One, as also in 2.4 [12].5.28–37. But what can it mean to be "cast out" of the Intelligible? Is it, perhaps, that matter is included in the first emanation from the One as a result of Otherness? Is it then only disclosed as matter because it remains unillumined in its own nature and, therefore, escapes the realm of

---

[52] Cf. Jonas, *The Gnostic Religion* (note 4), 62–65, 182–196. See also the *Ap. John* II 10; 18.

being to become, first, precosmic matter ("when the intelligible realities had come to an end, it appeared") and, finally, the substratum of the sensible world (cf. it is "caught by the things that come into being after it")? I am not sure if this is the correct interpretation, but it certainly seems to fit at least two difficult passages in the *Enneads* (2.4 [12].5 and 2.5 [25].5). Please observe that this interpretation does not deny that the partial soul generates matter, but rather puts this in the context of the integral emanation of the two lower hypostases, Intellect and Soul. The whole content of soul, and matter too, is implicitly contained within the first movement from the One, but since the partial soul, or the lowest creative part of the World Soul, is higher than the whole of physical existence, it is still the partial soul—a pure, partial soul—which generates and informs matter.

At any rate, this is how I interpret 2.4 [12].5.28–37:

> For Otherness There … makes (intelligible) matter; for this is the principle of matter, this and the primary Movement. For this reason Movement too was called otherness…. The Movement and Otherness which came from the First are undefined, and need the First to define them; and they are defined when they turn to it. But before the turning, matter, too, was undefined and the Other and not yet good, but unilluminated from the First. For if light comes from the First, then that which receives the light, before it receives it has everlastingly [ἀεί] no light; but it has light as other than itself, since the light comes to it from something else.

First, the matter of the Intelligible World is generated by Otherness (perhaps a significant difference from the *Chaldean Oracles,* frg. 34, where matter is generated directly from the "Source"), but in its conversion becomes a fully formed οὐσία. Plotinus refers to this as "the dark," but its darkness is different from that of lower matter, which is an "outcast" darkness—or at least so Plotinus tells us in 2.5 [25].5. Here in 2.4 [12].5 he remarks: "the depth [βάθος] of each thing is matter" (quite probably a reflection of frg. 163 in the *Chaldean Oracles*).[53] Whatever intelligible darkness is in 2.4 [12].5, then, it is related to the intelligible substratum that is formed substance.[54] Thus, the Infinite or "dark other" of later Neoplatonism that is "the principle of life, fecundity and creative expansion"[55]

---

[53] *Chald. Or.* frgs. 163–65: "Do not stoop [νεύσῃς] into the dark-gleaming world beneath which an abyss [βυθός] is spread, forever formless [ἄμορφος] and invisible, dark all around, foul, delighting in images [εἰδωλοχαρής], without reason [ἀνόητος] … forever revolving around its maimed depth [βάθος], forever wedded to an invisible shape [cf. *Enn.* 2.4 [12].10], idle, without breath" (Majercik). Cf. frg. 184.

[54] 2.4 [12].5.15–16, 19–23.

[55] A. H. Armstrong, "Dualism: Platonic, Gnostic, and Christian" (note 6), 42.

cannot be found in this passage.[56] Nonetheless, Proclus's later development of this concept is implicit here, as also in 6.7 [38].32, where Plotinus tells us that the formlessness in *Nous* springs from the formlessness of the One's power which is καλοῦ ἄνθος ... κάλλος καλλοποιόν (31–39—an echo of the *Chaldean Oracles?*).[57] Still more pertinent is 6.5 [23].12.1–11, where Plotinus describes the omnipresence of being as a single intelligible life whose matter is not the endlessness of discursive thought, but the infinite, tireless, and boiling life of the same power "infinite in depth" (βυσσόθεν ἄπειρον). Again, this is surely an echo of gnostic or Chaldean influence.[58] All in all, one may say then that Plotinus's notion of intelligible matter, formless Beauty, or infinite unrestricted power is a genuine source of later Neoplatonism's more positive evaluation of the "dark other."

However, the language of the above passage is puzzling. How can intelligible matter everlastingly have no light? Is this simply a way of saying that all intelligible moments must effectively be eternal? I suggested in my *Phronesis* article that lower matter is implicitly contained in this description, for only lower matter is truly in itself a *recipient eternally in the state of being before receiving*. I do not deny that Plotinus is talking primarily about intelligible matter (though, of course, *both* matters have been included in the discussion of the chapter up to this point), but since intelligible matter is defined in its οὐσία by the intelligible form that shapes it, while lower matter remains "other," indeed "alien" to the form that appears in it, I think it most likely that Plotinus implicitly includes lower matter in his thinking about the integral emanation of everything from the One through the First Otherness and First Movement.

In sum, the two forms of darkness, Intelligible and Sensible, are to be distinguished only by the form that renders them different, as Plotinus states very clearly in 2.4 [12].5.[59] Since distinction between the two is not a question of easy resolution within a single phrase or one description, I suggest that the whole of these two treatises, 2.4 [12] and 2.5 [25], are systematic rational attempts to explore this fundamental ambiguity of darkness either in relation to, or by contrast with, the form that shapes it.

---

[56] Proclus *In Tim.* I [24d–e], 176 Diehl; *In Parm.* 6.1119.4–11, 23–31; *Elem. Theol.* props. 89–92; *Platonic Theology* 3.7–9.

[57] *Chald. Or.* frgs. 1; 34 (connected with the birth of matter); 35; 37.15; 42; 49; and 130.

[58] See H. J. Krämer, *Der Ursprung der Geistmetaphysik* (Amsterdam: B. R. Grüner, 1967), 223–64, esp. diagram, 239; and B. A. Pearson, "The Tractate Marsanes (NHC X) and the Platonic Tradition," in *Gnosis: Festschrift für Hans Jonas* (ed. B. Aland; Göttingen: Vandenhoeck & Ruprecht, 1978), 373–84.

[59] 2.4 [12].5.12–15.

3.3. Consequences: The Development of a Pathology of Evil in 1.8 [51]: A Genuine Comparison and Dialogue with Gnostic Thought

Nonetheless, Plotinus's language in 2.4 [12].5 and, even more so, his gnostic description of an exiled matter in 2.5 [25].5 (effectively a description of the fall of matter) remain puzzling (particularly in the latter case, at the end of a discussion of potential and actual existence). Angels or souls or mental attributes may fall in gnostic or Platonic myths, but it is much more difficult to see how matter as nonbeing or privation can undergo such a fall. Can Plotinus actually be *interpreting* their own myths for the gnostics themselves, but along the lines of his own thought? If this is so, there is a price to be paid, for if Plotinus conducts such a hidden conversation in argument, description, or phrase, then the gnostics certainly have the right to ask whether his notion of matter is any more compelling or consistent than their own. If one refuses to anthropomorphize or personify ultimate evil, but nonetheless continues to employ anthropomorphic language, then the question how evil can actually have real negative effects becomes pressing. How can an absolutely indeterminate matter cause evil? The very notion seems unthinkable. And how could such nothingness be related to the soul? Can the soul or λόγος really remain pure in generating matter, and what really happens when the soul becomes evil?

These questions, indeed, Plotinus confronts right at the end of his life, in his fifty-first treatise (1.8), and I propose that this is partly because of his continued implicit conversation with the gnostics, as well as because of his explicit critique that we will examine separately below. At any rate, despite Heinemann and Thedinga's reservations about this late work,[60] Plotinus actually succeeds in creating an effective pathology of evil in 1.8 [51] by means of the notion of matter as antisubstance, which is surely made possible by Aristotle's language in *Gen. corr.* 3 and also by Alexander of Aphrodisias's notion of holistic fields of the virtues and vices opposed by their contrary natures.[61] Matter, Plotinus argues, can be nonsubstance or antisubstance, not as the negation of individual substance, but rather as the universal negation of all beings, by virtue of its universal opposition to form. Other contraries are either in the same species or genus and, therefore, have generic or quasi-generic "matter" to unite them (1.8 [51].6.36–38, 56–59; Aristotle *Metaph.* 1.1054b27–30).

---

[60] F. Thedinga, "Plotin oder Numenius," *Hermes* 54 (1919): 249–78; F. Heinemann, *Plotin: Forschungen über die plotinische Frage Plotinsentwicklung und sein System* (Leipzig: F. Meiner, 1921), 83ff.

[61] For Alexander, the different virtues (or vices) are contributory parts of the whole and are virtues or vices only in this relation. *De Anima. Liber Cum Mantissa* 155.21–28 (Bruns). Cf. Aristotle, *Eth. nic.* 1096b27–28.

But where the contrariety is between utterly opposed wholes, that is, between the complements of substance and those of nonsubstance, the real application of the term *genus* disappears;[62] as Plotinus says, "they are made up of opposites and they *make* opposites (58–59). So in *De generatione et corruptione* Aristotle envisages the possibility of a universal opposition between being and nonbeing, οὐσία and ὕλη, and argues: "If unqualified non-being signifies what does not exist at all, this will be a universal negation of all things, and, therefore, what comes to be must come to be out of nothing" (317b11–13). Whether or not Aristotle himself holds this view to be true, throughout chapter 3 of *De generatione et corruptione*, he treats being and nonbeing as a continuum from form and substance to privation and matter. Here in 1.8 [51].6 Plotinus argues that both do not constitute a single genus; hence they must be contrary species or antispecies. There is, therefore, no "way between them" and, thus, he cites Aristotle's *Metaph.* 1.4 in the closing lines of the chapter to indicate clearly that these two opposed groups form "the greatest difference."[63] And in the following chapters he develops a theory of the complements of these opposed wholes.[64]

Here, again, we uncover a hidden dialogue with Aristotle and the Peripatetics behind a text that looks primarily Platonic. Again, there is a subtle interweaving of latent strands from the thought of "ancient philosophy" into the development of a new and distinctive line of inquiry. I shall show that there is still another level of dialogue present even in this complex subtext, a dialogue—however indirect—with the gnostics. I shall cite only two examples that I think bear comparison.

3.4. The Affection of Soul and the Fall of Nous: 1.8 [51] and Gnostic Thought

It is sometimes remarked that there is nothing in Plotinus like the failure, weakness, ignorance, and sickness of the *Logos* in gnostic thought.[65] This may be true, but Plotinus nonetheless develops his own version of this at different levels of descent. Parallel to the curiosity of the Demiurge or the boldness and self-determination of the fall in gnostic thought,[66] are, of course, the τόλμα and self-determination (αὐτεξούσιος)

---

[62] Cf. Alexander of Aphrodisias *Quaestiones* 78.13 (Bruns).

[63] 1.8 [51].6.54–59.

[64] See esp. 1.8 [51].9.1–14; 11–13; 15.9–12 (this is presaged already in 3.16–17, 30–38; 4.20–22; 5.14–17).

[65] See, for example, A. H. Armstrong, "Dualism: Platonic, Gnostic, and Christian" (note 56), 45.

[66] See A.-J. Festugière, *La Révélation d'Hermès Trismégiste,* vol. 3: *Les doctrines de l'âme* (Études bibliques; Paris: J. Gabalda, 1953), 83ff.; Zandee, *The Terminology of Plotinus and of Some Gnostic Writings* (note 38), 26–27.

of the early *Enn.* 5.1 [10].1[67] and the busybody "restless nature" (φύσεως πολυπράγμονος) at rest in eternity of the late treatise 3.7 [45].11.15.[68] If gnostic elements are pronounced in the early treatises, they are equally present in the middle and late treatises, but perhaps in a more sophisticated, subtextual form. In 1.8 [51] Plotinus develops two variations on the fall of the λόγος, the first in relation to soul:

> That which does not stay like this (soul in perfect intentness upon Intellect) but goes out from itself because it is not perfect or primary but is a sort of ghost [ἴνδαλμα] of the first soul, because of its deficiency, as far as it extends, is filled with indefiniteness and sees darkness, and has matter by looking at that which it does not look at (as we say that we see darkness as well as the things we actually see). (1.8 [51].4.28–32)[69]

The second variation in relation to Intellect is even more pertinent:

> So this intellect which sees matter is another intellect which is not intellect, since it presumes [τολμήσας] to see what is not its own ... so intellect leaving its own light in itself and as it were going outside itself and coming to what is not its own, by not bringing its own light with it experiences [ἔπαθε] something contrary to itself that it may see its contrary. (1.8 [51].9.18–26)

In the early *Enneads* we hear of partial soul "as it were, walking on air and becoming more indefinite" (3.9 [13].3.11–12), and the problem of the cognition of nonbeing or darkness is part of Plotinus's thinking from 2.4 [12].10 onwards. Nonetheless, the idea that νοῦς has the τόλμα to undergo the affection of its opposite is a genuine development in Plotinus's thinking. It is equivalent to intellect de-intelligizing itself, and it seems to me that Plotinus is talking—perhaps indirectly—to gnostics in these passages. I propose that Plotinus may have in mind a strikingly parallel passage from *Zostrianos* (or one rather like it) which describes the scattering and return of man in remarkably similar terms:

> If he withdraws to himself alone many times, and if he comes into being with reference to the knowledge of the others, Mind and the immortal [Origin] will not understand. Then it has a shortage,... for he turns, has

---

[67] 5.1 [10].1.3–5: "The beginning of evil for them was the τόλμα and γένεσις and the first Otherness and the wish to belong to themselves."

[68] 3.7 [45].11.15–17: "But since there was a restlessly active nature [φύσεως ... πολυπράγμονος] which wanted to control itself and be on its own, this moved, and time moved with it."

[69] Cf. 5.2 [11].1.18–27.

nothing and separates from it and stands ... and comes into being by an alien [impulse...], instead of becoming one. Therefore, he bears many forms. When he turns aside, he comes into being seeking these things that do not exist. When he falls down to them in thought, and knows them in another way because he is powerless, unless perhaps he is enlightened, he becomes a product of nature. Thus he comes down to birth because of it and is speechless because of the pains and infiniteness of matter. Although he possesses an eternal and immortal power he is bound within the [movement] of the body. He is [made] alive and is bound [always] within cruel, cutting bonds by every evil breath, until he [acts] again and begins again to come to his senses. (*Zost.* VIII 45,12–46,15)

This passage[70] is, of course, much influenced by Plato's *Timaeus,* and there is also a hint in the phrase "infiniteness of matter" of the "bottomless sea of unlikeness" (*Pol.* 273d6–e1), which Plotinus cites in his description of the fall and eventual awakening of the soul in the "mud of Hades" in 1.8 [51].13. The focus of the passage, however, is different from Plotinus (if not Plato), for it appears to describe birth as a fall (whether literal or metaphorical one cannot tell), whereas Plotinus is concerned to show how νοῦς can experience that which nullifies and even transforms it. Nonetheless, there appear to be important points of agreement between *Zostrianos* and 1.8 [51]. In both, there is a first "fall" in thought and then a knowing "in another way." In addition, the "ultimate" cause of the fall in *Zostrianos* is perhaps nature, but more probably "the pains and infiniteness of matter," whereas the first cause seems to reside in the soul or λόγος, which results in ignorance and weakness.

But how precisely is the relation between matter and soul to be conceived, and where is the responsibility for any fall to be located? These problems Plotinus takes up directly in 1.8 [51].14. The pure soul, which is

---

[70] [Sieber-Layton's translation should be modified: VIII 45 [12] "When (this type) repeatedly withdraws [13] into itself alone [14] and is occupied with [15] the knowledge of other things, [16] since the intellect and immortal [soul] do [not] [17] intelligize, it thereupon [18] experiences deficiency, [19] for it too turns, has nothing, and [20] separates from it (the intellect) and [21] stands [apart] and experiences [22] an alien [impulse] [23] instead of becoming a unity. [24] So that (type of person) resembles many forms. [25] And when it turns aside, it [26] comes into being seeking those things that [27] do not exist. When it [28] descends to them in thought, [29] it cannot understand them [30] in any other way unless 46 [1] it be enlightened, and it becomes [2] a physical entity. Thus this type of person [3] accordingly descends into generation, [4] and becomes speechless because of the [5] difficulties and indefiniteness [6] of matter. Although possessing [7] eternal, immortal power, [8] (this type) is bound in the clutches of [9] the body, [removed], [10] and [continually] bound [11] within strong bonds, [12] lacerated [13] by every evil spirit, until [14] it once more [reconstitutes itself] and begins again [15] to inhabit it." JDT]

"not in matter as in a substratum"[71] (1.8 [51].14.33), is separate and its activity is unhindered (17–34). But the presence of matter obscures the illumination and darkens soul's vision (38–43). This is not ἀφάιρεσις, but the presence of something alien (ἀλλότριον) (33–34). Thus, all of the soul's powers are prevented from operation:

> matter hinders them from coming by occupying the place which soul holds and producing a kind of cramped condition, and making evil what it has got hold of by a sort of theft—until soul manages to escape back to its higher state. (1.8 [51].14.46–49)[72]

But at the conclusion of the chapter, Plotinus offers a slightly different answer to an implicit interlocutor:

> For even if soul herself had produced matter having undergone some affection, and if she had communicated with it and become evil, matter would have been the cause by its presence; for soul would not have come to it unless its presence had given soul the occasion of coming to birth. (51–54)

What sort of view does the hidden interlocutor hold? Certainly, as in the *Zostrianos* passage, he seems to take birth and the moral fall of soul to be equivalent, yet he also distinguishes between an original *pathos* of some sort and a subsequent fall. Perhaps too he holds that soul is primarily responsible for evil as well as for the generation of what comes after it. At the same time, however, he seems ready to acknowledge that matter also

---

[71] Cf. Alexander of Aphrodisias *Quaestiones* 17.8–19.15.

[72] The final conversion of soul, a pronounced Platonic motif, is to be found both here and in *Zostrianos*. Note too the emphasis on the "alien" (ἀλλότριον) in 1.8 [51].14.24 (cf. 3.36) and in *Zostrianos*. At 1.8 [51].15, in the unsettling of soul as it "touches upon" a lower nature, φαντασία is a πληγὴ ἀλόγου ἔξωθεν which is received by the soul because of its multiplicity (cf. *Zostrianos,* "bearing ["resembles" JDT] many forms," evidently influenced by the *Republic*) whereas "the impulse to *nous* is different" (cf. *Zostrianos* "eternal and immortal power," 1.8 [51].15.12–21). The "cruel ["strong" JDT] cutting bonds" of the latter become for Plotinus, in the final words of 1.8, "beautiful fetters" by which evil is hidden (1.8 [51].15.24–28). For almost the same conception as in Plotinus, however, see the *Apocryphon of John,* esp. II 10,14–19: "And she surrounded it [the consequences of her desire] with a luminous cloud [a hint of the Nephele story which gives birth to the centaurs?] and she placed a throne in the middle of the cloud so that no one might see it except the holy Spirit, who is called the mother of the living. And she called his name Yaltabaoth." For the bonds upon evil see also *Trim. Prot.* XIII 41,18.

plays a definite, if subordinate role. If this is a correct reading of the subtext, then the hidden interlocutor exactly matches the *Zostrianos* text. Plotinus, then, argues a similar case here in 1.8 [51].14 as he had done in 4.8 [6].6. Either the soul is pure, but the illumination becomes darkened by the presence of matter which begs like an *exclusus amator* for entry (1–50); or even if the soul does undergo some affection in generating matter, thus coming to birth, and subsequently still by a different kind of act or knowing becomes evil, still matter is the cause of its descent and fall. Although Plotinus does not express his meaning clearly, we might say that matter is the deficient cause *ex parte privationis,* soul the formal cause *ex parte boni.* The two go together, but even in the case of an evil soul the privation has to be traced to the matter. The conditional clause beginning with καὶ γὰρ εἰ αὐτὴ ἡ ψυχὴ is not unreal.[73] Plotinus can hold both of the above alternatives from different points of view: according to the first alternative, soul remains undescended; according to the second, soul proceeds from its abiding nature and does undergo an affection, but the affection itself is not a sinful fall. There are, indeed, examples of such an "affection" in the *Enneads.*[74] Plotinus's point, therefore, would seem to be this: whichever view of matter and evil the gnostics take (darkened illumination or psychic-noetic entity subject to affection or both), the cause of weakness and privation in the soul must be traced to the matter. The ambiguities of this passage and of others like it in the *Enneads,* then, are not due to Plotinus stating his own point of view or failing to do so, but rather to the fact that there is a hidden dialogue inside a dialogue, which sets out alternative strands of reasoning so that the hidden interlocutors can enter into the argument and make it their own.

First, then, I propose that the correlative positive-negative functions of matter analyzed in 2.4 [12].1–16 are also important for understanding how Plotinus approaches the tricky question of the derivation, generation, and yet abandonment of matter. Here we seem to be presented *prima facie* with apparently mutually exclusive positions. Both, however, come from different viewpoints and can therefore be embraced by a more comprehensive position. For Plotinus, in fact, they seem to form part of a persuasive argument against a variety of possible opponents, gnostics, Numenius, Plutarch, or Atticus. Second, I want to suggest that 1.8 [51] as a project arose out of a peculiarly gnostic challenge. Yaltabaoth, the personification of aggressive, demonic evil, is a much more likely evil champion than

---

[73] On this, see the works cited in note 39.

[74] See Corrigan "Is There More Than One Generation of Matter in the *Enneads?*" (note 39), 174–75 and notes 21, 22, 23. Cf. 3.7 [45].11.11–40; 4.2 [4].1.41–45; 5.1 [10].1.3–8; 4.8 [6].4.12–17; 5.24–27; 3.9 [13].3.7–16; 3.6 [26].17.4–5; 6.9 [9].5.29; 3.8 [30].8.32–36; 4.8 [6].5.16ff.

indeterminate matter. The challenge for Plotinus, therefore, was to establish the foundations for a morphology and pathology of evil (that is, how does evil "make" anything?). This he does, typically on developed Aristotelian terms, but with a clear eye for the central gnostic-character of the whole project. Finally, if I am right so far in this, then the context for understanding Plotinus's explicit critique of the gnostics becomes a little clearer. A rational framework, established on the basis of a dialogue with the thought of some of the major ancient philosophers, is the occasion in which a further dialogue, be it with the gnostics or Numenius, etc., can begin to emerge. Or, in other words, a dialogue within a dialogue forms a conversation in which criticisms can be immediately located in a comprehensible context and, therefore, have more force. If I am right, then this form should characterize the nature of the *Großschrift* as a whole. And if this is so, then I propose that we should be alive to the real possibility that all of the treatises after the *Großschrift*, especially those with cognate interests such as 6.7 [38] and 6.8 [39], will bear similar traces of such a dialogue. In which case, and in the sense we have specified, Plotinus is certainly influenced by the gnostics, for some of his most mature thought is shaped by an implicit conversation with them.

4. *The* Großschrift: *Ancient Philosophy (Aristotle), Productive Contemplation, and the Dialogue with the Gnostics*

What then of 2.9 [33] and its relation to other treatises of the *Großschrift?* Is the whole work or only 2. 9 [33] itself a critique of the gnostics? With the majority of recent critics[75] I support the first alternative. Even

---

[75] V. Cilento, *Plotino. Paideia antignostica: Ricostruzione d'un unico scritto da Enneadi III 8, V 8, V 5, II 9* (Firenze: F. Le Monnier, 1971); C. Elsas, *Neuplatonische und Gnostische Weltablehnung in der Schule Plotins* (Berlin and New York: de Gruyter, 1975), D. O'Meara, "Gnosticism and the Making of the World in Plotinus," in *The Rediscovery of Gnosticism: Proceedings of the International Conference on Gnosticism at Yale, New Haven, Connecticut, March 28–31, 1978,* vol. 1: *The School of Valentinus* (ed. B. Layton; Leiden: Brill, 1980), 364–78; A. P. Bos, "Worldviews in Collision: Plotinus, Gnostics, and Christians," in *Plotinus amid Gnostics and Christians* (ed. D. T. Runia; Amsterdam: VU Uitgeverij/Free University Press, 1984), 11–28—(note 4). I have not been able to take account of Karin Alt's book on 2.9 [33], nor have I had a chance to reread F. Garciá Bazán, *Plotino y la Gnosis* (Buenos-Aires: Fundación para la Educación, la Ciencia y la Cultura, 1981). Porphyry, of course, changes the title of 2.9 [33] in his systematic ordering at *Vit. Plot.* 24 from "Against the Gnostics" (*Vit. Plot.* 5.33) to "Against those who say that the Universe and its Maker are evil," but returns in his edition to the original title. Cilento and Henry (*Études plotiniennes,* vol. 1: *Les états du texte de Plotin* (2d ed.; Museum Lessianum, Section philosophique 21; Paris: Desclée de Brouwer; Brussels: L'Édition universelle, 1948), held that the second title was more in the style of

the positive exposition of the first three treatises is somehow a part of the whole critique. But if so, in what sense? I have suggested above that Plotinus establishes a rational context where conversation can take place and points of similarity or difference can be examined. Is this "dialogue within a dialogue" a fruitful (and demonstrable) way of understanding the whole work? Further, does the work tell us anything more about Plotinus's theory of matter-evil?

One brief question before we try to give an answer to the above: Are Plotinus's opponents Sethian gnostics or Valentinian, perhaps Ptolemaean gnostics?[76] I do not think that the scope of Plotinus's argument can be curtailed, for this argument has clear application to many groups. John Turner's comparison of Sethian texts and Plotinus is, to my mind, absolutely convincing.[77] Plotinus, then, is addressing a wider group, but he

---

Plotinus himself. Goulet-Cazé has recently suggested that Porphyry probably adopted the title to fit the subject matter of the second *Ennead* (L. Brisson et al., *Porphyre: La Vie de Plotin*, vol. 1: *Travaux préliminaires et index grec complet* [Histoire des doctrines de l'antiquité classique 16. Paris: J. Vrin, 1992], 302 n. 1).

[76] Igal ("The Gnostics and 'The Ancient Philosophy' in Plotinus," [note 8]) argues that Plotinus's oversimplification and reinterpretation of gnostic doctrine has the following significant features: (1) It is a four-storied system consisting of four main Aeons. (2) The first three recall Numenius's three Gods. (3) The fourth, which Plotinus names Soul, has *Sophia* in its orbit. (4) The Aeon *Sophia* is to be distinguished from her image in the nether world. (5) For Plotinus (2.9 [33].6.15–19, 55–56) the system derives for the most part from *Tim.* 39e but is impaired by misunderstandings (2.9 [33].6.19)—four, not three, Hypostases and inconvenient additions (superfluous growth of Aeons, cf. 2.9 [33].6.28–31, 56–57). Plotinus keeps the *Pleroma* doctrine separate from the cosmological theses (Igal, 142 and notes). This system, he goes on to argue, is different from anything in *Zostrianos, Allogenes,* or *Hypsiphrone,* being much closer to the Ptolemaean *Pleroma* of (1) The *Ogdoad*— "parent, root, and basis of all" (Irenaeus *Haer.* 1.1.1), (2) The *Ogdoad* named by four names: *Bythos, Nous, Logos,* and *Anthropos,* (3) *Sophia* as the youngest Aeon, belonging to the sphere of the fourth syzygy (Irenaeus *Haer.* 1.1.3), and (4) a double *Sophia,* an apparent innovation of Ptolemaeus (Igal, n. 43). In Ptolemaeus, the first Aeon is a Pre-Principle (*Proarchē*), the second is *Nous,* the third *Logos,* and the fourth *Anthropos-Ekklesia.* Igal suggests that Plotinus's equation of the fourth Aeon with Soul was because of his own identification of man with soul and his own conception of soul as one and many at all levels (Igal, 143–44).

[77] The arguments of Igal and Turner are not, in fact, incompatible. Turner ("Gnosticism and Platonism" [n. 6]), independent of Igal, argues by contrast that the treatises of the *Allogenes* group themselves derive the ontological structure of their transcendent world and of the visionary ascent through it, as well as their negative theology, from sources "at home in Platonism" (451). While Plotinus does not seem to attack the Sethian scheme of the unfolding of the divine world, nonetheless he accepts and rejects different elements in Sethian Gnosticism. He accepts the

is also, and perhaps primarily in certain places, thinking of Sethian texts, and I hope to be able to support this thesis from my own amateur reading of those texts in the Nag Hammadi library.

Plotinus himself gives us a small key to understanding the whole work at the end of 2.9 [33]. "Even if the Gnostics say that they alone can contemplate, that does not make them any more contemplative," he says in virtually the closing paragraph of the work (2.9 [33].18.35–36). In his view, the gnostics claim contemplation as their own in their private revelations,

---

Allogenes' notion of learned ignorance (*Enn.* 3.8 [30].9–10; NHC XI 59,30–32; 60,8–12; 61,2–3; 61,17–19; cf. Porphyry *Sent.* 25–26 Lambertz; *Parmenides* commentary, frgs. 2, 4), the notion that spiritual beings are simultaneously present in their entirety as "all together" in the Intellect (*Enn.* 5.8.7–9; NHC VIII 21; 87; 115–16), and the idea of the traversal of Life from the One into the Intellect (*Enn.* 3.8 [30].11; NHC XI 49,5–21). On the other hand, Plotinus rejects (1) the strong partitioning of the Intellect (*Enn.* 2.9 [33], cf. 3.9), (2) the idea that *Sophia* is derivative and alien (*Zost.* VIII 9,6–11,9; cf. *Enn.* 5.8 [31].5) or that Soul or *Sophia* declined and put on human bodies or that *Sophia* illumined the darkness, producing an image in matter, which in turn produces an image of the image, (3) the idea of a demiurge revolting from its matter and whose activity gives rise to "repentances," "copies" (ἀντίτυποι, i.e., the demiurge's counterfeit aeons) and "transmigrations" (*Enn.* 2.9 [33].6; the "alien earth," 2.9 [33].11; cf. *Zost.* VIII 5,10–29; 8,9–16; 12,4–21), (4) the unnecessary multiplication of hypostases, (5) the conception of a secondary knowledge that is the knowledge of yet a higher knowledge (*Enn.* 2.9 [33].1; cf. *Zost.* VIII 82,1–13), and (6) their magical incantations (*Enn.* 2.9 [33].4; cf. VIII, 52; 85–88; 127; XI 53,32–55,11; VII 126,1–17; X 25,17–32,5). Turner concludes that Plotinus's encounter with the gnostics may have caused him to tighten up his own interpretation of Plato's *Timaeus* (esp. 39e) and even provided "sources of doctrine, insofar as these treatises built their systems upon those of previous Platonists and Neopythagoreans" (457). Turner stresses the importance of the *Allogenes'* contribution of the triads Being-Life-Mind and Existence-Vitality-Mentality to the development of the Middle Platonic exegesis of *Tim.* 39e and *Soph.* 248c–e on the relation and mutual inclusion of intelligence and life. "Sources of doctrine" may be going too far, though Turner's precise qualification of this is important and attractive. I am, therefore, very much in sympathy with Turner's views. My own argument here (certainly compatible with Turner) is that the first three treatises of the *Großschrift* prepare for, and contextualize the critique (2.9). Thus, even where Plotinus rejects certain ideas, he does so already in a philosophical context in which his "opponents" might well agree with him. For example, the strong partitioning of Intellect and the reduplication of knowledge are already "prefigured" in the doubleness of intellect argument of 3.8.11 (even in elements of a shared philosophical language): ἔφεσις γὰρ καὶ ἐν τούτῳ καὶ σύννευσις πρὸς τὸ εἶδος αὐτοῦ. Again, the criticism of the "image of an image" (2.9.10–11) has its earlier philosophical echo at 3.8.2.22–34. Or, finally, even Plotinus's ridicule of magical incantations has to be offset by his quasi-Heideggerian etymology in 5.5.5 and even by the appeal to Egyptian, nondiscursive hieroglyphs in 5.8.6.

which have nothing whatever to do with the nature of the physical world and which result in a "private philosophy" of innovations ("outside of the truth," 2.9 [33].6.11–12).[78] It can hardly be accidental, then, that 3.8 [30]; 5.8 [31]; and 5.5 [32] argue for the view that contemplation, far from being private or external to the world, is *the* fundamental form of all natural making and, indeed, of all life (3.8 [30].1–8). Furthermore, unlike the action of an ignorant, fallen Sophia (cf. 2.9 [33].8.36–39; cf. 43–46; 1.19–33), which makes piece-meal, all artistic and natural objects contain within themselves the seeds of their own whole-formed making according to a *physical* σοφία (5.8 [31].5.1–8), and this has to be traced back internally to *Nous* so that one can appreciate the beauty of both worlds, and especially the *intelligible beauty* of the aesthetic star-gods (cf. 5.8 [31].3.20–36), which the gnostics, in Plotinus's view, disparage (2.9 [33].16.1–2). Thus, finally in 5.5 [32] Plotinus explores what it means to locate nature, soul, and *nous* "within" the truth (5.5 [32].1.32–36, 59–67; 2.1–20; 3.1–2, 16–24, esp. "the king there does not rule over *aliens,* but has the most just, *natural* power and *true* kingdom, since he is king of *truth* and the *natural* lord of his gathered [ἀθρόος, i.e., nonscattered] product").[79] External revelation and alienation from divinity are, in fact, for Plotinus, far from the natural, inner presence of the Good, which is *the* most familiar, *the* most natural and fundamental presence in us:

> One must perceive each thing by the appropriate organ.... And we must consider that men have forgotten that which from the beginning until now they want and long for. For all things reach out to that and long for it by necessity of nature [φύσεως ἀνάγκη] as if divining by instinct [ἀπομεμαντευμένα] that they cannot exist without it. The grasp of the beautiful and the wonder and the waking of love for it come to those who, in a way, already know it and are awake to it. But the Good, since it was there long before to arouse an innate [σύμφυτον] desire, is present even to those asleep and does not astonish those who at any time see it, because it is always there ... but people do not see it, because it is present to them in their sleep. (5.5 [32].12.5–14)

Thus, even cosmic slumber is already pervaded by the presence of the divine, "unknowable" one, and we are given a *reason* why He is unknown in terms of the unconscious or preconscious. Yet by contrast with the gnostic Unknowable, Invisible Spirit (and also with a lot of Plotinus's other writings!), "the Good is gentle and kindly and gracious, and present to anyone

---

[78] Cf. 2.9.9.27–36, 48–50.

[79] Ἀθρόος becomes a leitmotif of the whole work. Cf. 3.8 [30].9.22; 5.8 [31].6.9–10; 5.5 [32].3.19; 7.8.

when he wishes" (5.5 [32].12.33–34). Therefore, I propose that Plotinus develops a theory of natural wisdom and contemplation, shows how these are to be traced to the beauty and inner unity of Intellect, and finally grounds them in the natural, familiar presence of the Good. He does this clearly in contrast to elements in gnostic thought,[80] but also as an implicit and indirect dialogue with gnostics on matters with which they might well agree. After all, not all of them are solipsistic innovators (2.9 [33].6.10–12)! The ability even of the "innovators" to recognize the truth even in the investigation of their own doctrines is what Plotinus insists on when he attacks them directly: "For their 'illumination of the darkness,' if it is investigated," he states at 2.9 [33].12.30–32, "will make them admit the true causes of the universe."

But how does Plotinus go about his task? I want to take one example of this and then point out some hidden parallels with Sethian Gnosticism. As in the case of matter, so in that of nature and contemplation Plotinus starts with a reflection on Aristotle: if the final goal of all human desire is contemplation, as Aristotle indicates in the *Ethics,* and if this includes irra-tional animals, the power of growth in plants, and the earth itself, as Aris-totle reports that Eudoxus thought (*Eth. nic.* 1072b10), and as Aristotle himself might hold, if the Good is final cause of *all* motion, how are we to conceive of this internal productive contemplation at all levels of the universe? Plotinus goes on to argue that the formal-final cause complex in any organism is not only a part of its substance, but internally productive of that substance.[81] Nature is a λόγος, he states, "which makes another logos, its own product, which gives something to the substrate, but stays unmoved itself." The λόγος that is viewed in relation to the visible shape is "last, and a corpse, and no longer able to make another, but that which has life is the brother of that which makes the shape, and has the same power itself and makes in that which comes to be" (3.8 [30].2.28–34). So Plotinus distinguishes between the shape, the λόγος or εἶδος proper (what we might call the substantial form, in later terminology), and finally Nature herself, which cannot simply be identical with the productive λόγος of a particular nature. On recognizable Aristotelian grounds (the unified ἐνέργεια of agent and product, and the principle that motion takes place in the thing moved),[82] Plotinus can thus conclude that what comes to be

---

[80] Apart from the comparisons discussed above in note 76, Plotinus's attempt to engage in the philosophical interpretation of myth (see especially 5.8 [31].12–13; 5.5 [32].3) is significant for its evident subtext. Myth is common ground for Platon-ists, Platonist gnostics, and innovators. Lack of space here precludes any further development of this either in the *Großschrift* or in the rest of the *Enneads.*

[81] For a different development of this notion, see the later treatise, thirty-eight in the chronological order, 6.7 [38].1–3.

[82] *Phys.* 3.3; *Metaph.* 1050a23–b2.

is made both by an external cause and by its own internal finality, which is embodied insight or contemplation.[83] Therefore, if the λόγος is contemplation in the sense of already possessing and being what it is and, thereby, making simply by being itself, then making, being, and contemplation are coextensive,[84] and everything, it follows, will be either contemplation or a product of contemplation.[85]

In his fine essay on this treatise, John Deck has argued that Plotinus alters Aristotle's doctrine drastically by extending contemplation to brute animals and by contradicting Aristotle's explicit statement that contemplation is not productive (*Eth. nic.* 1178b20–21).[86] Plotinus develops, in Deck's view, a curious kind of causality, not formal or final, but a "real efficient causality" (Deck, 107–9). I think Deck is wrong. True it is that Plotinus is well aware of the seeming paradoxical nature of the thesis he advances,[87] but ποίησις and πρᾶξις still remain distinct from θεωρία even if a new context transforms our view of them.[88] I suggest instead that Plotinus is consciously developing a line of thought implicit and even important in Aristotle, but one that Aristotle did not himself develop. If the divine life of contemplation is the goal of all natural organisms, then how this finality actually operates in all of nature becomes a problem. Besides, contemplation is conspicuously productive for Aristotle. The productive νοῦς of *De an.* 3.5 must be a contemplative power, and σοφία, in *Eth. nic.* 7, whose function is essentially and comprehensively contemplative, is said to make in an internal way (1144a1–6). Whether this "making" is a form of efficient or formal-final causality is the subject of contemporary debate.[89] I propose that Plotinus adopts and develops the latter alternative and indicates that he is developing Aristotle's own thought by citing Aristotle at major stages of his conclusion. 3.8 [30].7.15–18 is just such a stage: "it was necessary, since the first principles were engaged in contemplation, for all other things to aspire to this state, granted that their originative principle is, for all things,

---

[83] From a different viewpoint, this is also the goal of the argument in 6.7 [38].1–13.

[84] 3.8 [30].3.14–23.

[85] 3.8 [30].7.1–15.

[86] John Deck, *Nature, Contemplation, and the One* (Toronto: University of Toronto Press, 1967), 107.

[87] See, for example, 3.8 [30].1.

[88] So in 5.8 [31].1–6 the Aristotelian triad, making-doing-seeing, is retained (as also in a different way in 3.8 [30].1–4: making in different senses; 6–8: doing as a prelude to seeing; 7–9: seeing).

[89] For a full discussion see R. A. Gauthier and J. Y. Jolif, *L'Ethique à Nicomaque: Introduction, traduction et commentaire* (2 vols.; 2d ed.; Louvain-Paris: Publications universitaires, 1970), 2:542–47.

the goal (τὰ ἄλλα πάντα ἐφίεσθαι τούτου, εἴπερ τέλος ἄπασιν ἡ ἀρχή)." *Nous* or contemplative wisdom is the source and goal (*Eth. nic.* 1143b9–11). In the *Ethics* (6.7) this passage (1143b9–11) is a difficult one, susceptible of different interpretations.[90] Aristotle even goes so far as to say that the *perception* of particulars is νοῦς[91] (a thought that Plotinus develops in 6.7 [38] 1–7). However, the major drift of Plotinus's interpretation and development of Aristotelian θεωρία is clear. The sensible world is unfolded from within νοῦς. Thus, one can explain why things are so, but one should not suppose that things are so because of the reason one gives, Plotinus argues later in 5.8 [31].7. Νοῦς is like the conclusion before the syllogism (36–41), before purposive thought (ἐπίνοια, 41–43). As in Aristotle implicitly (cf. *Phys.* 2.8), so in Plotinus in a much more developed form, finality is an external principle in and beyond the cosmos, but it is also included in the form of physical things in a way that is not mere conceptual transference or anthropomorphic mind-projection (this Plotinus spends a lot of time arguing against) or again vague spiritual strivings in nature (Plotinus devotes 3.8 [30]; 5.8 [31]; 5.5 [32]; 6.7 [38] and a part of 6.8 [39] to dispelling this view).[92] Thus, in 5.8.7 Plotinus is again thinking of Aristotle's doctrine of the unity of "reason" and "fact" in intelligible perception (cf. *An. post.* 2.19 and 5.8 [31].7.36–44; *Phys.* 188a27–30 and 5.8 [31].7.45) when he concludes that "what is ἀρχή and τέλος is the whole altogether and without deficiency" (5.8 [31].7.47). And, of course, this goes right to the heart of his critique of the gnostics, for they want to ask "why Soul made the world" or "why there is a soul" or "why the maker makes" (2.9 [33].8.1–2) and then explain this in anthropomorphic terms either in terms of change or some kind of discursive thought (2.9 [33].8.2ff.).

I, therefore, propose that if we superimpose these two pictures of the *Großschrift,* one gnostic and one Aristotelian (not to mention the much more evident Platonic dimension), we uncover precisely the form of an inner, implicit dialogue within a hidden dialogue as a kind of pervasive subtext to the free, creative line of argumentation that plays out, so to speak, the major melody. Once one sees this, a lot of other apparently

---

[90] For different interpretations of the reference of τούτων (διὸ καὶ ἀρχὴ καὶ τέλος νοῦς· ἐκ τούτων γὰρ αἱ ἀποδείξεις), cf. J. A. Stewart, *Notes on The Nicomachean Ethics* (repr. of 1892 ed.; New York: Arno, 1973), ad loc., with H. H. Joachim, *The Nicomachean Ethics* (ed. D. A. Rees; Oxford: Clarendon Press, 1951), 213; and J. Burnet, *The Nicomachean Ethics of Aristotle* (London: Methuen, 1900), 281.

[91] Cf. Burnet's comment ad loc. (see note 89 above), 281.

[92] On Aristotle's conception of teleology, see Martha Nussbaum, *Aristotle's De Motu Animalium* (Princeton, N.J.: Princeton University Press, 1978), 57–106; and Jonathan Lear, *Aristotle: The Desire to Understand* (Cambridge: Cambridge University Press, 1988), 15–42.

insignificant details become clearer. Take, for example, the following passage from 5.8 [31].5, where Plotinus traces *all* (the emphatic first word of the chapter) products of art or nature back to the wisdom of Intellect: "the craftsman goes back to the physical wisdom [σοφίαν φυσικήν] according to which he has come into existence, a wisdom which is no longer composed of theorems, but is one thing as a whole [ὅλην ἕν τι], not the wisdom made into one out of many components, but rather resolved into multiplicity from one" (4–8). Why should Plotinus write φυσικήν? Well, for Aristotle, σοφία is the ἀρετή of τέχνη (*Eth. nic.* 6.7),[93] and yet at the same time it is not piece-meal wisdom or a wisdom parcelled up into various species-interests.[94] Rather, it presides over the whole of reality and provides for the coming-to-be of practical wisdom and skill.[95] Plotinus, in the above passage, implicitly emphasizes that this recognizably traditional view concerns *physical* wisdom (not manipulative or artificial thinking), evidently with the purpose of excluding *any* fallen, demiurgic *Sophia* who seeks to contract or reconstruct the world in a discursive manner. For the world is made, Plotinus states, "in every way after the manner of nature [φυσικώτερον ... πάντως], rather than as the arts make; for the arts are later than nature and the world" (2.9 [33].12.17–18). If everything that comes to be is guided by this physical *sophia*, then there is no need for an ignorant, fallen *Sophia*. At the same time, Plotinus's theory of contemplation and the unconscious takes the problem of ignorance very seriously, but shows that the apparent gnostic view can be given a much more subtle interpretation than gnostic mythologists or at least than that segment of "innovative solipsists" give it.

This positive appeal to the wider group of gnostics is, in my view, reinforced by Plotinus's use of important images or ideas that are clearly shared by the gnostics. The visionary description of the "true earth" and "true heaven" in 5.8 [31].3–4, while of course deriving from *Phaed.* 109dff. and *Phaedr.* 247ff., is conspicuously parallel to *Zost.* VIII 48–55. Even more noteworthy is the famous image of the One as a spring in which all rivers have their source or as the life of a great plant, giving and yet self-standing (3.8 [30].10). To be sure, this is common enough. Similar images are found in Macrobius and the *Corpus hermeticum*.[96] Is it merely accidental, however, that the *Tripartite Tractate* has both images? "The Father brought

---

93 *Eth. nic.* 1141a12.

94 Cf. *Eth. nic.* 1141a20–1141b23.

95 Cf. *Eth. nic.* 1144a1–36.

96 Macrobius *In Somn. Scip.* 2.16.23: *fons ... qui ita principium est aquae, ut cum de se fluvios et lacus procreet, a nullo nasci ipse dicatur.* Cf. *Corp. herm.* 4.10.

forth everything, like a little child, like a drop from a spring, like a blossom from a [vine] ... like a <planting> ... in need of gaining [nourishment] and growth" (62,6–13). In both passages, the emergence of multiplicity from the One is under discussion, and the intimate relation between product and Source, which permits the product to know the Source but which leaves the Source "undivided" (3.8 [30].10.17–19) or "incomparable" (*Tri. Trac.* 63,15–16), is developed at some length (*Tri. Trac.* 60–64; 3.8 [30].10.12–35). Or again, is it accidental that Plotinus constantly uses the analogy of perception for understanding the nature of intellection both in itself and in relation to the One? This tends to ground the analysis in a shared "objective correlate" rather than a private apocalypse but at the same time would be readily comprehensible to readers of the Sethian texts, with their emphasis on light and vision. Indeed, a passage in 5.5 [32].7 that I have always found a little puzzling comes into a new focus because of this comparison with Sethian texts. After a prolonged analysis of perception, in which Plotinus effectively distinguishes four cognate moments of light,[97] Plotinus concludes:

> "Just so Intellect, veiling itself from other things [ἀπὸ τῶν ἄλλων καλύψας] and drawing itself inward, when it is not looking at anything will see a light, not a distinct light in something different from itself, but alone by itself in independent purity [αὐτὸ καθ᾽ ἑαυτο] suddenly appearing [ἐξαίφνης φανέν], so that Intellect is at a loss to know whence it appeared, from outside or within. ..." (31–34)

I had thought that ἐξαίφνης φανέν was a distant echo of the daughters of the sun pulling back the veils (καλύπτρας) from their faces in Parmenides' *Proem* (Diels-Krantz frg. 1.10; cf. Plato *Symp.* 210e4; cf. 212c6, 213c). However, I now cannot help thinking that Plotinus includes within his empirically based image an indirect reference to the gnostic triad Autogenes-Protophanes-Kalyptos, just as he unites being-having-seeing in one unified description of Intellect in dialogue with Numenius or Amelius.[98] Thus, Intellect's vision is no longer that of Allogenes ("one thing in another") but rather that of Kalyptos (veiling itself from others), a seeing of Autogenes ("itself in itself alone, pure") as Protophanes (i.e., self-generated and first appearing: ἐξ᾽ αὐτοῦ ... φανέν). Instead of a triad of distinct personified hypostases, there is one unified description of a dynamic multiplicity. This may seem

---

[97] Cf. the four aeons or lights of *Zost.* 126–28; *Gos. Eg.* 51,17–53,9; or the Father as "the eye of those who see," *Tri. Trac.* 66,26–27. For the four moments of light in 5.5 [32].7, see K. Corrigan, "Amelius, Plotinus and Porphyry on Being, Intellect and the One," *ANRW* 2.36.2:989.

[98] See Corrigan, ibid., 975–93, esp. 981.

oblique, but I believe it is characteristic of the sophisticated level of argument that Plotinus employs, and it reveals, I think, that at root some of the gnostics, or at least those "friends" in Plotinus's circle, influenced by gnostic ideas, are not so much opponents as potentially sophisticated interlocutors. This is not to minimize 2.9 [33] as a critique, but rather to acknowledge that the first three treatises are primarily directed to colleagues and gnostics, especially to those who hold to the "ancient philosophy."

Finally, the *Großschrift* presents probably the most positive view of matter in the *Enneads*. In fact, matter is difficult to find, so hidden is it under all the forms (5.8 [31].7.21–22). It is itself "also an ultimate form; so this universe is all form, and all the things in it are forms" (22–23). This may sound inconsistent, but Plotinus's positive-negative view developed from Aristotle permits him to speak of matter in this sense as a kind of "proximate" or "ultimate" form.[99] Perhaps even more remarkable is the thought-experiment Plotinus devises two chapters later (after reproving those who censure the visible world, 8.22–23):

> Let us then take in our thought [διάνοια] this universe, each of its parts remaining what it is without confusion, gathering all of them together into one as far as we can, so that when any one part appears first, for instance, the outside heavenly sphere, the imagination of the sun and, with it, the other heavenly bodies follows immediately, and the earth and sea and all the living creatures are seen, as they could all be seen ... inside a transparent sphere. Let there be, then, in the soul a shining imagination of a sphere, having everything within it.... Keep this, and apprehend in yourself another, taking away the mass: take away also the places, and the mental picture of matter in you, and do not try to apprehend another sphere smaller in mass ... but calling on the god who made that of which you have a mental picture, pray him to come. And may he come, bringing his own universe with him.... (5.8 [31].9.1–15)

Since Plotinus mentions this sphere again at the end of 2.9 (ch. 17.4–19), I take this to be the proposal of a direct contrast to the gnostic private revelation that comes directly from above and that ignores or despises the cosmos. Instead of the many spheres of Valentinian cosmology, for instance, and the subsequent separation from God, Plotinus presents the single sphere of traditional Greek cosmology as the immediate phenomenological space of individual consciousness.[100] Nothing is bracketed, but everything has to be included in consciousness: a unifying grasp of perception, discursive reason, appearance, imagination, and apperception. In *Zostrianos* there is an ambiguous but analogous insistence upon "going through everything," a phrase that

---

[99] *Metaph.* 1045b18: ἡ ἐσχάτη ὕλη καὶ ἡ μορφὴ ταὐτό.

[100] Cf. the spherical shape of soul in *Marsanes* pp. 25–26.

is repeated at least three times.[101] At the same time 5.8 [31].9 echoes certain
elements in the Sethian texts and transposes them into an empirically based
model: for example, seeking the Father of all in thought and perception (*Zost.*
2,13; 44,2–3), the use of productive imagination (10,10–14), or thought in
silence (24,10–17), or "in accordance with the pattern that indwells you,
know likewise [that] it is in this way in [all such matters] after this very pattern" (*Allogenes* 59,37–60,2), or especially prayer (*Zost.* 63; *Tri. Trac.* 66),[102]
which neatly indicates in terms clearly acceptable to the Sethian gnostics that
ascent, understanding, or production is not one's own private doing, but a
shared endeavor in which one's own activity calls forth to a cognate but superior power. However, Plotinus does not tell us to take away the matter, only
the "phantom of matter in you." Can it be that matter itself here is genuinely
part of form, even part of the intelligible? Plotinus, of course, cannot accept
gnostic ἀποκατάστασις or even the view that finally "the entire defilement"
will be saved (*Marsanes* 5,15), but he is surely sympathetic with the world-
affirming side of the Sethian texts: "<I have come to know> when <I> was
deliberating that in every respect the sense-perceptible world is [worthy] of
being saved entirely" (*Marsanes* 5,24–26). Thus far, all this seems compatible
with Plotinus's view of the generation of matter and matter's positive function
in *genesis*. But without the gnostics, would we really have been able to see
this side of Plotinus's thought so clearly in the *Enneads?* At any rate, this positive view is generally characteristic of subsequent treatises in the chronological order from 34 up to 50.[103] Plotinus's critique of the gnostics might well
have helped to make possible, for all I know, one of the strangest statements
in the whole of the *Enneads* in 6.2 [43].21, to the effect that since bodies are
in the intelligible, matter and qualities must be there too (52–53). What we
are to make of this I am not entirely sure. In the light of the criticism of Aristotelian-Peripatetic philosophy that comes both before and after this treatise,
however, 6.2 [43] is concerned to demonstrate how a Platonic intelligible
view of reality is more capable of explaining the rich, teeming, even sensual

---

101 *Zost.* 4,26–6,2; 44,5–22.

102 For the importance of prayer in connection with the *Three Steles of Seth*, see
the assessment of Hans-Martin Schenke, "The Phenomenon and Significance of
Gnostic Sethianism" (note 6), 602: "In short I cannot help seeing the *Three Steles*—
as a typical liturgical text. And the passage 127:6–21 ... is something like a rubric,
in which it is expressed how the three prayer formulas are to be used and what
results from performance of the ritual. Our text does not represent the pure formula, as it were, but has been stylized and framed as an etiology of the ritual."

103 Of the treatises in this chronological section, 3.5 [50] requires proper, separate attention, which it is not possible to give it here. For an interpretation of the
birth of *Eros*, see Corrigan, "Is There More Than One Generation of Matter in the
Enneads?" (note 39), 177–80.

diversity of all life rather than what we might call the poststructuralist, categorial mentality which begins with abstract categories and tries to fit everything into these. The latter view, I believe, is less characteristic of Aristotle than of the subsequent history of interpretation.[104] All in all, however, the interpretation of the "living creature" of the *Timaeus* that Plotinus offers in chapter 21 of 6.2 [43] is not dissimilar from Neopythagorean, Chaldean, or gnostic views of the unfolding of intelligible reality down to the ultimate sediment that is, in this perspective, a pretty desiccated "physical universe" (because the soul has been for whatever reasons subtracted from it).[105]

Given this general assessment, however, it is most probable that Plotinus develops his final analysis of the negative pathology of matter in continuing opposition to gnostics (among others) and even as a response to gnostic-related demands to create a coherent philosophical theory of the *action* of evil (on the basis of the "ancient philosophy") to replace their own more immediately plausible mythology of aggressive, demonic forces. In 1.8 [51], in particular, Plotinus clearly responds to the gnostic challenge of a fault, split, or "affection" in the spiritual world and argues that even if one grants some affection (which he does) of soul, his philosophical theory of matter-evil can still account for generation and, subsequently, for the emergence of evil in the world.

5. Conclusion

The results of this investigation, then, might be stated as follows. A positive-negative matter theory is characteristic of many schools and thinkers before Plotinus. What distinguishes Plotinus is the distinctive line of thinking he creates within the context of ancient Platonic philosophy. In much of Plotinus's thinking about the sensible world, but particularly in his works on matter, there is a hidden conversation with Aristotelian philosophy, whose object appears not to be procrustean reconciliation so much as the development of an inner dialogue in which latent possibilities in "the ancient philosophy" and in the subject of investigation itself can be scrutinized in a relatively open fashion. If this "dialogue within a dialogue" form is in the tradition of the "School of Gaius" and of Ammonius Saccas, then our analysis here will help to show that Plotinus's implicit readers were much more sophisticated than we have commonly supposed.

On the question of matter, I have argued that Plotinus's positive-negative analysis in 2.4 [12] is a Platonic development of latent-elements in

---

[104] To demonstrate this would require a separate treatment. For a similar view, however, see S. Strange, "Plotinus' Treatise 'On the Genera of Being,'" Ph.D. diss., University of Texas at Austin, 1981.

[105] Cf. 6.3 [44].1.19–31.

Aristotle by means of an inner dialogue with Aristotelian philosophy. Most of the features of Plotinus's later works are already there *in nuce,* but certainly not in developed form. This reciprocal positive-negative view of matter accounts for matter's "participation" in form, to the degree it is formed, and also for the thoroughly positive treatment of matter in the *Großschrift* (treatises 30–33) and most of the works of Plotinus's middle period, while it also accounts for the negative view developed further in 3.6 [26] and 1.8 [51]. This simultaneous positive-negative view according to different perspectives provides a context for understanding lower matter's generation by the partial soul and its implicit appearance as a consequence of primal Otherness in 2.4 [12].5 and its "banishment" in 2.5 [25].5. And if the darkness of the Intelligible is to be related to the infinite formlessness in *Nous* that springs immediately from the formlessness of the One's unrestricted Beauty as beauty-making power, then the later Proclan doctrine of the "dark other" or Intelligible infinite is presaged here in Plotinus.

In many of the passages relating to the generation of matter one also begins to uncover a critical, indirect dialogue with the gnostics or at least with those friends of the Plotinian circle influenced by Gnosticism. Plotinus's elaboration of alternative possibilities in 4.8 [6] and 2.9 [33] (matter's ultimate abandonment or its consequential connectedness with being) and his gnostic description of the "exile" of matter in 2.5 [25] are evidence of a subtextual critical reflection upon gnostic thought and even an implicit, indirect dialogue. The most conspicuous example of such a subtextual current is in the late work 1.8 [51], where a comparison with *Zostrianos* helps us to realize the extent and importance of this dialogue. Clearly Plotinus has developed his own thinking in order to show how the intelligible "affection" of soul is susceptible of philosophical explanation without making intelligible reality the cause of evil. At the same time, I proposed that Plotinus develops a subtle pathology of evil (again in subtextual dialogue with Aristotle and Alexander of Aphrodisias) as a direct philosophical response to an evident gnostic-type problem, namely, how an indeterminate indefiniteness can "do" anything or have any effects whatsoever. Here we come closest to uncovering a dialogue with the gnostics, within a dialogue with Aristotle, in the subtext of the work itself. I believe that this is of fundamental importance for understanding the place of the explicit critique of the gnostics within the *Großschrift*, for if I am right in this, then the implicit gnostic-influenced interlocutors capable of understanding what Plotinus is talking about (and clearly to be distinguished from mere "innovative solipsists") are highly sophisticated thinkers who must have formed part of the collegial circle of Plotinus's house in Rome.

In my treatment of the *Großschrift*, therefore, I have emphasized that the first three treatises—3.8 [30]; 5.8 [31]; and 5.5 [32]—establish a philosophical conversation with the gnostics, a conversation that we have seen here to be characteristic of Plotinus's method, a method that is ultimately inclusive just like his Intelligible Universe. This conversation is the framework for understanding the force of the explicit critique in 2.9 [33], and I have pointed out several comparisons with Sethian texts that serve to illustrate the positive, philosophical meeting ground that Plotinus may well be seeking to establish as the real basis for dialogue. I have argued in particular that the whole development of thought in the three earlier treatises occurs in the context of this gnostic project. If we ask ourselves what "doctrine" might mean for Plotinus, I think we have to answer that "doctrines" are not fixed epitomes of developed Platonic, Aristotelian, or Stoic insights but rather lines of thinking which take on their own organic form and reveal the many layers of their inception and development in the treatises of the *Enneads*. If this is so (even if it is only part of the truth), then gnostic thought (and particularly Sethian Gnosticism) is a genuine motive force for the critical development of Plotinus's own thinking, since clearly it is at least in part because of the gnostics that Plotinus is compelled to rethink, not only the interpretation of Plato's *Timaeus,* but also the central question of what divine creativity or creative making in general really is. Again true to "the ancient philosophy," he does this partly by means of an inner dialogue with Aristotle (and, of course, always Plato). Nonetheless, the gnostics, and Sethian gnostics, in particular, are at least implicit interlocutors in the development of one of the most distinctive lines of thinking in the *Enneads,* namely, the doctrine of internal, contemplative making, which Plotinus returns to over and over again in some of his greatest works. For example, the first chapter of the next treatise after the *Großschrift*, 6.6 [34].1, "On Numbers," might well begin with "a traditional Neo-Pythagorean view of evil," but the treatise's principal concern to provide "a more positive evaluation of multiplicity and number"[106] is very definitely related to the gnostic-project of the *Großschrift*. Even more conspicuous is Plotinus's major development of the thought of the *Großschrift* in 6.7 [38] and 6.8 [39]. I suggest that these two works are written directly as a response to colleagues and opponents (gnostic and others) who wanted to know after reading the *Großschrift,* first, how Plato's language in the *Timaeus* could properly be reconciled with Plotinus's doctrine of internal productive making[107] and, second, how Plotinus's One could in

---

[106] A. H. Armstrong, *Plotinus: Enneads* (7 vols.; LCL. Cambridge: Harvard University Press, 1966–1988), 7 (6.6 [34].1) ad loc.

[107] See the assessment of P. Hadot, *Plotin: Traité 38* (Paris: Cerf, 1987), 26: "Comme les traités 30–33 … comme peut-être aussi le traité 39, notre traité 38 au moins dans ses premiers chapitres, est dirigé contre les Gnostiques, ce qui signifie sans doute que la polémique antignostique a tenu une place importante dans les préoccupations de Plotin à cette periode de sa vie." See also 27–28.

any meaningful sense be a free and creative "God." Development of this part of my thesis is, however, not possible here. At any rate, what I hope to have shown is that there is an unexpected hidden dialogue, however indirect, between Plotinus and gnostic "representatives" that leads not only to the development of some of Plotinus's major doctrines in the middle and late works, but also to the strongest statements in the *Enneads* of a positive view of matter as well as to the development of a radical pathology of evil just before Plotinus's death.[108]

---

[108] The writing of this paper and the discussion in the seminar were invaluable in the preparation of my subsequent book, *Plotinus' Theory of Matter-Evil and the Question of Substance: Plato, Aristotle, and Alexander of Aphrodisias* (Recherches de Théologie ancienne at médiévale, Supplementa 3; Louvain: Peeters, 1996), which profited considerably from the suggestions of the participants.

After Aporia: Theurgy in Later Platonism[1]

Gregory Shaw
Stonehill College

> Those who would be Gods must first become human.
> — Isidore

> ... the truth of the matter gentlemen, is pretty certainly this, that real wis-
> dom is the property of God, and this oracle is his way of telling us that
> human wisdom has little or no value. It seems to me that he is not refer-
> ring literally to Socrates, but has merely taken my name as an example,
> as if he would say to us, "The wisest of you men is he who has realized,
> like Socrates, that in respect of wisdom he is really worthless."
> — Socrates (*Apology* 23a–b)

In the figure of Socrates, the Platonic tradition begins with a great deal of caution about what human beings can know of the divine. Not only did Socrates maintain that consciousness of his ignorance made him wisest by default, but in the *Alcibiades I*—the first dialogue studied in the later Platonic schools—the worst kinds of evil are said to be caused by those who claim to understand the best things: goodness, justice, and nobility (118a). A Socratic *aporia* and humility about human wisdom seem to have been the starting point for a genuine philosophic education, and this aporetic element continued to influence Platonic thinkers until it reached perhaps its highest expression in the writings of Damascius, the last head of the Platonic Academy in sixth-century Athens.

It is surprising, then, that Iamblichus, the fourth-century Syrian Platonist, has been so poorly appreciated by scholars. For not only did Iamblichus reassert the limits of the human soul against the opinion of his Platonic predecessors, he provided an explicit psychology to account for

[1] I would like to thank the members of the Gnosticism and Later Platonism Seminar who commented on this paper at the 1994 AAR/SBL meeting. Special thanks to John Finamore for his excellent suggestions and to Ruth Majercik for her support. An earlier version of this paper appeared in *The Journal of Neoplatonic Studies,* appearing in revised form here with the editor's permission.

these limits and developed a Platonism in which the acceptance of our incapacity, our *aporia,* became an integral part of contacting the gods in theurgic ritual. In contrast to Iamblichus's poor repute among us, the Platonists themselves saw him as divinely gifted, and it is Iamblichean Platonism—including the practice of ineffable theurgic rites—that dominated the later Academy, inspired the resurgence of Platonism in Ficino's fifteenth-century Florence, and led Ralph Waldo Emerson to write that he "expected a revival in the churches to be caused by the reading of Iamblichus!" What is it that Platonists saw in Iamblichus that we have not?

While it is now almost commonplace to explain Iamblichus's theurgical tendencies as a response to the influx of irrational forces in late antiquity—the *Chaldean Oracles,* the appeal of magic, or the growth of Christianity—I will argue that Iamblichus's introduction of theurgic rituals was tied directly to his understanding of Socratic *aporia* and that theurgy should be seen first as an *intra*-Platonic phenomenon that solved metaphysical and soteriological problems that had long vexed the Academy. Further, I will argue that it was Iamblichus's understanding of the soul specifically that led him to promote theurgy as a necessary and entirely coherent response to the needs of the embodied soul. Finally, after discussing Iamblichus's rationale for a Platonic theurgy, I will consider his soteriology in contrast to Plotinian and gnostic views of the soul's salvation.

1. The Platonic Background

The evidence of Plato's dialogues suggests that the "ignorance" of Socrates was the result of a profound moral and intellectual effort and that his *aporia* was—as Socrates himself says—a state of mind available to all human beings, but only reluctantly accepted. The simplicity of it, realizing that one's wisdom is entirely worthless, remains as terrifying for us today as it was in the fifth century B.C.E., and because it terrifies us we tend to diminish its importance or think that it applies to everyone but ourselves. Socrates is Plato's example of the soul no longer beguiled by fantasies of security or self-importance. He is the soul cleansed of self-deception, and throughout the first, or "cathartic," dialogues in the curriculum of the later Platonists: the *Alcibiades I,* the *Gorgias,* and the *Phaedo,* Socrates' probing questions cause his interlocutors, and Plato's readers, to recognize their own self-deceptions and experience the shock of *aporia.*[2]

---

[2] Westerink, who discussed the curriculum of the later Platonists based on the anonymous *Prolegomena* 26, writes: "After the (introductory) *Alcibiades,* the *Gorgias* deals with the civic virtues, then the *Phaedo* with the purificatory virtues, followed by seven others which contain, in systematic arrangement, the subject-matter for speculation (contemplative virtues): *Cratylus* and *Theaetetus* (epistemology),

As exemplified in Socrates, rational thinking for Plato has a purely cathartic function. Its purpose was to prune away deceptions, not to affirm or discover what is of the greatest importance for the soul. For the highest and most valuable subjects Plato says there can be no rational discourse, and in the *Seventh Letter* (341c–d) he writes:

> I certainly have composed no work in regard to it, nor shall I ever do so in the future, *for there is no way of putting it in words like other studies.* Acquaintance with it must come rather after a long period of attendance on instruction in the subject itself when, suddenly, like a blaze kindled by a leaping spark, it is generated in the soul and at once becomes self-sustaining.

After pointing out the inadequacies of the rational method to describe the subject to which he is most devoted, Plato portrays the soul's experience of it with a poetic image: "suddenly ... a blaze kindled by a leaping spark"; it is an evocation, not an explanation. Plato's evocative use of myths and images, seen, for example, in the *Phaedrus* and the *Timaeus,* were studied later in the Platonic curriculum and were the necessary complement to Socrates' cathartic cross-examinations prominent in the early dialogues. Cleansing, then awakening, was the way of Platonic *paideia,* and while a well-exercised skill in rational analysis was necessary to strip the soul of false beliefs, it could never awaken it to its innate dignity. For this, something more fundamental was needed, and again Plato has Socrates show the way.

Despite his profession of ignorance on virtually all matters, there was one thing, the only thing, that Socrates claimed to understand: *ta erōtika,* the mysteries of love and desire.[3] In the *Symposium* and the *Phaedrus* Plato lays out the fundamental importance of *erōs* for the soul in reestablishing its contact with the divine. *Erōs* was a more than human force, a divine magnetism that pulsed through the cosmos, and to the degree that human souls were carried by its higher currents, they experienced a heavenly rapture that was superior to all forms of knowledge and human wisdom.[4] For Plato, *erōs* was more fundamental than reason, and even in the most "rational" of souls, *erōs* secretly determined the goal and direction of its

---

Sophist and *Statesman* (physical world), *Phaedrus* and *Symposium* (theology), with the *Philebus* (on the Good) as the end of the series." This was followed by the perfect dialogues: the *Timaeus* and the *Parmenides.* See L. G. Westerink, *The Greek Commentaries on Plato's Phaedo I* (Amsterdam: North-Holland Publishing, 1976), 15.

[3] *Symp.* 177e.

[4] *Phaedr.* 244a.

thinking.[5] Since human knowledge, at its best, could reach only a Socratic *aporia,* to contact the divine something more than human was needed, something that penetrated our lives as an *a priori* force given by the gods. This is the *erōs* of the Platonic dialogues. Anterior to rational reflection, *erōs* slowly awakens in the human form, and when guided up the ladder of beauties described in the *Symposium* (241b–c), it reaches Absolute Beauty where the soul is fulfilled and rides again in the heavens with the gods.[6]

Plato warns his readers that such images cannot be taken as true descriptions of the soul's destiny, for such matters fall outside the certainty and artifice that the abstract sciences allow. The origins of the universe and the nature of the soul are matters that "only a god could tell,"[7] and Plato admits that his myths are but "likely stories" passed on by the wise.[8] In sum, I would characterize Plato's myth of the soul as follows: Created immortal and imbued with the generosity and creativity of its Maker, the human soul is coordinated perfectly with all the divinities and powers of the cosmos. In the trauma of human birth, however, the soul loses its innate coordination and becomes estranged from its original and divine nature. In the words of the *Phaedrus,* the soul "loses its wings" and identifies with its mortal body. Yet, through *paideia* the soul can reorient itself, see through its false identity, and regain the harmony that it lost at birth. Prior to *paideia,* the human soul is estranged both from itself and from the cosmos. Its thinking moves counter to divine thought, as Plato puts it, like a man walking backwards and turned upside down.[9] This is why *paideia* must arrest the soul's thinking with the shock of *aporia.* Only then can it begin to reorient itself to the thoughts and movement of the divine. In this, the visible cosmos plays an essential role, as Plato says:

> And the motions which are naturally akin to the divine principle in us are the thoughts and revolutions of the universe; these each man should follow, and by learning the harmonies and revolutions of the universe should correct the courses of the head which were corrupted at our birth, and should assimilate the thinking being to the thought.[10]

The assimilation of the soul to the harmonies of the universe required intellectual disciplines to purify the soul's *erōs* for its lost divinity. Yet lacking

---

[5] See comments by W. K. C. Guthrie, *A History of Greek Philosophy* (London: Cambridge University Press, 1975), 4:475–76.

[6] *Phaed.* 247b–e.

[7] *Phaed.* 246a.

[8] *Tim.* 29c–30a.

[9] *Tim.* 43d–e.

[10] *Tim.* 90c–d.

an awakened *erōs*, no amount of intellectual skill could benefit the soul. However brilliant it might be, such a soul remained fixed in the shadows cast by its own unrecognized *aporia*.[11] Although Plato's *paideia* was intellectually rigorous, it was even more demanding as a discipline of the heart, for it required souls to endure the insecurity and inferiority of not knowing. Yet from their conscious *aporia,* such souls began to follow a more ancient way, revealed in the stars, the seasons, and the lives of pious souls who preserved the myths of the wise.[12]

The evocative imagery of Plato's myths were not intended to inform but to awaken and guide the soul's *erōs* to its original nature. But what then? If Plato's soteriology may be described poetically as an ascent to the gods, what follows was just as important. The divinized soul had to return to mortality and fulfill the ancient pattern initiated by the Demiurge and portrayed suggestively throughout the dialogues. In the act of creation the Demiurge extends himself into the world in order to share his generosity.[13] The guardians who ascend from the cave imitate this benevolence by returning to the darkness.[14] *Erōs,* the agent of the soul's deification, is described as moving up and down between the gods and men.[15] And Socrates, the exemplary soul and avatar of *erōs*, is simultaneously attracted by, yet even more attractive to, his interlocutors.[16] While being constantly drawn upward to divine beauty, Socrates communicates that same divinity to his listeners, and not as a man—who would credit himself for it—but as something Alcibiades described as more than human.[17] Finally, the dialectic itself, after ascending to the first principle, is completed only when it descends into the many without losing touch with the Forms.[18] In Platonic *paideia* the soul's ascent to the gods was confirmed only when it descended and communicated that divinity to the mortal world.

Plato's *paideia* provided a rich legacy for his students, and while it continued to stimulate and sustain philosophic communities, it necessarily left many questions unanswered. The driving force of *paideia* was the soul's *erōs,* not *logos,* so the metaphysical framework of Plato's thought was left fluid, allowing it to be shaped to meet the needs of

---

[11] *Rep.* 516d.

[12] Plato suggests that this was more an intuitive than an intellectual attainment; see, e.g., *Phaedr.* 275b–c.

[13] *Tim.* 29e.

[14] *Rep.* 519d–520a

[15] *Symp.* 202e–203a.

[16] *Symp.* 216d–217a.

[17] *Symp.* 221c–222a.

[18] *Rep.* 511b–e.

other generations. The "likely stories" that provided the imaginative framework for *erōs* were left to be worked out by later Platonists in different contexts. Yet the needs of the soul remained the same regardless of changes in culture, and Platonic *paideia* continued to follow a twofold process: (1) to purify the soul with the shock of *aporia*, and (2) to nurture the soul's *erōs* for the divine, which united it with the generosity of the Demiurge.

2. The Puzzle of Plotinus

> I am puzzled how I could, even now, descend, and how my soul has come to be in the body.
>
> — Plotinus

Perhaps no one in the history of Platonism better exemplifies the fulfillment of *paideia* than Plotinus, the designated founder of Neoplatonism. He recognized the soul's *aporia* in our efforts to know the One and explained how we paint the One in the colors of our personal experience. He says:

> we run round it [the One] outside, in a way, and want to explain our own experiences [πάθη] of it, sometimes near it and sometimes falling away in our perplexities [ἀπορίαι] about it. The ἀπορία arises especially because our awareness of that One is not by way of reasoned knowledge or of intellectual perception, as with other intelligible things, but by way of a presence superior to knowledge. (*Enn.* 6.9.3.53–4.4 trans. Armstrong)

This presence superior to knowledge was the Platonic *erōs,* and Plotinus employed Plato's likely stories to convey the depths of his own erotic experience of the One. Following the imagery of the *Phaedrus* and the *Symposium,* Plotinus said that the soul's desire for the One was a more than human force bestowed on the soul by the One (and Good) that put the soul in a state of elevated passion. Describing this he says:

> Then the soul, receiving into itself an outflow from thence [the Good], is moved and dances wildly and is all stung with longing and becomes desire [ἔρως]. (*Enn.* 6.7.22.8–10)

This god-given *erōs,* Plotinus says, was implanted in souls "from the beginning,"[19] and he maintained that in its ascent to the One, the soul goes "out

---

[19] *Enn.* 6.7.31.18–19.

of its mind,"[20] is lifted on the wings of *erōs* "above knowing," and returns to the "giver of its love."[21]

Thanks to Porphyry we have a glimpse of how Plotinus communicated these experiences to others. In his seminars we see the image of a beatific sage. Porphyry writes:

> When he spoke, his intellect illuminated even his face. Of pleasing aspect, he was then even more beautiful to see. Sweating slightly, his gentleness showed as did his kindness while being questioned and his rigor.[22]

In addition to holding seminars devoted to philosophic matters, Plotinus lived with others where he attended to the daily needs of orphaned boys and girls given to his care.[23] He was the exemplar of the Platonic sage united to the Good while extending this beneficence to others. Yet, despite the power of his reveries on the ascent to the One or the example in his own life of the "return to the cave," Plotinus's doctrines on the soul and its place in the cosmos proved to be a stumbling block to later generations of Platonists. Iamblichus, in particular, who in most respects espoused a Plotinian Platonism, had significant differences with Plotinus's teachings on the soul as passed on to him by Porphyry.

The philosophic challenge that Plotinus faced as regards the soul was to account for the soul's union with the One as well as to explain the soul's identity with the divine *Nous*. The former problem was solved poetically by following Plato's notion of an *a priori erōs* implanted in the soul "from the beginning." But the soul's identity with the *Nous* was a problem that Plato did not need to address, for it was not part of his philosophic language. Plotinus inherited a Platonism that had already been shaped by the thinking and terminology of Aristotle. Most significantly, Plotinus inherited Aristotle's two conceptions of intellect: metaphysically, a divine intellect that was the first cause of the universe,[24] and psychologically, an active intellect (*nous poiētikos*) that either was or was not the property of the human soul.[25] Prior to Plotinus, Alexander of Aphrodisias had equated the two intellects and argued that the soul's ordinarily passive intellect (*nous pathētikos*) was able to habituate itself to the active intellect and share in

---

[20] *Enn.* 6.7.35.24.

[21] *Enn.* 6.7.22.19.

[22] *Life of Plotinus* 13; translation (modified) by Dominic J. O'Meara, *Plotinus, An Introduction to the Enneads* (Oxford: Clarendon Press, 1993), 6.

[23] *Life of Plotinus* 9.

[24] *Metaph.* 1072b.

[25] *De an.* 3.430a.

its divinity.[26] The *Nicomachean Ethics* supports Alexander's interpretation, for Aristotle suggests that although the active intellect may not be "human," it can nevertheless be engaged by the soul, and he distinguished the virtues of mortal life from the divine virtues that come from the *Nous*. He says:

> such a life will be too high for human attainment; for any man who lives it will do so not as a human being but in virtue of *something divine within him,* and in proportion as this divine element is superior to the composite [σύνθετον] being, so will its activity be superior to that of the other kind of virtue [i.e., moral virtues].[27]

The life of a soul that follows the *Nous,* Aristotle says, is elevated above human happiness, for it lives the life of a god and is engaged in godlike contemplation (*theōria*) like the Prime Mover itself.[28]

Since Plotinus incorporated Aristotle's noetic terminology into his Platonism and believed that the human soul was able to unite with the *Nous,* he had to explain how this was possible. Or, more to the point, if the *nous poiētikos* was always in activity and the soul, in its highest degree, was identical to it, how does it happen that the soul falls away from the active intellect and into body-bound passivity? This is the question that Plotinus asked himself in his treatise on the *Descent of the Soul.* He says:

> Many times, awakened to myself away from the body … believing myself then especially to be part of the higher realm, in act as the best life, having become one with the divine and based in it advancing to that activity, establishing myself above all intelligible beings, then going down from this position in the divine from Nous down to discursive reasoning, I am puzzled how I could, even now, descend, and how my soul has come to be in the body.[29]

In an effort to resolve this question Plotinus reviews the evidence of Plato's dialogues—which he rightly describes as ambiguous—and then formulated his own explanation for the soul's descent into a body. It was Plotinus's answer and its consequences to which Iamblichus and the later Platonists objected.

---

[26] See Philip Merlan's discussion, *Monopsychism Mysticism Metaconsciousness* (The Hague: Martinus Nijhoff, 1963), 47–50; and F. E. Peters, *Greek Philosophical Terms* (New York: New York University Press, 1967), 135–36.

[27] *Eth. nic.* 1177b; translation by J. A. K. Thomson, *The Ethics of Aristotle* (New York: Penguin, 1955).

[28] *Eth. nic.* 1178b.

[29] *Enn.* 4.8.1.1–10; O'Meara (modified), *Plotinus,* 104.

After reviewing various reasons for the soul's descent suggested by the *Phaedrus,* and after discussing both positive and negative consequences of this descent, Plotinus returns to the crux of his question based on his own experience of union with the *Nous*. For if he knew himself to be the *Nous,* and if the *Nous* was always active, then Plotinus himself must, somehow, have had two identities and two souls: the one in the body (which Plotinus came to call his "inferior companion")[30] and the other (his true self) outside the body in the intelligible world. Plotinus was aware of the eccentricity of this position from a Platonic point of view, and yet he writes:

> And, if one ought to dare to express one's own view more clearly, contradicting the opinion of others, even *our soul does not altogether come down,* but there is always something of it in the intelligible; but if the part which is in the world of sense-perception gets control, or rather if it is brought under control and thrown into confusion [by the body], it prevents us from perceiving the things which the upper part of the soul contemplates. (*Enn.* 4.8.8.1–6 Armstrong)

According to Plotinus, the soul's experience of the *Nous* depended on whether or not it could free itself from the "world of sense perception"; if successful, the soul-as-*Nous* realized that it had never really "come down," that it was never truly embodied.

In a different context, however, discussing self-knowledge, Plotinus admits that "the *Nous* is ours *and* not ours,"[31] and he draws careful distinctions between the soul and the *Nous* that is present to it.[32] Yet Plotinus continued to assert the notion of an undescended soul, which he described in evocative terms. Although souls are enticed into bodies by sensate images, he says, "their heads are firmly set above in heaven,"[33] and in one of his last writings, Plotinus described the soul's descent as an illumination (*ellampsis*). He writes:

> If the inclination [to the body] is an illumination [ἔλλαμψις] to what is below it is not a sin; what is illuminated is responsible, for if it did not exist the soul would have nowhere to illuminate. The soul is said to go down or decline in the sense that the thing which receives the light from it lives with it. (*Enn.* 1.1.12.25–29)

---

30 *Enn.* 1.2.6.28.

31 *Enn.* 5.3.3.27–28.

32 *Enn.* 5.3.3.

33 *Enn.* 4.3.12.5–6.

The Plotinian soul, then, does not truly incarnate but illuminates, from above, its mortal image. This portrayal of the soul's "descent" bears a striking resemblance to Plotinus's portrayal of the fall of Sophia, which he had condemned in his treatise *Against the Gnostics*. According to the gnostics, he says, the World Soul (i.e., Sophia)

> did not come down itself, did not decline, but only illuminated [ἐλλάμψαι] the darkness and so an image from it came into existence in matter. (*Enn.* 2.9.10.25–27)

Plotinus had faulted the gnostics for attributing the personal drama and characteristics of the particular soul to the World Soul and thus confusing ontological levels.[34] Yet his doctrine of the undescended soul seems to have done the same but from the other direction. Rather than attributing personal characteristics to the World Soul, Plotinus gave universal qualities to the particular soul. In effect, both the gnostics and Plotinus treat the particular soul and World Soul as functional equivalents. The undescended soul of Plotinus exhibits the same traits and is described with the same metaphors as the gnostic Sophia.

Is it possible that Plotinus's doctrine of the undescended soul was influenced by the gnostics against whom he so vigorously argued? Was the dualistic soteriology and acosmicism implied in this doctrine a reflection of gnostic belief or perhaps the influence of dualist Middle Platonists such as Numenius? Was the doctrine of the undescended soul an aberration rightly condemned by later Platonists? Before seeking supposed "influences" or sources for Plotinus's doctrine, I think we first need to understand its function. My view is that Plotinus's attempts to communicate his mystical experiences in the philosophic language of Plato and Aristotle should not be read as explanations, but as evocations offered to his students. Within the confines of Plotinus' s seminars, his descriptions of the soul with its "head in heaven" and "illuminating" the body from above would have evoked in his listeners an inkling of the transcendence that he had experienced. His beautiful face, then even more beautiful to see, and voice, resonant with his soul's depth, carried his listeners into verbal images of transcendence. In effect, Plotinus's explanations were erotic enchantments in the form of philosophic discourse, yet taken out of the context of his seminars his "explanations" were likely to have been misunderstood by a Porphyry, an Iamblichus, or even by Plotinus himself. So, while Plotinus's doctrine of the undescended soul was criticized for philosophic reasons by Iamblichus, we must remember that it was the "doctrine" of an undescended soul that was criticized and not the legitimacy of Plotinus's experience.

---

[34] *Enn.* 2.9.7.5–9.

One problem of the undescended soul doctrine is that Socratic *aporia* comes into play only at the highest level—when the *Nous* approaches the One. It is then that the soul-as-*Nous* reaches an utter *aporia* and must be carried by its god-given *erōs* to the Good. Prior to that, however, since the soul has been encumbered only by the camouflage of embodiment, it is able to recover its divinely noetic status through its own efforts. This would afford the human soul far more power than traditional Platonic *paideia* had given to it. While this difference may seen inconsequential and merely reflect Plotinus's use of Aristotle's terminology, the results were significant as regards the Plotinian philosopher's self-understanding and his view of the world. In this context, let us now turn to Iamblichus to examine his objections to this doctrine and to see how the introduction of theurgy to Platonic *paideia* was consistent with his understanding of the soul and the cosmos.

3. Iamblichean Paideia: Aporia to Theourgia

> When compared to divine action, even the perfect soul is imperfect.
> — Iamblichus

In his philosophic doxography, the *De anima*,[35] Iamblichus criticizes the opinion of those who blur distinctions among the incorporeals. He writes:

> There are some who maintain that all parts of this incorporeal substance are alike and one and the same, so that the whole exists in any part of it. They even place in the individual soul the Intelligible World, the Gods, the Daimons, the Good, and all Races superior to the soul.... According to this view, the soul, considering its entire essence is in no way different from the *Nous,* the Gods, or the Superior Races. (Stobaeus *Anth*. 1.365.7–21)

Iamblichus says that Numenius clearly held this view, as did Plotinus—though not entirely—as well as Plotinus's students: Porphyry, who sometimes rejected and sometimes revered it, and Amelius, who leaned toward it.[36] Iamblichus here was implicitly criticizing Plotinus's doctrine of the undescended soul, and in his *Commentary on the Phaedrus* he explicitly rejects the notion that the soul's highest element remains unfallen and unchanged. He writes:

---

[35] *De anima,* in *Stobaeus Anthologium* (ed. C. Wachsmuth and O. Hense; Berlin: Weidmanns, 1884–1912).

[36] Stobaeus *Anth*. 1.365.7–21.

> And if the charioteer is the highest element in us, and he, as is said in the
> *Phaedrus,* sometimes is carried aloft and raises "his head into the regions
> outside," while at other times he descends and (fills his pair) with lame-
> ness and moulting, it plainly follows that the highest element in us expe-
> riences different states at different times.[37]

According to Iamblichus, when the human soul enters a body it descends
entirely and does not leave its "head in heaven." In the *De anima*
Iamblichus explained that the soul is generated from the *Nous* as a subordinate and separate level of reality,[38] and he defined the soul's essence as

[1] the mean between divisible and indivisible,
     corporeal and incorporeal beings;
[2] the totality of the universal *logoi;*
[3] that which, after the Forms, is at the service
     of the work of creation, or
[4] that Life which has Life of itself, which
     proceeds from the *Nous,* or
[5] again, the procession of the classes of Real
     Being as a whole to an inferior status.[39]

For anyone who has studied the *Timaeus,* these definitions should sound
familiar, a point that Iamblichus himself made with a polemical retort:
"Indeed, he says, "Plato himself, Pythagoras, Aristotle and all of the
Ancients whose great names are praised for wisdom were absolutely con-
vinced of these doctrines ... as anyone would discover if he were to study
their teachings with care!"[40]

The *Timaeus* supports Iamblichus's position. In the creation of human
souls, each is coordinated with all the numerical *logoi* of the World Soul
and, as soul, each functions as an intermediary between the irreconcilable
extremes of same and different, indivisible and divisible, and immortal and
mortal, which allows the intelligible world to appear as sensible (*Tim.*
35a–36e). In the case of human souls, however, due to the dilution of their
essence, their mathematical *logoi* are broken apart and twisted when they
enter bodies (*Tim.* 43d–e). Human souls suffer a discontinuity in their
mediation not experienced by the Superior Races. It was this dividedness
and suffering that the doctrine of the undescended soul denied, yet to
deny the divisible in favor of the indivisible was to deny to the soul its

---

[37] *In Tim.* frg. 87.28–32; in *Iamblichi Chalcidensis* (ed. with trans. and commentary by John Dillon; Leiden: Brill, 1973).

[38] Stobaeus *Anth.* 1.365.22–25.

[39] Stobaeus *Anth.* 1.365.25–366.5.

[40] Stobaeus *Anth.* 1.366.6–11.

function as a mean between extremes. According to Iamblichus, all souls had to mediate, and in the case of human souls their mediation included the experience of suffering, dividedness, and mortality. Since the soul's original nature was immortal and coordinate with the gods it meant that— as human—the soul was alienated not only from the divinity of the gods but from its own divinity as well. And this alienation was not an accident or a temporary condition that could be rectified when the soul corrected the "error" of identifying with the body: *the experience of self-alienation constituted the soul's very essence as human.*

Yet the soul still contained the *logoi* of the World Soul, and by aligning its own *logoi* with the *logoi* of the visible world it could gradually transform its alienation. In order to regain its divinity the soul had to reshape its human identity into the rhythms and ratios of the visible world, as Plato put it: "the motions which are naturally akin to the divine principle in us..." (*Tim.* 90c). This was traditional *paideia,* and Plotinus himself encouraged it in his treatise *Against the Gnostics,*[41] but an undescended soul would have required no knowledge of the cosmos except the realization that it had never really fallen into it. The doctrine of the undescended soul, in effect, short-circuited traditional Platonic *paideia* because it no longer required the soul to realign itself with the cosmos. The unfallen soul needed only to return to a Self that Porphyry claimed was "the same as the *Nous.*"[42] While this, admittedly, exaggerates the intent of Plotinus's position, such distortions were perhaps inevitable. It would be difficult, for example, to imagine Socrates saying, with Porphyry, that "the philosopher is the savior of himself,"[43] but not so difficult if Socrates believed that his "self" was a god. When Plotinus's metaphor of the undescended soul was taken outside his seminars and was transformed into a metaphysical "doctrine," it became an invitation for rationalistic *hubris.* This, in particular, is what Iamblichus sensed in Porphyry's Platonism and in the questions posed in Porphyry's *Letter to Anebo.* It was simply too easy for the empirical self to misappropriate Plotinus's images and assume that one's ascent to the gods did not require passage through the humiliation and darkness of Socratic *aporia.* Iamblichus's understanding of the soul guaranteed that it did.

Thanks to the careful analysis of Carlos Steel in *The Changing Self,*[44] we can now appreciate the complexity and originality of Iamblichus's

---

[41] *Enn.* 2.9.18.31–35.

[42] Porphyry *Abst.* 1.29.4; in *Porphyre: De l'abstinence* (text, translation, and introduction by J. Bouffartigue and M. Patillon; Paris: Les Belles Lettres, 1977).

[43] *Abst.* 2.49.1.

[44] Carlos Steel, *The Changing Self* (Brussels: Palais der Academien, 1978).

psychology, why he opposed Plotinus's doctrines, and why, for philosophic reasons, Iamblichus turned to ritual theurgy for the soul's salvation. Like Plotinus, Iamblichus incorporated Aristotle's noetic terminology into his Platonism but with significant differences. Iamblichus seems to have taken Plato's description of the embodied soul in the *Timaeus*—walking backward and turned upside down—and explained its limitations in Aristotelian terms. Most notably, Iamblichus denied that the active intellect (*nous poiētikos*) was the property of the soul. Iamblichus followed Aristotle's more restrictive noetic terminology and believed that the *Nous* must enter the soul from without (*thurathen*),[45] and in the *De mysteriis* he consistently maintained that the gods come to us from without (*exōthen*), which was one rationale for performing rituals given by the gods. Iamblichus also employed the Aristotelian formula that essences (*ousiai*) are revealed by their activities (*energeiai*) and used it to identify the incorporeal classes, including the human soul.[46] This formula led Iamblichus to a conclusion especially difficult for a Platonist: because the *energeiai* of human souls are mortal and subject to change, so their *ousiai* must somehow be mortal and subject to change!

Steel cites Priscianus's *Commentary on the De Anima*, where he refers to Iamblichus's application of this formula. Priscianus writes:

> If, however, as Iamblichus thinks, a perverse and imperfect activity would not proceed from an essence which is impassive and perfect, the soul would be, even in its essence, somehow subject to passion. For in this view, the soul is a mean, not only between the divided and undivided, the remaining and proceeding, the noetic and irrational, but also between the ungenerated and generated....[47] *Thus, that which is immortal in the soul is filled completely with mortality and no longer remains immortal....*[48]

To think that part of "us" remains untouched by embodiment is, in Christian terms, a docetic form of Platonism. Iamblichus was clearly more Chalcedonian. Indeed, the paradox of the Chalcedonian Christ, being fully man and fully god, applies equally to the Iamblichean soul. As Priscianus

---

[45] *Gen. an.* 236b.28.

[46] The Aristotelian dictum that essences are known by their activities (*De an.* 2.4.415a16–20) had precedents in the Platonic dialogues (*Rep.* 477c; *Soph.* 247e).

[47] *In de anima* 89.33–37 (Berlin: Reimeri, 1882). For attributing this commentary to Priscianus rather than to Simplicius, see F. Bossier and C. Steel, "Priscianus Lydus en de 'In de Anima' van Pseudo(?)-Simplicius," *Tijdschrift voor Filosofia* 34 (1972): 761–882.

[48] *In de anima* 90.21–23.

remarked: "The definition of these matters is difficult because the soul is one and many in essence" (*In de anima* 14.7–8), and in his *Metaphrasis* (32.13–19) he again refers to Iamblichus's definition of the soul as a mean term to account for its self-contradictions. He says:

> According to Iamblichus, the individual soul embraces permanency and change equally, so that in this way its intermediate position is again preserved; for higher beings are stable, mortal ones are completely changeable. The individual soul, however, as middle, is undivided and multiplied together with mundane beings, and it does not only remain permanent but also changes because it lives through so many divisible lives. *And not only in its habits, but also in its substance.*[49]

There was no part of the Iamblichean soul unaffected by embodiment as Plotinus and Porphyry had maintained.[50] Even Proclus, who otherwise followed Iamblichus's teachings on the soul, could not accept that its highest part, the *ousia*, was changed in embodiment.[51] Damascius, however, supported Iamblichus's view by referring to Plato's definition of the soul as self-moved,[52] meaning, he says in his *Parmenides* commentary, "that both moved and mover are the same being."[53] "The soul," Damascius continues, "both changes itself and is always being changed, and thus it possesses its being by always changing itself through the transformation of its own essence."[54]

The soul endured such paradox because of its cosmogonic function as the mean between extremes. The loss of the soul's unity and stability caused it to suffer, but this was the only way for the human soul to imitate the Demiurge. To deny diversity and mortality to the soul would negate its role in cosmogenesis, yet because it was weakened by the dilution of its substance (*Tim.* 41d–e), the soul performed its demiurgy through a kind of self-alienation and shattering of its essence. In embodiment the soul became "other" to itself.[55] Thus Iamblichus:

---

[49] Translation (modified) by Steel, "Priscianus Lydus," 57.

[50] *Enn.* 1.1.7.1–7.

[51] Proclus *Elem. Theol.* props. 106–7; 191; text, translation and commentary by E. R. Dodds (Oxford: Clarendon Press, 1963).

[52] According to Iamblichus, *Myst.* 12.6–11, the self-movement (αὐτοκινησία; cf. *Phaedr.* 245c: τὸ αὐτὸ κινοῦν ~ αὐτοκίνητον) of the soul is "a simple essential movement that subsists from itself and not in relation to another."

[53] *Dub. et Sol.* 2.263.10 Ruelle.

[54] *Dub. et Sol.* 2.263.12–14 Ruelle; cf. C. Steel, *The Changing Self,* 110.

[55] *DA* 223.26.

> Our soul remains one and is multiplied at the same time in its inclination
> to the body; it neither remains purely nor is changed entirely but remains
> somehow and proceeds from itself, *yet when it is made other to itself, the
> sameness with itself becomes faint.*[56]

To borrow an Egyptian image, the embodied soul—like Osiris—was dismembered and its *logoi* were scattered throughout the world; to restore
itself the soul had to rediscover these *logoi* in nature, an important point
to which we will return.[57]

Since the Iamblichean soul was self-alienated and separated from the
divine *Nous,* it is not hard to see the importance of Socratic *aporia* for
Iamblichus. No matter how exalted or brilliant the human soul, as *human*
it was confined to a single form of consciousness[58] which made it "other
to itself" and cut off from the *Nous.* To recognize this was the first and perhaps most difficult task of Platonic *paideia,* particularly for the discursively
brilliant. To accept with Socrates the "worthlessness of our wisdom" would
mean remaining an "inferior companion" and accepting our existence as
"lowest, deficient, and imperfect" compared to all other immortal beings
(*Myst.* 21.2). Iamblichus acknowledges our inferior status when he says:
"...compared to divine activity, even the perfect soul is imperfect" (*Myst.*
149.111–12).

It is now almost commonplace to say that Iamblichus had a more pessimistic view of the soul and its capacities than did Plotinus. I think this
misses the point. The deification of the soul was as important to
Iamblichus as it was to Plotinus, but its description by Porphyry—who
claimed that Plotinus achieved it "four" times and himself "once"[59]—
risked making a caricature of the soul's *henōsis* and deification. An enumeration of *henōsis* makes no sense. By definition, a *henōsis* that can be
claimed, numbered, or known cannot be a true *henōsis,* and it was this
discursive counterfeit that Iamblichus attempted to overcome by distinguishing the human activity of philosophy from the *divine* activity of

---

[56] *DA* 223.28–32. Yet, as a mean, the soul "could never become entirely self-
alienated or it would cease to be soul" (*DA* 241.10–11).

[57] According to Plutarch, *Isis and Osiris* (nos. 53–54), Osiris represents the Platonic Forms; Isis, the pure material receptacle; and Horus, the "perceptible image
of the intelligible world." The embodied soul, born "crippled" like the elder Horus,
seeks with Isis to recover the hidden parts of Osiris, dismembered and buried by
the titanic Seth/Typhon.

[58] *Myst.* 148.12–14. The standard text and translation of the *De mysteriis* is that
of E. des Places, *Jamblique: Les mystères d'Egypte* (Paris: Les Belles Lettres,
1966).

[59] *Life of Plotinus* 23.13–18.

theurgy.[60] Iamblichus's distinction was not based on some kind of presumed supernatural authority but on sound philosophic reasoning. For when discursive language and terms such as "knowing," "seeing," or "grasping" are used to describe experiences that transcend all forms of knowing, seeing, or grasping, then one must take care not to confuse the content of the discursive statement with its evocative power.[61] To do so would reduce *henōsis* to a discursive experience. For Porphyry to have "counted" henadic events suggests that he failed to make this distinction and mistook Plotinus's poetry for prose.

Iamblichus was careful to avoid this confusion, and his psychology helped to buttress the distinction between the divine and human orders. For if the human soul does not merely seem to be embodied but truly is, and if its individual consciousness alienates it from divinity, then the soul— as human—cannot reach the divine of its own power. If it has contact with the gods this must be initiated by the gods themselves, from outside the soul. These restrictions need not reflect Iamblichus's pessimism about the soul or, as some would have it, his diminished capacity for mystical experience, but rather his concern that transcendent experiences be received properly and not confused with discursive fantasies. Iamblichus's promotion of theurgy, therefore, may be seen as a consequence of his philosophic precision about the limits of the discursive mind, limits that Plotinus did not always make explicit.[62] To oppose philosophy to theurgy or to see them as alternate routes to salvation is to misunderstand the role of philosophy for Iamblichus.

This misunderstanding is reflected in Porphyry's *Letter to Anebo*, where Iamblichus's former teacher presumes that theurgic rituals attempted to manipulate the gods. Although Porphyry himself had once practiced theurgy for the purpose of cleansing his "lower" soul, he felt that his "higher," undescended soul could be reached only by philosophic contemplation.[63] For

---

[60] J. Trouillard dismissed the portrayal of *henōsis* as a "state" subject to enumeration. According to Trouillard, Porphyry was a "disciple souvent exotérique" who misunderstood much of Plotinus's more profound teachings (J. Trouillard, *La purification plotinienne* [Paris: Presses Universitaires de France, 1955], 98).

[61] For example, when Iamblichus refers to the charioteer's "vision" of the Forms in his journey with the gods, he explains that the term is a metaphor for the soul's union with the intelligibles (*In Phaedr.* frg. 6, J. Dillon, *Iamblichi Chalcidensis*, 97). Plotinus makes the same point in *Enn.* 5.8.11.

[62] J. N. P. Lowry, *The Logical Principles of Proclus' STOICHEIÔSIS THEOLOGIKÊ As Systematic Ground of the Cosmos* (Amsterdam: Rodopi, 1980), 16–19.

[63] For a discussion of theurgy and the lower/higher soul distinction see R. Majercik, *The Chaldean Oracles: Text, Translation, and Commentary* (Leiden: Brill, 1989), 31–32.

Porphyry, theurgy was merely a *technē* for the philosophically immature, and he proceeds to discuss it like any other philosophical problem. It is more Porphyry's attitude than the content of his questions that seems to have irked Iamblichus, for to Porphyry's seemingly innocuous remark that the gods exist, Iamblichus replies:

> You say first that you grant that the Gods exist, but speaking in this way is not right. For the innate knowledge [ἔμφυτος γνῶσις] of the Gods preexists in our very essence; it is superior to all judgment and choice and exists prior to reason and demonstration. From the beginning it is established with the soul's essential desire [ἐφέσει] for the Good. (*Myst.* 7.12–8.1)

Iamblichus does not allow that gods may or may not be "granted" existence for the purpose of discussion. The gods are the vitality that allows such discussions to take place. They precede and sustain all forms of life, including cognitive states. As such, divinities cannot be "known" as one may know objects of thought. Porphyry should certainly have known this as Plotinus's student, but Iamblichus continues:

> If one must speak the truth, contact with the divine is not knowledge. For knowledge is separated from its object by a kind of otherness. But prior to this knowledge which understands the other as "other," there exists a self-generated ... uniform embrace, suspended from the Gods. One must not suppose that one has the power to recognize or not to recognize this contact, nor represent it as ambiguous (for it is always uniformly established in activity). (*Myst.* 8.3–9)

In these citations Iamblichus makes two points that reflect the principles of traditional Platonic *paideia:* (1) when it comes to knowing the gods we face an utter *aporia;* we are constitutionally unable to know them, and (2) the gods are *already* present to us, embedded in the very activity of our thinking and breathing, but especially revealed in our erotic yearning (*ephesis*) for the Good. As in traditional *paideia,* if the soul cannot first accept its *aporia,* it cannot engage its innate gnosis of the gods.

The closest Iamblichus comes to describing what attitude the soul must adopt to trigger the activity of the god is in his discussion of prayer. In response to Porphyry's remark that man's prayers are impure and unfit to be offered to the *Nous,* Iamblichus retorts:

> Not at all! For it is due to this very fact, that we are far inferior to the Gods in power, purity, and everything else, that it is of all things most critical that we do pray to them to the utmost. *For the awareness of our own nothingness* [οὐδενείας], *when we compare ourselves to the Gods, makes us turn*

spontaneously [αὐτοφυῶς] *to prayer.* And from our supplication, in a short time we are led up to that one to whom we pray, and from our continual intercourse with it we obtain a likeness to it, and from imperfection we are gradually embraced by divine perfection. (*Myst.* 47.13–48.4).

Iamblichus's awareness of our nothingness, like the worthlessness of Socrates' wisdom, or Plotinus's insight that all efforts to increase the soul diminish it, point to the need for the soul to accept and inhabit *aporia* before engaging the gods.[64] I would suggest that the spontaneous prayer that arises from this "nothingness" was the awakening of the soul's "essential desire" for the Good. When engaged in this way, prayers were themselves the active presence of the gods. Iamblichus says:

> At the moment of prayer, the divine itself is quite literally joined with itself, and it is not like one entity speaking with another that it is united with the spiritual conceptions in prayers.[65]

As in Socratic *paideia,* the purpose of discursive thinking was to reveal the soul's utter helplessness and *aporia* with respect to knowledge of the gods. By contrast, Porphyry's questions suggested that our connection to the gods was capable of being solved intellectually, and Iamblichus criticizes Porphyry for his excessive rationalism. Thus Iamblichus:

> You seem to think that knowledge of divine things and of anything else is the same, and that each step is derived from oppositions, as is usual with dialectical propositions; but it is nothing like that at all, for the knowledge of divine things is entirely different and is separated from all contradiction. (*Myst.* 10.1–7)

Of course, if Porphyry believed that his true self was the *Nous* he might also think himself capable of understanding divine mysteries. This kind of *hubris,* Iamblichus argued, was the cause for our failing to contact the gods. He says:

> For being unable to lay hold of the knowledge of the Gods through reasoning, but believing they are able to do so, men are entirely carried away by their own human passions and make assertions about divine things drawn from personal feelings. (*Myst.* 65.16–66.2)

---

[64] In another context, Iamblichus says that when the soul becomes aware of its "ugliness" apart from the gods it is drawn to divine beauty (*Myst.* 39.3–13).

[65] *Myst.* 47.9–11. Compare with *Myst.* 48.5–11 where Iamblichus says that theurgic prayers do not derive from human beings. These prayers, he says, are sent by the gods and are the tokens (*sunthēmata*) of the gods and therefore possess divine power.

We have seen that Plotinus had the same caution with respect to the One and said that our awareness of it comes not through reasoning but by a "presence superior to knowledge" (*Enn.* 6.9.4.3–4). Iamblichus followed Plotinus in this reserve but extended the soul's *aporia* to exclude knowledge of all divinities, not just of the One. For a completely descended soul, *aporia* was necessarily more significant and extensive.

But how was the soul to engage its innate yearning for the Good? How was it to awaken the presence superior to all reasoning? While Plato leaves this unexplained and portrays the engagement through erotic images, Iamblichus discovers this erotic power in theurgic rituals, that is, in traditional forms of worship: rites of sacrifice, divination, and invocations of the gods. While Iamblichus was probably introduced to the term *theourgia* by Porphyry, he refashioned its meaning to suit his understanding of *paideia*. The function of theurgic rites for Iamblichus was to awaken the soul's innate yearning for the divine, and since the soul was divided and scattered into the sensate world, this innate *gnōsis* could be awakened only through a complexity of rites that corresponded to the complexity and intensity of the soul's alienation.

Iamblichus believed that embodiment was essential to the soul's identity and served a cosmogonic function. The soul's inversion as well as its return expressed the will of the Demiurge (*Myst.* 272.2–12). As inverted and self-alienated, however, the soul could recover its immortality only by recovering the traces of its divinity in the generated world. Iamblichus believed that these traces had been deposited by the Demiurge throughout the world (*Myst.* 65.6) and that pious races like the Egyptians had preserved them in rites that allowed souls to reenter their immortality (*Myst.* 249.14–250.7).

The integration of traditional religious practices into *paideia* was clearly not a goal of Plotinus.[66] In addition to negating the soul's cosmogonic function as a mean between extremes, the doctrine of the undescended soul necessarily diminished the value of the sensible cosmos and the rites that venerated its powers. For if the soul's purpose was to escape from the illusion of embodiment, then the body and material world would be obstacles to the soul. From this perspective, it is not surprising that Plotinus referred to matter as "evil itself" (*Enn.* 1.8.3.39–40) or that Porphyry characterized the soul's salvation as a permanent escape from the cosmos "never again to find itself held and polluted by the contagion of the world."[67] In light of Platonic *paideia's* emphasis both on the soul's *return*

---

[66] This is perhaps best exemplified in Plotinus's remark to Amelius after he was asked to join him in worshiping the gods: "They ought to come to me, not I to them" (*Life of Plotinus* 10.35–36).

[67] Porphyry *De regressu an.* 40*.15–16 Bidez (1964).

to the world after its ascent and on the complementary descent of *erōs* from the gods to humanity, there is something new and unplatonic in Porphyry's remark. He is speaking from a dualist and anticosmic standpoint, so he was necessarily opposed to rituals that aligned the soul with cosmic powers. Yet this was precisely the function of theurgic rituals. Iamblichus held that it was only through these rites that the soul's innate *erōs* for the gods could be awakened.

If Iamblichus's understanding of the soul provides a rationale for the importance of *aporia* in Platonic *paideia,* then his explanation of theurgy may be seen as an effort to secure more effectively the soul's *erōs* for the Good by aligning it with traditional religious rituals. For Iamblichus, the old ways, the ancient forms of worship, were concrete expressions of a divine *erōs* for the gods, and in terms of the individual soul, this *erōs* played an essential role. The *Chaldean Oracles* speak of a "deep *erōs*" implanted in souls by the Creator to stir their desire for him.[68] Like the god-given *erōs* of Plotinus or the "soul's essential desire for the Good" of Iamblichus, this deep *erōs* was prior to all knowledge and conceptualization, so whether it was conveyed through the medium of intellectual discourse (e.g., Plotinus) or through ritual acts, its presence was ineffable, and I believe that Iamblichus favored ritual in order to protect the soul from intellectual self-deception in these matters.[69] According to Iamblichus:

> The Intelligible is held before the mind, not as knowable [ὡς γνωστόν], but as desirable [ὡς ἐφετόν], and the mind is filled by this, not with knowledge, but with being and every intelligible perfection.[70]

Iamblichus referred to this divine presence in the soul in a variety of ways. He says it is the "first principle in us" (*Myst.* 10.10), provides us with an "innate knowledge of the gods" (*Myst.* 7.14), and is the soul's "essential

---

[68] *Chaldean Oracles,* frgs. 43, 44 Majercik.

[69] In one sense, Iamblichus might be understood as attempting to preserve the intuitions of Plotinus against the more analytical approach of Porphyry. L. G. Westerink noted: "Iamblichus' purpose is to make Plotinus' belief of the superiority of intuition to reason the guiding principle of a new systematic approach to Plato. Intuition, which is a superior form of sight, does not proceed from point to point, but has a unified vision of the structure of all reality" (Westerink, *The Greek Commentaries on Plato's Phaedo I* [Amsterdam: North-Holland Publishing, 1976], 15). J. M. P. Lowry, *Logical Principles,* 21ff., similarly remarks: "What Iamblichus did was to develop this mystical side of Plotinus more systematically than Plotinus himself had done."

[70] Cited by Damascius *Dub. et Sol.* 1.154.9–11 Ruelle = Westerink-Combès, 2.104.20–23.

desire for the Good" (*Myst.* 8.1–2). Although Iamblichus was somewhat lax about what he called it, referring to it as the "divine, intelligible, and one in us" awakened in prayer (*Myst.* 46.13–15), or more simply as "the one in the soul,"[71] he was adamant in maintaining that this principle was *not* a property of the soul. As *archē,* this divine presence was not considered a higher part of the soul even in a Plotinian sense, for it transcended the order that it established.[72] Iamblichus claimed that this anterior principle, and not the soul, was the cause of every theurgic divination. It was, he says, "a certain divine good which is pre-established as more ancient [*presbuteran*] than our nature,"[73] and it was this presence that was awakened in theurgic rites.[74]

In the context of Platonic *paideia* I believe that theurgy may be best understood as Iamblichus's elaboration and ritualization of Platonic erotics. For just as different kinds of souls were attracted to different kinds of *erōmenoi* depending on their position on the ladder to Absolute Beauty,[75] so in theurgy, different souls employed different forms of theurgic ritual depending on their degree of intimacy with the gods. Plato's Beauty, the only Form that entered the sensible world to arouse our *erōs,* was transformed by Iamblichus into the magnetic will of the Demiurge, drawing souls back to their divinity. And just as the erotic madness of the *Phaedrus* appealed to the wise but not the learned,[76] so theurgy was honored by the pious but not by intellectuals like Porphyry!

Before summarizing theurgy's place in Platonic *paideia,* I would like to reconsider the two paths of Platonism as represented by Plotinus and Iamblichus. I believe that one reason Plotinus has been favored by recent

---

[71] *In Phaedr.* frg. 6 Dillon.

[72] A generally accepted Pythagorean principle discussed by Iamblichus in *De Communi Mathematica Scientia* 15.10–15 (ed. N. Festa; Stuttgart: Teubner, 1975).

[73] *Myst.* 165.18–19; cf. Stobaeus *Anth.* 2.174.9–16 where the *archē* that frees the soul from fate is described as *presbuteran.*

[74] Damascius, who claims to follow Iamblichus in these matters, refers to this principle as the soul's *huparxis,* which he describes as "the One itself, which pre-exists beyond all things and is the cause of every *ousia* but is not yet itself *ousia.*" See Pierre Hadot, "L'être et l'étant dans le Néoplatonisme," *Revue de théologie et de philosophie* 1 (1972): 110–11. According to Hadot, the technical use of this term was coined by Porphyry, and Ruth Majercik recently has argued that its use by Neoplatonists may have been the source for the prevalence of *huparxis* among Sethian gnostics. See R. Majercik, "The Existence-Life-Intellect Triad in Gnosticism and Neoplatonism," *CQ* 42 (1992): 478–79. [For discussion, see the essays of Corrigan and Turner ("The Setting") in this volume. JDT]

[75] *Symp.* 210c–e.

[76] *Phaedr.* 245c.1–2.

generations of scholars—if not by the Platonists themselves—is because his doctrine of the undescended soul, in a highly secularized form, more closely resembles our post-Enlightenment optimism (and *hubris*) about the capacities of rationality and our independence from ritualistic superstitions. Plotinus, then, is more like us! And Iamblichus, by contrast, is an oriental: an irrational Syrian priest and occultist who claims to possess "supernatural" power to control the gods! While the image of Iamblichus is obviously a caricature, the picture we have made of Plotinus is no less distorted. Both Platonists sought to communicate the depths of their experiences, and both were misunderstood. Plotinus's statements, for example, that the soul goes "alone to the Alone" or that the soul's "head remains above" were taken out of the context of his seminars as positive statements about the soul's relation with the divine rather than as invitations to experience it.[77] The consequences were an anticosmism and escapist dualism hardly reflected in Plotinus's own life. Iamblichus's theurgical doctrines suffered perhaps even more distortion, for by laying excessive emphasis on the power of the ritual act and forgetting Iamblichus's cautions about first purifying the soul, scholars have assumed that theurgy was the attempt to animate statues or manipulate gods,[78] and they have taken rogues like Maximus to be representative of Iamblichean theurgy. Both caricatures are false, and both are characterized by an unplatonic grandiosity and separateness of soul: the overly spiritualized Plotinian soul isolated and removed from the contagion of the world, and the Iamblichean theurgist-as-sorcerer who controls the spirits and threatens the gods. It is not surprising that both Plotinus and Iamblichus directed their harshest criticisms toward gnostics and sorcerers respectively, for the gnostic dualist (Plotinus) and the sorcerer (Iamblichus) were their own distorted reflections.

---

[77] For a correction to these distortions see A. H. Armstrong, "The Apprehension of Divinity in the Self and the Cosmos in Plotinus," in *The Significance of Neoplatonism* (ed. R. B. Harris; Norfolk, Va.: International Society for Neoplatonic Studies, 1976), 195ff.

[78] This despite Iamblichus's explicit condemnation of the practices of statue-makers (*Myst.* 160.15) and his repeated statements that theurgy in no way manipulates the gods, e.g., *Myst.* 42.2–5. E. R. Dodds, not Iamblichus, seems to be our source for this view. Dodds reported the polemical remarks of the Christian John Philoponus that Iamblichus tried to prove that "statues are divine" and then cited examples of this "theurgy" in the case of Maximus and others. See Dodds, *The Greeks and the Irrational,* Appendix II, "Theurgy" (Berkeley and Los Angeles: University of California Press, 1951), 295. On contemporary as well as ancient distortions of Iamblichean theurgy see P. Athanassiadi, "Dreams, Theurgy and Freelance Divination: The Testimony of Iamblichus," *JRS* 83 (1993): 123–29.

4. Conclusion

As a theurgist, Iamblichus believed the hieratic practices he performed were revealed by the gods and that no amount of human intelligence possessed the same degree of soteriological power. As a Platonist, he also knew this divine revelation was not limited to a particular time, place, or culture, but was revealed continually in all times and in all places as the cosmogenesis described in the *Timaeus*. The revelation of the gods was the ceaseless unfolding of numbers from the One into the Many, descending into the mathematical bases of the physical world. For the Platonic theurgist, nature was the material expression of the gods calling souls back to their role as cocreators with the Demiurge.[79] In Iamblichus's monistic vision, even sensible matter, the medium of creation, was believed to be rooted in the One and was necessary for our salvation.

The most complex and perhaps most original aspect of Iamblichus's Platonism was his doctrine of the soul. Based on Plato's description of the soul as a mean term made up of numerical *logoi,* Iamblichus found a unique place for human souls as the mean between the immortality of the gods and the mortality of created life. To recover one's immortality within the context and medium of mortal life—as theurgy required—meant that the soul's deification assumed the shape of a ritually embodied world. For the theurgist, therefore, this ritualization of cosmogenesis could be described as equally ascending or descending depending on one's perspective. From the perspective of the embodied soul, theurgy enflamed its god-given *erōs* and lifted it to the gods. Yet once elevated, and having ritually taken on the shape of the gods, the soul joined their cosmogony and descended demiurgically into the world. Theurgic rituals were designed according to the soul's capacity to receive the gods, so the rites varied, reflecting the variety of human souls. Yet all theurgies, from the densely material to the spiritually refined, required that the soul recognize its own "nothingness" before it was able to receive the god and take on another life. This, in sum, was Iamblichus's vision of a Platonic theurgy, but was it unique?

Iamblichus's explanation of *nomina barbara* and *asēma onomata* in theurgy, and the use of the same material in gnostic and magical texts, suggest that gnostics and magicians may have used the same techniques and materials as theurgists. Birger Pearson's suggestion that Iamblichus's theory

---

[79] Christian (Dionysian) theurgy fails to be "theurgic" in a Platonic sense because its revelation was limited to a unique historical "event" and was essentially opposed to nature. James Miller has argued that the elimination of nature achieved greater clarity for Christian theurgy and enhanced the authority of the church. In effect, the *ekklēsia* of Christian theurgy replaced the physical cosmos of pagan theurgy. See J. Miller, *Measures of Wisdom: The Cosmic Dance in Classical and Christian Antiquity* (Toronto: University of Toronto Press, 1986), 461.

of theurgy be applied to gnostic texts such as the *Marsanes,* the *Gospel of the Egyptians,* and the *Three Steles of Seth* helps to "make sense" of otherwise unintelligible material.[80] Pearson's study is fruitful in finding parallels between the ritualized ascent and descent described in *Three Steles of Seth* and Iamblichus's explanations of theurgic ascent and descent in the *De mysteriis*.[81] But I am not sure how far this takes us.

Iamblichus's understanding of the soul's ascent and descent in theurgy was surely not unique, as Pearson points out,[82] but it is unlikely that non-Platonists would have been as careful as Iamblichus to situate, let alone *explain,* their rituals in the context of an "orthodox" Platonism. Surely, the greater the number of parallels and shared terms that one finds between gnostic, magic, or Hermetic literature and that of Platonic theurgists suggests at least a cross-fertilization of ideas and possibly of ritual practices. Yet without more evidence it is not possible to know if these rituals had the same function.

In the case of Iamblichean theurgy, the ritual act could never be divorced from the proper preparation and purification of the soul. The evidence from Iamblichus suggests that the function of theurgic rites was to arouse the erotic presence of the One in the soul (the ascent) in a ritual mimesis of creation (the descent). While even these theurgical criteria might be found in gnostic material, what I don't find is an emphasis on the ineffability of the gods *and* its correlate: the *aporia* of the soul. In Platonic terms, without a clearly defined psychology to anchor our "titanic" impulse to discursive knowing, the soul can easily be led to think that it has fathomed divine mysteries and attained a heavenly status. Iamblichus's psychology ensured that the soul remained human and that divine acts, although performed by the soul, were attributed to the gods. His apparent diminishment of the soul and separation of ontological orders may well have been a pedagogical strategy to protect the soul's contact with the gods from discursive habits of self-interest. To be genuine, this contact had to change the soul utterly. As Plotinus puts it: "it is as if he [the seer] had become someone else and is not himself and does not count as his own

---

[80] Birger Pearson, "Theurgic Tendencies in Gnosticism and Iamblichus' Conception of Theurgy," in *Neoplatonism and Gnosticism* (ed. R.T. Wallis and Jay Bregman; Albany: SUNY Press, 1992), 253–76. Patricia Cox Miller has recently studied the *nomina barbara* and *asēma onomata* in the context of Platonic and Stoic theories of language and grammar. While she does not discuss theurgy, her study, like Pearson's, reveals the complexity of thought that was hidden in "unintelligible" spells. See Miller, "In Praise of Nonsense," in *Classical Mediterranean Spirituality* (ed. A. H. Armstrong; New York: Crossroad, 1989), 481–505.

[81] Pearson, "Theurgic Tendencies," 260–62.

[82] Ibid., 261–62.

There, but has come to belong to That" (*Enn.* 6.9.10.15–16). Iamblichus, similarly, says that in theurgy the soul "exchanges one life for another and gives itself to another order, *having entirely abandoned its former existence*" (*Myst.* 270.18–19). The separation of ontological levels and the limits given to the soul ensured that it genuinely experienced this exchange.[83]

There is in Iamblichus's Platonism a willingness to *identify* with the humiliation of the human condition that I am not aware of in gnostic or magical literature. Damascius's companion Isidore once remarked, after meeting a pretentious philosopher: "*Those who would be Gods must first become human!*"[84] For the hieratic Platonists the limits of our humanity must be fully realized in order to recover our lost divinity. The Socratic *aporia* and *oudeneia* central to Platonic *paideia,* seem somehow missing from the rarefied literature of the gnostics and even from the writings of certain Platonists. Yet it was the mystery of mortality and its nothingness that lay hidden at the heart of Iamblichus's Platonism. For, according to Iamblichus, the soul's immortality was recovered only through our mortality and the experience of nothingness (*oudeneia*) that terrifies us all.

---

[83] Cf. *Enn.* 1.2.7.25–28: "He will leave that [human] life behind, and choose another, the life of the gods: for it is to them, not to good men, that we are to be made like." What Plotinus came to identify with as his own undescended soul, Iamblichus left entirely as the property of the gods to be received—in exchange for human life—in the context of theurgic ritual.

[84] *Damascius: Vitae Isidori Reliquiae* (ed. C. Zintzen; Bibliotheca Graeca et Latina suppletoria 1; Hildesheim: G. Olms, 1967), *Epitoma Photiana* nos. 227, 292.

Ritual in Gnosticism

John D. Turner
University Of Nebraska-Lincoln

An action divorced from its primary practical context, ritual bears a symbolic or semiotic character. It usually serves to promote group formation and social solidarity and to negotiate understanding among members of the species. Such actions are religious when they signal a turning towards something extra-human or super-human; indeed the very act of turning away from the human context has an eminently social function. Usually this something is described as the sacred, something experienced as powerful, overwhelming, majestic, solemn, enchanting. This experience is portrayed symbolically by the juxtaposition of things threatening and alluring (pain, entrapment, exclusion, death, and sterility on the one hand, and nourishment, liberation, inclusion, life, and sexuality on the other); by gestures of submissiveness alongside displays of power; and by sudden alterations of darkness and light, covering and uncovering, stability and movement, sound and silence. This quasi-language signals and creates situations of anxiety in order to overcome them and leads from isolation and fear of abandonment to the establishment of solidarity and the reinforcement of status. Ritual helps to overcome situations of crisis by replacing the apathy of ordinary everyday experience with focused activity. Although religious ritual borders on magic (in the sense of the nonsalvific coercion of a particular outcome apart from divine sanction), particularly when consciously practiced by an individual, its primary character is social and collective, a way of participating in the often traditional framework of social communication, and its strongest motive is the fear of isolation from the greater whole.[1]

Although both gnostics and Platonists seemed to have sought this sense of integration and well-being primarily through conceptual means—the interpretation of texts and traditions, the use of analogy, argumentation, speculation, and mythical narrative—they also engaged in ritual activity, repeated patterns of behavior, both as individuals and groups.

---

[1] I have here paraphrased the admirably succinct definition of ritual given by W. Burkert, *Greek Religion* (trans. J. Raffan; Cambridge, Mass: Harvard University Press, 1985), 54–55.

Gnostics share with Platonists the notion that salvation is the ultimate extrication of the soul or inner person from the bodily realm coupled with an ascent to its point of origin in the divine world. After the example of Plato, many Platonists until the time of Plotinus and Porphyry could use visionary terminology associated with the mystery religions to characterize this ascent, but there is no evidence from this period that it was to be effected by ritual means. After the time of Plotinus, however, many Platonists adopted a form of ritual known as theurgy, in which embodied souls were brought into a sympathetic resonance with the divine λόγοι that informed the natural world; divine powers were invoked to enter the phenomenal world in the form of purified souls intended to reveal their divine source in the body and other physical objects, so as to assist the ascent of the practitioner's soul during this life as well as its final ascent.[2] In apparent contrast to this late Platonic theurgical ritual, the salvific rites offered in gnostic sources of the same period continue to appear as symbolic enactments of the more typically Neopythagorean and Plotinian goal of extricating every soul from the physical world altogether, even when one can detect in these sources a quite positive valorization of the psychic and spiritual cosmos.

This paper surveys ritual acts described or alluded to in various gnostic sources, original and heresiological, and where appropriate, to comment upon their relation to Platonic doctrine and ritual. These will include rites of lustration, investiture, chrismation, the sacral meal, sacral marriage, sexual sacramentalism, ritual verbal performances, and ascensional and contemplative practices in both individual and group endeavor. The paper will concentrate mostly on Sethian and Valentinian sources, adducing other material when appropriate.

The rituals practiced by the gnostics, most of which they share with—and sometimes derived from—Christians, are the result of transferring rather simple, everyday acts, such as washing, applying salves and balms, changing clothes, eating and sharing a meal, arising upon awakening, and engaging in sexual intercourse, into a symbolic setting and discourse. The main preoccupation of the gnostics seems to have been the overcoming of an experience of alienation, and isolation, and disenchantment with the *status quo,* and they developed a number of elaborate myths in which they, like other groups, elevated these otherwise rather common acts into rites that had the power to overcome this alienation, and achieve a sense

---

[2] Of course the ultimate goal of theurgists was the soul's return to its stellar origin (Proclus *Hymn* 3). Iamblichus (*Myst.* 5.26.9–18) describes the stages of prayer, whose efficacy lies entirely with the gods: initial contact and acquaintance with the divine, establishing a common noetic bond, petition for divine gifts, and finally the "sealing" of the ineffable union.

of solidarity and authenticity by realistic enactments of personal transformation and integration into a larger whole. Compared with nongnostic Platonists, they subjected a wider range of these ordinary acts to symbolic enactment, no doubt because they inherited many such enactments from other religious movements known to them, such as Judaism, Christianity, and the mysteries, or simply because many gnostics were already adherents of those movements and were merely applying a gnostic twist to them by an innovative exploration of their symbolic resources.

For gnostics as well as Jews and Christians of various stripes, the loss and recovery of a sense of integration and solidarity—personal, social, and cosmic—were expressed in two basic myths. One was the myth of a vertiginous fall from the heights, in which the human soul, like a bird having lost its wings, had plummeted to earth, losing direct contact with its native element; its only hope of return was the acquisition of a new set of wings, a task hindered by the beguiling conditions of its new environment, which led to a gradual forgetfulness of its homing instinct. The other basic myth was that of the primal androgyne, the supposed ultimate, bisexual progenitor of all of humanity, who underwent the primeval experience of being sundered in two, into male and female, thus creating an elementary crisis of estrangement and loss of the divine image and the need to heal this split by the reunion of the two sexes. This myth was extremely widespread. Platonists possessed a version of it in Aristophanes' famous encomium on Eros in Plato's *Symposium,* portraying Zeus's sundering and weakening of the original humans, creating their urge to reunite.[3] Jews and Christians read Gen 1:26–27 as portraying a masculofeminine Adam, made in the true image of the God who transcended gender altogether, an image that was lost in the fateful division into a separate male and female (Gen 2:21–22). These myths of division and alienation underlie many of the traces of gnostic ritual known to us, in particular the rites of baptism, investiture, chrismation, and sacral marriage. These rites serve to reverse that alienation: when the soul regains its wings and homing instinct, it is no longer a

---

[3] *Symp.* 189d–191a: "For in the beginning there were three races of men, not the two of male and female as now, but also a third sharing the nature of both, whose name is extant but the creature not. For at that time there was an androgyne, a single species and name shared by both male and female .... their strength and vigor was awesome and their arrogance was great.... taking thought, Zeus said, 'It seems to me that there is a strategy by which these humans might both survive and cease from their intemperance by becoming weaker; I propose to split them in half, and therewith they will be weaker.' ... having said this, he split the humans in two ... since their nature was bisected, each yearned to unite with its other half." The themes of original androgynous unity and its superiority, the divine jealousy, the split, the attendant weakness, and the urge to reunite all return in gnostic thought.

captive. When the primal image of God is restored, man is no longer divided—not even by the most fundamental division of all, male and female.[4]

Of these four fundamental rites, baptism, though its origins lie in the sphere of repeatable acts of lustration and purification, seems to be an initiatory rite generally—but not necessarily always—practiced only once as the initial break with one's flawed past and an entrance into a new state of reunification, while the other three seem to be repeatable acts of celebration and intensification of one's awareness of that reunification. Closely associated with baptism are the act of chrismation and investiture, which early Christian texts often treat as a postlude to baptism; indeed baptism and chrismation were both called "seals," marking one as reborn and belonging to God. While these rites mostly appear to be unrepeatable acts of initiation, the sacral meal, the Eucharist, though often following baptism, was repeatable. The sacral marriage known as the "bridal chamber," though its origins lie in biblical metaphor, seems to be a peculiarly gnostic ritual; although it usually had an eschatological reference, it could become repeatable, particularly when enacted as an explicitly sexual sacrament.

Besides these major rituals, gnostics share with all groups the ritual use of speech, especially prayer formulas (doxologies, aretalogies, petitions, etc.), hymns, aretalogies, recognition formulas, and ecstatic utterances (chants, syllables of power, glossalalia, etc.). Particularly intriguing is the rite of contemplative, visionary ascension; although one tends to think of this as the practice of isolated individuals, it acquired the status of a rite, not only among the devotees of Hermes Trismegistus, but especially among the Sethian gnostics, probably because it was originally developed in a baptismal context. Other forms of ritual behavior not easily characterized as specific rites may include certain explicit life-styles clearly separating an individual or community from the norm, mostly of an encratitic sort, which include fasting, eremitic withdrawal, celibacy, or the erection of images, statues, and cultic buildings.

---

[4] On this myth and its application to the Pauline baptismal reunification formula of Gal 3:8, see W. Meeks, "The Image of the Androgyne: Some Uses of a Symbol in Earliest Christianity," *HR* 13 (1974): 165–211. Among the references cited by Meeks (188 n. 102) are the Marcosians *apud* Irenaeus *Haer.* 1.18.2 = Epiphanius *Pan.* 34.16.4–5; Naasenes *apud* Hippolytus *Ref.* 5.7.7–15; *Ap. John,* BG 8502, 27,20–25 = NHC III,*1* 7,23–8,5; NHC II,*1:* 5,5–14; *Gos. Phil.,* passim; Simonians *apud* Hippolytus *Ref.* 6.18; *Exeg. Soul,* NHC II,*6* 127,24; the lists of paradoxes found in Hippolytus *Ref.* 6.17.3 and *Thund.,* NHC VI,*2* 13,16–14,5 ‖ *Orig. World,* NHC II,*5* 114,7–16 ‖ *Hyp. Arch.,* NHC II,*4:* 98,11–17. On the whole, see Jacob Jervell, *Imago Dei. Gen 1, 26 f. im Spätjudentum, in der Gnosis und in den paulinischen Briefen* (FRLANT NS 58; Göttingen: Vandenhoeck & Ruprecht, 1960), 161–65.

Because of its foundational significance for several associated rites and its widespread attestation in gnostic texts, I begin this survey with the baptismal rite as practiced by various gnostic groups.

1. Baptism

1.1. Sethian Baptism

The Sethian gnostic treatises from the Nag Hammadi library contain not only numerous accounts of visions of the transcendental world and its contents, but also numerous references to baptisms, washings, anointings, and sealings, and numerous instances of various prayers, doxologies, and hymns mentioning or directed to a rather fixed set of divine beings. Such references generally occur in stanzaic, even hymnic, passages to be found especially in the *Gospel of the Egyptians, Apocalypse of Adam, Melchizedek, Zostrianos, Apocryphon of John,* and *Trimorphic Protennoia.* They apparently refer to a sequence of ritual acts involving a kind of baptism, which the texts often designate by the term "the Five Seals." The Sethian texts providing the most detail about the Five Seals are the *Gospel of the Egyptians* and the *Trimorphic Protennoia,* but they do not reveal the precise ritual character of these Five Seals, with the result that the rite must be reconstructed from their rather allusive allusions to it. The texts contain no liturgical rubrics. Baptism is an extremely well attested rite in the early Christian world, where it and the various symbolic acts that comprise this rite are commonly called "seals." So the basic puzzle is the meaning of the term "five": does it refer to a single act performed five times, e.g., a quintuple immersion in contrast to the typically triple immersion of Christian baptism, or does it refer to five ritual acts comprising the rite, or to some mysterious transcendental Pentad of names (*Trimorphic Protennoia* NHC XIII 49,28–32) or aeons (*Apocryphon of John* NHC II 6,2–10)?[5] The texts do not tell us.

---

[5] The main passages are: *Gos. Eg.* (the series of prayers in III,*2* 65,26–68,1 and the doxologies in IV,*2* 59,13–29; III,*2* 49,22–50,17; 53,12–54,11; 55,16–56,3; 61,23–62,13); *Apoc. Adam* (the visions of the thirteen kingdoms, V,*5* 77,27–82,19, and the concluding sections in 82,19–85,31); *Melch.* (the aretalogies of Gamaliel and Melchizedek in IX,*1* 5,17–6,10 and 14,16–18,7 respectively); *Zost.* (esp. NHC VIII,*1* 5,11–7,22; 15,1–21; 47,1–63,9); the Pronoia hymn of *Ap. John* (II,*1* 30,11–31,25); *Trim. Prot.* (sporadically throughout the aretalogical passages and especially in the recitation of XIII,*1* 48,15–35 and in other, more expository passages, e.g., 36,5b–7a; 37,1b–3a; 37,35; 41,21b–24a; 45,12b–20; 46,16–19a; and 48,top–48,12a). The term "the Five Seals," mostly referring to some kind of baptism, occurs in *Ap. John* II,*1* 31,24; IV,*1* 49,4; *Gos. Eg.* IV,*2* 56,25; 58,6; 58,27–28; 59,27–28; 66,25–26; 74,16; 78,4–5; III,*2* 55,12; 63,3; 66,3; the Bruce untitled treatise 32,10 [Schmidt-MacDermot]; and *Trim. Prot.* XIII,*1* 48,31; 49,27–28; 47,29; 50,9–10).

By way of comparison, the normal Christian baptismal rite contained at least four procedures: removal of outer garments and renunciation of the devil, removal of all garments and anointing with oil, baptismal immersion, and reclothing in white garments; often this was supplemented by a fifth, the chrismation.[6]

The fundamental study of these remains that of J.-M. Sevrin, *Le dossier baptismal Séthien* (BCNHE 2; Québec: Presses de l'Université Laval, 1986). The Sethian rite of the Five Seals (investiture, baptism in the Living Water, enthronement, glorification, and enlightenment in *Trim. Prot.* 48,15–35; 45,12–20), appears to have been complete in itself and effective of salvation. It includes acts similar to those in *2 En.* 22 (stripping of earthly garments, anointing, investing, enlightening) and in *T. Levi* 8:2–10 (investing as priest and king, anointing, washing, feeding, drinking, further investing, and crowning). In *T. Levi* 18:6–7 at the advent of the eschatological priest, a star arises, emitting the light of knowledge, the Father's Voice issues from the heavenly temple, and the spirit of understanding rests upon him in the water. The similarity of these motifs to those of the synoptic accounts of Jesus' baptism is obvious. Similar baptismal motifs occur in the *Odes of Solomon* (11:7–16: drinking Living Water, stripping away of folly, investing with radiance and enlightenment; 24:1–5: the Voice of the dove above the Messiah and the opening of the abysses). The sequence of acts in the Sethian Five Seals is also nearly duplicated in the Mandaean *Maṣbuta* as summarized by Kurt Rudolph, *Die Mandäer*, vol 2: *Der Kult* (FRLANT NS 57; Göttingen: Vandenhoeck & Ruprecht, 1961), 88–89: investiture, entrance into the "jordan," triple self-immersion, triple immersion by the priest, triple signation with water, triple drink, crowning or wreathing, invocation of divine names, ritual handshake (*kušta*), and ascent from the "jordan." Like many of these baptismal materials, the Sethian baptismal materials seem consistently to link the descent of the savior (Seth or Christ as the Logos) into the world with the descent of the baptizand into the water or world of chaos, and the visionary ascent of the baptizand out of the water or world into the light with a sort of royal enthronement of the baptizand. The similar pattern of various of the NT christological hymns may also be seen against such a baptismal environment (e.g., Phil 2:6–11; Col 2:9–15; John 1:1–16).

6 By mid-second century, the Christian baptismal ritual comprised (with regional variations) approximately the following sequence of acts (in certain regions preceded by a two-day fast and an all-night vigil culminating with the rite performed in darkness): (1) renunciation of sin and Satan (later spoken with outstretched arms and facing westwards), sometimes coupled with removal of the outer garments, standing in penance on sackcloth or goatskin, and a prebaptismal anointing with olive oil (a gesture of healing) and cruciform signation on the forehead (either as a kind of exorcism or as an *epiclēsis* of the Holy Spirit); (2) an optional signation with oil on the forehead, after which the postulant strips naked (reminding the postulant of the primal nudity of Adam and Eve in the garden; in cases where there was a baptistery, stripping occurred after entrance into the inner chamber, called by Cyril the holy of holies); (3) an optional complete prebaptismal anointing with oil; (4) water baptism by immersion accompanied by invocation of "the Names"

The Sethian texts are unusual in that, perhaps to a greater degree than is the case with the corpora of other gnostic groups, they conceive the baptismal rite as a series of visionary experiences resulting in complete enlightenment and therefore total salvation. In spite of the allusions to ritual acts that could indeed be enacted by ordinary human beings, the importance of the rite lay primarily in the spiritual plane, an emphasis characteristic of Christian and probably non-Christian baptizing circles throughout the first century. The Sethian baptismal water was understood to be of a celestial nature, a Living Water identical with light or enlightenment. Although in earlier Sethian treatises this rite is usually said to be "received," later treatises portray a self-performable contemplative technique that could be enacted either by means of—or independently of—outward ritual actions. Terms that ordinarily refer to ritual acts, such as "baptism," "immersion," "disrobing," "enrobing," "stripping off," "putting on," "sealing," and the like, also designate acts of mental transformation, conceptual refinement and abstraction from the world of psychic and sensible experience, abstention from previous behavioral dispositions, "unlearning" of older and

---

(usually threefold and including affirmations of creedal interrogations, later spoken eastward); (5) emergence from the water (in which the baptizand is to imagine himself or herself as clothed in a radiant garment); (6) an optional postbaptismal anointing of various parts of the body with oil or myrrh (absent in the Syrian rite, and thus likely a secondary addition); (7) investiture (usually in white clothing, signifying receipt of the light of immortality, supplemented in Egypt much later with a crowning); (8) in the Western church, a postbaptismal anointing (chrismation) of the head by the priest or bishop with oil or myrrh; and (9) an imposition of hands, usually by the bishop, which may include a further anointing and "sealing" on the forehead. Any one of these acts, the anointings (prior to baptism conceived as apotropaic, after baptism as confirmation), the imposition of hands or the baptism itself might be called a "seal." To judge from *Acts Thom.* 26–27, the ascent from the water (Syriac version) or the chrismation (Greek version) may also involve luminous appearances of the Savior; Justin Martyr (*1 Apol.* 61.11–12) characterizes the baptismal washing as "enlightenment" (φωτισμός). See J. Ysebaert, *Greek Baptismal Terminology: Its Origins and Early Development* (Graecitus Christianorum Primeva 1; Nijmegen: Dekker & Van de Vegt, 1962); Hippolytus *Apostolic Tradition,* sec. 21 in the editions by both Dix (London, 1937) and Botte (Paris, 1946); the ancient Syrian liturgy reconstructed by A. F. J. Klijn from the Syriac "Life of John" and other sources ("An Early Christian Baptismal Liturgy," in *Charis kai Sophia: Festchrift Karl Rengstorf* [ed. U. Luck; Leiden: Brill, 1964], 216–28), and the convenient collection of texts in E. C. Whitaker, *Documents of the Baptismal Liturgy* [London: SPCK, 1970]; T. F. Finn, *The Liturgy of Baptism in the Baptismal Instructions of St. John Chrysostom* [CUA: SCA 15; Washington, D.C.: Catholic University of America Press, 1967], 50–54; P. F. Bradshaw, ed., *Studies in Early Eastern Initiation* [Alcuin/GROW Liturgical Study 8; Nottingham: Grove, 1988). Generally, this ceremony would be followed by a kiss of peace and the Eucharist.

adoption of new perceptions of self and world, and entrance into a higher state of enlightenment. It is natural to assume that such a mental transformation arose out of the individual experience of actual cultic and ritual praxis of a sort that could be taught and enacted either while participating in the physical setting and associated gestures of the rite or quite apart from them.[7] We do not know whether this rite was a once-for-all initiation, as it appears to be in earlier Sethian treatises, or was administered repeatedly; later treatises witness what seems to be a gradual extraction of the clearly repeatable visionary component from the baptismal setting.

In the earlier Sethian texts that portray the advent of salvation as coincident with the third and final manifestation in this world (the first two occur in primordial times)[8] of the divine mother Barbelo, she confers the

---

[7] Such stripping, disrobing, and attendant nakedness denote separation from the profane condition of ignorance and entrance into a liminal state. At this point, the initiate or the visionary is "neither this nor that, and yet is both" (V. W. Turner, "Betwixt and Between: The Liminal Period in Rites of Passage" in *Forest of Symbols* [Ithaca, N.Y.: Cornell University Press, 1967], 98), neither enlightened nor unenlightened, but inhabiting a liminal state of literal or figurative nakedness, humility, and passivity, with no claim to status or possession of knowledge. The third phase of the initiatory "rite of passage," aggregation, means incorporation not only into a new state of awareness and into the elect group that inhabits this state, but also the advent of a new cosmic situation, such as the defeat of the hostile cosmic powers and the dissolution of chaos. In the Sethian treatises, typical metaphors for aggregation are Pronoia's gathering of all her members, or in the contemplative ascent, "standing," and being assimilated to increasingly higher levels of reality. As Plotinus observed, such transformed persons thought themselves superior in rank to the very stars, even to the gods themselves (*Enn.* 2.9 [33].9.43–60).

[8] The Sethian scheme of salvation is centered around the supreme trinity of the Father, Mother, and Son: the Invisible Spirit, the male virgin Barbelo who is the Invisible Spirit's First Thought (Ennoia, Protennoia), and their offspring, the divine Autogenes (identified as Christ in the Christian Sethian treatises; in an unpublished paper, "The Virgin Became Male: The Feminine Principle in Platonic and Gnostic Metaphysics," I have tried to show that the Father-Mother-Son nomenclature is likely to be an adaptation of the Father, Mother, Child triad developed by Plato in *Tim.* 48–52, representing respectively the transcendent Forms as father, the receptacle and nurse of becoming as mother, and the images comprising the phenomenal world as child or offspring). The main agent of salvation is the Mother Barbelo, who in various guises descends into the world to rescue the spiritual substance that had been captured in human bodies through the ignorant act of the Archon Yaldabaoth, the aborted offspring of Barbelo's lower double, Sophia. Typically, Barbelo descends thrice into the world. First she projects the image of Adamas, the archetypal human, which the Archon undiscerningly incorporated into a psychosomatic human copy. Second, once the Archon had sundered Eve from Adam, the Mother (as the Epinoia of light) descends to enlighten the primeval couple by

gift of salvation in the form of a baptismal rite called the Five Seals. According to the so-called *Gospel of the Egyptians,* on the third and final descent of the heavenly Seth into the world to save his progeny ("seed"), he is equipped with a Logos-begotten body prepared for him "by the virgin" (the "male virgin" Barbelo), the Providence of the supreme deity, in order to "establish the holy baptism" (a reference to the inaugural baptism of Jesus?) and "put on" Jesus, through whose crucifixion he defeats the powers of the thirteen aeons. According to the *Trimorphic Protennoia,* Protennoia (Barbelo) descends for the third time as the Logos, confers the Five Seals, and finally puts on Jesus, removes him from the cross, and bears him and her seed aloft into the holy light. Similarly, the Pronoia aretalogy concluding the longer version of the *Apocryphon of John* (NHC II 30,11–31,25) depicts the figure of Pronoia (Barbelo) as conferring the Five Seals on her third and final descent. The primary actor behind the scenes is the divine Mother Barbelo, who appears to be a higher, unfallen double of Sophia, the divine wisdom. The imagery of water, light, ascent, and descent found in the Pronoia hymn and in the *Trimorphic Protennoia* seems heavily indebted to the hellenized Jewish wisdom tradition.[9] These two works appear to be old, likely contemporaneous with the Johannine prologue with which they share a common vocabulary and mythological structure, suggesting an early date for these works, perhaps the early second century C.E.

The Sethian text most replete with data for the reconstruction of the ritual acts that comprise Sethian baptism is the *Gospel of the Egyptians*

---

causing them to eat of the tree of knowledge and enabling them to produce their son Seth in the true image of God. Seth becomes the father of an "immovable race" of potentially enlightened people destined to live a perilous life among the mass of immoral humanity descended from Cain, the illegitimate son of the physical Eve by the Archon. Her third and final salvational act is her descent to the contemporary members of that race, the contemporary Sethian gnostics, taking on the form of the divine Logos, or Christ, or of Seth himself.

[9] According to it, the exalted Sophia is the fountain or spring (cf. Sir 15:3; 24:30; Philo, *Fug.* 195) from which flows the Word like a river (Philo, *Somn.* 2.242; cf. *Fug.* 97). She is also equated with the living water of which God is the source (cf. Prov 16:22; 14:27; Cant 4:15 and Bar 3:12 with Jer 2:13; 17:13 [LXX]; John 4:10; 7:38; and *Odes Sol.* 11:5–9; 30:1–6). She is the Mother of the Word through whom the universe came to be (Philo, *Fug.* 109), the mother of all creatures (Philo, *Det.* 115–16). To be baptized in her water is to receive true Gnosis. Her Voice is the revelation of the truth. The same sort of myth of descent applied to Barbelo or the First Thought in the Sethian treatises figures also in the story of Sophia in *1 En.* 42 and other sources—such as the Johannine prologue—where Wisdom (or the Logos) descends to find a place to dwell among men, but meeting with initial failure, reascends or tries again.

(NHC III,*2* and IV, *1*). In it, this baptism involves the begetting of the saints through invisible secret symbols, the "killing" (Coptic ϨⲰⲦⲂ, IV 75,3–4; III 63,3–12 has ϨⲰⲦⲡ, "reconciliation") and renunciation of both the world and the "god of the thirteen aeons," and the invoked (ἐπίκλητοι) presence of certain holy, ineffable beings along with the light of the Father. Although Seth is said to have appeared in the primeval world to deliver his race from the Archon's destructive acts (the flood and conflagration), the Mother now sends him for a third time. At his appearance along with certain divine beings or angels who are to guard the incorruptible race until the consummation of the age, the "great men of the great Seth" receive a vision of various spiritual beings whose names occur repeatedly in the baptismal sections of the Sethian treatises.[10]

Evidence of ritual activity abounds in this text. In NHC III 65,26–66,8 it is said that through the incorruptible man Poimael, those "who are worthy of (the) invocation [ἐπίκλητος], the renunciations [ἀποτάξεις] of the Five Seals[11] in the spring-baptism will know their receivers [παραλήμπτορες] as they are instructed about them." In III 66,9–68,1 there follows a long prayer in which the baptizand praises the Living Water "Yesseus Mazareus Yessedekeus" as the eternal Jesus who truly is, the glorious name that is now upon and within him, granting him immutability and the armor of light. Stretching out his hands while yet folded, the baptizand apparently symbolically portrays the containment of the inner light or the circle of all those who have received enlightenment, and praises the man (Seth?) who raises up the man (Jesus?) in whose name the baptizand will be purified. Having received the incense of life (the Holy Spirit?), the baptizand has mixed it with "water after the model of the archons" (presumably the earthly water of his baptism), now to live with the Savior in the peace of the saints.

Here one has a series of references to certain gestures and verbal performances capable of ritual enactment: renunciation, invocation, naming of holy powers, doxological prayer to the living water, receipt of incense, manual gestures, as well as baptismal immersion itself. Whether any of these acts, and if so, which ones, comprise the Five Seals is difficult to tell;

---

[10] They include: Yesseus Mazareus Yessedekeus the living water, Micheus, Michar and Mnesinous, who preside over the "spring of truth" or "the gate of the waters," Seldao and Elainos, who preside over the "mountain" (perhaps Charaxiô [III,*2* 68,13], "mountain [Heb. הַר] of the worthy [Gk. ἀξιῶν]"), the Four Lights Harmozel, Oroiael, Davithe, and Eleleth along with their "ministers" Gamaliel, Gabriel, Samblo, and Abrasax, and finally Yoel, who presides over the divine name with which one is baptized.

[11] Here one might interpret the Five Seals as five renunciations, but it seems to me unlikely.

certainly renunciation, invocation, and the extension of the arms were frequently part of the baptismal rite in the wider church.[12] Throughout, the use of the passive voice for ritual actions and the use of plural references to the saints begotten "through instruction" suggests a community ritual in which there were initiates and officiants, as well as a tradition of prescribed actions and declarations.

What is more, it may be that the entire *Gospel of the Egyptians* and not just its conclusion has a ritual or liturgical function. There are five doxologies (IV 59,13–29; III 49,22–50,17; 53,12–54,11; 55,16–56,3; 61,23–62,13) punctuating the completion of various stages of its cosmology, which invoke a fixed set of beings.[13] This doxological inventory has the fixity of a liturgical formula. If the term "Five Seals" originally designated a fivefold or five-stage baptismal procedure, it may be that the *Gospel of the Egyptians* was read aloud during the administration of each phase of the ritual: after the reading of each of the five sections of the cosmology, the baptizand might have repeated this doxology as a way of affirming the receipt of each of the Five Seals. A similar correlation between baptismal sealings and depictions of the structure and deployment of the transcendent world occurs also in *Zostrianos,* although there the sealings are clearly given a celestial, rather than earthly, setting.

Furthermore, in both the *Gospel of the Egyptians* and the *Trimorphic Protennoia,* the final act of salvation is the descent of Seth in the form of the Logos or of the Logos in the form of Christ, who "puts on," that is, appears in the form of, Jesus. The salvation of Jesus implied in these two texts certainly reflects Christian influence, but of an extremely polemical sort, since rather than being the Savior, Jesus becomes the one saved. In view of this Sethian christological reinterpretation, one would characterize the present form of these two texts as reacting to rather than merely submitting to Christian influence.

The *Apocalypse of Adam* contains a dream vision revealed to Adam by three glorious men who narrate a third saving mission conducted by an illuminator whose origin is unknown to the evil powers. Thirteen opinions of his origins are rejected; in reality he comes from a great aeon to enlighten his elect. The illuminator experiences neither birth nor generation, nor does he receive nourishment, glory, and power in the beyond

---

[12] The components are similar to those found in early Christian baptismal liturgies; see above, note 6.

[13] They include the Invisible Spirit, Barbelo, the thrice-male Child, the male virgin Youel, Esephech the Child of the Child, and the Doxomedon aeon. A similar set of beings are invoked in the doxologies of *Melchizedek* (IX, *1* 5,17–6,10; 14,16–18,7), there revealed by Gamaliel and pronounced by Melchizedek as he is baptized.

and then "come (down) to the water." The Illuminator is not first born into
the world and then baptized in the waters of the Jordan, which the author
or redactor regards as polluted and chaotic.[14] Instead, the Illuminator
remains above in the light where he resides with the three imperishable
illuminators Yesseus, Mazareus, Yessedekeus, the Living Water, and first
appears in the world not at his own "birth" or baptism, but at the time he
baptizes his "seed," who receive his name on the water.[15] At some point,
angelic beings will bring the truth to the earthly Sethians in a way independent of the written word of the evil creator, a truth that is communicated by a holy baptism through a logos-begotten illuminator who
descends to the water during baptism. Thus there is a distinction between
the holy baptism with Living Water and a baptism ordained by the creator
and practiced by his servants who have polluted the water of life.

Using nomenclature reminiscent of that found in the *Apocryphon of
John,* the *Trimorphic Protennoia* identifies the initiator and bringer of salvation, conferred on her third descent in the form of the Five Seals, as Protennoia or Barbelo, the First Thought of the Invisible Spirit.[16] At various
points throughout the *Trimorphic Protennoia,* the triple descent of Protennoia and the various forms in which she appears, namely as Voice,
Speech, and Word, are interpreted by means of concepts that are drawn

---

[14] In the Sethian theogony and cosmogony, a similar distinction is maintained
between the transcendent luminous living water in which Barbelo emerges as a
faithful reflection of the Invisible Spirit's thought (cf. *Ap. John* NHC II,*1* 4,18–28)
and the dark and chaotic waters below produced by the downward inclination of
Sophia, from which the demiurge produces the physical cosmos as merely a pale
and inauthentic reflection of the divine aeons (e.g., *Zost.* NHC VIII,*1* 9,16–10,18;
Hyp. Arch. NHC II,*4* 87,11–20 and parallels). See Hippolytus, *Ref.* 5.19.21, and
below on Justin's *Baruch.*

[15] Clearly these thirteen "birth stories" about the Illuminator are being reinter-
preted in the light of earlier traditions about the descent of the spirit upon Jesus at
his baptism. See below on the Basilideans, and J. M. Robinson, "On the *Gattung*
of Mark (and John)," in *Jesus and Man's Hope* (175th Anniversary Festival on the
Gospels at Pittsburgh Theological Seminary) *Perspective* 11.2 (1970): 99–129, especially 119–29.

[16] She appears in three successive forms: First, as Father, she is the divine but as
yet inarticulate Voice of the First Thought of the Invisible Spirit who presides over
the establishing of the heavenly dwellings for her members and descends to chaos
to loosen their bonds. Second, as Mother, she is the articulate Speech of the
Thought who overthrows the old aeon ruled by the evil powers and announces the
dawn of the new age. Third, as the Son, she is the fully articulate Logos who adopts
the guise of successively lower powers, descends to and enters the "tents" of her
members, puts on Jesus, thus rescuing him from the cross, and leads her members
back to the light by means of the celestial ascent ritual of the Five Seals.

from the Sethian baptismal terminology: the Voice is said to be the unpolluted spring from which flows Living Water, characterized as radiant light.[17]

Rather than designating a fivefold immersion in the Living Water, the Five Seals are interpreted as a five-stage ritual of ascension, which serves to strip the inner spirit of its chaotic psychic and material garments and reclothe it with shining light. The spirit is invested with the robes of light, enthroned, baptized by Micheus, Michar, and Mnesinous in the spring of Living Water, glorified with the Fatherhood, and raptured into the light (perhaps the Four Lights) by the servants of the Four Lights Kamaliel, [. . .]anen, and Samblo (XIII 48,15–35). Clearly the rapture into the light is the equivalent of the baptismal φωτισμός spoke of by Justin, Cyril, and other patristic authors. The five stages of this ascensional rite do not seem to follow in an intuitively obvious sequence (e.g., in 45,13–20 one has the following sequence: glorification, enthronement, investiture, baptism, and becoming Light). Indeed, since most cults practiced naked baptism, one might expect the order: baptism, investiture, enthronement, glorification, and final rapture (see above, note 6).

In the concluding section of the *Trimorphic Protennoia,* the Five Seals are equated with the "ineffable ordinances of the Father," taught by Protennoia to her "members," "the brethren." The Five Seals are said to be "complete by means of Nous." Whoever possesses the Five Seals "of these particular names"[18] has stripped away all ignorance and darkness and has put on a shining light, permanently free from ignorance and the power of the hostile archontic forces, and experiencing a mutual indwelling with

---

[17] Gnosis, or perhaps the seed of Seth; cf. *Gos. Eg.* III,*2* 56,4–13. Cf. the radiant light with which the Invisible Spirit is surrounded in *Ap. John* II,*1* 4,18–26, as well as the important place given to the Four Lights. The Word, bearing Living Fruit, pays the tribute of this Fruit to the Living Water, which it pours out upon Protennoia's "Spirit" (i.e., her gnostic "members" who share affinity with her), which originated from the Living Water but is now trapped in the soul (i.e., the psychic realm) below. The baptismal rite of the Five Seals is the celestial ascent by which one strips off the psychic and somatic garments of ignorance (cf. Col 2:11–15). It transforms and purifies Protennoia's members within those aeons from which Protennoia initially revealed her masculine likeness (XIII 43,20–25; probably in the form of the Autogenes who established the Four Lights), and it clothes them with radiant light (48,7–14).

[18] NHC XIII,*1* 49,29–30: ⲧⲧⲉ ⲛ̄ⲥⲫⲣⲁⲅⲓⲥ ⲛ̄ⲧⲉ ⲛⲉⲉⲓⲣⲁⲛ ⲉⲧⲉ ⲛⲁⲓ̈ ⲛⲉ. The use of the Coptic relative clause ⲉⲧⲉ ⲛⲁⲓ̈ ⲛⲉ in the absolute seems odd; perhaps it once had a predicate, now lost, providing a more specific gloss on the Five Seals. As it stands, its antecedent is "these names," presumably the names of the beings named in 48,15–35. The effect of this phrase is to identify the Five Seals with a (ritual) invocation of the names of these spiritual beings, the baptizers, guardians, investitors, rapturers, glorifiers, enthroners, and others associated with the baptismal rite.

Protennoia until the time when she gathers all her members into her eternal kingdom. Here the Five Seals are connected with communicable doctrine and the ability to name and experience the presence of certain spiritual beings, a doctrine that entails the stripping away of the ignorance of common perception and the adoption (putting on) of an appropriate way of seeing things. The rite is the dramatization of this process, and the Sethian myth its narratization. The fact that this text refers to the recipients of the baptismal ascent ritual in the first person plural and as "brethren" suggests a (Sethian) community with a well-established tradition of water baptism that has been conceived as a mystery of celestial ascent, and which brings Gnosis (NHC XIII 48,33–34) and total salvation.

In many ways, the Sethian text that most abounds with baptismal imagery is *Zostrianos,* although the extant remains do not mention the Five Seals, and the imagery has been divorced from any actual water rite. Throughout the first sixty or so pages, it seems that Zostrianos is baptized at least twenty times in the course of his ascent, once at the airy earth (the atmosphere below the moon), seven times in the copies of the aeons (the planetary spheres), once in the Transmigration (παροίκησις, probably the sphere of the fixed stars), and six times in the Repentance, for a subtotal of fifteen. At the level of the Self-begotten Ones he is baptized four times by the traditional Sethian baptizers and purifiers, each time standing as an angel upon the level of each of the Four Lights, and again for a fifth time at the level of Autogenes, where he becomes divine and enters the Aeon of Barbelo. In a further baptism at the level of the Triple Male Child, he becomes truly existing, and lastly, it seems that he is baptized once again at the level of Protophanes, where he becomes perfect, for a subtotal of seven, and a grand total of some twenty-two baptisms, washings, and sealings. Although the fragmentary state of the text precludes certainty on the total number of baptisms or their precise significance, here baptism has become interpreted as a metaphor for the process by which a visionary becomes assimilated to the being and nature of each level of the transcendent realm to which he ascends.

Zostrianos portrays a visionary and auditory experience that has no explicit ritual setting. Terms which may once have had a ritual reference now serve only as means to articulate the various stages of a visionary ascent. Celestial baptisms denote stages of increasing spiritual enlightenment, while the earthly experience of the nonspiritual mass of humanity is regarded as a "baptism with death" (NHC VIII 131,2). Perhaps *Zostrianos* lies at the terminus of a process of development in which a traditional practice of visionary ascent that originally arose in the context of Sethian baptismal practice as it is reflected in the *Apocryphon of John,* the *Trimorphic Protennoia,* and the *Gospel of the Egyptians* was subsequently transformed from an original practice of water baptism into a self-contained and self-performable contemplative practice engaged in either by lone individuals or by groups (as the *Three Steles of Seth*, NHC VII 126,31–127,22 makes clear). Perhaps it is merely a later expression of an original but alternative trajectory of visionary practices that developed alongside but independently of the Sethian communal water rites. Knowledge of the nature of the Sethian encounter with both Platonism and Christian forms of gnostic Sethianism would certainly help to resolve this puzzle.

As an immersion in water, baptism may also have a negative connotation, especially when it signifies immersion in materiality, symbolized by the chaotic waters underlying the natural cosmos. Gnostics applied this negative connotation to what they considered to be the lower baptism undergone by nongnostic Christians. Like the *Apocalypse of Adam* (NHC V 84,4–85,30) and *Zostrianos* (NHC VIII 131,2–5), the *Paraphrase of Shem* (NHC VII 30,21–27; 37,19–38,6) speaks also of an impure baptism in a dark water that enslaves, evidently a polemic against ordinary water baptism. The Archontics, whom Epiphanius (*Pan.* 40.2.6–8) presents as an offshoot of the Sethians, reject completely the baptism and sacraments of the church as deriving from the inferior law-giver Sabaoth; to shun baptism is to enhance the prospect of acquiring of the gnosis enabling their return to the Mother-Father of the All.

1.2. Valentinian Baptism

The patristic accounts of the Valentinian baptismal practices agree on three basic features of Valentinian baptismal practice.[19] The first is the presence of two separate baptisms among the Valentinians. The "psychics" had access to the "normal" Christian one, while the "pneumatics" could gain closer contact with the divine by a second rite, which Irenaeus and Hippolytus called the "redemption." Rather than devaluing the standard, psychic baptism, as Irenaeus thinks, both the Nag Hammadi sources and patristic sources, such as Clement of Alexandria's *Excerpta ex Theodoto*, demonstrate great concern for the psychics. Secondly, patristic accounts all agree that these rituals were salvific sacraments, and thirdly, they associate baptism (perhaps both baptisms) with the remission of sins. The *Excerpta ex Theodoto* (76–86) characterize the first, water baptism as a "sealing" done in the name of the Father, the Son, and the Holy Spirit, which gives psychic Christians power over sin, allowing them to be reborn, control the impure spirits, and gain entry to the marriage feast in the end times. Baptism affords access to saving knowledge, as *Exc.* 78 states:

---

[19] According to the detailed analysis of M. R. Desjardins, "Baptism in Valentinianism," a paper delivered at the 1987 Annual Meeting of the Society of Biblical Literature.

Until baptism, they say, Fate is effective, but after it the astrologers no longer speak the truth. It is not the washing alone that makes us free, but also the knowledge of who we were, what we have we become, where we were, into what place we have we been cast, whither we are hastening, from what we are delivered, what birth is, and what rebirth.

According to Hippolytus, (*Ref.* 6.41), Marcus taught that a second washing or baptism, called the "redemption" (ἀπολύτρωσις), was available to Christians through him. It normally required special and extensive instructions beforehand, but a bishop could also administer it to those who were on their deathbed. Anyone undergoing the rite of redemption belonged to "the perfect power and inconceivable authority" and was no longer affected by sin. According to Irenaeus (*Haer.* 1.21.2), psychic baptism is said to have been inaugurated by John the Baptist with a view to repentance and instituted by the visible Jesus for the remission of sins. Redemption, on the other hand, was brought by Christ descending on Jesus, with a view to perfection; this is another instance of the widespread gnostic adoption of the traditions about Jesus' inaugural baptism, in which he sees the heavens opened and receives both the Spirit and adoption as Son of God. Hippolytus (*Ref.* 6.35.5) attests that the Italian Valentinians considered Jesus' body to be psychic, but made pneumatic and raised from the dead at his baptism by the Spirit, said to be the Logos of his mother Sophia. As in the Sethian treatises, traditions about the descent of the Spirit upon Jesus at his baptism justify the distinction; indeed Irenaeus speaks of the Valentinian tendency to gather Gospel allusions (e.g., Luke 12:50; Matt 20:20) to support the necessity of another baptism. The remission of sins is linked to baptism, and thence to repentance, the psychics, and the ministries of John and the visible Jesus. Redemption, on the other hand, is linked to pneumatics, perfection, and Christ descending on Jesus.

According to Clement of Alexandria's *Excerpta ex Theodoto* (22.1), the male angelic counterparts of Valentinian Christians are themselves baptized through the redemption of the same name that descended to redeem Jesus at his own baptism. These angels are baptized "for the dead," that is, for the earthly Valentinians, imparting to them the name of the son by which they are enabled to pass through the Limit into the Pleroma. The imposition of hands, apparently in connection with the baptismal rite, confers the angelic redemption, tantamount to being baptized in the same name as was one's angelic counterpart.

For the *Tripartite Tractate* (NHC I 127,25), Valentinian baptism is equivalent to the redemption, the second baptism (the baptism "in the fullest sense" as opposed to "the baptism which we previously mentioned"). Redemption occurs when one confesses faith in the names of the Trinity and is equivalent to entering a state of tranquillity, enlightenment, and immortality; it is the bridal chamber. It is the ritual that above all others that functioned as the seal of the union between the author's community and the Father, who grants knowledge of himself in exchange for the believer's confession of faith.

According to the *Gospel of Philip*, becoming perfect by acquiring the spiritual resurrection while yet on earth enables Christians to bypass post-mortem suffering in the Middle (μεσότης) and proceed directly to the Father and his rest. Such perfection is enabled by no less than five sacraments.[20] In baptism, one strips off the old self and puts on a spiritual body; the chrism confers the Holy Spirit, creating the spiritual or pneumatic person; the Eucharist does the same, except using the symbols of bread and a cup of wine mixed with water, probably on a repeated basis. The redemption seems to be an oil rite, perhaps a sort of confession or extreme unction (like the Mandaean *Masiqta*), or perhaps a post-baptismal chrismation as was customary in the Western (but not Syrian) church. The bridal chamber seems to be a proleptic enactment of one's final entrance into the Pleroma, perhaps symbolized by a ritual kiss (cf. the kiss of peace in the *Apostolic Constitutions* and the ritual handshake [*kušta*] in the Mandaean *Maṣbuta*).

The *Gospel of Philip* (NHC II 67,28–30) names these five sacraments, evidently in order of importance, although their distinctiveness is often blurred, perhaps because they are understood as being all interdependent. As Meeks observes, it illustrates the tendency of motifs originally connected with baptism to become distinct rituals, as the mythical context of these motifs also becomes more elaborate.[21] Thus, while the receiving of

---

[20] For sacraments in the *Gospel of Philip,* see R. M. Grant, "The Mystery of Marriage in the Gospel of Philip," *VC* 15 (1961): 129–40; H.-M. Schenke [and Johannes Leipoldt], "Koptisch-gnostiche Schriften aus den Papyus-Codices von Nag-Hammadi," *TF* 20 (1960): 35–38; Eric Segelberg, "The Coptic-Gnostic Gospel according to Philip and Its Sacramental System," *Numen* 7 (1960): 189–200; idem, "The Baptismal Rite according to the Coptic-Gnostic Texts of Nag Hammadi," in *Studia Patristica V* (ed. F. L. Cross; TU 80; Berlin: Akademie Verlag, 1962), 117–28; idem, "The Gospel of Philip and the New Testament," in *The New Testament and Gnosis: Essays in Honour of Robert McL. Wilson* (ed. A. H. B. Logan and A. J. M. Wedderburn; Edinburgh: T&T Clark, 1983), 204–12; D. H. Tripp, "The 'Sacramental System' of the Gospel of Philip," in *Studia Patristica in Three Parts* (ed. E. A. Livingstone; 3 vols.; Oxford: Pergamon, 1982), 1:251–60; Wilson, *The Gospel of Philip,* 17–23; C. Trautmann, "Organization communautaire et pratiques rituelles," *Histoire et archéologie* 70 (1983): 44–51; and H. Green, "Ritual in Valentinian Gnosticism," *JRH* 12 (1982): 109–24. Cf. especially the doctoral dissertations of H.-G. Gaffron, "Studien zum koptischen Philippusevangelium unter besonderer Berücksichtigkeit der Sakramente" (Bonn, 1969) and J.-M. Sevrin, "Practique et doctrine des sacraments dans l'Evagile selon Philippe" (Louvain, 1972).

[21] "The Image of the Androgyne," 190–91.

the garment or body of light is still connected with baptism in some of the sayings in the *Gospel of Philip* (75,21–24; cf. 76,25–30), in others the clothing with light is effected by the chrism (74,12–22) or the bridal chamber (78,5–9). Christ's own participation in baptism and Eucharist (by instituting the Last Supper) of course renders these sacraments of particular importance. These rites are arranged in an ascending order (69,14–29), e.g., the chrism is superior to the baptism (74,12–13), yet baptism can include redemption (69,25–26), and chrism the Eucharist (74,36–75,11), although the supreme rite is the bridal chamber (64,31–70,22).[22] Because of this overlapping, it is really impossible to tell whether these were enacted separately or in combination.

It seems likely that the first three rites (baptism, chrism, and Eucharist, perhaps unrepeatable) were included in same initiation ceremony, while the redemption and bridal chamber constituted a sort of second baptism (cf. 75,1–2) and were capable of repetition. According to Desjardins,[23]

> Baptism, reinforced by chrism (the "second baptism" done with olive oil—73,17–18), actually provides immortality. In these two rites, purification occurs visibly through water and invisibly through fire and light (57,22–28). Jesus has purified and perfected the water at baptism (77,7–9) and God has "dyed it" (63,25–30), yet it is still possible for someone to emerge from the water baptism without having received the Holy Spirit 64,22–31). So, "it is fitting to baptize in the two, in the light and the water. Now the light is the chrism" (69,11–13). This dual baptism provides the resurrection (69,25–26) and perfection: "He who has been anointed possesses everything. He possesses the resurrection, the light, the cross, the Holy Spirit; the Father gave him this in the bridal chamber" (74,18–22). In turn, this resurrection requires a spiritual flesh, which the eucharist provides (56,26–57,22; cf. also 75,14–24).

According to 69,14–70,4, just as the Jerusalem temple supposedly consisted of a succession of enclosing chambers, the holy enclosing the holy of the holy, which in turn encloses the holy of the holies, so also baptism includes the resurrection and the redemption, which latter occurs in the bridal chamber. In turn, this resurrection requires a spiritual flesh, which the Eucharist provides (56,26–57,22; cf. 75,14–24). Both resurrection and baptism must be received while one is still alive (73,1–7); likewise, if one

---

[22] So M. R. Desjardins, *Sin in Valentinianism* (SBLDS 108; Atlanta: Scholars Press, 1990), 95. It may be that the very positive evaluation of baptism in *Gos. Phil.* II 61,12–20; 64,22–31; 69,4–14; 73,1–8; and 75,21–25 belongs to an early stratum of this work in contrast with other material that deprecates baptism in favor of chrism and especially the bridal chamber.

[23] *Sin in Valentinianism,* 95–96; "Baptism in Valentinianism," 18.

does not actualize the resurrection by receiving the bridal chamber here in this realm, one will not be able to receive it in the other place (86,5–7). Truth does not appear naked but in sacramental types and images (67,9–11). Each sacrament effects union by overcoming separation; by means of baptism, Eucharist, or resurrection, Christ's soteriological function is to overcome the original separation of woman from man, whose separation results in death (70,11–16), but whose reunification is effected only through enacting sacraments in this world. To receive a sacrament transforms one from a Christian into a Christ (67,27–27; cf. Augustine, *Homily on John* 21.8: *non solum nos christianos factos esse, sed Christum*).

In agreement with the *Gospel of Philip,* the liturgical supplements to *A Valentinian Exposition* (esp. 41,21–38) clearly distinguish a second baptism differing from the ordinary Christian baptism, though it does not describe it. Like the *Gospel of Philip, A Valentinian Exposition* understands the first baptism as the forgiveness of sins, but whose effect seems to be the same as the "redemption" or second baptism described in patristic sources: it elevates the recipient out of the world into the aeon. In both treatises the first baptism seems to be connected with an anointing and a Eucharist, although the significance of the latter seems to be attenuated. In the *Gospel of Philip,* which seems to refer to the rites of redemption and bridal chamber as a sort of second baptism, the chrism becomes the central part of the baptismal rite, overshadowing the eucharist altogether.

Just as the treatise *Zostrianos* portrays Sethian practice of visionary ascent as a series of baptisms, washings, and sealings, the *Gospel of Philip* (69,4–14) draws an explicit connection not only between vision and baptism, but also vision and the chrism, and further associates both with rebirth and the restoration to the condition of the primal androgyne: "Through the holy spirit we are indeed begotten again, but we are begotten through Christ in the two. We are anointed through the spirit. When we were begotten we were united. None can see himself either in water or in a mirror without light. Nor again can you see in light without water or mirror. For this reason it is fitting to baptize in the two, in the light and the water. Now the light is the chrism." For the *Gospel of Philip,* sacraments occasion an assimilation of the participant to the nature of the participated:

61 [20] It is not possible [21] for anyone to see anything of the things that actually exist [22] unless he becomes like [23] them. This is not the way with man [24] in the world: he sees the sun without being a sun; [25] and he sees the heaven and the earth and [26] all other things, but he is not these things. [27] This is quite in keeping with the truth. But you (sg.) saw [28] something of that place, and you became [29] those things. You saw the spirit, you [30] became spirit. You saw Christ, you became [31] Christ. You saw [the father, you] shall become father. [32] So [in this place] you see [33]

everything and [do] not [see] yourself, [34] but [in that place] you do see yourself—and what [35] you see you shall [become].

1.3. Other Testimony concerning Gnostic Baptism

Many other gnostic groups practiced baptism. According to Irenaeus (*Haer.* 1.23.5), Menander's disciples were baptized into his own name, receiving resurrection in the form of agelessness and physical immortality. According to Clement of Alexandria (*Strom.* 1.21.146.1–4), the disciples of Basilides calculated the date of Jesus' baptism, which they celebrated on the fifteenth of Tybi (January 6) by spending the previous night in Scripture readings; it is possible that this sect witnesses the first known instance of a 365-day lectionary year that began with the Epiphany celebration of Jesus' baptismal enlightenment (φωτισμός) at the Jordan.[24] The Naasenes (Hippolytus, *Ref.* 5.7.19; 5.7.40; 5.9.18) understood baptism as a spiritual birth ("from water and the spirit," John 3:5) and entrance into immortality through Jesus the "true gate" (cf. John 10:9); it included washing in "living water" (the water above the firmament) and an anointing from a horn "at the third gate."[25] The gnostic Justin's book of *Baruch* (apud Hippolytus *Ref.* 5.27.1–4) distinguishes between the water below the firmament belonging to the evil creation and the springing well of living water above the firmament belonging to the Good one; only pneumatic persons drink of—that is wash in—the latter, while the psychic and material wash in the former. Here the sapiential metaphor of drinking from the water of wisdom is interpreted as baptism,[26] yet one notes again the strong distinction between ordinary Christian baptism and pneumatic baptism as expressed in the dual baptism of the Valentinians and the harsh polemic against water baptism in the *Apocalypse of Adam* (NHC V 84,4–85,30; cf. *Zost.* NHC VIII 131,2–5). In the

---

[24] See D. Vigne, "Enquête sur Basilide," in *Recherches et Tradition: Mélanges patistriques offerts à Henri Crouzel, S.J.* (ed. A. Dupleix; ThH 88, Paris: Beauchesne, 1992), 285–313. Basilidean Christology is based, not on the passion, but the baptism of Jesus; according to Hippolytus (*Ref.* 7.26.8–10), the third Sonship receives the light from the Holy Spirit descending with a fragrant ointment like a bird from the Ogdoad at the time of his baptism, which Hippolytus misinterprets as the coming of the Spirit on Mary at the time of Jesus' birth (a similar confusion appears in the *Apocalypse of Adam*).

[25] Perhaps an allusion to the eastern gate of the heavenly temple through which the glory of the Lord entered, as envisioned in Ezek 43:1–5.

[26] The Hermetica (*Corp. herm.* 4.3–6, "The Cup") interprets the receipt of Gnosis as a baptism in the "cup" of intellect (νοῦς) reserved only for a few, who by immersing themselves become perfect men, able to see the Good, despise the body, and hasten upward to the One.

second *Book of Jeu* (chs. 45–52) one finds a most elaborate baptismal rite that affords entry into the Treasury of Light. In a ritual setting featuring a table set with bread, pitchers of wine and water, herbs, and incense, the disciples of Jesus don linen robes and myrtle crowns to receive a sequence of three baptisms (in living water, fire, and the Holy Spirit) in which they acquire certain ciphers and names as "seals" allowing them to ascend through the aeons. Unfortunately, the manuscript ends before Jesus reveals the great "mystery of the forgiveness of sins" required for ultimate entrance into the Treasury of Light.

Simonian Gnosticism illustrates the central role of the ritual recovery of the androgynous image (here called the undifferentiated "root" power, Hippolytus, *Ref.* 6.18.2; 6.18.4). The separation and reunion of the male and female elements in humankind underlies the legend of Simon and his consort Helen, which was already known before the time of Justin Martyr.[27] The later *Apophasis Megale* quoted by Hippolytus (*Ref.* 6.17.1) suggests that it may have taken the form of a baptismal ritual:

> According to Simon, then, that blessed and incorruptible being lies hidden in every being potentially [δύναμει], not actually [ἐνεργείᾳ]; that is he who stands, took his stand, and will stand [ὁ ἑστώς, στάς, στησόμενος]: who stands on high in the unbegotten power, who took his stand below in the chaos of waters when he was begotten in an image [εἰκών], who will stand on high with the blessed infinite power if he be fully formed [ἐξεικονίσθη]. For, he says, there are three that stand, and without there being three that stand, the [un]originate being, who (they say) hovers over the water [cf. 6.14.4], is not set in order, the perfect heavenly being who is recreated according to the likeness, who becomes in no respect inferior to the unoriginate power. This is the meaning of their saying, "I and thou are one, thou art before me, and I am after thee." This, he says, is one power, divided as being above (as infinite) and below [as λόγος?], self-generating,... its own mother, its own father, its own sister, its own consort, its own daughter, its own son,... unity, the root of all things.

Being (re)-formed in the image, equated with "being begotten" and occurring "in the stream of waters," suggests a cultic act like baptism, as in *Exc.* 68: "As long as we were children of the female only, as of a dishonorable union, we were incomplete, childish, without understanding, weak, and without form, brought forth like abortions, in short, we were children of

---

[27] See E. Haenchen, "Gab es eine vorchristliche Gnosis?" in *Gott und Mensch: Gesammelte Aufsätze* (Tübingen: Mohr Siebeck, 1965), 289–91, 297–98; contra K. Beyschlag, "Zur Simon-Magus-Frage," *ZTK* 68 (1971): 395–426; and R. Bergmeier, "Quellen vorchristlicher Gnosis," in *Tradition und Glaube* (ed. G. Jeremias et al.; Göttingen: Vandenhoeck & Ruprecht, 1971), 200–20.

the woman (i.e., Sophia). But having been given form (μορφωθέντας) by the Savior, we are the children of the man (husband) and of the bride-chamber."[28] In fact, Hippolytus (*Ref.* 6.19.5) says the Simonians called a rite of apparent sexual promiscuity in imitation of Simon (and Helen) "the holy of holies," the same metaphor used for the rite of the bridal chamber in *Gos. Phil.* 69,14–70,4. It therefore likely that the Simonians possessed rituals analogous to the Valentinian baptism and bridal chamber, which might account for the report in Pseudo-Clement (*Homilies* 2.23–24) that Simon was a disciple of John the Baptist.

A striking parallel to the Simonian legend is the myth of the soul's abuse, transformation, and joining to her heavenly "bridegroom" found in the Nag Hammadi treatise the *Exegesis on the Soul,* which seems to have Simonian affinities. It regards what seems to be the vehicle of the soul as its womb, surrounding it as a dirty and polluted garment (cf. esp. NHC II 131,13–132,2). The restoration of the soul's former nature, which it possessed before it had fallen into the body and prostituted itself to the materialistic life, is called the baptism of the soul; the "womb of the soul" is on the outside like male genitals until purified by baptism, when it is "turned inward" to regain the freshness of its former nature.[29]

Among the Sethians, Simonians, and especially the Valentinians, the sacramental means of restoring the androgynous wholeness of the inner person through ritual acts centered on baptism presupposes a cultic community with a strong sense of corporate identity. In other gnostic circles, however, the same quest and its mythical justification could be focused

---

[28] According to Meeks, "The Image of the Androgyne," 191–93, the primary allusion is the anthropogony of Gen 1, but in the clause, "if he be fully formed [ἐὰν ἐξεικονίσθαι]," the verb (ἐξ)εικονίζεσθαι (be "iconized") appears to be a technical term in the *Megale Apophasis,* equivalent to "to become perfect" (γενόμενος τέλεσιος, *Ref.* 6.18.1).

[29] Meeks, "The Image of the Androgyne," 193–94, connects this peculiar simile with the metaphor of making "the inner like the outer" in *Gos. Thom.* 22: "When you make the two into one, and when you make the inner like the outer and the outer like the inner, and the upper like the lower, and when you make male and female into a single one, so that the male will not be male nor the female be female, when you make eyes in place of an eye, a hand in place of a hand, a foot in place of a foot, an image in place of an image, then you will enter [the kingdom]." Variant forms of this saying occur in Clement of Alexandria *Strom.* 3.13.92 (citing the *Gospel of the Egyptians* and Julius Cassianus), *2 Clem.* 12.2, and, without mention of male and female, *Acts Pet.* 38 and *Acts Phil.* 140. Meeks also cites logion 106, "When you make the two one, you shall become sons of man"; logion 11, "On the day when you were one, you became two. But when you have become two, what will you do?" and logion 4, "Many who are first shall become last and they shall become a single one."

exclusively upon a subjective transformation of consciousness leading away from sect-formation and toward a radical isolation of the individual. Within Sethianism, the exclusive concentration on the singular experience of an individual visionary like Allogenes or Zostrianos or Marsanes in the Platonizing Sethian treatises might lend itself to such a development, although the *Three Steles of Seth,* apart from Seth's initial praise of his father Geradamas, is explicitly cast in the first person plural as a communal exercise in contemplative ascent.

The trend towards individual isolation is evident in the *Gospel of Thomas* and in the encratite Christianity of eastern Syria, where most scholars locate the Thomas tradition. The theme of "making the two one" in the *Gospel of Thomas* likely derives from baptismal liturgies, particularly Syrian ones.[30] But its ideal of "singleness," expressed in the Coptic ογⲁ ογⲱⲧ or the Greek μοναχός, signifies celibacy and isolation from society. Indeed, the Nag Hammadi *Testimony of Truth* (esp. IX 69,8–24) specifies that true baptism is the renunciation of the world, rather than a ritual sealing of one entering the faith administered by the (defiled!) fathers of the world: the Son of Man baptized no disciples.

1.4. Jesus' Inaugural Baptism As a Paradigm for Visionary Enlightenment

The baptismal lore of many of the foregoing groups, especially the Sethians and those associated with Valentinus and Basilides, make a good deal out of the traditions of Jesus' inaugural baptism.[31] Within the NT,

---

[30] J. Z. Smith, "The Garments of Shame," *HR* 5 (1965): 217–38, shows that the main elements of logion 37, undressing, being naked without shame, treading upon the garments, and being as little children, all point to an origin of this saying "within archaic Christian baptismal practices and attendant interpretation of Genesis 1–3" (218).

[31] In Mark 1 par. Jesus is baptized in the Jordan by John, and, coming out of the water, he sees the heavens opened and the spirit of God descending upon him and hears the heavenly voice pronounce him as Son of God. The parallel in Matthew agrees but has reservations about Jesus' submission to John's baptism. The Fourth Gospel, like Luke, suppresses Jesus' explicit baptism by John and furthermore demotes John to a mere voice of one crying in the wilderness, whose only subsequent function is to bear witness to the descent of the Spirit upon Jesus (cf. Heracleon frg. 5, apud Origen *Comm. Jo.* 6.20–21). Rather than being the subject of John's water baptism, the Fourth Gospel (John 4:7–15) understands Jesus as the source of Living Water, which to drink means eternal life; although he has baptized Judean people in water (3:22; 4:1), there will be a time when he will baptize with the Holy Spirit, which the author identifies with living water (John 7:37–39). In John 3:3–5, rebirth as a condition of seeing the kingdom is equated with being born of water and spirit; one thus reborn through baptism is uniquely empowered to "see" the Kingdom. While the obvious reference seems to be to Johannine Christians, the

visionary experience is connected not only with heavenly ascensions but also with baptism, especially the inaugural baptism of Jesus; outside the NT, it is also connected with the manifestation of light (e.g., frg. 4 of the *Gospel of the Ebionites;* Epiphanius *Pan.* 30.13.7; Justin *Dial.* 88.3 [fire]). The widespread attestation of this phenomenon suggests that the feast of Epiphany originally celebrated the incarnation in context of Jesus' baptism rather than his virginal birth; unlike the passion, this was an event that could be shared by almost all Christians, including gnostic Christians.

As we have seen, with its awesome associations with death and rebirth, baptism becomes a principal occasion for visionary experience. A notable instance is the baptismal vision of King Gundaphorus in the *Acts of Thomas.* According to the Syriac version (20), when the baptismal party enters the bathhouse, Jesus appears, but only his voice was heard "since they had not yet been baptized." After the initial anointing, the invocation of the Name and the Spirit, and baptism proper, as the participants were emerging from the water, there appeared a luminous youth carrying a blazing torch whose light overpowers the illumination afforded by the many oil lamps illuminating the proceedings. The Greek version (26–27) does not explicitly mention the baptism proper: during the night, before the anointing and baptism of Gundaphorus, the participants received an audition from the Lord, but not a vision, "not having received the added sealing of the seal." When Gundaphorus receives the chrism in oil, Christ, the Holy Spirit, Wisdom, and the five rational faculties are invoked, whereupon the Lord appears briefly as a luminous youth with a burning torch. In both versions, upon daybreak, after the candidate was again clothed, the apostle celebrated the Eucharist. The Syriac version makes it clear that the occasion was the nocturnal baptism of Gundaphorus and that the audition came prior to baptism, while the vision of the Lord occurred immediately upon their emergence from the water.[32]

Fourth Gospel's lack of explicit accounts of Jesus' birth and baptism on the earthly plane combine with this conception of being born from above as an additional reference to the untraceable—and thus divine—origin of the Savior who brings light into the world. The parallel with the explanation of the origins of the Illuminator in the *Apocalypse of Adam* is obvious. Like the Johannine Gospel's conception of Jesus as the one who will provide living water, the *Trimorphic Protennoia* regards the Logos who descends with the Five Seals as the one who pours forth Living Water upon the Spirit below out of its source, which is the Father/Voice aspect of Protennoia, called the unpolluted spring of Living Water. Perhaps it would not be going too far to suppose that Johannine and Sethian conceptions of baptism had a common origin.

[32] E. Peterson, "Einige Bemerkungen zum Hamburger Papyrus-Fragment der Acta Pauli," in *Frühkirche, Judentum und Gnosis* (Rome: Herder, 1959), 194–96, collects numerous texts recounting epiphanies of Jesus at baptism in the form of a παιδίον, νεανίσκος, or the like.

2. Investiture

Investiture typically follows upon naked baptism. The metaphor of replacing an old garment with a new one, which occurs repeatedly in gnostic baptismal contexts, can signify several religious acts: a shift from a life of vice to one of virtue, religious conversion, a change of life-style, and initiation, where it signifies the death and rebirth of the initiate and assimilation of divine power.[33] In baptismal contexts, the garment that is discarded (cf. the "garments of skin," Gen 3:21) signifies the physical body, while donning the "robe of light" signifies the restoration of the lost image of God.[34] The "Paraphrase of Seth," which Hippolytus (*Ref.* 5.19.22) attributes to the Sethians, understands baptism as washing in and drinking from a cup of living, springing water by which the believer, like the Savior, puts on the form of a servant, escapes earthy ties, and is reclothed with a heavenly garment.

The *Trimorphic Protennoia* also applies the motif of putting on garments to the Savior's salvific descent. On her third descent as the divine Logos, when Protennoia reveals herself to her members in human likeness ("in their tents," NHC XIII 47,13–25; cf. John 1:9–14), she makes herself invisible to and unrecognized by all the celestial powers by wearing their "garments" until she reveals herself to her brethren by conferring the Five Seals. Similarly in the *Gospel of the Egyptians* (NHC III 63,23–64,3), Pronoia causes Seth to establish the holy baptism of the Five Seals through a "logos-begotten" body, Jesus the living one, whom Seth put on. To be compared is the depiction of the descent of the initially unrecognized Logos in the Johannine prologue, which may have arisen in a baptismal context.

Likewise, in the *Second Treatise of the Great Seth* (NHC VII 56,20–59,18), the revealer undergoes an incognito descent (changing his likeness

---

[33] Meeks ("Image of the Androgyne," 184) cites examples; behavioral change: Col 3:8; Eph 4:17–24; Philo *Somn.* 1.224–25; *Acts Thom.* 58; *Teachings of Silvanus* (NHC VII,4 105,13–17), *T. Levi* 8:2; donning armor for the eschatological holy war (Isa 59:17; Sir 5:18–20): 1 Thess 5:8; Rom 13:12; Eph 6:10–17; *Gos. Eg.* NHC III,2 67,2–3; shift in life-style from indulgence to austerity: Col 2:11; 3:9–10; Philostratus *Vit. Apoll.* 4.20; *Acts Thom.* 58; initiatory investiture: Apuleius *Metam.* 11.24.

[34] I repeat some useful references from Meeks, "The Image of the Androgyne," 183–88; for the "garments of skin" signifying the body: Philo *QG* 1.53; Clement of Alexandria *Exc.* 55.1 and *Strom.* 3.95.2; Irenaeus *Haer.* 1.1.10; Tertullian *Res.* 7; *Apoc. Mos.* 20:1–3; *Val. Exp.* (NHC XI,2 38,14–21); the garments of light: *Acts Thom.* chs. 112–13; *Odes Sol.* 25:8; Tertullian *Bapt.* 5; Pseudo-Clement *Homilies* 17.16; Mandaean *Canonical Prayerbook* (Drower) no. 51, p. 47, no. 49, pp. 43–44 (*Masiqta*), no. 9, p. 8 (*Maṣbuta;* cf. E. Segelberg, *Maṣbuta: Studies in the Ritual of Mandaean Baptism* [Uppsala: Almqvist & Wiksells, 1958], 115–30). See A. F. J. Klijn, "An Early Christian Baptismal Liturgy," 216–28; and of course J. Z. Smith, "The Garments of Shame," 224–30.

at each cosmic level), his "third baptism in a revealed image," in which he appears in the form of Jesus in order to defeat the cosmic powers through their ignorant attempt to crucify him. The Docetics (according to Hippolytus *Ref.* 8.10.6–8) considered Jesus to have two bodies, his fleshly body acquired through his human parent Mary, and another body, received at his baptism in the Jordan as the type of the former; the former body was nailed to the cross, deceiving the archons and powers, yet his nakedness was covered by his baptismal body, perhaps to be understood as an ethereal garment or subtle body rather like the vehicle (ὄχημα) of the soul. Even the *Gospel of Truth* (NHC I 20,28–28), which proclaims that Jesus, although clothed with eternal life, died on the cross, states that he nevertheless stripped himself of the "perishable rags," put on imperishability, and ascended to heaven, invulnerable to the powers stripped naked by forgetfulness.

Putting on clothes appropriate to the cosmic level one occupies so as to make one invulnerable or invisible to the powers applies not only to the descending revealer, but also to an enlightened being as it ascends into the aeonic world. A fine example is the royal garment sent to the revealer in the "Hymn of the Pearl" (*Acts Thom.* 108–13). The new garment is often so luminous and brilliant that it blinds the cosmic powers that oppose the soul's ascent (*Pistis Sophia* ch. 59 [p. 74 Schmidt]). According to the *Gospel of Philip* (NHC II 58,15–16; 70,5–9; 76,22–28), in the union of the bridal chamber, one sacramentally acquires a garment of light that makes one invisible to the hostile powers; unlike earthly garments, such heavenly garments put on "by water and fire" (baptism and chrism) are better than those who put them on (57,19–23). In *Allogenes* (NHC XI 50,10–34; 58,26–37), the metaphor of changing clothes is applied to Allogenes' ecstatic removal from the fleshly (and psychic?) garment of ignorance and investiture with a "great power," enabling him to know things unknown to the multitude and obtain a vision of the Luminaries of the Aeon of Barbelo. A non-Sethian example of stripping and reclothing in the context of an ascent is offered by the *Authoritative Teaching* (NHC VI 31,24–64,3), where the soul, come to her senses, strips off this world, replacing it with her true garment, her bridal clothing, in which she enters the fold and unites with her true shepherd.

Alongside the metaphor of being invested with a new garment, one sometimes finds the royal image of being crowned. In *Zostrianos* (NHC VIII 129,12–16; cf. 57,13–24), when Zostrianos descends from the Kalyptos the Protophanes level in the Aeon of Barbelo, he joins "those who are unified," blesses the higher powers, becomes παντέλειος, is written in glory, sealed, and receives a perfect crown. In chapters 11 and 12 of the untitled text of the Bruce Codex, Setheus, by means of a λόγος δημιουργικός (i.e., Christ), sends forth ray-emitting crowns, which are awarded to believers; they are crowned with a seal of glory on the right and a triple-powered fount (πηγή) in their midst. In a nonritual context, the royal image of investiture, coronation, and enthronement occur side-by-side in the *Teachings of Silvanus* (NHC VII 87,11–13; 89,10–34; 112,10–27), where one is urged to put on the shining robe of wisdom and holy teaching, the crown of Paideia, and sit on the throne of perception; those who contend well will gain dominion, unlike the fools, who are invested with folly, crowned with ignorance, and sit on the throne of nescience.

3. Chrismation

3.1. The Sethians

Although the Sethians do not appear to have had a ritual of chrismation, they used the term as a metaphor in two basic contexts. The first is that of the anointing of the third member of the Sethian Trinity of Father, Mother, and Son with the "goodness" (χρηστία, a pun on χριστός and χρίσμα) of the Father, the Invisible Spirit immediately after his conception by the Mother Barbelo, found in the *Apocryphon of John* (NHC II 6,23–26 and parallels), the *Gospel of the Egyptians* (NHC III 44,22–24), and the *Trimorphic Protennoia* (NHC XIII 37,30–35). This is probably based on an interpretation of the Gospel accounts of Jesus' baptism, when he is established as Son of God. The second occurs in the conclusion of Eleleth's revelation to Norea, wife-sister of Seth in the *Hypostasis of the Archons* (NHC II 97,1–5), where it is promised that the Father will send the "true man," probably Seth, within three generations to anoint the souls of his progeny, the undominated generation, with the unction of eternal life.

3.2. Valentinian Chrismation

The relation of the Valentinian chrism to the baptismal rite has been discussed above. The *Gospel of Philip* (NHC II 57,22–28; 67,2–9; 69,5–14; 78,1–10; 85,21–86,18) understands the chrism as fire, in the sense of intense light that gives form and beauty. One is begotten again (reborn) by baptism in water and anointing with the chrism through the Holy Spirit as a sort of "baptism" in light. It seems that this is the same light that is kindled in the bridal chamber. The doxology appended to *A Valentinian Exposition* (NHC XI,2a 40,1–29) refers to the Valentinian rite of anointing, which was performed either before the first baptism or simultaneously with it, enabling the recipient to overcome the power of the devil, who dominates the flesh and struggles against God.

Marcus (Irenaeus *Haer.* 1.21.5) also practiced a rite of unction by pouring ointment or a mixture of water and oil of balsam upon the heads of his flock, which had the effect of making one invulnerable to the powers and authorities, allowing the inner person to ascend to the invisible by sloughing off the soul (to be delivered to the Demiurge) and the body (to be left behind on earth). Evidently some Valentinians perform the unction in connection with baptism, while others claim that going to the water is unnecessary. Irenaeus calls this casting away of the chain of the soul the redemption. Epiphanius (*Pan.* 36.2.4–8) adds that the followers of Heracleon perform this unction upon the dying so that the "inner man" of those who receive it will become invisible to and untouchable by the principalities and authorities on high as they ascend, leaving the body on earth and consigning the soul to the Demiurge. The inner man, a son of the preexistent Father, appeals to the motherless mother Sophia, the mother of Achamoth, as its source, while the inferior powers and the Demiurge know nothing higher than Achamoth, a female created from a female.

4. Sacral Meal

4.1. The Valentinian Eucharist

In the *Gospel of Philip* (NHC II 75,15–24), it is said that the eucharistic cup of water and wine contains the Holy Spirit; to drink it conveys the perfect man; in 53,21–24, the Eucharist is identified with the crucified Jesus (who brought bread from heaven, II 55,6–15), which may explain why this rite seems underplayed in the *Gospel of Philip* (e.g., II 74,1–2). In the act of baptism, the living water is a body that replaces the body stripped off in the act of prebaptismal disrobing.

The Valentinian Marcus (Irenaeus *Haer.* 1.13.1–5) celebrated a Eucharist with a cup mixed with a wine that was understood to be the purple and red blood of Grace and was repeatedly administered in large doses to wealthy women, making them deranged. Moreover, Marcus is said to have proclaimed himself to be this Grace as well as the bridegroom whose luminous seed a woman, as bride, is to receive "in her bridal chamber" in order to enter together with him into the One. Women are induced to acts of prophecy by being allowed to babble nonsense spontaneously, supposedly repaying this gift of prophecy by granting their possessions and bodies to Marcus.

4.2. Other Instances of the Eucharist: Ophites, Carpocratians, and Borborites

Epiphanius (*Pan.* 37.5.6–7) describes a curious ritual meal practiced by the Ophites in which they worship a snake (Irenaeus says they identified the paradisical snake with the devil!) as a royal source of knowledge by offering it bread:

> For they have an actual snake, and keep it in a sort of basket. When it is time for their mysteries they bring it out of the den, spread loaves around on a table, and call the snake to come; and when the den is opened it comes out. And then the snake ... crawls onto the table and coils up on the loaves. And this is what they call a perfect sacrifice. And so, someone has told me, not only do they break the loaves the snake has coiled on

and distribute them to the recipients, but they each kiss the snake besides
... and they offer a hymn to the Father on high-again, as they say,
through the snake—and so conclude their mysteries.

Finally, Clement of Alexandria (*Strom.* 3.2.10.1) reports that the Car-
pocratians celebrate an apparently nocturnal common meal that he calls
a "love feast," after which they extinguish the lamps and command the
women present to engage in sexual intercourse as a divine duty. Epiphanius reports similar activity on the part of the Borborites, whom he connects with the Sethians (see below on sexual sacramentalism); in
particular, he mentions two communal meals of theirs: a Eucharist consisting of offering up and consuming menstrual blood and spent semen
withheld from intercourse as the blood and body of Christ, and a Passover
meal devoted to the consumption of a mangled fetus extracted from any
woman who accidentally happens to become pregnant during such sexual exchange (*Pan.* 26.4.5–5.6).

5. Sacral Marriage

The metaphor of marriage and the bridal chamber in gnostic usage can
refer both to the experience of spiritual reunification as well as to overtly
sexual union. In either case, the underlying myth is that of the re-creation
of the primal androgyne through the union of male and female, whether
that be taken as man and woman, intellect and soul, or the earthly seed and
its angelic counterpart. As enlightened beings, the gnostics generally considered themselves alone capable of understanding the true significance of
sexual union, considering the nongnostic as worldly and animalistic, experiencing not love, but only lust: "A bridal chamber is not for the animals,
nor is it for the slaves, nor for defiled women; but it is for free men and virgins" (*Gospel of Philip* NHC II 69,1–3; cf. Irenaeus *Haer.* 1.6.3; Clement of
Alexandrai *Exc.* 68). While the question of gnostic sexual practices will be
discussed under the heading of sexual sacramentalism, here I want to comment on its use as a metaphor for spiritual unification.[35]

The application of the concept of human marriage to the achievement
of unity with a transcendent reality is frequent in classical Judaism, where
God is the husband of his bride Israel; the metaphor of marriage also
appears in the NT, not only where Jesus refers to himself as the bridegroom, but especially in the Pauline corpus (1 Cor 6:15–17; 2 Cor 11:1–2;
Eph 5:22–23) as a symbol for the relation of Christ and the church.
Although Christian gnostics likewise draw on these biblical concepts,

---

[35] See especially J.-M. Sevrin, "Les noces spiritualles dans l'Evangile selon
Philippe," *Museon* 87 (1974): 143–93.

uppermost in their minds as well as those of Jewish gnostics was the notion of the primordial unity of humankind as expressed in Gen 1:26–27, according to which Adam was created as a single masculo-feminine being in the image of God.

The primordial sin or fault underlying human existence that had to be overcome was the creator's ignorant act of separating this originally androgynous into separate male and female persons. In the act of physical union, the offspring was thought to receive the human form from the male, while its physical and emotional essence was provided by the female. The same held for the spiritual world as well; spiritual perfection lay in androgyny, so when a spiritual being such as Sophia undertakes to produce offspring without a male consort, the result is defective, a formless abortion lacking the male element of form. This being the character of her offspring, both her son, creator of the natural world, and his cosmic product are likewise defective. The rectification of the creation depends on introducing into it a potential source of its reunification.

The Sethian myth conceives this to be accomplished when the image of God (Adamas), the original human androgyne, is primordially projected as the archetype upon which the creator unwittingly bases his own human copy. Once he realizes that his androgynous copy is superior to him, he splits it into male and female, but it is too late. In spite of the creator's attempts to subvert the primal couple, by reuniting themselves they can now re-create their original androgyny, which they do in the birth of Seth, the "other seed." Like the divine Adamas, he is a true ("triple," i.e., androgynous) male Child, as is the "immovable race" he engenders.

While a few gnostic groups such as the late Sethian Borborites sought to replicate this primeval union through nonreproductive sexual union, most, like the earlier Sethians, eschewed sexual union, which they considered to typify the adulterous race of Cain. One might therefore effect a symbolic union on the transcendent plane through ritual means, the Sethians through baptismal ascension, and the Valentinians by an eschatological sacred marriage, the bridal chamber.[36] In the latter act, recourse was had not only to the myth of the primal androgyne and the NT notions of the marriage of Christ and the church, but also to Neopythagorean speculation on the properties of unity.[37]

---

[36] The Sethians effected the return to androgyny by stripping away the "psychic and corporeal thought" in the acts of baptism and contemplative ascent, by which they could "flee from the madness and the bondage of femaleness and choose the salvation of maleness" (*Zost.* NHC VIII, *1* 131,5–8).

[37] Even quantities could always be divided in such a way as to leave a space in the middle capable of receiving an extra member (x x), while the division of odd quantities always left over precisely such a single member in the middle (x x x).

In the Valentinian view, having abandoned her male consort, Sophia's ultimate human offspring from Adam and Eve onward, both males and females, were regarded as weak female seed lacking the element of form, which could only be restored by an ascent to the Pleroma and marriage with the male angels that the savior had prepared for them. In this way they could eternally enjoy the harmonious syzygetic union experienced by all the undescended aeons there. As in the metaphysics of the Platonic psychology of the individual, every human was a split personality. One's higher rational, active—and thus masculine—aspect of the self had been primordially sundered from one's emotional, passional, receptive, and thus essentially feminine aspect of the self. The natural link with the divine world, the intellect or highest part of the soul was still resident in the transcendent world, although cut off from the soul and body now that formed one's link with the everyday physical world. The goal of life was therefore to recover this lost unity, which would involve detaching a soul overly enamored of its bodily vehicle from the body, or detaching the rational part of the soul from its irrational and impassioned psychic vehicle, so as to effect its reunion with the higher intelligence.

For the gnostics who appropriated such views, the reunion of the psyche with one's intellect was thus tantamount to coming together in an act of marriage, whether enacted through contemplative union, symbolic rites, or actual physical union. The following Valentinian citations make the point clear:

> As long as we were children of the female only, as of a dishonorable union, we were incomplete, childish, without understanding, weak, and without form, brought forth like abortions, in short, we were children of the woman. But having been given form by the Savior, we are the children of the man (husband) and of the bride-chamber. (Clement of Alexandria *Exc.* 68)

> If the woman had not separated from the man, she would not die with the man. His separation became the beginning of death. Because of this Christ came to repair the separation which was from the beginning and again unite the two, and to give life to those who died as a result of the separation and unite them. But the woman is united to her husband in the bridal chamber. Indeed those who have united in the bridal chamber will no longer be separated. Thus Eve separated from Adam because it was not in the bridal chamber that she united with him. (*Gospel of Philip* NHC II 70,9–22)

The number one, being indivisible, was thought to embrace both these properties and thus was androgynous, while even quantities were female and odd quantities were male. Thus the unity of the One could best be approximated by the union of male and female. In the ideal realm of the Pleroma, all spiritual beings dwelt in the form of syzygetic pairs.

In the *Exegesis on the Soul* (NHC II 132,2–133,9), which seems to have certain Simonian affinities, the restoration of the helpless female soul wallowing apart from her spiritual home in the brothels of materiality is effected by the advent of the marriage of the female soul with her intellectual masculine counterpart, her true husband. The reunification of the irrational, passionate aspect of the soul with her celestial, intellectual component as her true husband and master, from whom physical embodiment has separated her, is interpreted as a reversal of the primordial separation of Eve from Adam in the garden of Eden: "They will become a single flesh" (Gen 2:24; 3:16; cf. 1 Cor 6:15; 11:1; Eph 5:23). The *Testimony of Truth* (NHC IX 31,24–32,16; 34,32–35,23), which also seems to have certain Simonian affinities, likewise uses the imagery of the soul as the bride who strips off this world and learns from the evangelists about the inscrutable One, adorning herself for this her true shepherd with her bridal clothing "in beauty of mind," whereupon:

> She found her rising. She came to rest in him who is at rest. She reclined in the bride-chamber. She ate of the banquet for which she had hungered. She partook of the immortal food. She found what she had sought after. She received rest from her labors. (NHC IX 35,8–16)

The image of entrance into the bridal chamber and receipt of the new, imperishable wedding robe occurs also in the *Second Treatise of the Great Seth* (NHC VII 57,7–58,4) as a metaphor for the soul's receipt of Intellect and entry into the heavens. It is called a "mystery" effected by the revealer's incognito descent (changing his likeness at each cosmic level), his "third baptism in a revealed image," to defeat the cosmic powers through the crucifixion and resurrection of Jesus.

5.1. The Valentinian Mystery of the Bridal Chamber

Of course, it was the Valentinians who made the most extensive use of the metaphor of marriage as a designation for the eschatological reunion of the Savior Jesus with Sophia and of her spiritual seed with the male angels of the Savior:[38]

> When the whole seed is perfected, then, they say, will the mother, Achamoth leave the place of the Middle, enter into the Pleroma, and receive her bridegroom, the Savior, who came into being from all (the aeons), with the result that the Savior and Sophia, who is Achamoth, form a pair (syzygy). These then are said to be bridegroom and bride, but the bridal chamber is the entire Pleroma. The spiritual beings will divest themselves of their souls and become intelligent spirits, and, without

---

[38] See R. M. Grant, "The Mystery of Marriage in the Gospel of Philip," *VC* 15 (1969): 129–40.

being hindered or seen, they will enter into the Pleroma, and will be
bestowed as brides on the angels around the Savior. The Demiurge passes
into the place of his mother Sophia, that is, into the Middle. The souls of
the righteous will also repose in the place of the Middle, for nothing psychic enters the Pleroma. When this has taken place, then (they assert) the
fire that is hidden in the world will blaze forth and burn: when it has consumed all matter it will be consumed with it and pass into non-existence.
According to them the Demiurge knew none of these things before the
advent of the Savior. (Ptolemaeus apud Irenaeus *Haer.* 1.1.7.1; cf. Clement
of Alexandria *Exc.* 63–65)

The Savior and Sophia are interpreted as the bridegroom and bride, and
the place of their union is the "bridal chamber," the divine realm of the
Pleroma of spiritual aeons. Thus the Pauline metaphors of the church as
bride and Christ as bridegroom are combined with the story of the fall and
restoration of Wisdom, the cosmic soul, and the restoration of the individual psychic beings created by her. As Christians, the Valentinians maintained the Christian rites of baptism, Eucharist, and the chrism but seem to
have developed their own ritual enactment of their expected eschatological marriage to their celestial angelic counterparts.

In *Haer.* 1.13.1–21.5, Irenaeus describes some of the Valentinian rituals known to him. In so doing he polemically contrasts the disagreement
among the gnostics with the supposed unified practice of his own church.
They include a mystic rite with certain invocations designed to effect a
spiritual marriage, mirroring the syzygetic union of the pleromatic aeons,
in a bridal chamber prepared beforehand. Others perform a water baptism
in the name of the Father of All, Truth the Mother of All, and the Christ
who descended on Jesus. Some utilize Hebrew invocations of Achamoth
to effect redemption as a communion with the pleromatic powers, and others replace this with a "redemption" in which a mixture of oil and water is
poured on the head with certain invocations. Some boast an angelic
redemption or restitution (ἀποκατάστασις) featuring an anointing with balsam oil in the names of Iao (Yahu) and Jesus of Nazareth that frees one's
soul from the powers of this age. Still others, he says, reject all such tan-
gible symbolic acts involving the body or soul which derive from deficiency, claiming that the true redemption occurs only through inner,
spiritual man's knowledge of the ineffable Greatness.

In the Nag Hammadi corpus, the *Tripartite Tractate* (NHC I 122,12)
portrays the Pleroma as the bridal chamber in which the elect spiritual
beings will experience ultimate restoration as the bride of the Savior, while
those "called" psychic humans, the "men of the church," will serve as atten-
dants outside the Pleroma in the aeon of "images," until they receive
instruction, upon which all will receive the restoration together; in Irenaeus's account of the Ptolemaic theology (*Haer.* 1.7.1), the lower Sophia,

Achamoth, enters the Pleroma or bridal chamber as the bride of the Savior, while the spiritual ones put off their souls, enter the Pleroma and unite with the Savior's angels. In the *Tripartite Tractate* (NHC I 128,30), the bridal chamber is also identified with baptism, as another expression of the agreement and indivisible union of the knower (the Valentinian gnostic) with the known (the Savior).

In the *Gospel of Philip,* the sacral marriage has multiple symbolic referents. The fundamental mythical motif of the restoration of the broken unity of Adam is still present (NHC II 68,22–26; 70,9–22), but, as in the introductory quote from Irenaeus, the biblical legend is now overshadowed by theogonic myths of the Valentinian school. The sacramental union in the bridal chamber has its archetype in the union of the Savior with the previously barren Sophia. According to II 71,3–15, the body of Jesus the Savior was produced in the pleromatic bridal chamber from the union of the Father of the All with the "virgin who came down," presumably the higher Sophia before her fall from the Pleroma; from this origin, it descended to establish this union of bride and bridegroom as the way for his true disciples to enter into his pleromatic rest.[39] This union is perhaps represented on another level by the legends of Christ's association with Mary Magdalene[40] and its fulfillment in the eschatological union of the gnostic's true self (the female bride, or "seed," or εἰκών) with its corresponding male "angel" as bridegroom (II 58,10–14; 65,23–25). According to the *Gospel of Philip* (II 86,1–18), becoming a son of the bridal chamber is the only means to receive the light. Although in this world it is present only as an image of the truth, this light grants absolute imperturbability throughout the rest of this life as though he were already living in the Pleroma. The theme of restoration of man's primeval unity is thereby projected onto the macrocosmic plane, where it symbolizes the reintegration of the Pleroma to its precosmic state.

---

39 *Gos. Phil.* 63,30–32; cf. Irenaeus *Haer.* 1.1–8; Clement of Alexandria *Exc.* 43–65; H.-M. Schenke [and Johannes Leipoldt], "Koptisch-gnostiche Schriften aus den Papyrus-Codices von Nag-Hammadi," 35–38.

40 This is a typical example of the favored or "beloved" disciple theme found in Matt 16, throughout the Fourth Gospel, and in the Thomas literature (*Gos. Thom.* 14, the *Book of Thomas the Contender*). Meeks, "The Image of the Androgyne," 190 n. 111, refers to *Gos. Phil.* 63,30–32: "[Sophia], called the barren, is the mother of the angels, and the consort [κοινωνός] of [Christ] is Mary Magdalene." In *Gos. Phil.* 61,10–11, κοινωνία means sexual intercourse, though perhaps not physical; in 63,30–36 Christ is said to love Mary and to have kissed her often, presumably impregnating her (as the Savior, in the Valentinian scheme, made the barren lower Sophia pregnant), since "it is by a kiss that the perfect conceive and give birth. For this reason we also kiss one another. We receive conception from the grace [χάρις] which is in one another" (59,1–6).

The *Gospel of Philip* (II 84,14–85,21) represents the bridal chamber or Pleroma, Christ, and the spiritual elect with the imagery of the heavenly temple and high priesthood similar to that found in the NT letter to the Hebrews (6:19–20; 9:2–5). The reality of the Pleroma, symbolized as the holy of holies, has been concealed from those inhabiting the outer courts of the cosmos from the time that the inferior creator fashioned the world, available to those outside only in types and images. But now the veil separating the holy of holies from the outer courts of the cosmos has been rent, and these outer courts of the templelike cosmos will be destroyed. Their creator, the demiurge, will not enter the holy of holies, but will ascend to the Hebdomad below Horos, the lower boundary of the Pleroma. When the outer precincts of the cosmic temple are destroyed, the merely psychic members of the Valentinian community will be saved by the church, symbolized by the ark, while the truly pneumatic members, those belonging to the priesthood, will be able to go through the veil into the Pleroma in the company of the high priest, the Savior.

The actual ritual involved in the sacred marriage of the Valentinians cannot be determined with certainty. Given its eschatological reference, Gaffron considers it to have been the believer's last sacrament, a "death sacrament" rather like the Mandaean *Masiqta*.[41] As one might expect of any mystery rite, the *Gospel of Philip* (NHC II 82,7–26) makes it clear that the mystery of the bride chamber is reserved for the pneumatic members of the Valentinian community alone. The intercourse of bride and bridegroom is private, pure, and undefiled; the pneumatic bride may reveal her true nature only to those who may enter the bridal chamber every day: her father, mother, and the friend and sons of the bridegroom. The *Gospel of Philip* (II 69,1–5) specifies that "a bridal chamber is not for the animals, nor is it for the slaves, nor is it for defiled women; but it is for free men and virgins." Meeks notes the parallel in *Gos. Thom.* 75: "The μοναχοί are the [only] ones who will enter the bridal chamber," but here the bridal chamber seems only a metaphor, rather than a cultic anticipation, of "the kingdom."[42] Although no cultic acts are described in the *Gospel of Thomas,* baptism is presumably presupposed. "Male and female" are to be made "one," but it is an unequal union, since the female must become male if she is to become a "living spirit" (logion

---

[41] Gaffron, "Studien zum koptischen Philippusevangelium," 191–222.

[42] Meeks, "The Image of the Androgyne," 193–96, citing also the parallel in logion 49. "Blessed are the solitary [μοναχοί] and elect [or, "blessed and elect are the solitary"] for you shall find the Kingdom... because you come from it (and) you shall go there again" (trans. Guillaumont et al.). The gnostic conception of "the kingdom" here is reinforced by the following logion, "We have come from the Light, where the Light has originated through itself. It [stood] and it revealed itself in their image."

114).[43] As Meeks notes, the μοναχός in the *Gospel of Thomas* is beyond sexuality, "like a little child" (*Gos. Thom.* 22), whose innocence of sexuality is portrayed in the removal of clothing without shame—like Adam before the fall (logion 37, cf. logion 21).[44]

The heresiologists, most of whose information about ritual details was likely inferred from reading gnostic treatises, concluded, sometimes correctly, that the rite of the bride chamber involved physical sex relations.[45] The *Gospel of Philip* disparages actual cohabitation, even though it is an "image" of the true union "in the Aiōn."[46] As early as 1959, H.-M. Schenke speculated that the outward symbol of the Valentinian rite of the bridal chamber was the "holy kiss," on the basis of the *Gospel of Philip* NHC II 59,2–6 ("For it is by a kiss that the perfect conceive and give birth. For this reason we also kiss one another. We receive conception from the grace which is in one another") and 63,30–64,2 naming Mary Magdalene as Christ's most beloved disciple, whom he often used to kiss.[47] The popular practice of the wider church tends to confirm that the kiss did have an important place.[48] As Meeks concludes, "whatever the Gnostics did in the marriage sacrament, it clearly distinguished them, in their opinion, from those who were merely baptized and anointed. It was the sacrament of the elite, the *teleoi*."[49]

---

43 The phrase "become a living spirit" is perhaps an allusion to Gen 2:7, possibly even a pun on "Eve." In Clement of Alexandria *Exc.* 79 the female "seed" becomes male when it is "formed" (μορφωθέν).

44 "The Image of the Androgyne," 194, referring to J. Z. Smith's "The Garments of Shame," comparings the homilies of Theodore of Mopsuestia, who contrasts nudity at baptism, when shame is still felt, with an eschatological nudity without shame. Meeks also adduces logion 21, where clothing represents the physical body by which one is connected temporarily to the world, "the field."

45 Grant thinks this likely ("The Mystery of Marriage in the Gospel of Philip," 139). *Gos. Phil.* 61,5–12 redefines adultery as "κοινωνία between those who are not alike," i.e., between gnostics and nongnostics (cf. 78,25–79,12). See below under sexual sacramentalism.

46 64,30–65,1; 76,6–9; 85,29–86,4. Clement of Alexandria *Strom.* 3.29 describes the Valentinian "marriage" as "spiritual."

47 Schenke, "Das Evangelium nach Philippus," *TLZ* 84 (1959): 1–26, and "Koptisch-gnostiche Schriften aus den Papyrus-Codices von Nag-Hammadi," 38, contra Grant, "The Mystery of Marriage in the Gospel of Philip," 139.

48 Cf. 58,30–59,6. According to the *Apostolic Tradition* of Hippolytus, only those are admitted to the kiss of peace who have received both baptism and chrismation. The catholic rite, however, keeps men and women separate for the kiss (18.3–4; 22.3.6).

49 Meeks, "The Image of the Androgyne," 191.

6. Sexual Sacramentalism

6.1. The Simonians and Valentinians

While many gnostic groups of the second and third century advocated and practiced a sexual and dietary encratism approaching a true demonization of sexuality, other groups rejected such a practice as ineffective and deceptive, transforming the moral indifference typical of its libertine opposite, free sexual exchange, into sacred ritual. According to Irenaeus (*Haer.* 1.23.4), the Simonians worship images of Simon Magus and Helen, as well as engage in various occult practices, including exorcisms, incantations, philters, and erotic magic. Hippolytus (*Ref.* 6.19.5) specifies further that this erotic magic took the form of sexual intercourse as a means of experiencing spiritual union. In *Haer.* 1.13.1–5, Irenaeus indicates that the Valentinian Marcus interpreted the rite of the bride-chamber in a sexually explicit way, claiming himself to be the Grace whose luminous seed should be deposited "in her bridal chamber" as a way of imitating the pleromatic syzygetic union of male and female aeons, thus entering into the One together with him.

6.2. A Sethian Offshoot: The Borborites

According to Epiphanius (*Pan.* 26.3–12), the later Sethians, whom he calls Borborites, Barbelites, Phibionites, Stratiotici, and Coddians, engaged in a thoroughgoing sexual sacramentalism. Their symbolic actions included a ritual handshake (featuring tickling beneath the palms of joined hands), a love feast in which spouses were exchanged, homosexual intercourse on the part of a special class called Levites, naked prayer featuring the elevation to the 365 Archons (e.g., Iao, Saklas, Seth, Daveithai, Eloaeus, Yaldabaoth, Sabaoth, Barbelo, the Autogenes Christ, and the supreme Autopater) of hands smeared with semen and menstrual blood (apparently symbolizing the elevation of the host and wine commemorating the "passion" of Christ), and consumption of the same as a form of Eucharist. If one of the women accidentally conceived, the fetus was extracted and sacramentally consumed to prevent the further dispersal of the divine spirit in another human body.

According to Stephen Gero,[50]

> the central, distinguishing feature of the sect, its devotion to the so-called *sperma* cult, described by [Epiphanius] in vivid detail, can hardly be dismissed as a prurient invention. In the simplest of terms it involved the

---

[50] S. Gero, "With Walter Bauer on the Tigris: Encratite Orthodoxy and Libertine Heresy in Syro-Mesopotamian Christianity," in *Nag Hammadi, Gnosticism, and Early Christianity* (ed. C. W. Hedrick and R. Hodgson; Peabody, Mass.: Hendrickson, 1986), 293–94.

extraction, collection and solemn, sacramental consecration and consumption of bodily fluids, male and female, which contributed to the further propagation of the human race, and thus to the continued entrapment of the divine substance by the evil archons. In these fluids is concentrated the spiritual element, found scattered in the world, in particular in food-stuffs (including meat!), of which the initiates can and should partake. The mythology proper is a version of the Barbelo-gnostic myth, as known from Irenaeus and the *Apocryphon of John*.

Although Epiphanius does not say that they called this rather unrestrained ritual sex a "mystery" or rite of the bridal chamber, it seems clear that its intent was the same, effecting a restoration of the lost primordial unity by physical coupling and attempting to reverse the natural course of the propagation of the species.

7. Verbal Performances

A large and varied class of ritual expression can be loosely gathered under the head of ritual speech, which can include glossalalia, traditional verbal formulas, spells, oaths, conjuration, invocations, evocations, *voces mysticae,* συνθήματα, and prayers of various sorts addressed to transcendent powers, good and evil alike.

The Basilideans (Irenaeus *Haer.* 1.24.4) are said to engage in magic, conjuring of the dead, spells, calling up of spirits, and the invocation by name of each of the angelic beings belonging to the 365 heavens: "The person who has learnt these things, and knows all the angels and their origins, becomes invisible and incomprehensible to all the angels and powers." In his *Contra Celsum* (6.31), Origen describes numerous verbal formulas employed by the Ophites as passwords used by the ascending soul to mollify the hostility of the heavenly rulers blocking their entrance into the divine world. These formulas bear a striking resemblance to the first person self-predicatory recognition formulas attributed to the gnostic revealer who likewise used them in the course of his own descent and reascent to disarm the hostile cosmic powers. As the ascending soul traverses the spheres of the powers (the solitary king, Yaldabaoth/Saturn, Iao, Sabaoth, Astaphaios, Ailoaios, Horaios), it announces to the respective rulers its special status as purified and freed from the archontic powers, possessing the divine light and life, imbued with the power of the Mother. Thus:

> But you, archon Yaldabaoth, to whom power belongs as first and seventh, I go with confidence as a ruling Logos of pure Nous, as a perfect work for the Son and the Father, bearing by the imprint of a stamp the symbol of life, having opened for the world the gate which you had by your aeon closed; as a free man I go past your power. Grace be with me, yes, Father, be it with me. (*Cels.* 6.31)

Irenaeus (*Haer.* 1.21.5) also attributes similar formulas to Valentinians who, in the context of a death-bed anointing, are provided with recognition formulas by which they identify themselves to the demiurge as a son of the preexistent Father who invokes the higher Sophia as the supreme Mother, whose power greatly transcends that of the demiurge's mother, the lower Sophia Achamoth.

The ultimate ancestor of this genre of passwords seems to be found either in the dialogues of the Egyptian *Book of the Dead* or, more likely, in the Orphic-Bacchic gold leaves inscribed with hexameter instructions to the dead about the path to be followed in the other world, such as this one from Hipponion:[51]

> In the house of Hades there is a spring [i.e. Lethe, of forgetfulness] to the right; by it stands a white cypress. Here the souls, descending, are cooled. Do not approach this spring! Further you will find cool water flowing from the lake of recollection. Guardians stand over it who will ask you in their sensible mind why you are wandering through the darkness of corruptible Hades. Answer: "I am a son of the earth and of the starry sky, but I am desiccated with thirst and am perishing; therefore quickly give me cool water flowing from the lake of recollection." And then the subjects of the Chthonic King (?) will have pity and will give you to drink from the lake of recollection.... And indeed you are going a long, sacred way which also other *mystai* and *bacchoi* gloriously walk.

In gnostic literature, one finds verbal formulas, often in the context of ecstatic prayer and praise, that are clearly intended as syllables of power. Sometimes these syllables are enigmatic abbreviations for articulate utterances, sometimes they have nearly the character of Hindu mantras, as in the chanting of strings of vowels in seminumerical groupings, where the emphasis seems to lie in the sonority and repetitiveness of the verbal performance. In this regard, the following passage from the *Gospel of the Egyptians* (NHC III,*2* 66,9–68,1) is exemplary:

> ιн ιεγc нω оγ нω ωγλ! Really truly, O Yesseus Mazareus Yessedekeus, O living water, O child of the child, O glorious name, really truly λιων ο ωн (i.e., "O existing aeon"), ιιιι ннннн εεεε οοοο γγγγ ωωωωω λλλλ{λ}, really truly, нι λλλλ ωωωωω, O existing one who sees the aeons! Really truly, αее ннн ιιιι γγγγγγ ωωωωωωωωω, who is eternally eternal, really truly, ιнλ λιω, in the heart, who exists, γ λει εις λει, ει ο ει, ει ος ει (or:

---

[51] The recording of such revelations and passwords only on gold leaves but also in authoritative books under the authority of figures like Orpheus and Musaios (Plato, *Rep.* 364B–365A) effectively detaches them from an exclusively ritual setting and makes them available to literate persons without cultic mediation.

Son forever, Thou art what Thou art, Thou art who Thou art)! This great
name of thine is upon me, O self-begotten Perfect one, who art not outside
me. I see thee, O thou who art visible to everyone. For who will be able
to comprehend thee in another tongue? Now that I have known thee, I
have mixed myself with the immutable. I have armed myself with an armor
of light, I have become light. For the Mother was at that place because of
the splendid beauty of grace. Therefore I have stretched out my hands
while they were folded. I was shaped in the circle of the riches of the light
which is in my bosom, which gives shape to the many begotten ones in the
light into which no complaint reaches. I shall declare thy glory truly, for I
have comprehended thee, ϲογ ιнϲ ιλε λειω λειε οιϲ, O aeon, aeon, O
God of silence! I honor thee completely. Thou art my place of rest, O son
нϲ нϲ ο ε, the formless one who exists in the formless ones, who exists,
raising up the man in whom thou wilt purify me into thy life, according to
thine imperishable name. Therefore the incense of life is in me. I mixed it
with water after the model of all archons, in order that I may live with thee
in the peace of the saints, thou who exists really truly for ever.

This presentation of ecstatic prayer is notable in that it mentions the bodily gesture, rather like a Hindu *mudra,*[52] of extending one's hands in the
act of prayer (cf. 3 Macc 2:2; in *Odes Sol.* 21, 27, 37, 42 a sign of the crucifixion), indeed, while they are folded, forming a circle to symbolize one's
containment of the inner light. The prayer also contains an apparent reference to water baptism, in which ordinary physical water ("in the type of
the archons") is converted into living water by mixing it with the spirit
("incense of life") possessed by the baptizand; rather than being purified
prior to baptism by invocation of the Spirit or by holy oil, the baptismal
water is here purified by the one undergoing baptism, since he has already
received the light.

In the gnostic treatises one finds also extended doxologies in praise of
the aeonic powers. In the Sethian treatises, there are the four particularly
striking parallel doxologies in *Allogenes* (XI 53,32–54,37), the *Three Steles
of Seth* (VII 126,5–13), and *Zostrianos* (VIII 51,6–52,25 and 88,9–25). They
recite a traditional list of *nomina barbara* designating divine beings
invoked in the course of the mystical ascent through the Aeon of Barbelo.[53] In fact the entire *Three Steles of Seth* is essentially an extended doxology in praise of the Sethian Father, Mother, and Son triad, praising the

---

[52] E.g. the very ancient *anjali-mudra* is a gesture of adoration and prayer with
hands joined; see R. Poduval, *Kathākil and the Diagram of Hand Poses* (Trivandrum: Department of Archaeology, Travancore State, 1930).

[53] The names of these beings stand out in contrast to most Sethian *nomina barbara* by the fact that most of them are Greek compounds in *-eus, -os, -is,* and *-ios,*
in keeping with the Graecicizing, Platonizing terminology of these treatises.

powers and deeds of Autogenes, Barbelo, and the supreme Invisible Spirit; it appears to have been composed for use in a community-oriented practice of contemplative ascent.

Aretalogical doxologies also are found in the Hermetic Corpus. In the Nag Hammadi library, the *Prayer of Thanksgiving* (NHC VI, 7), which occurs also in Greek (Papyrus Mimaut) and at the end of the Latin *Asclepius,* is a combination of petitions with doxological praise, which is concluded by a mutual embrace (ἀσπάζεσθαι, cf. the "kiss of peace) and a communal meal of "sacred food that has no blood in it" (VI 65,3–7). This prayer follows the Hermetic treatise *The Discourse on the Eighth and the Ninth,* which itself contains the extended prayer of an unnamed initiate to his spiritual father Hermes Trismegistus. Having attained the Hebdomad, Hermes guides the initiate towards the Ogdoad and Ennead, where he sees that his guide is Intellect itself and, along with other angels and souls, he sings a hymn of praise to the Father in silence. The prayer seems to be regarded as a "spiritual sacrifice" (cf. Rom 12:1) and contains petition, aretalogical doxology, and ecstatic chanting of vowels spoken in the first person plural; it is followed later by a hymn with a similar chant in the first person singular (NHC VI 55,23–61,18). Taken with other Hermetic prayers (*Corp. herm.* 1.31–32; 13.16–20; *Asclepius* 41), these prayers indicate an established community ritual in which visionary experience is expressed in prayers of praise, thanksgiving and ecstatic formulas, and celebrated in a meal. There is also the very similar doxological *Prayer of the Apostle Paul* included in the front of the Jung Codex (NHC I, 1).[54]

Three of the five supplements to *A Valentinian Exposition* (NHC XI, 2a; XI, 2d; and XI, 2e) are prayers, separated by two short catacheses on the nature of baptism. The first is a prebaptismal invocation of Christ to anoint baptismal candidates with the power to "trample on the heads of snakes and scorpions and all the power of the Devil" (Luke 10:19; cf. Clement of Alexandria *Exc.* 76); this is very similar to the prebaptismal practice of exorcising the devil through the acts of anointing with oil and penitence by standing on sackcloth or goatskin.[55] The other two prayers are pre-eucharistic thanksgivings. Although not part of a ritual setting, two other prayers might be mentioned, which are petitions for release from the troubles of this life, one at the conclusion of the *Book of Thomas the Contender* (NHC II 145,8–16), and James's prayer for a speedy death at the conclusion of the *Second Apocalypse of James* (NHC V 62,13–63,29).

---

[54] On prayer in gnostic sources, see E. Segelberg, "Prayer among the Gnostics? The Evidence of Some Nag Hammadi Documents," in *Gnosis and Gnosticism: Papers Read at the Seventh International Conference on Patristic Studies (Oxford, September 8th–13th, 1975)* (ed. M. Krause; NHS 7; Leiden: Brill, 1977), 55–69.

[55] See Smith, "The Garments of Shame," 225–33.

The frequent use of *nomina barbara,* syllables of power, and phrases in languages other than one's own (cf. the Aramaic baptismal formulas quoted in Irenaeus *Haer.* 1.21.3) is succinctly explained in *Corp. herm.* 16.2 (Asclepius to King Ammon):

> Expressed in our own native (Egyptian) tongue, the discourse [λόγος] keeps clear the meaning [νοῦς] of the words [λόγοι] [at any rate], for its very quality of sound, the very intonation of the Egyptian names, have in themselves the actuality [ἐνέργεια] of what is said. So as far as you can, O King—and you can do all things—keep this our discourse from translation, in order that such mighty mysteries may not come to the Greeks, and the disdainful speech of Greece with all its looseness and its surface beauty, so to speak, take all the strength out of the solemn and the strong—the energetic speech of Names. The Greeks, O King, have novel words, effecting demonstration only; and thus is the philosophizing of the Greeks—the noise of words. But we do not use words; we rather use sounds filled full with deeds.

As Socrates says in the *Cratylus* (439a; 424bc), "names rightly given are the likenesses and images of the things they name." He who would imitate the essence of things in speech must give them a name; to analyze them, one must "separate" the syllables and letters, "first the vowels, and then the consonants and mutes, into classes according to the traditional distinctions of the learned, also the semivowels, which are neither vowels nor yet mutes, and distinguish into classes the vowels themselves." Of course, more desirable is a kind of knowledge that grasps reality directly, without names.

The most striking instance of gnostic texts containing words and symbols of power is the *Books of Jeu* in the Bruce Codex. Nearly every page portrays tables and lists of divine names, powers, and attributes in the form of *voces mysticae et barbara* intended to be pronounced, as well as numerous graphic images that were perhaps intended to be gazed upon until a trancelike state resulted. The graphic συνθήματα (tokens), appearing as they do on the pages of a codex, seem to presuppose private appropriation on the part of the reader rather than communal recitation and thus approach the phenomenon of the "reading mystery" (*Lesemysterium*), a term coined by Reitzenstein to characterize the gradated reading of the *Corpus hermeticum.*

Although apparently independent of ritual contexts, the alphabet mysticism and magic scattered throughout the pages of gnostic literature are to be used as words of power.[56] It consists of mysterious combinations of

---

[56] See F. Dornseiff, *Das Alphabet in Mystik und Magie* (2d ed.; Berlin: Teubner, 1925); and A. Dieterich, "ABC-Denkmäler," *Rheinisches Museum für Philologie* 56 (1901): 77–105.

letters, syllables, the seven vowels and seventeen consonants of the Greek alphabet, and the twenty-two letters of the Hebrew alphabet, which are arranged in various sequences and patterns (κλίματα), where each permutation of order is significant, as is the pronouncing of these sounds. Particularly important is the use of names, especially the Tetragrammaton and other Semitic formations such as Sabaoth and Abrasax, names for the δαίμονες of the planetary Hebdomad, as well as a multitude of φρικτὰ ὀνόματα and ὀνόματα ἄσημα καὶ βάρβαρα, whose significance is hard to ascertain.[57] The primary example of these is of course the Greek magical papyri.

Although space and complexity forbids treating these phenomena in any detail, perhaps the most extensive gnostic examples are Irenaeus's account (*Haer.* 1.13–22) of the alphabetic and numerical speculations of the Valentinian Marcus and the unfortunately very fragmentary phonological, arithmological, and astral speculations on the shape of the soul in the Sethian treatise *Marsanes* (NHC X, *1*). The Valentinian Marcus "the Magician" reports a "decree of the Tetrad" concerning the highest divine principles:

> Understand the twenty-four letters that you have as symbolic emanations of the three powers that contain the entire number of elements on high. The nine mute consonants belong to the Father and Truth because they are voiceless, that is, inexpressible and unutterable. The eight semivowels belong to Logos and Life, since they occupy as it were the intermediate position between the unvoiced and the voiced, and they receive the effusion of those above them and elevate those beneath them. The vowels, seven in number, belong to Man and Church, since a voice went forth from Man and formed all things, for the echo of the voice gave them form. (Irenaeus *Haer.* 1.14.5)

The theurgical intent of this alphabetic speculation is nicely summed up by Nicomachus of Gerasa, who makes clear the relation between the elements of the alphabet (letters, vowels, and consonants), the elements of number and geometrical shape, and both musical and spoken sounds:

> For indeed the sounds of each sphere of the seven, each sphere naturally producing one certain kind of sound, are called "vowels." They are ineffable in and of themselves, but are recalled by the wise with respect to everything made up of them. Wherefore also here (i.e., on earth) this sound has power, which in arithmetic is a monad, in geometry a point, in grammar a letter (of the alphabet). And combined with the material letters, which are the consonants, as the soul is to the body and the

---

[57] See P. C. Miller, "In Praise of Nonsense," in *Classical Mediterranean Spirituality: Egyptian, Greek, Roman* (ed. A. H. Armstrong; New York: Crossroad, 1986), 481–505.

musical scale is to the strings—the one producing living beings, the other pitch and melody—they accomplish active and mystic powers of divine beings. Wherefore when especially the theurgists are worshipping such (a divine being), they invoke it symbolically with hissing sounds and clucking, with inarticulate and foreign sounds.[58]

In *Marsanes,* this symbolic power of the letters applies not only to the powers of the zodiacal signs, but also to various "configurations" (σχή-ματα) of the soul.[59] The rather better preserved section (NHC X 18,14b–39,17) on the alphabet and its relation to the configurations or shapes of the soul seems to reflect portions of Plato's discussion of the structure of the world soul and the embodiment of soul into body in *Tim.* 35A–44D. Of particular importance seem to be three fundamental ("first," "second," "third") and two minor ("fourth," and "fifth") configurations of the soul in relation to various components of the alphabet: the seven "simple" vowels (αεηιουω) and their combination into diphthongs; the seventeen consonants and their various subcategories (the semivowels—liquids [λμνρσ] plus double consonants [ζξψ]—and the mutes—aspirate [θφχ], inaspirate [κπτ] and "intermediate" [βγδ]); and the combination of all of them into syllables. In addition to these five "configurations" of the soul, the author also seems to think in terms of two "nomenclatures" (ὀνομασία): one for the "gods and angels" (X 27,13–14; cf. 30,3–9) that has to do with natural phonological combinations, and an "ignorant" nomenclature (X 30,28b–31,4) which apparently has to so with certain unnatural combinations of the seven vowels and seventeen consonants.

Apparently, the vowels and diphthongs symbolize the three highest conditions of the soul—cosmic as well as individual—apart from somatic embodiment, while the syllabic combinations of the consonants—perhaps symbolizing corporeality—with the vowels seem to symbolize the "fourth" and "fifth" configurations of the soul, perhaps as an embodied entity. Just as the vowels are "influenced" by consonants, so also are souls influenced by the body, just as both souls and bodies are influenced by the "angelic"

---

[58] Nicomachus apud C. Janus, ed., *Musici Scriptores Graeci* (Leipzig: Teubner, 1895; repr. Hildesheim: Olms, 1962), 276–77, trans. and cited by B. A. Pearson, "Gnosticism As Platonism," in *Gnosticism, Judaism, and Egyptian Christianity* (SAC 5; Minneapolis: Fortress, 1990), 161, referring also to the treatment of theurgy in E. R. Dodds, "New Light on the Chaldaean Oracles," in H. Lewy, *Chaldean Oracles and Theurgy: Mysticism, Magic, and Platonism in the Later Roman Empire* (Recherches d'archéologie et de philosophe et d'histoire 13; Cairo: Institut français d'archéologie orientale, 1956; new ed., ed. M. Tardieu; Paris: Études Augustiniennes, 1978), 700 n. 31.

[59] See my forthcoming introduction to *Marsanes* in W.-P. Funk, P.-H. Poirier and J. D. Turner, *Marsanès (NH X,1)* (BCNHT 25; Québec: Presses de l'Université Laval; Leuven-Paris: Peeters, 2000), 54–81.

powers of the seven planets and the stellar powers of the dominant zodiacal signs. But since the powers of these astral objects are also regarded as somehow present in the fundamental "elements" of reality in much the same way as the soul is present in the body, knowledge of how their symbolic counterparts—the letters (as στοιχεῖα)—combine and mutually influence one another at the levels of syllable and word apparently gives the knower some measure of control over the apparently external powers of the zodiac, stars, and planets, and the gods and angels embodied in them. These five configurations of the soul involving vowels alone might be summarized as follows:

1. first outer (spherical?) configuration = αεηιουω = only begotten soul—unitary, androgynous soul
2. second spherical configuration = εηιου "from diphthongs" = self-begotten soul—dyadic, feminine soul
3. third spherical configuration = <ααα>, εεε, <ηηη>, ιιι, οοο, υυυ, ωωω—triadic, male soul
4. fourth (spherical?) configuration = combinations of vowels = visible, perceptible soul
5. fifth (spherical?) configuration = combinations of vowels = visible, perceptible soul

This lengthy passage seems to constitute an alphanumeric interpretation of the psychogonia of Plato's *Tim.* 35A–44D. The first three configurations of the soul would represent the cosmic soul in terms either of its three basic ingredients (Being, Difference, and Sameness) or, more likely, in terms of the spherical or circular configurations into which the demiurge divided it (36C2): an outer spherical envelope signifying the motion that revolves invariantly in the same place (the sphere of the fixed stars), containing two inner circles, that of the same (the celestial equator defining the plane of this revolution), and the circle of the different (the ecliptic or zodiacal belt within which the movements of the sun and other planets is confined), which is subsequently subdivided into the individual orbits of the seven planets. If so, then the fourth and fifth configurations would represent the "second and third" portions (41D5) remaining in the mixing bowl from which individual souls were made and sown into each star, thus becoming visible (not the souls themselves, but their "bodies," Plato, *Laws* 898DE; Proclus *In Tim.* 3.255.10–16) and "revealing" visible things (X 29,2–6). At this point, the younger gods are assigned the task of incarnating these souls into mortal bodies—which *Marsanes* seems to symbolize by the consonants—crafted from the four elements (42E–44C). The shock of being incarnated into a foreign element causes such souls to undergo perturbations that result in the loss of their original innate capacity to perceive clear and distinct ideas and thus to distinguish between things and name them according to the appropriate nomenclature. Incarnation results in the initial loss of the soul's natural or innate "nomenclature" (the one for gods and angels) and its replacement by an unnatural (ignorant) "nomenclature." In this way, *Marsanes* establishes direct relationships between, on the one hand, the various conditions of the soul and its relative knowledge and ignorance, and on the other, the ability to understand the appropriate combination of the letters of the alphabet.

8. Ascensional and Contemplative Practices

8.1. The Sethian Platonizing Treatises

In the treatises *Allogenes, Three Steles of Seth, Zostrianos,* and *Marsanes,* salvation is not brought from above to below by divine visitations but rather occurs through the gnostic's contemplative ascent through ever higher levels of the divine realm. Here one finds an exemplary visionary, Allogenes or Marsanes (probably alternative designations for Seth), utilizing a self-performable technique of successive stages of mental detachment from the world of multiplicity and a corresponding assimilation of the self to the ever more refined levels of being to which one's contemplation ascends, until one achieves an absolute stasis and cognitive vacancy characteristic of deification. The *Three Steles of Seth* presupposes a three-stage ascent to the Autogenes, the Aeon of Barbelo, and the supreme One. Allogenes depicts a similar three-stage ascent but begins at the Aeon of Barbelo and adds an ascent through the supra-intelligible levels of the Triple-Powered One of the Invisible Spirit, culminating in a "primary revelation" of the Unknowable One. A similar ascent is portrayed in *Zostrianos,* except that it has been supplemented by a series of initial stages within the sense-perceptible realm, and each successive stage of ascent after these is associated with a certain baptismal sealing. *Marsanes* merely comments on certain features of the ascent, which its author claims to have already undergone.

The text that most warrants the treatment of this contemplative ascent as an established ritual is the *Three Steles of Seth,* in which the aretalogical doxologies of Seth in honor of his father Geradamas, the Aeon of Barbelo, and the ultimate preexistent One are provided for the use of both individuals and a community: "Whoever remembers these and always glorifies shall be perfect among those who are perfect and impassive beyond all things; for individually and collectively they all praise these: and afterward they shall be silent. And just as it has been ordained for them, they will ascend. After silence, they will descend from the third, they will bless the second, and afterward, the first. The way of ascent is the way of descent" (NHC VII 127,6–21). In the first Stele, Seth praises his father Geradamas as his intellect, then as the Autogenes ("self-generated"), the "Mirotheid" offspring of Barbelo (Mirothea is the mother of Adamas in *Gos. Eg.* NHC III

49,1–12 and *Zost.* VIII 6,30) who presides over Seth's "alien" seed, the immovable race; then both Seth and Geradamas praise the thrice-masculine aeon Barbelo who came forth to the middle to empower and bestow crowns and perfection upon them. The second stele is directed by the "perfect individuals" to Barbelo as their three-in-one source, the source of all multiplicity, the projected image ("shadow") of the "first pre-existent One," the bestower of divinity, goodness and blessing; the "individuals" petition her to save them by uniting them. The third stele is directed to the preexistent One, the only and living Spirit, the Existence, Life, and Mind of the All, whom they entreat to present a "command" that they might be saved; at that point, the petitioners recognize that they have been saved and therefore offer praise and glory. Each stele marks a stage on the contemplative ascent to the One. Just as Seth, spiritual ancestor of the Sethians, praised and joined his father Adamas in the praise of the Mother Barbelo and of her source, the preexistent One, so the members of the Sethian community are to follow the same pattern in their own ascent to the Aeon of Barbelo and receive the revelation of the Invisible Spirit.

The treatise that most likely contains the key to the ritual origins of the Sethian ascensional rite is *Zostrianos,* since, as noted above, it marks the various stages of Zostrianos's visionary ascent with certain baptisms, sealings, washings in various "waters." It is perhaps also significant that *Marsanes* (NHC X 2,12–4,24) enumerates the entire sequence of the ontological levels underlying these treatises as thirteen "seals."

Of these texts, it is *Allogenes* that most clearly portrays the method of this ascent, so it will form the basis of the following exposition, even though it narrates the ascent as that of an individual and enumerates the levels of ascent slightly differently than the others.

The cosmology of these treatises is tripartite but belongs to the four-level ontology of Speusippus, the Neopythagoreans, and Plotinus, which posits a highest realm beyond even being itself, below which one finds an atemporal, intelligible realm of pure being, followed by a psychic realm, characterized by time and motion, and finally a physical realm at the bottom of the scale. The following summary of the ontology of *Allogenes* will suffice to indicate the ontological structure of the entire group.

The highest being, corresponding to the Plotinian One, is the Unknowable One or Invisible Spirit, characterized by nonbeing existence, silence, and stillness; he is not an existing thing and is completely unknowable (XI 62,23–64,14; *Marsanes* [X 2,12–23] adds yet another level, the "unknown, silent One" beyond even the Invisible Spirit).

The second major level is that of the Aeon of Barbelo, the First Thought of the Invisible Spirit, characterized as a nondiscriminating, incorporeal, [timeless] knowledge (XI 51,10–11). The Barbelo Aeon is subdivided into three levels that correspond to aspects of the Plotinian hypostases of Intellect and Soul: (1) the domain of "the authentic existents" (τὰ ὄντως ὄντα, the νοητά) presided over by Kalyptos (the Hidden One, a sort of νοῦς νοητός) rather like the Plotinian Intellect; (2) the domain of "those who are unified" (i.e., "exist together," cf. *Enn.* 4.1.1: ἐκεῖ [ἐν τῷ νῷ] ὁμοῦ μὲν πᾶς νοῦς ... ὁμοῦ δὲ πάσαι ψυχαί) presided over by Protophanes (the First Appearing One, a sort of νοῦς θεωρητικός), rather like the Plotinian cosmic Soul; and (3) the domain of the "(perfect) individuals" (perhaps individual souls) presided over by Autogenes (the Self-Begotten One, a sort of demiurgic νοῦς διανοούμενος), who operates to rectify the realm of Nature, rather like the Plotinian individuated soul.

The third level, Nature, is merely mentioned in passing as a realm whose defects are continually rectified by Autogenes and appears to hold no interest for the author of *Allogenes,* although the treatise *Marsanes* (X 5,23–26) regards this realm as "entirely worthy of preservation."

The mediator between the Invisible Spirit and the Aeon of Barbelo is an entity called the Triple-Powered One. This being is mentioned sometimes independently and sometimes in conjunction with the Invisible Spirit.[60] By a static self-extension, the Invisible Spirit through his Triple-Powered One becomes the Aeon of Barbelo (XI 45,21–30; cf. *Zost.* VIII 76,7–19; 78,10–81,20; *Steles Seth* VII 121,20–122,8; *Marsanes* X 8,18–9,28). Thus the Triple-Powered One is the potency (δύναμις) of the Unknown One and/or Invisible Spirit by which he unfolds himself into the world of Being and Intellect. It is said to consist of three modalities or phases: That-which-is (Being or Existence), Vitality, and Mentality (XI 49,26–38).

In *Allogenes,* the Triple-Powered One is identical with the Invisible Spirit in its Existence-phase, discontinuous with the Invisible Spirit but identical with Barbelo in its Mentality-phase, and in its emanative or Vitality-phase, it is simultaneously continuous and discontinuous with both the Invisible Spirit and Barbelo. *Allogenes* attributes also to the Unknowable One/Invisible Spirit a similar triad of attributes but characterizes them as

---

[60] The Invisible Spirit and the Triple-Powered One are mentioned sometimes separately (*Zost.* VIII 15,18; 17,7; 24,9–10; 93,6–9; 124,3–4; *Allogenes* XI 45,13–30; 52,19; 52,30–33; 53,30; 61,1–22; and *Marsanes* X 4,13–19; 6,19; 8,11; 9,25; 14,22–23; 15,1–3), sometimes as identical with or in close conjunction with the Invisible Spirit (*Zost.* VIII 20,15–18; 24,12–13; 63,7–8; 74,3–16; 79,16–23; 80,11–20; 87,13–14; 97,2–3; 118,11–12; 123,19–20; 128,20–21; *Allogenes* XI 47,8–9; 51,8–9; 58,25; 66,33–34; *Steles Seth* VII 121,31–32; *Marsanes* X 7,16–17 [the "activity" of the Invisible Spirit]; 7,27–29; 8,5–7), often as "the Triple-Powered Invisible Spirit" or "the invisible spiritual Triple-Powered One," and sometimes in conjunction with Barbelo (*Steles Seth* VII 120,21–22; 121,32–33; 123,18–30; *Marsanes* X 8,19–20; 9,7–20; 10,8–11). As the activity of the Invisible Spirit, the Triple-Powered One is perhaps identical with all three in *Marsanes* X 7,1–9,29.

acts rather than qualities or substances: "he exists, lives and knows without mind, life or existence" (XI 61, 32–39).

In reality, all three levels are only separate phases of the unfolding of the Invisible Spirit by means of its Triple-Powered One into the Aeon of Barbelo. Rather than being a triad of principles distributed vertically among different planes of reality, the Existence-Life-Intellect triad is seen as a dynamic three-in-one principle in which each phase of the triad, while containing the other two, is named by the phase of the triad that predominates at each stage of its unfolding:

Unknowable One/Invisible Spirit	*Exists*	Lives	Knows
Triple-Powered One/Eternal Life	Existence	*Vitality*	Mentality
Barbelo/First Thought	Being	(Life)	*Mind*

In the accompanying diagram, the italicized term indicates the relative predominance of one of the three modalities. The first phase coincides with the Invisible Spirit and the third phase with the Aeon of Barbelo, in effect giving rise to a median phase in which the Triple-Powered One is discontinuous with both the Invisible Spirit and Barbelo, having a quasi-hypostatic character of its own.

8.2. The Visionary Ascent in *Allogenes*

Allogenes (XI 58,26–61,21) tripartitions the contemplative ascent into separate but successive stages in accord with the tripartitioning of its general ontology, since the object of the ascent is to become assimilated with each higher level of being through which one passes. Each stage of the ascent is prefaced by instruction from a revealer. The technique of the initial ascent through the lowest level of the intelligible realm, the Aeon of Barbelo is revealed by the "male virgin" Youel (57,29–58,26). The technique of the culminating ascent through the Triple-Powered One is revealed by the three "luminaries of the Aeon of Barbelo" (58,26–61,22) and is structured in terms of the tripartite nomenclature previously applied to the Triple-Powered One in 49,26–38. The technique of the final union with the Unknowable One, however, cannot be conveyed by a positive descriptive revelation, but only by a "primary revelation of the Unknowable One"; this turns out to be the long negative theology in 61,32–64,36, by which one acquires the saving gift of learned ignorance. On completion of the ascent and revelation, Allogenes' appropriate response will be to record and safeguard the revelation (68,16–23) and entrust its proclamation to his confidant Messos (68,26–end).

Stage 1: The Ascent through the Aeon of Barbelo. The revealer Youel instructs Allogenes concerning the initial part of the ascent to "the God who truly [preexists]," which requires a perfect seeking of the Good within oneself, by which one knows oneself as one who exists with the preexistent God. According to 50,10–36, the wisdom conveyed by Youel's initial revelation of the Aeon of Barbelo and of the Triple-Powered One will restore Allogenes to his primordial, unfallen condition. It will invest Allogenes' "thought" with the power requisite to distinguish between "immeasurable and unknowable" things, the contents of the Barbelo Aeon and the principles beyond it, causing Allogenes to fear that his learning has exceeded normal limits. One notes again the metaphor of putting on a garment.

In 52,7–21, after Youel's initial revelation of the contents of the Aeon of Barbelo, Allogenes reports that his soul went slack with disturbance. Turning to himself, he sees the light surrounding him and the Good within him and becomes divine, which Youel interprets as a completion of wisdom sufficient to receive a revelation of the Triple-Powered One.

Interpreted in the light of the ontology of the treatise, it seems as if Allogenes has become successively assimilated to the various levels of the Barbelo Aeon: first, to the level of the "individuals" within Autogenes, and second, to the level of "those who are unified" within Protophanes, and third, to "those who truly exist" in Kalyptos.

In her fifth discourse (55,33–57,24), Youel promises Allogenes that, after an incubation period of a "hundred years" (during which he presumably is to engage in self-contemplation, experiencing "a great light and a blessed path," 57,27–58,7), he will receive a revelation from the "luminaries of the Aeon of Barbelo." This revelation will convey only so much as is necessary to know without Allogenes forfeiting his own kind. If Allogenes is successful in this, he will receive a conception (ἔννοια) of the preexistent One and know himself as one "who exists with the God who truly preexists" (56,18–36), which will make him divine and perfect.

At the conclusion of the "hundred years" of preparation, Allogenes reports that he saw Autogenes, the Triple Male, Protophanes, Kalyptos, the Aeon of Barbelo, and the "primal origin of the One without origin," that is, the Triple-Powered One of the Invisible Spirit (57,29–58,26). One should probably understand this as Allogenes' ascent through the various levels of the Aeon of Barbelo up to and including the lowest aspect ("blessedness" or Mentality) of the Triple-Powered One, which would be identical with the entirety of the Aeon of Barbelo itself. Up to this point, Allogenes still bears his earthly "garment" (58,29–30).

This initial vision culminates with Allogenes' receipt of a luminous garment by which he is taken up to "a pure place" (58,31), where he transcends ("stands upon") his knowledge (characterized by blessedness and self-knowledge) of the individual constituents of the Barbelo-Aeon. He is now ready for "holy powers" revealed to him by the "luminaries of the Aeon of Barbelo" to encourage him to "strive for" an even higher knowledge toward which he had already "inclined," namely "the knowledge of the Universal Ones, the Barbelo Aeon" (59,2–3).

Stage 2: The Ascent through the Triple-Powered One. The ascent beyond the Aeon of Barbelo to the Unknowable One is first revealed to Allogenes by holy powers (59,4–60,12) and then actually narrated (60,12–61,22) by Allogenes in a way quite similar to the revelation, yielding what amounts to two accounts of the ascent. Having surpassed his active, earthly knowledge and inclining toward the passive knowledge of the Universal Ones (the Triple-Powered One and the Invisible Spirit, 59,2–3), Allogenes attains first the level of blessedness (i.e., Mentality), at which one knows one's proper self, sees the good in oneself, and becomes divine (59,9–13; 60,14–18). Next, as he "seeks himself," he ascends (ἀναχωρεῖν) to the level of Vitality, characterized by an undivided, eternal, intellectual motion, a supra-eidetic realm where one achieves partial stability (he stands not firmly but quietly, 59,14–16; 60,19–28). Finally Allogenes achieves the level of Existence, characterized by a completely inactive "stillness" and "standing" (59,19–26; 60,28–37). He is filled with a "primary revelation of the unknowable One" that empowers and permanently strengthens him, enabling him to receive an incognizant knowledge of the Unknowable One.

At this point, having assimilated himself to the primal modality of the Triple-Powered One, Allogenes can no longer ascend to any higher level; only in the case that he becomes afraid can he further withdraw and that only "to the rear because of the activities" (59,34–35; cf. Plotinus *Enn.* 3.8.9.29–40; 6.9.3.1–13). He must not "seek incomprehensible matters" but must avoid any further effort lest he dissipate his inactivity and fall away from the passivity, concentratedness, and instantaneousness of the primary revelation to follow (59,26–60,12; cf. 64,14–26; 67,22–38). Allogenes is told to be "incognizant" ("ignorant" or "nonknowing") of the Unknowable One, that is, not to exercise any faculties of the active intellect, lest this activity initiate a movement that would destroy the stability he has achieved. Even to fear this extreme inertness is such a mental activity and necessitates a withdrawal to a previous level of contemplation. Once he receives the primary revelation, he must therefore "still himself" and remain completely self-concentrated ("do not further dissipate") and refrain from any exercise of the active intellect, even if it should be a "luminous ἔννοια," which might replace and therefore destroy the inactivity conveyed to him by the Unknowable One.[61] In a state of utter passivity, Allogenes receives a "primary revelation of the Unknowable One" (59,28–29; 60,39–61,1) characterized as a cognitively vacant knowledge of the Unknowable One

---

[61] Cf. Plotinus *Enn.* 5.8.11.23–24, 33–34.

(59,30–32; 60,8–12; 61,1–4). This knowledge can be articulated only by an extensive negative theology (61,32–62,13; supplemented by a more affirmative theology, 62,14–67,20).

The sequence of Allogenes' mental states therefore moves from relative to permanent stability, and from self-knowledge to mental vacancy: (1) At the level of Mentality, characterized by silent stillness, he "hears" the Blessedness of true self-knowledge. (2) At the level of Vitality, characterized by the eternal circular ("undivided") motion of the supra-eidetic realm, and still seeking himself, he achieves partial stability. (3) At the level of Existence, characterized by total stability and inactivity, he achieves a complete stability, permanently strengthened by the indwelling of the Triple-Powered One. (4) Allogenes is filled with the "primary revelation of the Unknowable One," which allows him to know the Unknowable One and his Triple-Powered One insofar as he maintains a state of complete incognizance and mental vacuity.

The sequence of Allogenes' mental states is also the reverse of the sequence of the dominant phases or ontological modalities in which the Triple-Powered One unfolds into the Aeon of Barbelo. His initial state is called Blessedness, a condition associated with a silent (nondiscursive?) self-contemplation characteristic of "Mentality," which designates also the lowest phase of the Triple-Powered One's three phases of Mentality, Vitality, and Existence. He is then instructed to move from this state to a less stable state, that of "Vitality," which is characterized by an eternal circular motion that still includes a "seeking of oneself." Then, in order to gain a state of ultimate stability, he is to move on to the level of Existence, the phase in which the Triple-Powered One is identical with the Invisible Spirit, who is absolutely at rest and contains all in total silence and inactivity. In each case, the contemplation of entities on ever higher ontological levels is characterized as a form of the contemplator's self-knowledge, suggesting that the consciousness of the knowing subject is actually assimilated to the ontological character of the level that one intelligizes at any given point.

Allogenes thus presents two levels of knowing: One is achievable in the world and is characterized by the actual vision of what was communicated in the auditory revelations imparted by the emissary-revealer Youel; it suffices to have a vision of each of the beings comprising the Aeon of Barbelo up to and including the lower aspect of the Triple-Powered One. The other is achievable, not in the world, but only after elevation to a pure place, and is to be imparted by an apophatic "primary revelation" from the Luminaries of Barbelo's Aeon; it enables one to experience directly the realm beyond intellect and even being itself occupied by the upper levels of the Triple-Powered One and the Unknowable One. The first level of knowing is active and discursive, involving knowledge of oneself as well as the ability to experience one's assimilation to the various levels comprising the intellectual and psychic realm of the Barbelo Aeon (58,38–59,3; 59,9–16): from individuated soul to unity with the cosmic soul to the intellectual domain of the authentic existents. The second level of knowing is passive; strictly speaking it is not knowledge at all but culminates in a nonknowing, nondiscursive knowledge with no awareness of distinctions, even that between knower and known, an utter vacancy of the cognitive intellect, a "learned ignorance" (59,30–35; 60,5–12; 61,1–4) called a "primary revelation of the Unknowable One" (59,28–29; 60,39–61,1).

Stage 3: The Primary Revelation. The extensive negative theology occupying the last third of *Allogenes* exhibits a close relationship between the negative ontological (apophatic) predications of the Invisible Spirit and the noncognitive contemplation of him.[62] It turns out that the primary revelation conveying the ultimate vision of the supreme reality is identical with its object: the Invisible Spirit is the very primary revelation by which he is known (63,9–19). The Invisible Spirit is so unknowable that he is in some sense his own unknowable knowledge and forms a unity with the ignorance that sees him; in fact he seems to be equated with the state of mental vacancy itself (63,28–64,14). Yet one cannot simply use the equation between the unknowable deity and the primary revelation or incognizant knowledge by which he is known as a way of knowing or speaking about him. To equate him with either knowledge or nonknowledge is to miss the goal of one's quest (64,14–36). It is nevertheless clear that *Allogenes* assumes that it is possible to achieve a consubstantiality between the known, the means of knowledge, and the knower: the unknowable deity is united with the ignorance that sees him, which is identical with his own self-knowledge. By implication, he is also united with the nonknowing visionary as well. Thus there is an isomorphism, indeed an identity, between both the epistemic and ontic states of the knower, the known, and the means of knowledge at each stage of the ascent.

The prototype of this threefold ascent is found in Plato's *Symposium* (210a–212a), in the speech where Socrates recounts the path to the vision of absolute beauty into which he had been initiated by the wise Diotima. The method consists of a three-stage qualitative and quantitative purification or purgation of the soul by a redirection of Eros, the moving force of the soul, away from the lower realm to the higher.[63] The qualitative

---

[62] See R. T. Wallis, "The Spiritual Importance of Not Knowing," in *Classical Mediterranean Spirituality: Egyptian, Greek, Roman* (ed. A. H. Armstrong; New York: Crossroad, 1986), 460–80; as Wallis notes, the knowledge of God as divine silence in *Corp. herm.* 10 is similar.

[63] See the analysis of E. O'Brien, *The Essential Plotinus* (New York: Mentor, 1964), 16–17.

purgation is a progressive shift of attention from the sensible to the intelligible realm in three levels of knowing, which correspond to three levels of experience: physical beauty, moral beauty, and intellectual beauty; these are the objects respectively of the bodily senses, the ethical components of the soul, and the intelligizing, contemplative faculty of the reflective soul. The quantitative purgation is a shift of attention away from individual instances of beauty, to the ideal beauty of all forms, and finally to absolute beauty itself, which then discloses itself as a sudden and immediate intuition. The next higher stage is therefore achieved by a purifying and unifying synthesis of the experience of the lower stage. As in the *Symposium,* so also in the *Republic* (532A–B) the final moment of attainment is conceived as a revelation of the supreme form. After long preliminary effort, one's soul or mind has transcended discursive science, dialectic itself, for an unmediated vision of or direct contact with the object sought. No longer does one "know about" the object things that can be predicated of it, but one actually possesses and is possessed by the object of one's quest.

In the first four centuries of our era to which the Barbeloite treatises belong, the Platonic tradition regarded metaphysics or theology as the highest of the three stages of enlightenment or spiritual progress.[64] It corresponded to the highest stage of initiation into the mysteries and was in fact called ἐποπτεία, the supreme vision of the highest reality, tantamount to assimilating oneself to God insofar as possible (Theaetetus 176B).[65] This traditional Platonic quest is found not only in Plato but also later in Philo of Alexandria (who however shunned the notion of assimilation to God), Numenius, Valentinus, Albinus (i.e., Alcinous, the *viae analogiae, negationis, additionis* and *eminentiae* of *Did.* 10.5–6; cf. 28.1–3), Clement of Alexandria (*Strom.* 5.11.70.8–71.5), Origen (*Cels.* 7.42) and especially Plotinus (*Enn.* 6.7 [38].36). What is generally common to these visionary ascents is initial purification, usually through some form of instruction involving the use of analogies, negations, and successive abstraction until the contemplative mind has become absorbed in its single object (the One, the Good, the Beautiful, etc.) at

---

64 P. Hadot, "La métaphysique de Porphyre," in *Porphyre* (Entretiens sur l'antiquité classique 12; Vandoeuvres-Geneva: Fondation Hardt, 1960), 127–29 (citing Calcidius *In Tim.* 272; 335; and Proclus *In Tim.* 1, p. 202 Diehl), points out that Porphyry's systematic arrangement of Plotinus's *Enneads* conforms to this scheme (*Enn.* 1 = ethics; *Enn.* 2, 3 = physics; *Enn.* 4, 5, 6 = epoptic, the objects of contemplation), as do certain Neoplatonic prescriptions for the order of the study of Plato's dialogues (*Republic* = ethics; *Timaeus* = physics; *Parmenides* = theology).

65 See Plutarch *Is. Os.* 382D–E; Clement of Alexandria *Strom.* 1.28.176.1–3; Theon of Smyrna *Exp.* 14.18–16.2; Origen *Cant.* 75.6 Baehrens.

which point one "suddenly" sees the ultimate source of all these;[66] here philosophy and intellection give way to ecstasy.

9. Concluding Observations

By way of conclusion, it can be seen that the purpose of gnostic ritual was uniformly salvific, a means to restore the primordial unity of the human person. This process might be conceived on a relatively more biblical basis, as uniting the male and female components of an original androgyne that wrongfully underwent a primeval division. Or, on a more Platonic basis, as the restoration of the soul to the original psychic substance from which its ungrudging maker extracted and incarnated it; its (metaphorically feminine) irrationality acquired from contact with materiality must be subjected to its higher, undescended, rational or intellectual (metaphorically masculine) component. The gnostics illustrated the original perfection of the soul by the pairing and agreement of the pleromatic aeons, and its degradation is illustrated by the lack of cooperation between male and female at the moment of the inception of the physical cosmos and its creator, which become characterized by victimization and oblivion on the one hand, and by presumption and antagonism on the other. The physical bodies into which the divine substance was thereby incarnated must be stripped away like an old garment and replaced with the luminous garment made of that substance; they must be thoroughly washed away and the inner person immersed in the living water of wisdom, anointed with the fragrance of the divine spirit, and wed with its other but higher self.

In contrast to gnostic rites of baptism, investiture, chrismation, and the sacral meal—whose effect depends on a combination of divine initiative and revealed insight (Gnosis)—the practice of ritual speech, sexual sacramentalism, and to some extent contemplative ascent come closest to the kind of ritual acts which effect their own work (*ex opere operato*). Baptism, investiture, chrismation, and even the sacral meal are typically said to be received or undergone. Similarly, the rite of sacral marriage is usually portrayed as an eschatological gift, something to be awaited. On the other hand, ritual sex, speech, gesture, and contemplative ascent depend much more on individual initiative and technique. In this sense, they border on theurgical rites insofar as they exploit acquired knowledge of certain cosmic sympathies and/or properties of physical actions that serve to assimilate oneself to transcendent forces or levels of reality. Simonian, Valentinian, and especially Sethian materials witness both self-actualized and conferred ritual procedures and portray salvation sometimes as "self-help" and "other help" process. Particularly notable is the distinction

---

[66] So also Plotinus *Enn.* 6.7.34.8.

between Sethian texts that portray the advent of salvation as brought from above to below by the supreme Mother and those that portray it as the result of a self-actualized contemplative ascent. To be sure, a divine revelation showing the path is required; Allogenes is still dependent on divine powers like Youel and the luminaries of the Aeon of Barbelo to reveal to him the way of ascent, yet once he receives the revelation, he makes the ascent in an unaided fashion. Of course, in almost all texts that portray an ascent to the supreme One, gnostic and Platonic alike, the final vision of the One is ultimately vouchsafed. Nevertheless, the salvific goal seems to involve the transfer of one's inner essence from below to above, rather than conjuring the manifestation of the divine powers here below. Vivid manifestations of divine beings occur in the gnostic texts, yet they are uninvoked, free manifestations of the divine unrelated to any causal connection or affinities innate to the created realm and usually are witnessed by august figures who themselves have a heavenly origin (Seth, Jesus) or by figures who are singled out by divine choice (Zostrianos, Marsanes, Allogenes, Thomas and other disciples of Jesus). Salvation is achieved by the return of the soul to its original state, not by a rectification of the physical world it has come to inhabit or by a final overthrow of antidivine powers. This is not merely to repeat the old adages about the anticosmicism and antisomaticism often ascribed to the gnostics, many of whom valued corporeality as a vehicle of revelation.[67]

---

[67] Cf. the veneration of the visible Jesus in the Valentinian *Gospel of Truth* and *Gospel of Philip*, in the "Carpocratian" Marcellina's worship of Christ's image (Irenaeus *Haer.* 1.25.6), and Zostrianos's willing postascensional readoption and invigoration of his "image" so as to preach the truth (NHC VIII, *1* 130,5–9). Indeed, according to the *Gospel of Philip* (77,2–6), "the holy person is completely holy, even including his body. Taking up bread, he makes it holy, as also the cup or anything else that he takes up and sanctifies. Then how will he not sanctify the body too?" To be sure, one can find anticosmic passages, particularly in the earlier Sethian texts, yet in this corpus one also finds Marsanes at the conclusion of his ascent saying "<I have come to know> in detail the entire realm of incorporeal being, and <I> have come to know the intelligible world. <I have come to know>, while deliberating, that in every respect the sense-perceptible world is [worthy] of being saved entirely" (NHC X, *1* 5,19–26). The demiurgic activity of the divine Autogenes in *Allogenes* (NHC XI,*3* 51,25–35), by which he rectifies the defects of nature, likewise affirms the value of the cosmos without overlooking its problematic nature (which Platonists, including theurgists like Iamblichus, also recognized). Late Sethian ritual, such as the sexual rites of the Borborites, is ambiguous: on the one hand, the unrestrained practice of intercourse seems affirmative of bodily existence, yet the practice of *coitus interruptus* and consuming the aborted and mangled bodies of accidentally conceived fetuses is certainly a denial of the value of bodily life. Real contempt for the body arises mostly in the encratite movement with which

Because of the wide variation of gnostic attitude and implementation, the relation of gnostic ritual to later Platonic, especially theurgical, ritual cannot be simply characterized. It cannot be said that one is fundamentally based on biblical motifs and the other on Platonic concepts. Although the theurgists do not seem to employ the myth of the primal androgyne, even given its fundamental significance for gnostic myth and ritual, it cannot be said that all gnostics employed it. Nor can it be said that one is anticosmic while the other is procosmic, or that one is individualistic and noetic while the other is communal and dependent on revelation, or that the one is self-actualized while the other is divinely initiated.

As stated in the introduction, it may be taken that theurgy is a ritual practice in which embodied souls were brought into a sympathetic resonance with the divine *Logoi* that informed the natural world and that these divine powers were invoked to enter the phenomenal world in order to reveal their divine source. And yet, apart from an appeal to a Posidonian doctrine of cosmic συμπαθεία, that seems precisely the intent of the invocation of the numerous divine beings, the living water itself, and those who preside over it and the Name, and the receivers, guardians, and purifiers necessary to effectuate the Sethian baptismal rite. Indeed, it remains that ultimate salvation in both outlooks is ultimately a matter of revelation and divine initiative, for at the summit of all ritual and contemplative effort, the Supreme "suddenly" manifests itself, as both Plato and the gnostics discovered.

Judas the Twin was associated; witness the uncompromising hatred of the body and its natural passions in the *Book of Thomas the Contender*: "Woe to you who love intimacy with womankind and polluted intercourse with them! Woe to you in the grip of your bodily faculties, for they will afflict you! Woe to you in the grip of the evil demons! Woe to you who beguile your limbs in the fire!" (NHC II,7 144,91–94). And yet the underlying core of this text is an *epitome* of Plato's teaching on the transmigration of the soul gathered principally from the *Phaedo, Phaedrus, Republic,* and *Timaeus* that has undergone a radical encratite reworking. Persons of this stripe would have no truck with Platonic theurgists who sought to embody the demiurgic powers of nature through ritual means. Any hint of cosmic sympathies and affinities would be attributed by them to demonic forces; theirs was a dualism of absolute opposition, not mimetic dependence.

PLATONISM AND GNOSTICISM. THE ANONYMOUS *COMMENTARY* ON THE *PARMENIDES:* MIDDLE OR NEOPLATONIC?

Kevin Corrigan
University of Saskatchewan

For the past hundred years and more, scholars have supposed that an anonymous commentary on Plato's *Parmenides,* originally published by W. Kroll (1892), must be post-Plotinian. Suggestions for authorship have ranged from Porphyry to Plutarch of Athens and Proclus.[1] The present

---

[1] The philosophical sophistication of the *Commentary* and some elements of its technical vocabulary (particularly the use of the word ὕπαρξις) suggest that it is at the very least post-Plotinian. For this reason B. Peyron ("Notizia d'un antico evangeliario bobbiese che in alcuni fogli palimpsesti contiene frammenti d'un greco tratato di filosofia," *Rivista di filologia e di istruzione classica* 1 [1873]: 53–71) supposed the author to be from the school of Alexandria, probably Proclus, while W. Kroll ("Ein neuplatonischer Parmenides-kommentar in einem Turiner Palimsest," *Rheinisches Museum für Philosophie* 48 [1892]: 599–627) argued that the *Commentary* presupposes the thought of Iamblichus and should therefore be traced to the second half of the fourth century C.E. Kroll's thesis was founded on the view that it was Iamblichus who first introduced the term "life" in between "existence" and "thought" in order to establish the triadic structure of the intelligible world, both vertically and horizontally. M. Wundt ("Platons Parmenides," *Tübinger Beiträge zur Altertumswissenschaft* 25 [1935]: 24–26), while recognizing that traces of the triad already appear in Plotinus and Porphyry, eliminated Iamblichus and Syrianus as possible authors and suggested Plutarch of Athens rather than Porphyry, with the proviso that a definitive identification could not be made, given the little we know. R. Beutler ("Plutarchos von Athens," PW 21:974–75), by contrast, directly assigned the authorship to Plutarch on the grounds that the details of the interpretation of the *Parmenides* in the *Commentary* are distinctively Plutarchan, though he admitted the important influence of Alexander of Aphrodisias, Plotinus, and Porphyry (cf. also Evrard, "Le maître de Plutarque d'Athènes et les origines du néoplatonisme athénien," *L'Antiquité classique* 29 [1960]: 391–406). Later views, including those of D. P. Taormina (*Plutarco di Atene. l'Uno, l'anima, le forme: saggio introduttivo, fonti, traduzione e commento* [Catania: Università di Catanio; Rome: L'Erma di Bretschneider. Centro di studi sull'antico Cristianésimo, Università di Catania, 1989]) and A. Linguiti ("Commentarium in Platonis «Parmenidem»," in *Corpus dei Papiri Filosofici Greci e Latini,* part 3:

work argues for the first time that the *Commentary* is pre-Plotinian, quite possibly from the hand of a member of the "school" of Cronius and Numenius, and consequently presents a rather new view of the place of Plotinus in the history of thought and indicates the need for a rethinking of some of the principal features of Middle Platonism and of the relation between the Plotinian circle and Gnosticism.

A word of caution is necessary. At the outset several different scenarios seemed possible and plausible: either Porphyry, or a pupil of Porphyry, or someone later still, could well have been the author of the *Commentary*. Nonetheless, it began to dawn upon me that a pre-Porphyrian authorship was more plausible than any other hypothesis, but only, of course, if one could show that Pierre Hadot's thesis, based as it is upon Plotinus as a *terminus a quo,* could be shown to be ill-founded.[2] So, among other things, I here argue that a pre-Plotinian authorship for the *Commentary* should not only *not* be ruled out, but ought to be taken seriously—and at least as seriously as Pierre Hadot's thesis. However, the present work goes somewhat beyond this, for it also argues that on the basis of all the positive evidence it is most plausible to suppose (1) that the *Commentary* could *not* have been written by Porphyry and that it must be earlier than Plotinus, (2) that the Sethian gnostic texts[3] of the Nag Hammadi library, to which Porphyry

---

Commentari [Firenze: L. S. Olschki, 1995], 63–202), have rejected Beutler's thesis while arguing generally for a late date, in the case of Linguiti, for example, "*un neoplatonico posteriore a Porfirio che abbia operate nel pieno del IV secolo*" (91). Hadot (*Porphyre et Victorinus* [2 vols.; Paris: Études augustiniennes, 1968]), by contrast, has shown that the triad existence-life-thought already plays an important role in Porphyry's thought and in his exegesis of the *Chaldean Oracles,* and he has traced the influence of similar ideas to those in the *Commentary* in the works of Victorinus. Porphyry, in fact, was reproached by Damascius for identifying the "Father" of the intellectual triad with the First "One," and the author of the *Commentary* has a similar view to Porphyry. Furthermore, the moments of the triad are not yet hypostatized as in Iamblichus, but form parts of the unified, internal structure of intellect—a view that is much closer to Plotinus (see also n. 8 below).

[2] P. Hadot, *Porphyre et Victorinus.*

[3] On the determination of Sethian thought, see, for example, H.-M. Schenke ("The Phenomenon and Significance of Gnostic Sethianism," in *The Rediscovery of Gnosticism: Proceedings of the International Conference on Gnosticism at Yale, New Haven, Connecticut, March 28–31, 1978,* vol. 2: *Sethian Gnosticism* [ed. B. Layton; SHR 41; Leiden: Brill, 1980], 588–616); R. Majercik ("The Existence-Life-Intellect Triad in Gnosticism and Neoplatonism," *CQ* 42 [1992]: 475–76 and n. 2); and on the specific subgroup of "Platonizing" Sethian texts within the Sethian corpus (i.e., *Zostrianos, Allogenes,* the *Three Steles of Seth,* and *Marsanes*), see especially J. D. Turner, "Sethian Gnosticism: A Literary History," in *Nag Hammadi, Gnosticism, and Early Christianity* (ed. C. W. Hedrick and R. Hodgson; Peabody,

appears to refer in the *Life of Plotinus* (*Vit. Plot.*) chapter 16,[4] are dependent upon the *Commentary*, (3) that some version of these texts (and necessarily a *philosophical* version) was the subject of Amelius's refutation in forty volumes (as Porphyry tells us in the *Life of Plotinus*),[5] and (4) that Plotinus "replies" in the four works of the *Großschrift*[6] to gnostic doctrine in general and also, probably in part, to some version of the gnostic texts. I therefore make the *Commentary* Middle Platonic (of Neopythagorean provenance),

---

Mass: Hendrickson, 1986), 55–86; idem, "Gnosticism and Platonism: The Platonizing Sethian Texts from Nag Hammadi in Their Relation to Later Platonic Literature," in *Neoplatonism and Gnosticism* (ed. R. T. Wallis and J. Bregman; Albany: SUNY Press, 1992), 425–59; idem, "Typologies of the Sethian Gnostic Treaties from Nag Hammadi," in *Les textes de Nag Hammadi et le problème de leur classification: Actes du Colloque tenu à Québec du 15 au 22 Septembre, 1992* (ed. L. Painchaud and A. Pasquier; Québec: Les Presses de l'Université Laval; Louvain: Peeters, 1995), 208–11; and B. Pearson, "The Tractate *Marsanes* (NHC X) and the Platonic Tradition," in *Gnosis: Festschrift für Hans Jonas* (ed B. Aland; Göttingen: Vandenhoeck & Ruprecht, 1978), 373–84.

[4] On this general question see C. Schmidt, *Plotins Stellung zum Gnosticismus und Kirchlichen Christentum* (TUGAL 20; Leipzig: J. C. Hinrichs, 1901); C. Elsas, *Neuplatonische und Gnostische Weltablehnung in der Schule Plotins* (Religionschichtliche Versuche und Vorarbeiten 34; Berlin and New York: de Gruyter, 1975); J. H. Sieber, "An Introduction to the Tractate *Zostrianos* from Nag Hammadi," *NovT* 15 (1973): 133–40; idem, "Introduction" to *Zostrianos* (NHC VIII, *1*) in *Nag Hammadi Codex VIII* (ed. J. H. Sieber; NHS 31; Leiden: Brill, 1991), 19-25; M. Tardieu, "Les trois stèles Seth," *RSPT* 57 (1973): 545–75; James M. Robinson, "*The Three Steles of Seth* and the Gnostics of Plotinus," in *Proceedings of the International Colloquium on Gnosticism, Stockholm, August 20–25, 1973* (ed. Geo Widengren; Kungl. Vitterhets Historie ock Antikvitets Akademiens Handlingar, Filologisk-filosofiska serien 17. Stockholm: Almqvist & Wiksell; Leiden: Brill, 1977), 132–42; B. A. Pearson, "The Tractate *Marsanes*," 373–84; idem, "Introduction" to *Marsanes* (NHC X) in *Nag Hammadi Codices IX and X* (ed. B. A. Pearson; NHS 15; Leiden: Brill, 1981), 244–50; idem, "Gnosticism and Platonism: With Special Reference to *Marsanes* (NHC 10, *1*)," *HTR* 77 (1984): 55–73; J. D. Turner, "The Gnostic Threefold Path to Enlightenment," *NovT* 22 (1980): 324–51; idem, "Sethian Gnosticism: A Literary History," 55–86; idem, "Gnosticism and Platonism," 425–60; idem, "Typologies of the Sethian Gnostic Treatises," 208–11; P. Claude, *Les trois stèles de Seth* (BCNHT 8; Québec: Presses de l'Université Laval; Louvain-Paris: Peeters, 1983), esp. 26–33; Luise Abramowski, "Marius Victorinus, Porphyrius und die römischen Gnostiker," *ZNW* 74 (1983): 108–28; and Ruth Majercik, "Existence-Life-Intellect Triad," 475–88.

[5] *Vit. Plot.* 16.

[6] This is a single work, the "large work," recognized as such by R. Harder, "Ein neue Schrift Plotins," *Hermes* 71 (1936): 1–10, which was divided by Porphyry into four separate treatises: 3.8 [30]; 5.8 [31]; 5.5 [32]; 2.9 [33].

put the Sethian gnostic texts after the *Commentary,* and place the *Großschrift* and subsequent treatises in the *Enneads* as in some measure developing innovative philosophical solutions in reply to gnostic, and other, challenges and problems. This theory has the two virtues: (1) that it takes Porphyry's own witness (*Vit. Plot.* 16) about these Sethian texts seriously and (2) that Plotinus's own express view[7] that there is little or no *doctrinal* originality in his work can now be seen to be true, without our losing sight of the *philosophical* originality that marks every page of the *Enneads.*

My paper for the seminar is divided into two parts (part 1 dealing with the *Anonymous Commentary* and part 2 chiefly with Plotinus and the Sethian gnostic texts) and is too lengthy for inclusion here. So I shall simply summarize some of the major arguments in each part, adding such detail as is necessary.

1. The Anonymous Commentary on the Parmenides

1) Hadot's view is based, in large measure, upon an interpretation of Plotinus and Porphyry.[8] For Porphyry, the One is the "Father" of the intellectual triad, Father-Power-Intellect, and thus the One becomes in a sense its "idea," form, preexistence or pure indwelling unrestricted being. The doctrine of the *Commentary* presupposes the Plotinian One and Intellect but derives Intellect from the One in a way that is unfamiliar to Plotinus. I argue that this is not the case. In many different ways—e.g., the doctrine of Intellect, the First One as "idea" of the Second One, the doctrine of "participation," the distinction between infinitival and participial being, and the use of triads—the *Commentary* can be seen to be much closer to the thought of Plotinus and Amelius. Let me first take up some major points in the interpretation of Plotinus by comparison with the *Commentary:*

In Plotinus—as in Middle Platonism—the "One" is sometimes conceived as "Absolute Being" (unrestricted being or seeing) or real self, not only in 6.8 [39], where Plotinus stresses the One's positive, unrestricted being as pure activity and free creative, selfhood, but also in more orthodox passages, against the background of a stricter negative theology. For example, 6.8 [39].14.42: καὶ γὰρ πρώτως αὐτὸς καὶ ὑπερόντως αὐτός; 6.7 [38].40.41: καθαρὸν δὲ ὂν νοήσεως εἰλικρινῶς ἐστιν ὅ ἐστιν; 5.5 [32].9.13–15: ὥστε ἔστι καὶ οὐκ ἔστι, τῷ μὲν μὴ περιέχεσθαι οὐκ οὖσα, τῷ δ' εἶναι παντὸς ἐλευθέρα οὐδαμοῦ κωλυομένη εἶναι.[9] In 5.5 (32).7 (as elsewhere in the

---

7 *Enn.* 5.1 [10].8.

8 See below Appendix I: "The Theses of Pierre Hadot on the Anonymous *Parmenides Commentary* and Porphyry."

9 6.8 [39].14.42: "for he is primarily self and self beyond being"; 6.7 [38].40.41: "But being clear of thought is purely what it is"; 5.5 [32].9.13–15: "so it is and is

Enneads) intellect withdraws into itself and finds pure unalloyed selfhood there within, a selfhood that transcends duality and yet is problematic in that it transcends all forms of determinate signification: "it was outside and again not outside"; there is no "whence": "it appears and does not appear." This veiling of intellect from other things and its simultaneous self-gathering (ἀπὸ τῶν ἄλλων καλύψας καὶ συναγαγὼν εἰς τὸ εἴσω) is a vision of pure light, not "one in another" (i.e., accidental attribution) but αὐτὸ καθ᾽ἑαυτὸ μόνον καθαρὸν ἐφ᾽ αὐτοῦ ἐξαίφνης φανέν.[10] Transcendent selfhood is, therefore, the intimate, self-dependent, but indwelling root of all other selves. In the *Commentary* the Second One substantializes itself by participation in the First One, which is being for it, but the First One remains the ground of its being and identity.[11]

On the question of self-substantiation, Plotinus is very close to this view, but that the First One is the ultimate ground of all identity is a fundamental (if ambiguous) part of Plotinus's thinking. The transcendent One is often only one step of discourse away (e.g., 6.3 [43].8.18–20; 9.3ff.; 11.25–27), the implicit underpinning of the whole argument who, nevertheless, sometimes shines through explicitly. This is particularly true of significant parts of the great work on the omnipresence of being, "one and the same simultaneously," 6.4–5 [22–23]. At the beginning of 6.5 [22].1, for instance, Plotinus makes the startling statement that all human beings spontaneously recognize that the God in each and every one of us is one and the same. This can help us, he suggests, to reflect upon the omnipresence of real being.[12] The principle upon which he bases this is Aristotle's law of noncontradiction, which Plotinus understands to be a law of intelligible identity[13] and which he holds is prior to all particulars and even the first postulate of practical reason, which states that all things desire the good; for this latter principle is itself

---

not; it is not because it is not in the grasp of anything, but because it is free from everything it is not prevented from being anywhere." All translations of Plotinus will be taken from the seven-volume Loeb edition by A. H. Armstrong, though they may occasionally be adapted.

[10] 5.5 [32].7: "But since Intellect must not see this light as external, we must go back again to the eye; this will itself sometimes know a light which is not the external, alien light, but it momentarily sees before the external light a light of its own, a brighter one.... Just so Intellect, *veiling itself from other things and drawing itself inward,* when it is not looking at anything will see a light, not a distinct light in something different from itself, but *suddenly appearing, alone by itself in independent purity,* so that Intellect is at a loss to know whence it has appeared...."

[11] P. Hadot, *Porphyre et Victorinus,* vol. 2, frgs. 13–14, 106–12.

[12] Cf. K. Corrigan, "Amelius, Plotinus and Porphyry on Being, Intellect and the One," *ANRW* 2.36.2: 984 n. 37.

[13] As does Aristotle, in *Metaph.* 1010b19–37.

founded upon unity and the desire for unity. Plotinus then goes on to make
the transition from unity to identity explicit, and the ultimate ground of this
transition is pure selfhood which is "the good": Τὸ γὰρ ἓν τοῦτο προϊὸν μὲν
ἐπὶ θάτερα, ἐφ' ὅσον προελθεῖν αὐτῷ οἷόν τε, πολλὰ ἂν φανείη τε καί πως καὶ
εἴη, ἡ δ' ἀρχαία φύσις καὶ ἡ ὄρεξις τοῦ ἀγαθοῦ, ὅπερ ἐστὶν αὐτοῦ, εἰς ἓν ὄντως
ἄγει, καὶ ἐπὶ τοῦτο σπεύδει πᾶσα φύσις, ἐφ' ἑαυτήν. Τοῦτο γάρ ἐστι τὸ
ἀγαθὸν... (6.5 [22].1.14–19).[14] Clearly, this unity that proceeds into multiplicity belongs in a discourse that relates to the intelligible universe; yet it
also implies the immanent presence of the transcendent Unity, which is that
universe's fundamental principle (18–21).

My point then might be stated as follows: were we only to possess
the above passages of the *Enneads,* we might quite legitimately suppose
in these a Middle Platonist view of the One as a primary Self, transcendent, yet immanent in a different way in the being of everything derivative. The two sets of fragments in the *Commentary* have a similar
framework of reference, but they are also modeled, I suggest, upon
another principle to be found in Plotinus, and one that must surely have
been essential to the pre-Plotinian Platonic tradition. The "First One" or
"First God" must for Moderatus, or Numenius for that matter, remain
immobile and transcendent "in its own place." But if the Second One is
genuinely to come from the First, then the transcendence of the First has
to be jeopardized when one comes to articulate what this derivation
means. In other words, what is unthinkable in a universe of discourse
that proclaims the utter transcendence of the First One has to become
thinkable if the Second One emerges from the First One and if its being
remains grounded in That One.[15] The derivation-problems, therefore, in
both the *Enneads* and the *Commentary* are similar. In other words, Plotinus's doctrine of intellect is not unique to him. Plotinus too holds that
this doctrine is not his own, and according to the testimony of Porphyry,
he believed that Amelius *shared* his views.[16] What we see in Plotinus is
not a new list of innovative doctrines so much as an unusually creative
way of *doing philosophy,* that is, of thinking out problems of interpretation, and problems of philosophy, by comparing problems and
attempted solutions in a whole host of ancient texts (Plato, Aristotle,

---

[14] 6.5 [22].1.14-19: "For this one, proceeding to the others as far as, and in the
way in which it can proceed, would appear as many and even, in a sense, be many;
but the ancient nature and the desire of the good, that is of itself, leads to what is
really one, and every nature presses on to this, to itself. For this is the good...."

[15] Cf. K. Corrigan, "Plotinus, *Enneads* 5, 4 (7) 2 and Related Passages. A New
Interpretation of the Status of the Intelligible Object," *Hermes* 114.2 (1986):
195–203; idem, "Amelius, Plotinus and Porphyry," 989–90.

[16] See *Vit. Plot.* 18.13–14.

Stoics, etc.), but above all by coming up with a creative dialectical way of thinking through these problems so that all of the underpinnings of a reasonable solution become lucid. Plotinus is not a doctrine-maker, but a philosopher.[17]

The logical order of generation too in the *Commentary* is similar to that in Plotinus.[18] In fragment 12, (1) the One is first utterly transcendent (104.23–25: ἐπέκεινα οὐσίας καὶ ὄντος); it is neither determinate being nor substance nor act (ἐνέργεια); yet (2) it is pure unrestricted activity (25–26: "but rather it acts and is itself pure activity," ἐνεργεῖ δὲ μᾶλλον καὶ τὸ ἐνεργεῖν καθαρόν), i.e., not determinate act or noun-thing, but pure activity— (τὸ εἶναι with the infinitive form); so that (3) there is implicit duality between infinitive and noun forms of "being" ("so that it is itself being which is before being," ὥστε καὶ αὐτὸ τὸ εἶναι τὸ πρὸ ὄντος); and (4) the full consequence is that the Second One by participating in this has from it derived being (Οὗ μετασχὸν τὸ <ἓ>n ἄλλο ἐξ αὐτοῦ ἔχει ἐκκλινόμενον τὸ εἶναι), which is what it means to participate in being (μετέχειν ὄντος). The commentator then goes on to elaborate on this double meaning: "So that being is double, the one preexists determinate being, while the other is that which is led out from the One which is transcendent of determinate being and which is being in the absolute sense and like the idea of determinate being, in which by participating another One has come to be to which is linked the being borne out from it" (106.29–35: Ὥστε διττὸν τὸ εἶναι, τὸ μὲν προϋπάρχει τοῦ ὄντος, τὸ δὲ ὃ ἐπάγεται ἐκ τοῦ ὄντος τὸ ἀπόλυτον καὶ ὥσπερ ἰδέα τοῦ ὄντος, οὗ μετασχὸν ἄλλο τι ἓν γέγονεν, ᾧ σύζυγον τὸ ἀπ᾽ αὐτοῦ ἐπιφερόμενον εἶναι).

First, the idea that being is led out of the One itself to which is linked another "one" and the duality of intellect is thereby constituted is a frequent feature of Plotinian arguments (even if in these contexts other terms are substituted for μέθεξις). In 5.3 [49].10 and 11, the state of "not yet being intellect" is one of "prethinking" (προνοοῦσα) and of touching (θιγγάνοντος); in the development of thinking, it "explicates" (ἐξελίττει), "will split itself" (διχάσει), so that "it comes out having taken something else in itself and made it many" (ἐξῆλθε δὲ ἄλλο λαβοῦσα ἐν αὐτῇ αὐτὸ πολὺ ποιήσασα 10.41–11.8).

Again in 5.5 [32].5.16-19 primary being "proceeded, so to speak, a little way from the One, but did not wish to go still further, but turned inwards and took its stand there [ἔστη] and became substance [οὐσία] and hearth [ἑστία] of all things." Or in 5.6 [24].2, the One appears as an intelligible object not in the sense that it thinks, but rather in that it is

---

[17] This is the assessment of both Plotinus (5.1 [10]) and Porphyry (*Vit. Plot.* 14).

[18] For the *Commentary,* see P. Hadot, *Porphyre et Victorinus,* 2:102–12.

primarily substantial for something else to think it; but what thinks it cannot *think* it as the purely One; rather it has to reach out to it and "take and hold the intelligible object which it thinks" (2.11) (clearly a form close to "participation"). What characterizes intellect, however, is that the intelligible object "is linked" (συνέζευκται) inextricably with every intellect (3.8 [30].9.8).[19]

Second, the notion of an implicit duality emerging out of pure unity and becoming established as the linking of a third "one" with a second "one" is clearly present in what appears to be a formulaic argument in Plotinus based on the μέγιστα γένη of Plato's *Sophist* and perhaps also on a development of the concept of κίνησις from Aristotle's *Physics*.[20] The argument occurs in 6.7 [38].13.16–21 and runs as follows: "If a simple moves, it holds that alone," Plotinus argues, "and either it is the same and has not proceeded or, if it has proceeded, another remains, so that there are two." As far as I can see, this first series of premises necessarily envisages (1) an immobile motion of super-motion; (2) a moment of identity based on *stasis;* and (3) a moment of burgeoning duality based on motion and *otherness.* Plotinus continues: "And if 'this' is the same as 'that,' it remains and has not gone forward; but if different, it has gone forth with difference and made from something same and something different, a third One." In the second part of the argument, Plotinus seems to suppose first a moment of abidingness (μονή), now internal to the implicit duality uncovered in the first series of premises, and coupled with a second moment of subsequent procession and autoconstitution. If this is correct, the whole argument functions as a series of disjuncts by which the total possible configuration of the emergence of a new duality is plotted.[21] As in the *Commentary,* Plotinus explores the ambiguity of the traveling subject in the logic of generation, a subject that specifies itself and its whole structure in the course of the argument. A similar argument appears in 6.2 [43].8: pure self-directed activity or seeing is not οὐσία; for οὐσία to arise there has to be a division of itself into τὸ ἀφ' οὗ (i.e., The One, but as object for itself) and εἰς ὅ, and thus it splits its suprasubstantial identity into "that" and "itself" and joins the two together in its movement (cf. 6.7 [38].39.2–9). As in the *Commentary,* so too in 6.7 [38].13 and 6.2 [43].8, there is a highest moment of identity with the First (prior to implicit and then explicit conversion) that remains a necessary facet of the self-articulating subject whose fullest development as a second

---

[19] Cf. 5.6 [24].2; 5.8 [31].4; etc.

[20] On the importance of major items in Aristotle's *Physics* to Plotinus's thought, see, for example, A. C. Lloyd, "Plotinus on the Genesis of Thought and Existence," in *Oxford Studies in Ancient Philosophy* (ed. Julia Annas; Oxford: Clarendon Press, 1987), 155–86.

[21] See K. Corrigan, "Amelius, Plotinus and Porphyry," 990.

principle is unspecified until the conclusion (cf. 5.3 [49].10.21–29). I suggest that such arguments in Plotinus are quite likely already formulaic in the Neopythagorean tradition of deriving a dyad from a monad and that they provide a similar sort of context to compare with the argument in fragments 11 to 14 of the *Commentary*.

The context for this sort of reflection about the derivation of intellect that the commentator undertakes is familiar to the commentator quite possibly from Plotinus,[22] but it is more plausible to suppose that the milieu for such reflections is pre-Plotinian, for Plotinus's language about the procession and conversion of being is clearly not his own invention and the idea that the First is transcendent while intellect's vision of the First as a duality is a function of the coyoking of intellect and intelligible object already has a formulaic ring to it even in Plotinus, as well it might, for the idea is already perfectly current in the *Chaldean Oracles* (even if the view of the *Oracles* is ambiguous). The highest intelligible object, frg. 1 of the *Oracles* informs us, is transcendent and beyond human thought: "you must not perceive it intently, but keeping the pure eye of your soul turned away, you should extend an empty mind toward the Intelligible in order to comprehend it, since it exists outside mind" (ἐπεὶ νόου ἔξω ὑπάρχει). One therefore has to grasp it by a form of nonknowing and by the "flower of mind" (νόου ἄνθει), that is, by the highest power of the soul akin to the apparently fiery essence of the First God. At the same time, according to frg. 20, "intellect does not exist without the intelligible, and the intelligible does not exist apart from intellect" (Οὐ γὰρ ἄνευ νοός ἐστι νοητοῦ, καὶ τὸ νοητὸν οὐ νοῦ χωρὶς ὑπάρχει).

Either these two fragments contradict each other[23] or the first refers to human cognition and the second to the ontological situation of the *Oracles'* Second Intellect.[24] The latter seems more plausible: these intelligibles, sown throughout the cosmos, frg. 108 informs us, are "inexpressible beauties" (κάλλη ἄφραστα) from the perspective of human cognition; from the perspective of the Second Intellect, intelligible object and subject are necessarily linked together.

If we now turn to the *locus classicus* in Plotinus for the derivation of intellect from the One, we can see at a glance that even here the structure is similar to that of the *Commentary*. In 5.2 [11].1.7–9, (1) the One is so perfect (2) that it overflows and (3) its superabundance has made

---

[22] See ibid., 991–93.

[23] Cf. E. R. Dodds, ed. and trans., *Proclus: The Elements of Theology* (Oxford: Clarendon Press, 1963), 287.

[24] As R. Majercik supposes, *The Chaldean Oracles: Text, Translation, and Commentary* (Studies in Greek and Roman Religion 5. Leiden: Brill, 1989), 140.

"another" (ἄλλο) (which from the point of view of the new implicit duality or, in other early texts in the *Enneads,* the "indefinite dyad," is still indefinite or not fully formed); then (4a) the product turns back to the One (and to itself—εἰς αὐτό without the appropriate breathing should probably refer to both, that is, to the One and to itself),[25] (4b) is filled (ἐπληρώθη), and (4c) becomes Intellect by looking towards it (αὐτό is again ambiguous).[26] (4a), (b), and (c) are equivalent in structure to the triad of fragment 12 of the *Commentary,* ὕπαρξις-ζωή-νοῦς, since (4a) logically entails a moment of pure being-as-object for intellect, (4b) articulates the content of that vision as a power in intellect for substantial multiplicity, and (4c) finally recognizes intellect itself as an explicit functional reality.[27]

What appears to be new in the *Commentary* is the distinction between infinitival Being and determinate, participial being (τὸ εἶναι and τὸ ὄν). Yet this too is an implicit part of Plotinus's theory. Τὰ ὄντα are the determinate entities that constitute intellect and, from one perspective, τὸ ὄν is the first determinate moment of intellect's own being (cf. 6.6 [34].8). By contrast, the One is beyond οὐσία or ὄν. The One is pure unrestricted, infinitival being: the One's τὸ εἶναι is not a determinate activity but an acting, creative power which comes by and from itself (cf. 6.8 [39].33ff.), in which what it is to be (essence) and pure being (existence) are *one.*[28] From this perspective, the first moment of what intellect will be is coincident with the infinitival being of the One, but distinct because it will culminate in intellect. Otherwise, as Plotinus quite often claims, there would be no distinction.[29] I shall return briefly to this question (see items 4 and 5 of part 2 below) because it bears upon Hadot's claim that there is no distinction between essence and existence in Plotinus and that the rudimentary beginnings of such a distinction are to be found in the *Commentary.*[30] This is in fact not true. Here, however, I wish to make a smaller claim, namely, that the background to an infinitive-being and a participial-being distinction is an implicit but necessary part of Plotinus's theory of derivation. The

---

[25] See K. Corrigan and P. O'Cleirigh, "The Course of Plotinian Scholarship from 1971 to 1986," *ANRW* 2.36.1: 590–92. Cf. 5.1 [10].6–7.

[26] 5.2 [11].1: "the One, perfect because it seeks nothing, has nothing, and needs nothing, overflows, as it were, and its superabundance makes something other than itself. This, when it has come into being, turns back upon the One and is filled, and becomes Intellect by looking towards it."

[27] Cf. K. Corrigan, "Amelius, Plotinus and Porphyry," 989.

[28] On this, see K. Corrigan, "Essence and Existence in the Enneads," in *The Cambridge Companion to Plotinus* (ed. L. P. Gerson; Cambridge and New York: Cambridge University Press, 1996), 103–29.

[29] See, for example, 6.7 [38].41.8–14.

[30] P. Hadot, *Porphyre et Victorinus,* 1:489–93.

superabundance of the One that is experienced by intellect as the shock of purest intensity and identity *is* pure identity and unrestricted Being in the One, and this is also indefinitely intuited by the implicit duality that emerges from the One's overflowing power. However, for intellect, it is the highest defined object that constitutes its intellectual being. Plotinus's "light-metaphysic" is perhaps the simplest example of this.[31] Light is different from the form and cause of the form's being seen, but it is seen "in" and "upon" the form (5.5 [32].7.1–6). Even when it is grasped intuitively on its own without an accompanying object, it is seen because it is founded upon something else (ibid., 8–9). Only when it is alone (μὴ πρὸς ἑτέρῳ) does it escape perception. Light, pure seeing, or transcendental identity of subject and object, is pure unity itself. Light "based" (ἐπερειδόμενον, 5.5 [32].7.9) on another is "being." In itself it is supra-intelligible, but for intellect it is substance (5.6 [24].2.8–10). As Plotinus argues in 6.2 [43].8.14–18, purely self-directed activity is not οὐσία, but being (ὄν) constitutes the termini, thus constituting the unity in distinctness of the two:

> For its self-directed activity is not substance, but being is that to which the activity is directed and from which it comes: for that which is looked at is being, not the look [τὸ γὰρ βλεπόμενον τὸ ὄν, οὐχ᾽ ἡ βλέψις]; but the look too possesses being [τὸ εἶναι] because it comes from and is directed to being [ὄν]. And since it is in act, not in potency, it gathers the two together [συνάπτει] and does not separate them, but makes itself that and that itself.

Pure light or the unrestricted activity of the One coincides, as it were, with purely self-directed activity, that is, not activity as a determinate act but pure creative effulgence (as we also find in the *Commentary*), which gives rise to an indefinite duality that the power of the One is *in it* to make substance (cf. 5.1 [10].6–7).[32] This purely self-directed activity that

---

[31] See generally R. Ferwerda, *La signification des images et des métaphores dan la pensée de Plotin* (Groningen: J. B. Wolters, 1965), 46–61; W. Beierwaltes, *Selbsterkenntnis und Erfahrung der Einheit: Plotins Enneade V.3. Text, Übersetzung, Interpretation, Erläuterungen* (Frankfurt am Main: Klostermann, 1991), 334–62; K. Corrigan, "Light and Metaphor in Plotinus and St. Thomas Aquinas," *The Thomist* 57 (1993): 187–99.

[32] On this see especially M. Atkinson, *Ennead V.1: On the Three Principal Hypostases: A Commentary with Translation* (Oxford and New York: Oxford University Press, 1983); F. M. Schroeder, "Conversion and Consciousness in Plotinus. Enneads 5, 1 (10) 7," *Hermes* 114 (1986): 186–95; K. Corrigan and P. O'Cleirigh, "The Course of Plotinian Scholarship," 590ff.; J. R. Bussanich, *The One and Its Relation to Intellect in Plotinus* (Leiden: Brill, 1988); P. A. Meijer, *Plotinus on the Good or the One (Ennead VI, 9): An Analytical Commentary* (Amsterdam classical monographs 1; Amsterdam: J. C. Gieben, 1992).

overflows to make another is then the pure existence of the One as the highest object *for Intellect* of Intellect's own self-constituting vision in which a world of determinate intelligible objects emerges as Intellect's own content and identity.[33] There is, therefore, a higher moment of pure indeterminateness in Intellect's generation that acts internally as developing *subject* and as a power for life and substantiality. This moment, however, as *object* of Intellect's own seeing is determinate being (τὸ ὄν) which embraces the determinate content (τὰ ὄντα) of Intellect's pluralizing vision. The roots then of the distinction between determinate being or beings and unrestricted being or activity are certainly to be found in Plotinus, and this distinction is not simply between intellect and the One, but there is an indeterminateness like the One at the origin of intellect that is *not* the indeterminateness simply of the substrate: intelligible matter.[34]

One further item in the *Commentary* is worth picking out: the One as the "idea of being" and the question of a participation of the intelligible world in both the First One and in what is effectively the highest moment of itself. Both of these items are not only Plotinian but recognizably Middle Platonic. In Plotinus, the One appears as the limit (πέρας) of intellectual beauty (6.7 (38).32.34), and since the limit of intellect is also the ἰδέα ἐν στάσει (6.2 (43).8.23–25),[35] the commentator's ὥσπερ ἰδέα τοῦ ὄντος— if post-Plotinian—is hardly innovative. In Numenius, the First Intellect or αὐτοάγαθον is the "idea" of the Second Intellect or demiurge because the latter is good by participation in the first. So this apparently Porphyrian innovation is decidedly Middle Platonic.

In other words, Hadot's thesis is not a necessary or the best interpretation of the evidence. Let me now take up the other major remaining points in turn.

2) Nothing prevents the so-called Plotinian Structure—One/Intellect/Soul—and the interpretation of the *Parmenides* associated with it from being Middle Platonic, as Plotinus tells us it is (in *Enn.* 5.1 [10]). So the account of Moderatus's thought in Simplicius[36] strongly suggests a much earlier origin for the Plotinian structure; and even if this account is glossed by Porphyry and refers to an interpretation of Plato's *Second Letter*,[37] not

---

[33] Cf. 5.2 [11].1; 6.2 [43].8; 6.7 [38].16.

[34] 6.7 [38].33 ad fin.

[35] Cf. Numenius frg. 16 des Places.

[36] See Simplicius *In phys.* 230.34–231.27 Diels.

[37] This is the view of H. D. Saffrey and L. G. Westerink, eds., *Proclus: Théologie platonicienne* (6 vols.; Collection des universités de France; Paris: Les Belles Lettres, 1968–1997), 2:xxx–xxxv, against Dodds, "The *Parmenides* of Plato and the Origin of the Neoplatonic 'One,'" *CQ* 22 (1928): 129–42.

the *Parmenides*, this does not eliminate (apparently *a silentio*) a Middle Platonic or earlier need to interpret the *Parmenides*. There is no explicit mention of the *Commentary* in Proclus's *Commentary on the Parmenides*,[38] but in discussing the "logical" and "metaphysical" interpretations of the *Parmenides*, Proclus appears to refer to Albinus on occasion and perhaps also to Origen the Platonist.[39] And in the *Life*, Porphyry cites Longinus as saying that Numenius, Cronius, Moderatus, and Thrasyllus wrote on the first principles of Pythagorean and Platonic philosophy.[40] If we put this together with Moderatus and other testimony about Neopythagorean thought, it becomes more plausible to suppose that this dialogue was not only interpreted "logically" by Middle Platonists, but also given a "metaphysical" exegesis in Neopythagorean circles. On balance, it is reasonable to suppose that some form of relatively continuous "metaphysical" interpretation of the *Parmenides* and other dialogues (e.g., *Theaetetus*) is older still. Surely, for instance, the system of Speusippus requires such an interpretive foundation.[41]

3) The *Commentary* espouses a (somewhat obscure) participation of the Second One in the First One, which amounts to a participation by developing intelligible reality in the highest idea of itself. Syrianus and Proclus make it clear that according to Porphyry there was only *one* participation—of αἰσθητά in intelligible reality, whereas in Numenius, Cronius, Amelius, and Plotinus there is also an intellectual participation.[42] So if the *Commentary* holds a similar "Middle" Platonic view, namely, an intellectual participation, then it *cannot* be by Porphyry.

4) In addition, there is one further feature of the *Commentary* that, in my view, necessitates a date earlier than Porphyry. Fragment 4 takes up the question of the One's relation to posterior realities and concludes with a strong statement of the One's transcendence, with the sole provision that

---

[38] Cf. J. M. Dillon, ed. and trans., *Proclus: Commentary on Plato's Parmenides* (Princeton, N.J.: Princeton University Press, 1987), xxivff.

[39] Proclus *In Parm.* 630.37–640.17 Cousin.

[40] *Vit. Plot.* 20–21.

[41] See J. M. Dillon, *The Middle Platonists, 80 B.C. to A.D. 220* (London: Duckworth; Ithaca, N.Y.: Cornell University Press, 1977), on Speusippus; T. Szlezák, "Speusipp und die metaphysische Deutung von Platons 'Parmenides,'" in *En kai Plêthos: Festschrift für Karl Bormann zum 65. Geburtstag* (ed. L. Hagemann; Würzburg: Echter, 1993), 339–73; C. Horn, "Der Platonische *Parmenides* und die Möglichkeit seiner prinzipientheoretischen Interpretation," *Antike und Abendland* 41 (1995): 95–114.

[42] Syrianus *In Metaph.* 109.21ff. Kroll; Proclus *In Tim.* 248e–249b; 3.32ff. See below Appendix II: "Intellectual Participation in the Anonymous *Parmenides Commentary*, Plotinus (and Numenius and Amelius), but Not in Porphyry.

"he never remains in ignorance of future events and has known past events" (2.78.32–34). Even if we take into account the author's possible concern here to explicate the temporal language of Plato's *Parmenides,* it is still not plausible to suppose that the most knowledgeable pupil and colleague of Plotinus could have written the above sentence after the detailed critique of a temporal, anthropomorphic paradigm for creative demiurgy that Plotinus had undertaken in 5.8 [31].7 and 6.7 [38].1–13 and that is crucial for understanding the major currents of his thought.

5) The existence-power-intellect triad, although not occurring explicitly in Plotinus, is more than likely pre-Plotinian: ζωή, for example, appears already as a middle term between being and intellect in Plotinus;[43] ὕπαρξις denotes existence in Sextus Empiricus, Galen, Alexander of Aphrodisias;[44] the verb ὑπάρχειν occurs in Numenius and the *Chaldean Oracles;*[45] and compounds of ὑπάρχειν occur in Plotinus to denote original existence or preexistence.[46] Damascius's attestation of an explicit Chaldaic triad, existence-power-intellect, weights the balance in favor of this view in spite of Hadot's unproven suggestion that, although ὕπαρξις may already have been substituted for πατήρ in the *Oracles,* the technical usage originated with Porphyry.[47]

6) Against the view that the gnostics in Rome (in light of the Plotinian circle criticism mentioned in *Vit. Plot.* 16) revised their revelations to

---

[43] 3.8 [30].8–10.

[44] Sextus Empiricus *Math.* 9.29–194; Galen *Institutio Logica* 2.5 Kalbfleisch; Alexander *De An.* 90.2–5 Bruns.

[45] Although ὕπαρξις does not occur in the extant fragments of the *Chaldean Oracles,* the verb occurs three times in relation to the First Principle: frgs. 1.12: ἐπεὶ νόου ἔξω ὑπάρχει; 20.2: Οὐ γὰρ ἄνευ νοός ἐστι νοητοῦ, καὶ τὸ νοητὸν οὐ νοῦ χωρὶς ὑπάρχει...; 84.3: for (the first connector) encompassing all things (in the singular summit of his own existence [ὑπάρξεως, Proclus]...) exists, himself, entirely outside (αὐτὸς πᾶς ἔξω ὑπάρχει). In the fragments of Numenius, the verb ὑπάρχειν occurs frequently (see especially frg. 12.5: φάσκοντες δεῖν τὸν πρότερον ὑπάρξαντα οὕτως ἂν ποιεῖν ἔχειν διαφερόντως).

[46] Although the later triad does not occur in the *Enneads,* ὕπαρξις in the sense of existence in connection with the One or with the primary existence of the object of thought is a feature of Plotinus's vocabulary, e.g., 6.6 [34].11.9–11: the one nature predicated of many must exist in itself (καθ' αὐτὸν ὑπάρχειν) before being contemplated in many; 6.7 [38].8.6: for it is already clear that the thought of horse existed (ὑπάρχειν) if (God) wanted to make a horse; 6.8 [31].6.17–18. Furthermore, the compound verbs συνυπάρχειν and προϋπάρχειν are used sometimes in contexts that suggest original existence, coexistence, preexistence, and consequently some kind of basic existential attribution (cf. 6.6 [34].10.49; 13.17, 48; 6.8 [39].9.28–29).

[47] See below Appendix III: "Did the Existence-Life-Mind Triad Originate with Porphyry?"

conform more closely to the teachings of the great Porphyry,[48] I argue the following:

First, there had to be something *philosophically* objectionable to Plotinus's circle in the first place (to trigger a forty-volume refutation by Amelius). These treatises might later have been revised, but they must have contained a *casus belli* to start with, i.e., a sophisticated but objectionable appropriation or straightforward use of the παλαιὰ φιλοσοφία (i.e., the "traditional" ancient philosophy).[49]

Second, the explicit gnostic triads are plausibly pre-Plotinian, Platonic elaborations in the Chaldean tradition of the type that Amelius develops, and the method of paronyms (as well as the principles of predominance and implication) is also familiar to Middle Platonism—in, for example, Sextus Empiricus, Albinus, the *Corpus hermeticum,* etc.[50]

Consequently, a Middle Platonic authorship for the *Anonymous Commentary*[51] is the *simplest* and most plausible hypothesis on the basis of both the direct and the indirect evidence. So the *Anonymous Commentary* cannot have been written by Porphyry, but the most reasonable interpretation of the evidence is that the fragments of the *Commentary* we possess were a common source both for the gnostics and for Plotinus, Amelius, and Porphyry (which does not automatically preclude further "exchanges of ideas" or further redactions of the gnostic texts we now possess). Whatever the case might actually have been, and however many revisions might have been made to these gnostic treatises before their eventual burial in the Egyptian desert, the texts we possess are (1) most likely to be *in nuce* what Plotinus, Amelius, and Porphyry actually read and (2) to have been dependent upon some earlier or contemporary Platonic commentary on the *Parmenides* such as was also available and read in the Plotinian school. So the *Commentary* may well have been one of those works that were read in the meetings of the Plotinian circle. Porphyry mentions the names of Severus, Cronius, Numenius, Gaius, Atticus, Aspasius, Alexander, Adrastus, and others. We can eliminate Severus, Gaius, Atticus, Aspasius, Alexander, and Adrastus for obvious reasons.

---

[48] R. Majercik, "Existence-Life-Intellect Triad," 486.

[49] On the παλαιὰ φιλοσοφία, see esp. J. Igal, "The Gnostics and 'The Ancient Philosophy' in Plotinus," in *Neoplatonism and Early Christian Thought: Essays in Honour of A. H. Armstrong* (ed. H. J. Blumenthal and R. A. Markus; London: Variorum, 1981), 138–49, and for some of its content for the Plotinian circle see *Vit. Plot.* 14.

[50] See below Appendix IV: "The Pre-Plotinian Character of the Gnostic Triads."

[51] Ὕπαρξις, προέννοια, and other such terms, are all significantly pre-Plotinian. The apparently distinctive Porphyrian ὁ ἐπὶ πᾶσιν θεός occurs in the *Commentary* (Hadot, *Porphyre et Victorinus,* vol. 2, frg. 10.96.14). It seems highly unlikely, however, that we can base any reasonable case upon the restriction of such an obviously Platonic phrase to so late a Platonist as Porphyry.

Numenius himself would have been too well known for a commentary at his hand to become "anonymous." Cronius might seem to have the qualifications we seek: Platonist, lesser well-known companion of Numenius, Neopythagorean background; but probably similar considerations apply to him as to Numenius. So, we simply do not know who the author was, and this has the virtue of keeping it "anonymous," while placing it in the general Platonist-Neopythagorean milieu of the late second or early third century, which would provide sufficient time for it to have exerted the influence it certainly appears to have had on the Platonizing gnostic texts.

2. Plotinus and the Sethian Gnostic Texts

In part 2 of my original paper, I went on to develop a different approach to the problems of these texts in order to determine what relation there might be between the *Commentary*, Sethian gnostic texts, Middle Platonism, and Neoplatonism. Here I shall give a brief summary of part 2. I argued for the plausibility of the following theses: (1) that the Sethian gnostic texts (*Allogenes* and *Zostrianos,* in particular) are dependent upon the *Commentary* rather than vice versa; (2) that we need a much wider view of Middle Platonism than has been hitherto supposed; that in Middle Platonism, especially Numenius, Albinus, even Amelius, one of the hidden problems of *Timaeus*-interpretation, possibly prompted by gnostic attacks and appropriation of Plato, was the development of a prefigurative intelligible biology within which the interpretation of Aristotelian thought in the service of Plato started to figure more prominently; (3) that this trend, evident in the *Commentary* and to a lesser extent in the existence-essence distinctions in the Sethian gnostic texts, led to a new and much more developed distinction between essence and existence in Plotinus; (4) that this Plotinian distinction is to be related in the first place (i.e., chronologically) to the *Großschrift* as a whole and that it most likely presupposes (a) the more rudimentary version of the triadic distinction of the *Commentary* and (b) the more varied version of the Sethian gnostic texts; and finally (5) that important elements in the structure of the *Großschrift* presuppose significant motifs, images, and ideas in the Sethian gnostic texts (e.g., θεωρία, φύσις, the intelligible earth-sky-air motif, etc.). My view of the *Großschrift* is that the first three treatises prepare for and contextualize the overt critique of 2.9 [33].

Let me sum up several of the more important matters in turn:

1) First, a comparison between *Allogenes* XI,3 48,6–49,37 (and also *Zost.* 64,7–75,11) and fragments 13–14 of the *Commentary* demonstrates that these texts are dependent upon the *Commentary* or its equivalent (for the ultimate provenance of the thought must be Platonic-Pythagorean, given the emergence of a second One as an indefinite movement that by conversion knows both itself and its principle).

2) Second, in Albinus, Numenius, the *Anonymous Commentary, Chaldean Oracles,* and Amelius, there appears to be a growing interest in the problem of how being, life, and thought (from both Platonic and Aristotelian viewpoints) come to be prefiguratively articulated in an eternally actual intellect in such a way that the natural compounds of our experience (architects and artisans) bear that intelligible imprint at the very root of their own creativity.[52] A similar process is clearly also at work in the Neopythagorean linking of monad and triad to the Aristotelian *dynamis-hexis-entelechy* progression.[53] We find elements of this Aristotelian and Platonic language in both the *Commentary* and the Sethian gnostic texts, but the triadic schemata of the former are relatively simple, set out in serial succession, whereas in the latter they are more complex; there are interlinking moments such as we find in Amelius and a greater variety and proliferation of triads, an indication that the Sethian gnostics are working innovatively with an earlier Platonic text or texts and with what they take to be, at least, a shared tradition. In Plotinus again, there is a more developed form of triadization or the linking of δύναμις and ἐνέργεια, for Plotinus is not concerned with schemata but with the linking of the generative process and the dynamic nature of a hypostasis by means of a single thought pattern, which articulates the complexity of the hypostasis.[54]

---

[52] See below Appendix V: "Numenius and Amelius."

[53] The process of Aristotle-interpretation starts long before Plotinus, and there were presumably many forces at work in its inception, not least, one might hope, open-mindedness. As early as the second century C.E. in the Platonic-Pythagorean tradition, some sort of Aristotle-interpretation is clearly at work (if the terminology of later testimonies can be trusted) in the equivalence of μονάς to potency/ seed/power and τρίγωνον or triad to ἐντελέχεια/fully realized activity. Theon of Smyrna, a Platonist of the early second century, argues that the monad is said to be triangular not κατὰ ἐντελέχεια but κατὰ δύναμιν, for as the seed (σπέρμα) of all numbers, the monad possesses a triaform power (τριγωνοειδῆ δύναμιν) (*Exp.* 37.15–18 Hiller). His contemporary, Nichomachus of Gerasa, expresses a similar view: ἵνα καὶ τρίγωνος δυνάμει φαίνηται ἡ μονάς, ἐνεργείᾳ δὲ πρῶτος ὁ γ' (*Arith. Intro.* 2.8, p. 88, 9–10 Hoche).

[54] 6.7 [38].17 argues that intellect's life is the trace of the giver, which "shines out" from the One as "manifold and unbounded" (17.20–21: πολλῆς καὶ ἀπείρου οὔσης, ὡς ἂν παρὰ τοιαύτης φύσεως ἐκλαμψάσης). It was (ἦν) indefinite in so far as it *looked* to That (βλέπουσα), but in so far as *it had looked* (βλέψασα) it became limited in itself without implying any limit in the One. The tenses, imperfect, present, and aorist, are an interesting and typical feature of Plotinian discourse (e.g. 6.7 [38].16.31–35; 4.8 [6].1.1–11, etc.), which tends to distinguish phases or moments in the complex generation of intellect by use of different tenses (often within a single, interlacing sentence) rather than by serial representation (such as we find in the *Commentary*). The effect is a sort of stereoscopic picture rather than a serial,

3) Third, in 6.7 [38].1–42, Plotinus develops a new and highly subtle distinction between essence and existence (or determinate and unrestricted being), one that will surely help to determine and shape all subsequent thought on this question, but one that links together over the course of some forty chapters (a) the Aristotelian Nous with *dynamis-entelechy* theory,[55] (b) a prefigurative intelligible biology in relation to the *Timaeus* and gnostic claims about the making of the world,[56] (c) the hyper-intelligible significance of ordinary things (e.g., breathing, existing, desiring, loving, living, etc.),[57] and (d) the different extensions of being, life, and thought.[58] This distinctive Plotinian view about existence and life forms an integral part of Proclus's approach in his own *Commentary on the Parmenides*[59] but is conspicuously lacking from the anonymous *Commentary*. Had this commentary been written by Porphyry, it is impossible to believe that such a theory would have been absent.

4) Fourth, this later essence-existence distinction is foreshadowed significantly (and for the first time in the *Enneads*) in 3.8 [30].9 and 5.5 [32].12 of the *Großschrift,* and in both cases there is a certain resonance with gnostic thought. For Plotinus—at least in part by contrast with *some*

---

planispheric representation. A particularly good example is 6.7 [38].16.20–21: πληρωθεὶς μέν, ἵν᾽ ἔχῃ, ὃ ὄψεται. It is worth noting that this technique, particularly that of the single interlacing sentence, runs right through the *Enneads.* The early 5.2 [11].1.7–13, effectively a single sentence, unites all the moments of generation in one complex thought process. By contrast, the approach in the anonymous *Commentary* is less subtle and more *seriatim,* which is a further indication that the *Commentary* is pre-Plotinian. By and large, Plotinus avoids schematic triads, for he is concerned to link the generative process and the dynamic nature of a hypostasis by means of a single thought pattern that articulates the complexity of the hypostasis. For a different reason I date the Platonizing Sethian gnostic texts after the *Commentary*. The triadic schema of the *Commentary* is relatively simple, and both major versions of it (Existence-Life-Thought/Being-Vitality-Mentality) clearly relate to Middle Platonic preoccupations as evinced particularly in Albinus, the *Chaldean Oracles,* and the Neopythagoreans. In the Sethian gnostic texts, there is some evidence of the same sort of linking of moments we have found in Amelius (see especially *Zost.* VIII 15,1–20; 17,1–5; cf. *Chald. Or.* frg. 4), and in addition there is much more variety and proliferation of triads, an indication that the Sethian gnostics are working innovatively, and according to the already established gnostic manner, with an earlier Platonic tradition.

[55] See 6.7 [38].40 and generally K. Corrigan, "Essence and Existence," 105–29.

[56] See 6.7 [38].1–13; P. Hadot, *Plotin: Traité 38. VI. 7* (Paris: Cerf, 1988), 26–28.

[57] See K. Corrigan, "Essence and Existence," 122.

[58] Ibid., 116–22.

[59] *Corpus Platonicum Medii Aevi: Plato Latinus,* vol. 3 (ed. R. Klibansky and C. Labowsky, London: Warburg Institute, 1953), 54.

typical gnostic thought—(a) contemplation is an internal, creative process (not an apocalyptic *ab extra* spectator sport);[60] (b) the διάνοια must have something concrete and experiential upon which to ground itself;[61] (c) there is something in us that extends beyond intellect which is simultaneously grounded in the One's presence anywhere and everywhere even in the physical world "to anyone" (not just the "initiated");[62] (d) the power of the Good is the most extensive power *naturally* at work throughout the universe;[63] and (e) the full range of human faculties must be brought to bear to *test* the experience of ascent, for knowledge is a contemplative process of transformation and consubstantiality, not *praxis* or the performing of ritual *actions.*[64] Equally, Plotinus is concerned to distance himself from the gnostic view that there is an intelligible form of learned ignorance.[65] In other words, it is reasonable to suppose that Plotinus has

---

[60] 3.8 [30].1–7.

[61] 3.8 [30].9.16ff.

[62] 5.5 [32].9–12.

[63] Cf. 5.5 [32].12; 7.18.

[64] 3.8 [30].1–7; cf. 2.9 passim.

[65] In the case of ἀγνοεῖν, Plotinus is concerned not simply to argue that ignorance is possible only when the object remains outside, that ignorance should not be attributed to the Good, and that ignorance is ultimately ugliness (cf. 3.8 [30].9.15; 5.8 [31].2.33; 8.13; 10.37; 13.22); he also tries to point out how our own experiences can easily mislead us into thinking that ignorance has a spiritual, intelligible origin: "In the higher world, then, when our knowledge is most perfectly conformed to Intellect, we think we know nothing because we are waiting for the experience of sense-perception, which says it has not seen" (5.8 [31].11.33–35). In other words, Plotinus wants to repudiate the view that there is an essentially *intelligible* form or source of ignorance (at least in this content) (cf. 5.2 [11].1; 6.2 [43].8; 6.7 [38].16) but at the same time to provide a plausible explanation for anyone who can understand why people have supposed that an ignorant Demiurge or fallen *Sophia* are in some sense responsible for the ugliness of this world. This betrays a deeper and more comprehensive form of dialogue. Polemic is only a small part of this deeper critique, which wishes to show to the potential or implicit participant what the supposed meaning of his apparent philosophical beliefs and motives actually is. The gnostics might well be a group with whom one cannot have any sort of genuine conversation, and yet if they could be brought to question their own views, they would see why their present beliefs are inadequate yet at the same time plausible. To grasp the inadequacy of what one thinks and yet simultaneously to understand how one could have held such views is to have developed a more subtle and comprehensive view of reality and to be capable of living in a "bigger" world. In this sense, I think, while Plotinus's direct address in the first three treatises of the *Großschrift* excludes the gnostics, the wider scope of the subtext itself implicitly includes them.

inter alia a whole range of gnostic doctrines in mind here, and among them some of the Sethian gnostic texts mentioned by Porphyry.

5) Fifth, is this too subtle an interpretation of Plotinus? Not according to Hadot's own view of Plotinus's condensed, allusive interpretation of the Theogony myth, for example.[66] Furthermore, the levels of direct and indirect addressee are plainly to be uncovered in the text, and Plotinus's creative use of Aristotle at important moments (how he thinks through an Aristotelian problem in his own creative way) is perfectly demonstrable.[67]

So which comes first?—Sethian gnostic texts or the *Großschrift?* In my view, comparisons of the descriptions of the "living earth" in *Zostrianos* and *Allogenes* and *Enn.* 5.8.3–4, and of the "three-men" theories in the gnostic texts and in *Enn.* 6.7 [38].6–7, show as closely as one is going to get that the gnostic versions are not based on Plotinus, for nothing of Plotinus's real thought appears in those texts.[68] In other words, I suggest that in these works Plotinus—with the gnostics (and other Platonists) in mind—wants to show that even if we accept Platonic world-renunciation, the shadow-being of sensible things, and the call to ascend from things here, this does not commit us to the dead ranks of the unsaved, lost in the abyss of the sensible world, or to a spectacular, but external-Hollywood landscape of the elite, liberated, psychic human being. Liberation has to start from where one actually is situated, and the intrinsic connectedness of the physical human being with the higher levels of one's being, and even with the totality of intellect, must be a function, first, of the way one has been made, second, of one's proper definition, and, third, of one's present being.

So, I see the *Großschrift* as, in part, reacting to details in one or more of the Sethian texts (among other forms of Gnosticism) rather than the other way round, and I suggest that were it not for the challenge of Gnosticism to be an authentic interpreter of Plato and Aristotle, as well as of the myths that are so profound a part of the *Dialogues,* we might not have had the spectacular course of philosophical inventiveness we in fact do have in the middle to late *Enneads,* at least not in the form we now have them, showing as they do the simplicity and beauty of even the most ordinary and taken-for-granted, physical things.

My conclusion then is (1) that the *Anonymous Commentary* cannot be ascribed to Porphyry but must be pre-Plotinian, probably of

---

[66] P. Hadot, "Ouranos, Kronos, and Zeus in Plotinus' Treatise *Against the Gnostics,*" in *Neoplatonism and Early Christian Thought* (ed. H. J. Blumenthal and R. A. Markus; London: Variorum, 1981), 124–37.

[67] Generally on this question, see K. Corrigan, "'Solitary' Mysticism in Plotinus, Proclus, Gregory of Nyssa, and Pseudo-Dionysius." *JR* 76 (1996): passim.

[68] See below Appendix VI: "Plotinus's Independence from *Zostrianos* and *Allogenes.*"

Neopythagorean provenance (possibly from the "school" of Numenius and Cronius); (2) that the Sethian gnostic texts (in some form) predate the *Großschrift* and rely upon the *Commentary;* and (3) that we need to revise our standards of "originality" in order to appreciate the philosophical originality and subtlety of Plotinus more accurately and at the same time to situate the birth of Neoplatonism, as also of the more philosophical gnostic treatises, less stratigraphically or rigidly, and more in the context of so called "Middle Platonism" and "Neopythagoreanism," two rather fluid categories that serve in part to redeem our ignorance and the silences of the past.

Appendix I
The Theses of Pierre Hadot on the
Anonymous *Parmenides Commentary* and Porphyry

What are the essentials of Hadot's view (see bibliography for select list of major publications)? According to Hadot, Porphyry initiated the attempt to interpret and harmonize the teaching of Plotinus with the "divine revelation" of the *Chaldean Oracles*.[1] Like Numenius later, the *Oracles* recognize the existence of two intellects: a contemplative First Intellect or Father and a dyadic Second Intellect, both contemplative and demiurgic.[2] The *Oracles* describe these intellects in Stoicizing Middle Platonic terms as "fiery" in nature and situated in a transcendent *empyrean* realm (*Chald. Or.* frgs. 3, 5, 6, and 10 Majercik). There is also a third principle, a feminine Power (δύναμις) that links the Father Intellect and the Intellect fully actualized that emerges from him: "For power is with him [σὺν ἐκείνῳ], but Intellect is from him [ἀπ' ἐκείνου]" (*Chald. Or.* frg. 4).

On the basis of this oracle, the later Neoplatonists—beginning with Porphyry[3]—found in the *Oracles* a primal triad of Father-Power-Intellect in accordance with the three-in-one principle or triadic monad operative in every ordering (frg. 27: "For in every world shines a triad, ruled by a monad"; cf. frg. 22) and in the triadic ordering of the Platonic ideas (frg. 22: "For the Intellect of the Father said for all things to separate into three..."). The triad, existence (ὕπαρξις)-power-intellect does not occur explicitly in the extant fragments, although Damascius frequently attributes such a triad to the *Oracles* (*Dub. et sol.* 2.3.5–6; 2.36.2–6; 2.71.1–6 Westerink and Combès). Consequently, Hadot suggests the strong possibility that the word ὕπαρξις was already a substitute for πατήρ in the *Oracles*.[4] Although the existential use of ὕπαρξις and ὑπάρχειν occurs in Stoic, Epicurean, and Middle Platonic

---

[1] Hadot, *Porphyre et Victorinus,* 1:482–85.

[2] Numenius frg. 18 des Places (*Numénius: Fragments* [Collection des Universités de France; Paris: Les Belles Lettres, 1973]); *Chaldean Oracles,* frg. 7 Majercik (*The Chaldean Oracles: Text, Translation, and Commentary* [Studies in Greek and Roman Religion 5; Leiden: Brill, 1989]).

[3] *De regressu an.* 36.15–19; 38.7–10 Bidez; Hadot, *Porphyre et Victorinus,* 2:96 n. 2.

[4] Hadot, *Porphyre et Victorinus,* 1:267 n. 7.

usage as well as in Plotinus, the technical usage is to be attributed to Porphyry, who uses the term in the *Parmenides Commentary* to signify the idea of pure, unrestricted being prior to substance or οὐσία, i.e, determinate, substantial being.[5] This usage is also to be found in Marius Victorinus, where it is translated by the Latin word *exsistentia* to distinguish it from *substantia*.[6] Since *exsistentia* is not attested in Latin before Victorinus, then it is most likely to be attributed to Porphyry's philosophical usage. For Porphyry, then, ὕπαρξις as pure unrestricted being was equivalent both to the Plotinian One and the Chaldean Father, and the result was a coordination of the two triads at the level of the First Hypostasis: Father-Power-Intellect and Existence-Life-Intellect.[7] So according to frg. 9.1–8 of the *Commentary*, Porphyry interprets frg. 3 of the oracles ("the Father snatched himself away and did not enclose his own fire in his intellectual power") to mean that although the One "has snatched himself away from all that is within him, nevertheless his power and intellect remain co-unified in his simplicity." This Porphyrian solution results in a conception of the Chaldean First God as a three-in-one deity and was very congenial later to both Synesius and Marius Victorinus, but it was rejected by all later Neoplatonists who located the Chaldean triad beneath an utterly transcendent One.[8] According to Proclus, Porphyry was the first to give these triads a formal structure on the basis—at least in part—of his reflection upon the *Oracles* (*In Tim.* 3.64.8–65.8).

This provides an overview of the context of Hadot's view. On what principles precisely is his assessment of Porphyry's authorship of the *Commentary* founded? As we have seen in part, the fragments of the *Commentary* express, for Hadot, a doctrine more in line with Porphyrian than Plotinian metaphysics. According to Porphyry, the One is the "Father" of the intellectual triad, Father-Power-Intellect, and thus the One becomes in a sense its "idea" form, preexistence, or pure indwelling unrestricted being. This dual nature of the One—transcendent and yet immanent—is to be found in the earlier fragments of the *Commentary* in which, while there is an emphasis upon the One's transcendence and the superiority of negative theology over positive affirmations about God, the One is also "the only true being" (τὸ μόνον ὄντως ὄν) and everything apart from the One is unreal.[9] The One is even "really itself" (ὄντως ἑαυτός) (*Abst.* 3.27.226.16; 1.29.107.7, 8 Nauck).

---

[5] Ibid., 1:112–13; 267ff.

[6] *Ar.* 3.7.9 in ibid., 2:29, text 40; cf. also Calcidius *In Tim.* 289.3 and C. H. Kahn, "On the Terminology for Copula and Existence," in *Islamic Philosophy and the Classical Tradition: Essays Presented By His Friends and Pupils to Richard Walzer on His Seventieth Birthday* (ed. S. M. Stern, A. Hourani and V. Brown. Columbia, S.C.: University of South Carolina Press, 1972), 155 and n. 22.

[7] Cf. Kahn, "On the Terminology," 151–58; Hadot, *Porphyre et Victorinus*, 1:260–72; Proclus *In Tim.* 3.64.8–65.8; and J. M. Dillon, *Iamblichi Chalcidensis: In Platonis Dialogos Commentariorum Fragmenta. Edited with Translation and Commentary* (Philosophia Antiqua 23; Leiden: Brill, 1973), 356–58.

[8] Cf. Majercik, "Existence-Life-Intellect Triad," 476–86; *Chaldean Oracles*, 138–42.

[9] Hadot, *Porphyre et Victorinus*, vol. 2, frg. 4.76, esp. 26–28; cf. Corrigan, "Amelius, Plotinus and Porphyry," 985.

In the final fragments whose subject is the One-Being (τὸ ἕν ὄν), that is, the second hypothesis of the *Parmenides*, the Porphyrian character of the thought, so distinct from that of Plotinus, is even more emphatic. The One-Being is said to be in one sense identical with the One, in another not. For as a product and image of the One it has something of the One's nature; but as a One-Being it is no longer purely "One."[10] A particularly difficult statement from Plato's *Parm*. 142b, "if the One is, it participates in Being [οὐσία]," is interpreted to mean that the One in its pure activity is itself Being (τὸ εἶναι) prior to determinate being (πρὸ τοῦ ὄντος). Here the commentator introduces the celebrated distinction between unrestricted, infinitival being (τὸ εἶναι), that is, the article with the infinitive of the Greek verb, and determinate, participial being (τὸ ὄν), that is, the article with the neuter participial form of the verb to express being as a determinate or dependent entity.[11] In this relation, the One becomes the idea of the Second One; in Hadot's words, it becomes "sa pré-existence, son être et, puisque le second Un est l'Étant, le premier Un devient l'Être absolu, conçu comme un pur agir qui engendre la Forme."[12] As Hadot sees it, this new development, so foreign to Plotinus, helps to reconcile the absolutely simple Plotinian First Principle with the First God of the *Oracles*, who contains within Him a preexistent Power and Intellect (see above on *Oracles* frg. 3), and this development is supplemented by a distinction between two states of intellect (a rudimentary form of which we find already in Numenius), one in which intellect is perfectly unified and another in which it is explicitly deployed as the intellectual triad, existence/ὕπαρξις–life/ζωή–thought/νόησις.[13] As we have observed above, the first of these states is beyond the subject-object distinction and is identical with the First One. The second is no longer one and simple except in its first moment, pure existence, in which it is identical with the One itself.[14] Now while both Plotinus and Porphyry posit two states of intellect, corresponding to Numenius's First and Second Intellect-Gods, the difference, according to Hadot, is that in Plotinus these states are never intended to explain the generation of intellect, whereas in Porphyry "il s'agit de montrer que l'Intelligence pré-existe dans l'Un avant de se distinguer de lui."[15] Hadot even goes so far as to claim that Porphyry did not understand Plotinian doctrine or that he took the impression that Plotinus and the *Oracles* were teaching the same thing under different formulas.[16]

For Hadot, moreover, the distinction between τὸ εἶναι and τὸ ὄν involves two transpositions that are altogether characteristic of Porphyry: first, a transposition of the Stoic relation between ὕπαρξις and ὑπόστασις, and second, a transposition of the Aristotelian distinction between the being of a thing and the thing itself. According to the former, the Stoic understanding of ὕπαρξις as belonging to the incorporeal,

---

[10] Hadot, *Porphyre et Victorinus*, vol. 2, frg. 9.98.7–9)

[11] Ibid., frgs. 9–12, 98–108.

[12] Ibid., 1:484.

[13] Ibid., vol. 2, frgs. 13–14.

[14] Ibid., vol. 2, frg. 14.110.5–111.34

[15] Ibid., 1:484.

[16] Ibid., 1:482–83.

predicative order, and dependent upon the ontological fullness of substance, is transposed into the transcendent preexistence that ὕπαρξις now signifies. According to the latter, the opposition in Aristotle is one between the concept of a thing and its concrete reality. This is now transposed into a new Platonic understanding in which the concept becomes the existential predicate defining the essence of the thing.[17] Consequently, in Hadot's assessment, the distinction between τὸ εἶναι and τὸ ὄν in Porphyry does not yet signify a full distinction between essence and existence so much as a new step on the road to such a distinction, and one that points to the discovery of Being "comme actualité transcendante."[18]

Porphyry, therefore, according to this account, seems to be the only candidate for authorship of the *Commentary*. But why does the *Commentary* have to be post-Plotinian? There are several fundamental reasons why Hadot thinks that this is the only reasonable interpretation of the evidence. First, it must be post-Plotinian because it presupposes the Plotinian doctrine of the One. The principle that guides the exegesis of the *Parmenides* is in accord with Plotinian thought. In particular, the correspondence between the first hypostasis (The One) and the first hypothesis (of the *Parmenides*), and the second hypostasis (Intellect) and the second hypothesis is characteristic of Plotinian *Parmenides*-interpretation.[19] Second, the *Commentary's* doctrine of intellect presupposes that of Plotinus insofar as the commentator seems to paraphrase a passage on pure thought from *Enn.* 6.9 [9].6 as well as to depend on hints in Plotinus of a state of intelligence in which this transcends itself and coincides with the One;[20] but at the same time Porphyry goes much further than this and tends to distinguish "two intelligences": "Il semble bien que Porphyre ait voulu, par cette doctrine, rendre compte de la procession de l'Intelligence, en faisant coincider avec l'Un l'Intelligence 'qui ne peut rentrer en elle-même,' pour marquer ensuite fortement la continuité entre cette Intelligence originelle et l'Intelligence en acte, qui s'engendre elle-même comme Intelligence."[21] Third, while Plotinus in *Enn.* 6.9 [9].6 does not affirm that the One is pure thought, Porphyry supposes an absolute, simple, transcendent knowing that has no object and which is identical to the One itself.[22] Fourth, the commentator uses the being-life-thought triad to describe the dynamic process of Intellect's "autoposition" in a way that is clearly post-Plotinian insofar as this derives from Plotinus's doctrine of the internal identity of subject and object, a unity-in-duality, which springs from intellect's contemplation of the One itself.[23] For these fundamental reasons, therefore, Hadot places the date of the *Commentary* between 270 c.e. and the first half of the fifth century: the *Commentary* presupposes the Plotinian doctrine of the One

---

[17] Ibid., 1:487–90.

[18] Ibid., 1:493.

[19] Ibid., 1:104.

[20] Ibid., 1:122–24, 134; cf. *Enn.* 6.9 [9].3.27; 5.5 [32].8.24; 6.7 [38].35.30; 6.8 [39].18.21; 5.3 [49].14.14.

[21] Ibid., 1:135.

[22] Ibid., 1:124.

[23] Ibid., 1:104, 139ff.

and Intellect, as well as the Plotinian interpretation of the *Parmenides,* but in such a way as to go well beyond Plotinus's views, transforming, developing, perhaps even misunderstanding and degrading them, but maintaining simultaneously a dependence upon and clear connection with them.[24]

Finally, on the basis of evidence from the *Commentary* and Marius Victorinus, Hadot has tried to reconstruct Porphyry's metaphysics. At the top of Porphyry's metaphysical system there was an ennead or three triads, each designated ὕπαρξις-δύναμις-νοῦς, expressing the transition from the One to Intellect. In the first triad, equated with the One, ὕπαρξις predominates, while δύναμις and νοῦς are implicit or virtual. In the second triad, which represents the moment of unlimited movement away from the One, δύναμις predominates, and in the third triad there is the return and definition of νοῦς as such. According to Hadot, the members of this *Ennead* were also identified with various entities from the *Chaldean Oracles.*[25]

---

[24] Cf. ibid., 1:124ff., 482–83.

[25] Ibid., 1:361–75.

Appendix II
Intellectual Participation in the Anonymous *Parmenides Commentary,* Plotinus (and Numenius and Amelius), but Not in Porphyry

On this question, what Syrianus (*In Metaph.* 109.21ff. Kroll) and Proclus (*In Tim.* 248e–249b = 3.33.31ff.) appear to deny to Porphyry is not a participation of intellect in the One but a participation of the intelligibles in the ideas. At first sight, the *Commentary* would seem only to espouse a participation in the First One, not a participation of intelligible reality *in itself.* Closer inspection, however, yields a different picture. True it is, as Hadot indicates, that the commentator offers two different explanations of participation without attempting to reconcile them (something characteristic of Porphyry), namely, that the phrase "the one participates in substance" means, first, that the One is mingled (συνηλλοίωται) with substance and, second, that the second One participates in being which is the First One.[1] Nonetheless, according to the latter interpretation, the Second One receives being from the idea of being which is the First One, which is to say that participation in the First One is simultaneously participation in the generative idea of intellect which is the first moment of intellect's own being; and this is surely to make the equivalent claim that determinate being or beings participate in the highest object of their own vision, i.e., the ideas *qua* unified in the Good. Thus, the commentator tells us that such participation is not participation in a "one," but in a one "participating in being (τὸ ὄν), not because the first was being [ὄν], but because an otherness from the One has turned it around to this whole one-being" (104.17–20). Thus, by participating in the idea of itself "another one has come to be to which is yoked to

---

[1] Hadot, *Porphyre et Victorinus,* vol. 2, frgs. 11–12, 98–106.

the being borne out from it" (106.33–35). All of this is not very clear—which is a very good reason for supposing that it is more primitive than Plotinus, who despite considerable obscurities is generally far less oracular; but it seems much closer to Numenius's notion of participation or even that of Amelius, both of whom introduce participation into the intelligible world (Numenius frg. 16 [μετουσία] des Places). The second Intellect "participates" in the First or, according to Syrianus, the intelligible participates in the highest ideas.

However, elements in Plotinus's thought suggest a similar participation. At 6.5 [23].4.17–24 τὸ μετέχον participates both in the One and in τὸ μετ' αὐτό. That Plotinus is thinking of intelligible reality is confirmed by the "first, seconds, and thirds" (τὰ ὄντα) "in the intelligible" in the line immediately following and by the circle analogy of chapter 5, in which each radius is an extension of its center in all the centers (6.5 [23].4.17–24: "For even if we may be talking about something else after the One itself, this again will be together with the One itself and what is after it [τὸ μετ' αὐτοῦ] will be around that One and directed to that One and like something generated from it in close touch with it, so that what participates in what comes after it has also participated in that One [τὸ μετέχον τοῦ μετ' αὐτὸ κἀκείνου μετειλη-φέναι]. For, since there are many things in the intelligible, firsts and seconds and thirds, and they are linked like one sphere to its one center, not disparted by distances, but all existing together with themselves, wherever the thirds are present, the seconds and firsts are present as well" (cf. 6.5 [23].5 passim). Similarly in 6.6 [34].10.13–15, the sentence "when number already existed the things which came to be participated in the 'so many'" (μετέσχε τὰ γενόμενα τοῦ τοσαῦτα) is difficult, but τὰ γενόμενα in this context must refer to all beings, sensible and intelligible, for the focus of the discussion has been upon the movement of essential number from unity to multiplicity among real beings (and so τοσαῦτα at lines 10, 12, 13 is specified by τὰ ὄντα at line 9 and αἴτιος προών at line 13): "If then they are not as many as they are just casually, number is a cause which preexists their being so many: that is, it was when number already existed that the things which came to be participated in the 'so many' [μετέσχε τὰ γενόμενα τοῦ τοσαῦτα], and each of them participated in the 'one' so that it might be one" (ἕκαστον μὲν τοῦ ἕν μετέσ-χεν, ἵνα ἕν ᾖ). Again, in 6.7 [38].32.30ff., intellect is specifically τὸ μετέχον, and in participating in Beauty, it participates not only in the shapeless Beauty of the One but in the unshaped beauty of the product of One itself (i.e., intellect), which beauty is not "in" intellect (as in a substrate) but strictly speaking in itself: "Therefore, the productive power of all is the flower of beauty, a beauty which makes beauty. For it generates beauty and makes it more beautiful by the excess of beauty which comes from it.... But since it is the principle of beauty it makes that beautiful of which it is the principle, and makes it beautiful not in shape; but it makes the very beauty which comes to be from it to be shapeless, but in shape in another way; for what is called this very thing [shape] is shape in another, but by itself shapeless. Therefore, that which participates in beauty [τὸ ... μετέχον] is shaped, not the beauty." Thus the participant intellect participates in the highest moment of itself, which would be identical with the One were it not πρὸς ἑτέρῳ (to use the language of 5.5 [32].7): "but when there is nothing there but the medium, the eye sees [the light] by an instantaneous immediate perception [ἀθρόᾳ προσβολῇ], though even then it sees it based upon something different, but if it is alone and not resting on something else [μόνον δὲ αὐτὸ γενόμενον, μὴ πρὸς ἑτέρῳ], the sense is not able to grasp it."

It would seem, therefore, that there is a similar theory of intellectual participation to be found in Numenius, Amelius, Plotinus, and the *Commentary,* but not in Porphyry.

Appendix III
Did the Existence-Life-Mind Triad Originate with Porphyry?

On the basis of Damascius, Hadot tentatively suggests that ὕπαρξις may already have been substituted for πατήρ in the *Oracles,* as we have seen above, but traces the technical usage of ὕπαρξις to Porphyry.[1] Nonetheless, the positive evidence of Damascius is surely crucial in this issue (in the absence of anything to the contrary), whereas the argument that the technical sense originates in Porphyry is inconclusive, to say the least, and fraught with serious difficulties, at best. In the *Sententiae* Porphyry distinguishes the hypostases clearly (e.g., *Sent.* 10.4.8–10; 12.5.7–8; 25.15.1–2) and in a fragment of the *Historia Phil.* he refuses any kind of coordination (συναριθμεῖσθαι ... συνκατατάττεσθαι) between the One and intellect (frg. 18.15.8–12 Nauck). In his commentary on the *Oracles,* however, he seems to have identified the One and intellect. As Damascius tells us, "the principle of all things" (the One) is identified with the "father of the noetic triad" (intellect) (*Princ.* 1.86.9ff. Ruelle). As if to complicate matters further, Proclus tells us that intellect, according to Porphyry, is eternal, but possesses something preeternal in it (προαιώνιον) which links it (συνάπτειν) to the One (*Plat. Theol.* 1.11.51.4–11 Saffrey-Westerink), and in the fragment of the *Historia Phil.* cited above there is also a reference to a preeternal phase of intellect (frg. 18, 15, 1–3 Nauck). Hadot links these with Victorinus and the anonymous *Commentary,* and on the basis of Lydus's testimony that Porphyry put an ennead at the top of his metaphysics in dealing with the *Chaldean Oracles* (*Mens.* 157.5–8) attempts to reconstruct Porphyry's metaphysical system.[2] If we add to this the work being done on Arabic sources that contain several doctrines apparently similar to those in Hadot's Porphyry-Victorinus comparison (e.g., the first cause is τὸ εἶναι and is the cause of the being of things and of their form, whereas intellect is cause only of form), then Hadot's argument for Porphyry seems quite strong.

But is this necessarily so? The question is: Did Porphyry bring this interpretation to his study of the *Oracles* alone, or did he then apply it to his own metaphysical system? As Andrew Smith has pointed out,[3] we may also ask whether our evidence derives from Porphyry's *Commentary on the Chaldean Oracles* or "also from casual citations (with interpretation) of the *Oracles* in otherwise straight

---

[1] Hadot, *Porphyre et Victorinus,* 1:267–68, 112–13.

[2] Cf. A. Smith, "Porphyrian Studies Since 1913," *ANRW* 2.36.2:739–40.

[3] Ibid., 740.

metaphysical expositions." Furthermore, did Porphyry's enneadic interpretation of the *Oracles* arise out of a solution to the "purely metaphysical problem of transcendence," or was this complex structure prompted by the *Oracles* in the first place, or did some cross-fertilization of ideas take place? Given the present state of our evidence, we shall probably never be able to give a definite answer to these questions, but I suggest that in his own metaphysical system Porphyry followed a recognizably Plotinian view of the relation between the One and intellect according to which there was a preeternal, transcendent phase of intellect from which intellect in the proper sense derived. It is not necessary to suppose that the evidence about a preeternal phase necessarily relates to Porphyry's *Commentary on the Chaldean Oracles,* for it is clearly Plotinian. Συνάπτειν is a verb Plotinus commonly employs in similar contexts. Although Plotinus does not use the word προαιώνιος, and although he rejects a rigid dichotomy of intellect in 2.9 [33].1, a prenoetic, pre-eternal phase in the unified totality of intellect's generation from the One is a part of his thinking. On the other hand, Damascius's vexation with Porphyry's Chaldeanism might easily he explained by the sources Damascius had available to him or by allusions to the *Oracles* (with interpretation) "in otherwise straight metaphysical expositions."[4] Consequently, on the basis of the positive evidence before us, there seems little reason to suppose that the technical sense of ὕπαρξις and the triads, ὕπαρξις-ζωή-νόησις/ὕπαρξις-δύναμις-νοῦς, should have originated with Porphyry. All the positive evidence indicates that they are most probably pre-Plotinian.

[4] Ibid.

Appendix IV
The Pre-Plotinian Character of the Gnostic Triads

The explicit gnostic triads are much more plausibly pre-Plotinian Platonic elaborations in the Chaldean tradition, of the type, for instance, that Amelius develops in a Neopythagorean manner.[1] Second, all the positive evidence, as we have argued above, points to the pre-Plotinian origin of some variant of the ὕπαρξις-δύναμις-νοῦς triad. Third, the method of paronyms that seems to give rise to the ὀντότης-ζωότης-νοότης triad is surely also familiar in Middle Platonism. Αὐτότης and ἑτερότης are attested to in "Pythagorean" thought by Sextus Empiricus (*Math.* 2.248–84), and in Albinus (*Did.* 10.164), in a section on God, there occurs a triad of adjectival epithets (αὐτοτελής-αὐτοτελής-παντελής) followed by five substantial ones: divinity (θειότης), substantiality (οὐσιότης), Truth (ἀλήθεια), Symmetry (συμμετρία), Good (ἀγαθόν). Θειότης and οὐσιότης also occur in the *Corp. herm.* 12.1. So the method of paronyms is also conspicuously Middle Platonic and so too are the principles of predominance and implication, an admittedly rudimentary version of which we find in the passage immediately following in the *Didaskalikos:* the primary god is the

[1] On the impossibility of effectively distinguishing "Neopythagorean" and "Middle Platonic," see J. M. Dillon, *The Middle Platonists,* 341ff.

Good because he benefits all things according to their capacities, the Beautiful insofar as he is in his own nature perfect and commensurable, and Truth because he is
the origin of truth (164.32–40). There follows a passage that looks not unlike the
three principles of the *Oracles,* on the one hand, and that, on the other, also seems
to be involved in the same sort of demiurgic considerations that might have led
Amelius later to derive the triad, ὁ βουληθείς-ὁ λογιζόμενος-ὁ παραλαβών, from *Tim.*
30a (apud Proclus *In Tim.* 1.398.15ff.):

> he is Father [πατήρ] through being the cause of all things and bestowing
> order on the heavenly Intellect and the soul of the world in accordance
> with himself and his own thoughts. By his own will [βούλησιν] he has
> filled [ἐμπέπληκε] all things with himself, rousing up [ἐγείρας] the soul of
> the world and turning it towards himself [εἰς ἑαυτὸν ἐπιστρέψας], as being
> the cause of its intellect [αἴτιος ὑπαρχῶν]. It is this latter that, set in order
> by the Father [κοσμητείς], itself imposes order [διακοσμεῖ] on all of nature
> in this world. (*Did.* 10.3.164.40–165.4)

God is "Father" by virtue of his being and his thought; by virtue of his will all things
are filled; and by virtue of his power to convert the soul of the world, soul is finally
linked back through intellect to the Father. This compares quite strikingly with the
view of Amelius, presumably shaped by Chaldean and Numenian influences, as
reported by Proclus *In Tim.* 1.362.2–4: οὐκοῦν καθὸ μὲν νοῦς ὁ δημιουργός, παράγει
τὰ πάντα ταῖς ἑαυτοῦ νοήσεσι, καθὸ δὲ νοητόν ἐστιν αὐτῷ τῷ εἶναι ποιεῖ, καθὸ δὲ
θεός, τῷ βούλεσθαι μόνον (cf. also Proclus *In Tim.* 1.361.26–362.9). One might also
remark incidentally that in this relatively early passage in Albinus it is not overfan-
ciful to see rudimentary possibilities of triadic, even enneadic structures that are later
important, perhaps even controversial in Amelius, Plotinus, and others. Here, for
instance, the "Father" by his very *being* (αἴτιος ὑπάρχων) orders everything (intellect and the soul of the κόσμος), i.e., at the level of transcendent order. On the level
of *will,* however, the transcendent operation reaches into the content of everything,
wakes it up, and turns it back to the Father as its intelligibility. Finally, as a result of
the ἐπιστροφή, the soul of the world is rendered intellectual (*Did.* 165.2–30) and,
being properly ordered, herself sets the world in order (κοσμηθείς … διακόσμει).
Each movement is demiurgic, not entirely unlike the three demiurgic intellects in
Amelius later. Of course, they are not really distinguished in Albinus and, in addition, Amelius like Plotinus will emphasize the single primacy of existence and will
together. Nonetheless, the comparative similarity is worth remarking.

However this might be, if we can find important paronyms and rudimentary
versions of later triadic schemata, as well as of the principle of predominance, in
Albinus, not to mention Moderatus, Theon of Smyrna (*Exp.* 37.15–18 Hiller), Nicomachus of Gerasa (*Arith. Intro.* 2.8, p. 88, 9–10 Hoche), the *Chaldean Oracles* (frgs.
27, 26, 28, 29, 31; cf. frgs. 12, 23), Numenius, as well as the Stoics, and especially
Philo (*Abr.* 11.62–63),[2] which are related—according to admittedly later testimony—

---

[2] See also P. Hadot ("Être, vie, pensée chez Plotin et avant Plotin," in *Les sources de
Plotin* [Entretiens sur l'antiquité classique 5; Vandoeuvres-Genéve: Fondation Hardt,
1960], 126–28): Physics-Logic-Ethics/Nature-Doctrine-Practice/being-intelligence-life.

to triads in and enneadic interpretations of the *Chaldean Oracles,* there is less reason still to suppose that variant triadic terms in the Sethian gnostic texts must be
post-Plotinian. Finally, therefore, the supposition that we have only later philosophical versions of earlier primitive revelations, revised in the light of Porphyry's
criticisms, becomes much less plausible. And indeed it should perhaps be noted,
again in relation to the *Commentary,* that the enneadic structure of Porphyry's interpretation of the *Oracles* does not, in fact, appear there.

Appendix V
Numenius and Amelius

Numenius evidently thinks of divine intellectuality as analogous to the development and operation not only of human intellectuality, but also to the internal
operative functioning of the whole organism. In other words, at least one of the
problems that must have exercised Numenius was the problem of how mind, soul,
and body are prefiguratively distinguished, but also unified in the divine thinking—
a problem of no small philosophical and theological significance: How are we to
think of the total prefigurative unity of the living, sensible world in terms of the
intelligible world and its origin? And how are we to make this concrete and philosophically accessible in terms of the complex unity of what it means to be a human
being, and of what it means to be both other-knower and self-knower, after the
manner of the *Alcibiades* 1, while avoiding simple-minded anthropomorphism? In
Albinus this question is already tackled in relation to the tripartite prefiguration of
the tripartite embodied soul (*Did.* 178.40–45 Hermann; κριτικόν, ὁρμητικόν, οἰκει-
οτικόν). The first two of these parts even characterize aspects of the soul of the
Second God in Numenius (frg. 18 des Places). In the tradition of Albinus, this
becomes the problem of seeing the concrete relation between two or three intellectual activities and their implementation in the order of the physical universe.
Such a concern in Numenius is effectively the problem already of how to conceive
a primordial, intelligible biology in such a way that physical zoology and taxonomy
flow from it, since the world of the divine already pre-includes in its own way the
various articulations of the physical universe (cf. frg. 15.1; εἰσὶ δ'οὗτοι βίοι ὁ μὲν
πρώτου, ὁ δὲ δευτέρου θεου.... 9–10, ἀφ' ἧς ἥ τε τάξις τοῦ κόσμου καὶ ἡ μονὴ ἡ
ἀίδιος καὶ ἡ σωτηρία ἀναχεῖται εἰς τὰ ὅλα). Compare the striking down-to-earth
(Platonic) analogies for understanding the divine life: frg. 14, the giver and the gift;
frg. 13, the farmer and the planter; frg. 12, the spontaneous creation of life and the
animation of bodies from the glance of the divine (cf. the myth of Plato's *Politi-
cus*); frg. 18, the demiurge as pilot at sea (from the *Republic* and *Laws,* etc.). A strikingly similar conception of this prefigurative intelligible biology (very much in
accord with the passages on divine demiurgic activity in Albinus's *Didaskalikos*) is
also to be found in the *Chaldean Oracles* (see especially frg. 8 Majercik). In Numenius, then, we find, in a rudimentary way, an intelligible, explanatory schema of
the origin of life that takes account of all the major activities (thinking, deciding,

impulse, action, etc.) in the physical world and that attempts to reveal the divine in the simplest and most ordinary of physical activities.

According to a rather indirect testimony of Proclus, Amelius placed his three intellects or demiurges immediately after the One (unlike Theodore of Asine, who placed three distinct triads, intelligible, intellective, and demiurgic respectively, after the One; *In Tim.* 1.309.14–16). The testimonies of Proclus and Damascius do not provide very much evidence for any systematic reconstruction of Amelius's thought, and several different interpretations have prevailed at various times; for example, either that the demiurges are the three hypostases (King, Intellect, and Soul), each containing a triadic structure within itself and constructed according to will, contemplation, and demiurgic action in the strict sense;[1] or that there are three distinct noetic hypostases that Amelius multiplied because he could not understand the subtlety of Plotinian intellectual theory;[2] or that in Amelius we find instead of a tripartition of intellect, "fresh logical distinctions within each hypostasis," much like the logical realism of later Neoplatonism;[3] or finally that in Amelius's positing of three intellects there are really three different levels of a single hypostasis that betrays a unity in diversity very reminiscent of the Plotinian Intellect.[4] For a variety of reasons, this final interpretation almost certainly makes the best sense of a difficult issue. Amelius's "triad of demiurgic intellects" (Proclus *In Tim* 3.103.18–23) looks back to Numenius (on whom Amelius was *the* expert) but also bears a strong affinity to Plotinus's theory that intellect is a diversity-in-unity and betrays also some similar philosophical preoccupations to the thought of Plotinus, who was, after all, the close and valued colleague of Amelius.

Amelius divided intellect into three phases: "he who is," "he who has," and "he who sees." His theory was, in part, an interpretation of *Tim.* 39e, for Proclus tells us that he termed the first intellect "he who is" from the "really existing Living Creature," the second "he who has" from the phrases "dwelling in" (ἐνούσας) and third "he who sees" from the word καθορᾶν (*In Tim.* 3.103.18ff.; Plato *Tim.* 39e: "According then as intellect sees forms dwelling in the really existing Living Creature, such and so many as exist therein did he think that this world should also have"). Iamblichus criticized Amelius on the grounds that the "really existing Living Crea-

---

[1] Cf. J. Simon, *Histoire d'l'école d'Alexandrie* (2 vols.; Paris: Joubert, 1843–1845).

[2] Cf. E. Vacherot, *Histoire critique de l'école d'Alexandrie* (3 vols; Paris: Lagrange, 1846–1851; repr., Amsterdam: Adolf M. Hakkerty, 1965); E. Zeller, *Die Philosophie der Griechen in ihrer geschichtlichen Entwicklung,* vol. 3, ii (5th ed. rev. E. Wellmann; Leipzig: O. R. Reisland, 1923).

[3] Cf. A. H. Armstrong, ed., *The Cambridge History of Later Greek and Early Medieval Philosophy* (Cambridge: Cambridge University Press, 1967), 264; R. T. Wallis, *Neoplatonism* (London: Duckworth, 1972), 94.

[4] Cf. M. Massagli, "Amelio Neoplatonico e la Metafisica del Nous," *Rivista di filosofia neo-scolastica* 74 (1982): 225–43; K. Corrigan, "Amelius, Plotinus and Porphyry," 975–93; L. Brisson, "Amélius: Sa vie, son oeuvre, sa doctrine, son style," *ANRW* 2.36.2:793–860; H. J. Krämer, *Der Ursprung der Geistmetaphysik: Untersuchungen zur Geschichte des Platonismus Zwischen Platon und Plotin* (2d ed.; Amsterdam: B. R. Grüner, 1967), 87–88.

ture" is not different from the subject in which the forms indwell (*In Tim.*
3.103.18–28); and indeed in Amelius the precise function of a "possessing" intellect
that "does not exist, but they [i.e., the indwelling ideas] exist in him" (ibid., 22: οὐ
γὰρ ἔστιν ὁ δεύτερος, ἀλλ' εἴσεισιν ἐν αὐτῷ) remains obscure. At any rate, a certain
similarity with the three gods of Numenius must have been sufficiently clear
because Proclus goes on immediately to summarize the Numenian account according to which the first god functions as the really existing paradigm, the second acts
by πρόσχρησις as intellect (κατὰ τὸν νοῦν), and the third, again, by πρόσχρησις of
the second with the third, as demiurgic and reflective, strictly speaking (κατὰ τὸν
διανοούμενον) (ibid., 28–32).

In another passage (*In Tim.* 1.431.26–28) Proclus tells us that Amelius effectively identified the first of these demiurgic intellects with the intelligible object (τὸ
νοητόν) and saw the second and third as receiving definition within the sphere of
being. A more detailed explanation appears at *In Tim.* 1.306.1ff.:

> The first intellect is really what he is, the second is the object of thought
> in him but he has the object which is before him and participates alto-
> gether in that and for this reason is second; and the third is also the object
> of thought in him—for every intellect is the same as the object of thought
> linked to it [πᾶς γὰρ νοῦς τῷ συζυγοῦντι νοητῷ ὁ αὐτός ἐστιν] but he has
> the object of thought in the second intellect and sees the first [ἔχει δὲ τὸ
> ἐν τῷ δευτέρῳ καὶ ὁρᾷ τὸ πρῶτον].

What is striking about Amelius's view of the three intellects (τὸ ὄντα, τὸν ἔχοντα,
τὸν ὁρῶντα) that Amelius identified with the three Kings of Plato's *Second Letter*
(312e) and also with the Orphic triad, Phanes-Ouranos-Kronos (*In Tim.* 1.306.2,
10–14), of whom Phanes is demiurgic in the fullest sense (ibid., 13–14), is that from
the outset intellect is not an *object* as such, but first and foremost a *subject*. This
may well be a reflection upon Numenius's "Mosaic" notion of being (while being
is not characterized in the fragments as "I am who am," Numenius refers to Plato
as nothing other than Μωσῆς ἀττικίζων, frg. 8 des Places), but it also seems
designed to avoid an abstract or artificial, purely objective moment in the unfolding of intellect as a demiurgic whole, for Amelius is clearly concerned to interlace
the respective functions of the three intellects so that they represent a functional
totality, but one that remains grounded in the first instance upon a subject that in
turn is an object to be "held" by the second and third intellects, and to be seen as
fully expressed thinking only in the third. In other words, Amelius would appear
to have held the view (not unlike Plotinus), first, that intellect must be a traveling
subject, not simply an apparently independent *object* of thought; second, that subject and object cannot be linked retrospectively unless they are linked together in
identity from the beginning and in a subject that unfolds as a persistent but developing identity. The principle, that every intellect is identical with the object of
thought linked to it, makes this persistent identity clear. Third, it would also appear
that Amelius seeks to express (despite his reputation for long-windedness) in the
simplest and most accessible manner (being, having, and seeing) the necessary
logical and biological steps involved in the development of *anything* that possesses
more than minimal or rudimentary organization. In general, "to be" or "to exist"
is the most universal characteristic of all things, whereas "to have" is already to

possess in some measure a determinate constitution or potentiality for future determinate complexity; and "to see" or "to discern," in turn, is the fully realized activity of the earlier potentialities of "being' and "having."

It is therefore quite plausible to suppose that in Amelius (apart from exegesis of the relevant Platonic texts or of Neopythagorean doctrine and Platonic commentaries) there is also the remnant of a deeper philosophical reflection upon the Stoic triad, φύσις–ἕξις–ψυχή, and even more so upon the Aristotelian triad, δύναμις–ἕξις–ἐνέργεια, in so far as this is to be understood in relation to intellect itself. Implicit again behind this is a further hidden, and now lost, reflection upon the character of Aristotle's or Alexander of Aphrodisias's Νοῦς. Unlike Aristotle or Alexander, Amelius omits all mention of potentiality, passivity, or materiality in the context of intellect (at least as far as Proclus reports), but clearly behind the debate that prompts such a theory there must somewhere have been a concern to interpret the process or movement language in regard to intellect in Aristotle himself; as for example, at *Metaph.* 1072b13–20 in which: (a) intellect thinks itself κατὰ μετάληψιν τοῦ νοητοῦ; (b) *becomes* intelligible and identical with the intelligible in virtue of being the *recipient* of substance and intelligible object, and thus acts in *having* them (τὸ γὰρ δεκτικὸν τοῦ νοητοῦ καὶ τῆς οὐσίας νοῦς, ἐνεργεῖ δὲ ἔχων); and (c) the activity is "seeing" (θεωρία). As so often later in Plotinus and probably in Amelius, so also in Aristotle human mind and Divine Mind converge implicitly into one discourse.[5] At any rate, what we seem to see in Amelius is, first, some sort of *interpretation* of the being-having-seeing language (and attendant vocabulary) that Aristotle employs conspicuously (if somewhat strangely) of his own Νοῦς, and second, some concern to take into account the basic components that go to make up a fully realized ἐνέργεια or ἐντελέχεια, but now transposed or prefigured on the intellectual plane. If I am right, this is an important indication of a philosophical trend already rooted in Albinus's identification of God with the Aristotelian intellect and implicit perhaps in the double intellect or ἐνέργεια theory (i.e., "standing" and "moving") in Numenius (frg. 15 des Places). In Middle Platonic thought up to and including Amelius and Plotinus, the interpretive transposition of Aristotelian (and presumably Stoic) doctrines is a signal feature of basic philosophical practice, and of course the anonymous *Commentary* fits well into this milieu, for the interpretation of the structure of intellect is simultaneously Platonic and *Aristotelian.*[6]

Is this interpretation borne out by the rest of what we know about Amelius? There is no further confirmation regarding the interpretation of or reflection upon Aristotle, but that Amelius had in mind the intelligible prefiguration of later formal and material compound totalities is corroborated by other features of his thought preserved in Proclus. The first intellect is demiurgic by his very *existence* and by his *will* (as also in Plotinus's great work on Divine creativity and freedom, *Enn.* 6.8 [39]):

> in so far as the demiurge is intellect he brings all things forward by his thoughts [παράγει τὰ πάντα ταῖς ἑαυτοῦ νοήσεσι]; in so far as he is an intelligible object, he makes by his very existence [αὐτῷ τῷ εἶναι ποιεῖ]; in so far as he is god, he makes by his own will alone. (*In Tim.* 1.362.2–4).

---

[5] Cf. K. Corrigan, "Amelius, Plotinus and Porphyry," 983 n. 35.

[6] See especially Hadot, *Porphyre et Victorinus,* vol. 2, frg. 14.

If pure existence, will, and being *qua* νοητόν characterize the first intellect (which is described as οὐσιώδη, *In Tim.* 1.309.17), the second is an "intellectual substance" and "generative power" (*In Tim.* 1.309.17 ἡ δύναμις γεννητική), which apparently "reasons" or "takes account of" things (λογιζόμενος), for it makes by thinking and by the fact of thinking" (τῇ νοήσει καὶ τῷ νοεῖν, *In Tim.* 1.398.24) or by command alone" (ἐπιτάξει μόνον, *In Tim.* 1.362.24). This is presumably analogous to the Stoic λόγος ἐνδιάθετος and λόγος προφορικός, dependent as they quite probably are on the two kinds of discourse Plato discusses in the *Phaedrus* (cf. *SVF* 2:43.18; 74.4; *Phaedr.* 276a); which is to say that at the highest level, willed intention is equivalent to creation, whereas at the second level the expressed word becomes and makes reality. At this level, then, the second intellect is ranged in the category of the architect (κατὰ τὸν ἀρχιτέκτον, *In Tim.* 1.361.30–362.1).

At the third level, which, Proclus tells us, is the "truly demiurgic intellect" (*In Tim.* 1.309.24–25), the "intellect which sees" is the "source of souls" (πηγή ψυχῶν, 1.309.18) in the sense that it has "made its division right into the particulars" (1.309.19–20: τὸν δὲ καὶ τὴν εἰς τὰ καθ᾽ ἕκαστα διαίρεσιν πεποιημένον). (It should be noted that 1.309.14–20 appears to refer to Theodore, not Amelius directly.) What this means is unclear, although a comparison with *Enn.* 6.2 [43].21–22, and other treatises by Plotinus, might reasonably suggest that anything whatsoever that is in any way conformable to a λόγος (a reasonable "account" or "definition") could be regarded as intelligible in principle or as part of the prefigurative power of the third strictly demiurgic intellect. This intellect, then, is "that which has taken over" the physical world (*In Tim.* 1.398.23: ὁ παραλαβών) in the sense apparently that it enfolds that world inside soul and inside itself and in this way "fashions in cooperation the universe" (1.398.25–26: τίθησι μὲν γὰρ νοῦν ἐν ψυχῇ, ψυχὴν δὲ ἐν σώματι καὶ οὕτω συντεκταίνεται τὸ πᾶν) "by the work of his hand" (μεταχειρίσει) (1.398.25) and so is to be ranged in the category of work for himself" (κατὰ τὸν αὐτουργὸν τεχνίτην) (1.361.29–30). Amelius then is clearly concerned to develop an intelligible biology that reaches right down into the heart and content even of particular existences and prefigures the work of productive τέχνη or craft (in something of the way that Pseudo-Dionysius will later say that the more dissimilar an epithet from the life of God the more appropriate may be its attribution to divinity).

Amelius's view of Phanes seems to confirm this interpretation. Zeller thinks Phanes is the highest level of intellect; Massagli argues cogently that he is the lowest.[7] Whatever view one adopts, it seems clear from Proclus's accounts that Amelius sees intellect as including from within all that follows it, namely soul, the physical world, and all its content. Consequently, our interpretation of the intelligible prefiguration of the physical formal-material compound totality (by means of the Platonic notion of τέχνη) seems to be confirmed by other passages in Proclus. Furthermore, the view of Massagli that Amelius's three intellects are really three different perspectives of a single hypostasis is also confirmed by the evidence before us.[8] Despite Amelius's identification of these intellects with Plato's three Kings,

---

[7] For the former, see K. Corrigan, "Amelius, Plotinus and Porphyry," 983; on the latter, M. Massagli, "Amelio Neoplatonico," 233–37.

[8] M. Massagli, "Amelio Neoplatonico," 239–40.

Proclus speaks of one τριὰς τῶν δημιουργικῶν νοῶν (*In Tim*. 3.103.18–23), in other passages clearly envisages a unity of demiurgic activity (1.361.26–362.4; 398.19–21) to the point of echoing Plotinus (1.398.21–22: καὶ γὰρ οἱ πάντες εἷς εἰσι καὶ ὁ εἷς πάντες), identifies one of the levels of intellect as demiurgic *stricto sensu* (1.306.13–14; 336.22–23), and even reproaches Amelius for obscurity in treating the three as one subject (1.398.15–26). Amelius, we may reasonably conclude, is concerned with the problem of how being, life, and thought (both from Platonic and Aristotelian viewpoints) come to be prefiguratively articulated in an eternally actual intellect in such a way that the natural compounds of our experiences (architects and artisans) bear that intelligible imprint at the very root of their own creativity.

This is not a notion which starts with Amelius. It is present already in Albinus, Numenius, the anonymous *Commentary,* not to mention the *Chaldean Oracles* where the "flower of intellect" plays an archetypal role for the whole subsequent tradition (and the language of life and growth, if not the term ζωή itself, assumes a new intelligible significance; *Chaldean Oracles,* frgs. 37; 39.4; 16; 17; 33; 68 Majercik). Again, in the Hermetic and gnostic systems "life" assumes the role of a divine principle.[9] What we see by contrast in "late Middle Platonism" is a new attention to the prefigurative power of the Intelligible Universe and to its philosophical meaning. As a consequence, Aristotelian (and Stoic) thought clearly starts to assume greater significance.

---

[9] *Corp. herm.* 1.9, 12; 13.9; *Myst.* 267.4; E. R. Dodds, ed. and trans., *Proclus: The Elements of Theology* (Oxford: Clarendon Press, 1963), 253 n. 3.

Appendix VI
Plotinus's Independence from *Zostrianos* and *Allogenes*

First, *Allogenes* XI 59,10–61,32 furnishes indirect but strong support that Plotinus in 3.8 [30], and later, has this or a similar passage in mind, for the verbal parallels in Plotinus have a significantly different philosophical import than in *Allogenes* ("withdrawing to the rear," repeated three times; "placing oneself," "silently abiding"; "enlightened ignorance," etc.). Consequently, it makes no sense to suppose that the writer of *Allogenes* modeled himself on the *Enneads,* for almost nothing of the real, inner thought of the treatises we have been considering is contained in *Allogenes,* and if the writer had so modeled himself upon the *Enneads* we should have expected at least some reflection of this. It makes a lot more sense, therefore, to suppose that Plotinus's adaptation of philosophical motifs in *Allogenes* (themselves probably influenced by Middle Platonic thought: the *Chaldean Oracles,* for instance: retreat, looking both ways, etc.) is part of the creation of a complex, subtle appeal to people who, like him, were already familiar with these works.

Second, additional confirmation can be supplied by a comparison between *Zost.* VIII 48,3–26 and 3.8 [30].1–8 and 5.8 [31].3–4, from the descriptions of the "living earth." The *Zostrianos* passage runs as follows:

> Corresponding to each one of the Aeons I saw a living earth and a living water and (air) made of light, and fire that cannot burn [...], all being simple and immutable with trees that do not perish in many ways, and tares [...] this way, and all these and imperishable fruit and living men and every form, and immortal souls and every shape and form of mind, and gods of truth, and messengers who exist in great glory, and indissoluble bodies and an unborn begetting and an immovable perception.

> [Sieber's translation needs correction: VIII 48 [3] At each of the [4] aeons I saw a living earth, a [5] living water, luminous [air] [6] and an [unconsuming] fire. [7] All [these], being [8] simple, are also immutable [9] and simple [10] [eternal living creatures], [11] possessing a variety [of] beauty, [12] trees [13] of many kinds that do not [14] perish, as well as plants [15] of the same sort as all these, [16] imperishable fruit, [17] human beings alive with every species, [18] immortal souls, [19] every shape and [20] species of intellect, [21] gods of truth, [22] angels dwelling in [23] great glory with an [24] indissoluble body [and] [25] ingenerate offspring and [26] unchanging perception. JDT]

What we appear to have here, as John Dillon points out, is a comprehensive archetype of the physical world, right down to the tares among the wheat. There are also noetic archetypes of body, begetting (both of which Plotinus himself includes in the second of his great logical works, 6.2 (43).21–22, when he describes the teeming vitality and fecundity of the intelligible world—see especially 21.52–59), and perception (which forms part of the subject matter of 6.7 (38).1–7: αἴσθησις is a dim form of νόησις). Some of the details of this description are repeated at *Zost.* 55,15–25 and 113–17. The former passage (55,15–25) includes animals (which is again the subject of 6.7 [38].1–13, especially the problem how irrational animals are to be conceived as part of the content of intellect; 6.7 [38].9–10), and the latter (113–17) appears to describe the whole world contained within the Aeon, down to the "simple elements of simple origins" (cf. Plotinus's analysis of the simple elements κατὰ λόγον in 6.7 [38].11–12), and appearing quite remarkably similar to Plotinus's intelligible world: "All of them exist in one, dwelling together and perfected individually in fellowship and filled with the aeon which really exists" (*Zost.* VIII 116,7). What are we to make of this?

Let us compare the following passage from 5.8 [31].3–4, bearing in mind that much of the early chapters of 6.7 [38] might also profitably be compared with *Zostrianos.*

> ... but the gods in that higher heaven, all those who dwell upon it and in it, contemplate through their abiding in the whole of that heaven. For all things there are heaven, and earth and sea and plants and animals and men are heaven, everything which belongs to that higher heaven is heavenly ... for it is "the easy life" [cf. Homer, e.g., *Il.* 6.138] there, and truth is their mother and nurse and substance and nourishment—and they see all things, not those to which coming to be, but those to which real being belongs, and they see themselves in other things; for all things there are transparent, and there is nothing dark or opaque; everything and all things are clear to the inmost part to everything; for light is transparent to light. (5.8 [31].3.30–4.6).

Apart from the scriptural motifs in *Zostrianos* (e.g., "fire that cannot burn"; "tares") and a presumed dependence upon an earlier apocalyptic tradition, both passages are clearly dependent upon two of Plato's most famous myths, *Phaedr.* 247ff. and, especially, *Phaed.* 109dff. But beyond a striking general similarity, the two passages are really quite different. *Zostrianos* describes a remarkable edifying *spectacle* in which the subject ecstatically *perceives* an object of vision. Plotinus, on the other hand, reverses the mistake that Plato asserts people habitually make (i.e., "just as if someone seeing the sun and the stars through the water, should think the sun *was* the sky"; *Phaed.* 109c); we do make this mistake, but we make it in a sense because of the perfect transparency of the intelligible medium in which every intelligible object is manifested in and through every other. Plotinus, therefore, represents a *philosophical* picture, developed carefully as we have seen above throughout these treatises, in which subject and object are mutually transformed so that "they see themselves in others" (ἑαυτοὺς ἐν ἄλλοις): "everything there *is* heaven." Now it is striking that not one direct reflection of Plotinus's view of this sort of mutual transformation is to be found in any of the three *Zostrianos* passages. The idea of all things existing in one fellowship and filled with the aeon is perfectly Middle Platonic and gnostic. Consequently, if *Zostrianos* is modeled on Plotinus or even dependent in some minimal fashion, it is a resounding failure. Yet we have no reason to suppose that the author of *Zostrianos* was philosophically unsophisticated or incapable of recognizing a major philosophical difference, had he or she seen it. We must conclude, therefore, either that the resemblance between the *Enneads* and *Zostrianos* is purely coincidental or that Plotinus had read *Zostrianos,* wished to indicate *sotto voce* that this so-called vision is fundamentally Greek (which is at least partly why, I suggest, he quotes Homer, after his similar treatment of Hesiod's *Theogony*), and that there is more involved in such a vision than just a special kind of "intelligible" perception. If perception is at root intelligible and intellection aesthetic, this will have to be analyzed out in a different way in relation to the making of the physical universe and the nature of the intelligible universe, an analysis that Plotinus undertakes later in 6.7 [38]. However, it is also not plausible to suppose that there is only a coincidental resemblance between *Zostrianos* and the *Enneads,* because, for one thing, we have external, independent confirmation that Plotinus knew directly of this treatise. A reasonable conclusion is therefore that, 5.8 (31).3–4 is a subtle indirect critique and philosophical correction of *Zostrianos.*

THE SETTING OF THE PLATONIZING
SETHIAN TREATISES IN MIDDLE PLATONISM

John D. Turner
University of Nebraska-Lincoln

1. The Position of the Platonizing Treatises within Sethianism

Over the last decade, I have attempted to develop a hypothesis concerning the origins of Sethian Gnosticism on the basis of the topological and prosopographical similarities and differences exhibited by the various texts that are commonly agreed to form the Sethian corpus. It appears that the Sethianism of the Nag Hammadi treatises are the product of two distinct but not entirely unrelated speculative movements within or on the fringe of Hellenistic Judaism: (1) that segment of the wisdom tradition that was in conversation with contemporary Platonism, which I take to be the originating milieu of the "Barbeloite" speculation on the divine Wisdom and Name, and (2) the rather more eschatologically oriented form of speculation on the traditions concerning the primordial figures of Adam and Seth that gave rise to the sacred history of the Sethians. The name "Barbeloite" is inspired by Irenaeus's ascription of the theogonical and cosmogonical doctrine he describes in *Haer.* 1.29 to a group he calls "Barbeloites," a doctrine recognized by contemporary scholars as being nearly identical with that found in the four versions of the foundational statement of Sethian mythology, the *Apocryphon of John.*

The first movement conceived the receipt of revelation as a kind of baptism in wisdom, conceived as light or knowledge conferred on the recipient by the Logos or Voice or First Thought (Barbelo) of the supreme deity, who was conceived as a divine trinity, the supreme Invisible Spirit as Father, his First Thought Barbelo as divine Mother, and the divine Autogenes as her self-generated Child. Sometime in the first century this movement was influenced by Christian baptizing groups, causing these "Barbeloites" to identify this Autogenes Child with the preexistent Logos or Christ and construe him as the mediator of this saving baptism. The second group, which I call "Sethites" (in distinction from "gnostic" Sethians), conceived of revelation as deriving from certain ancient records containing the sacred history of the enlightenment of their primordial ancestors, Adam and Seth, records of which had been brought to light by a recent reappearance of Seth, the original and chief recipient of this revelation. The fusion of this group with the former group of previously Christianized "Barbeloites" resulted in an identification between Seth and Jesus found in several of the Sethian gnostic treatises.

It seems as if the baptismal rite was originally foreign to the pre-Sethian-gnostic Sethites and was adopted by them in the course of their contact with other baptismal movements, probably Christian or Christian-influenced, especially the "Barbeloites" responsible for the production of the theogonies featuring the figure of Barbelo as found in the *Trimorphic Protennoia* and the *Apocryphon of John*. At that point, the baptismal rite, called the "Five Seals," and its associated mythologumena became central to the self-definition of the Christian Sethianism reflected in treatises such as the *Trimorphic Protennoia,* the *Apocryphon of John, Melchizedek,* and especially the *Gospel of the Egyptians*. A central feature of the baptismal experience was the receipt of divine wisdom revealed in the course of immersion in ordinary water that also symbolized receipt of its celestial counterpart, the "living water" of divine illumination; it enabled an experience of transcendental vision resulting in total salvation.[1]

There are, however, certain Sethian treatises like *Allogenes* and the *Three Steles of Seth* that, although centered on the figure of Barbelo, not only lack Christian features typical of other Sethian treatises, but also define Sethian religious praxis in terms of a rite of contemplative ascent in which there appears to be no reference to an actual earthly baptismal rite. A median position in this spectrum of ritual practice is represented by the likewise non-Christian treatise *Zostrianos,* which conceives the stages of this visionary ascent as marked by nonearthly, celestial baptisms in the name of various transcendental beings, which suggests that the baptismal rite was the cultic setting within which the apparently nonbaptismal visionary ascension in Sethian treatises like *Allogenes* and the *Three Steles of Seth* arose. In the latter two texts, it appears that the ascensional rite has become detached from the older baptismal mystery, while in *Zostrianos* (and perhaps in the closely related treatise *Marsanes*) it is still associated with the baptismal rite, or at least interpreted in terms of it. None of these texts, however, mentions the "Five Seals."

---

[1] See J.-M. Sevrin, *Le dossier baptismal Séthien: Études sur la sacramentaire gnostique* (BCNHE 5; Quebec: Presses de l'Université Laval, 1986); my "Ritual in Gnosticism," *SBL Seminar Papers, 1994* (SBLSP 33; Atlanta: Scholars Press, 1994), 136–81, reprinted in the present volume; and my "To See the Light: A Gnostic Appropriation of Jewish Priestly Practice and Sapiential and Apocalyptic Visionary Lore," in *Mediators of the Divine: Horizons of Prophecy and Divination in Mediterranean Antiquity* (ed. R. M. Berchman; South Florida Studies in the History of Judaism 163; Atlanta: Scholars Press, 1998), 63–113.

Such detachment from the ritual practice defining a religious group's traditional understanding of the salvific process seems a rather radical step. Instead, in these four texts—including the two that maintain some baptismal conceptuality—the process of enlightenment is now presented in a new conceptual framework derived from a contemporary practice of contemplative, visionary ascent that seems modeled upon the vision of ultimate Beauty presented in Plato's *Symp.* 210A–212A, whose ascending stages of conceptual abstraction lead to a vision of ultimate Beauty.

Within the Sethian corpus, one therefore is justified in speaking of a specific subgroup of texts, the "Platonizing" Sethian treatises *Zostrianos, Allogenes,* the *Three Steles of Seth,* and *Marsanes.* What is most striking about these treatises is that they introduce into Sethian literature an entirely new fund of metaphysical conceptuality that draws heavily on the technical terminology of Platonic philosophy.

Assuming that comparisons between the Sethian treatises are not to be explained by interdependencies between versions to which we have no access, the obvious conclusion seems to be that these four texts represent a departure from an older Christian Sethianism in which both the baptismal rite and the Sethite primeval history played a fundamental role. Such a departure would most likely have been occasioned by an "orthodox" Christian rejection of the Sethian identification of Christ with the Autogenes as the preexistent Son of Barbelo and the Invisible Spirit, and of their notion that Barbelo had accomplished her third and final saving descent as the Logos—perhaps appearing as the figure of Seth in the guise of Jesus—bearing the celestial baptismal rite of the Five Seals. In such a situation, Sethian authors may have been forced to seek a less Christian and ritual-oriented interpretation of the transcendental theology of the Barbeloite tradition than that offered by baptismal rites or the Sethite speculation on Gen 1–6 typical of such texts as the *Apocryphon of John,* the *Trimorphic Protennoia,* and the *Gospel of the Egyptians.* The most hospitable environment for such a venture would be certain groups other than Christians who were committed to the philosophical articulation of biblical and other traditional wisdom along Platonic lines, such as the wing of contemporary Neopythagorean Platonism represented by Philo of Alexandria, Numenius, the *Chaldean Oracles,* and various members of Plotinus's seminars in Rome.

2. The Triadic Metaphysics of the Platonizing Sethian Treatises

The metaphysics of these Platonizing Sethian treatises is laid out on four levels, a highest realm beyond even being itself, below which one finds an atemporal, intelligible realm of pure being, followed by a psychic realm, characterized by time and motion, and finally a physical realm at the bottom of the scale.

The highest being, corresponding to the Plotinian One, is the Unknowable One or Invisible Spirit, characterized by nonbeing existence, silence, and stillness; it exists (in the Stoic sense of a τί, an actual entity), yet acts without mind, life, or existence or nonexistence, superior even to its own character, and is completely unknowable (*Allogenes* XI 61,32–64,14). It is "a unity of all that which [exists] in it and [outside] it and [remains] after it ... [the power of] all those [that exist, principle of every principle], fore[thought of] every thought, [power] of every power" (*Zost.* VIII 64,13–65,10).[2]

The second major level is that of the Aeon of Barbelo, the First Thought of the Invisible Spirit, characterized as a nondiscriminating, incorporeal, [timeless] knowledge (*Allogenes* XI 51,10–11). According to *Allogenes,* Barbelo is a tripartite Aeon that is subdivided into three levels resembling the Plotinian hypostases of Intellect and Soul: (1) the domain of "the authentic existents" (τὰ ὄντως ὄντα, the νοητά) presided over by Kalyptos, the Hidden One, a sort of νοῦς νοητός rather like the Plotinian Intellect; (2) the domain of "those who are unified" (i.e., "exist together,")[3] presided over by Protophanes, the First Appearing One, a sort of νοῦς νόερος rather like the Plotinian cosmic Soul; and (3) the domain of the "individuals" (perhaps individual souls) presided over by Autogenes (the Self-Begotten One, a sort of νοῦς διανοούμενος) who operates to rectify the realm of Nature, rather like the Plotinian individuated soul.[4]

---

[2] In *Marsanes,* there is even a yet higher entity, "the Unknown Silent One," beyond the Invisible Spirit and his Triple-Powered One, much the same as Iamblichus posited an "altogether ineffable" principle beyond even the Plotinian "absolutely One" that, together with a duality of principles (Limit and Unlimited, or the One and the Many), heads the noetic triad (apud Damascius *Princ.* 1.86.3–6; 101.14–15; 103.6–10 Ruelle).

[3] Cf. *Enn.* 4.1 [42].1.5–7: ἐκεῖ [ἐν τῷ νῷ] ὁμοῦ μὲν πᾶς νοῦς ... ὁμοῦ δὲ πᾶσαι ψυχαί.

[4] As cosmic Mind, Barbelo contains both those things that truly exist (the Ideas) as well as their types and images, which constitute the image of the Hidden One, Kalyptos. Unlike Plotinus's Nous, Barbelo is not only the aeonic place of the Ideas, but also that of their images. Three such images are named: Kalyptos, Protophanes and Autogenes. Barbelo thus contains (1) the truly existing objects (ΝΗ ΕΤϢΟΟΠ ΟΝΤⲰⲤ) of intellection, the Ideas, as the image of Kalyptos, (2) "the intellectual principle [Porphyry defines Nous as an incorporeal νοερὸς λόγος, *Sent.* 42.12] of these things (Ideas)," as the image of Protophanes (the domain of those who are "unified," ΝΗ ΕΤϨΙΟΥΜΑ), who apparently intelligizes the Ideas in Kalyptos and operates (ἐνεργεῖν) with them on the individuals (ΝΙΚΑΤΑ ΟΥΑ), which in turn are (3) the image of Autogenes, who acts successively and step-by-step to master (ΤΑϨΟ, "to set straight") the defects of the realm of φύσις, tantamount to taking on the demiurgic role of the cosmic soul. In this sense, the Aeon of Barbelo seems to be

The third level, Nature, is merely presupposed by the *Three Steles of Seth* as the perceptible realm where the seed of Seth dwells and mentioned in passing by the author of *Allogenes* as a realm of defects to be rectified by the divine Autogenes. In *Zostrianos* and *Marsanes,* however, the realm extending from the Aeon of Barbelo to the (sublunar) atmospheric realm is articulated into distinct levels, populated with various kinds of souls and spiritual beings. Directly below the Aeon of Barbelo, presided over by the divine Autogenes, are the Self-Begotten Aeons (apparently consisting of four levels defined by the Four Luminaries of earlier Sethian mythology and populated respectively by the archetypes of Adam, Seth, Seth's antediluvian seed, and their progeny), the Repentance (containing souls of those who sin yet repent), the Sojourn (containing those who are not self-directed but follow the ways of others), and the three lower realms *Marsanes* calls the "cosmic and material," but which *Zostrianos* specifies as the Aeonic Copies (ἀντίτυποι) of the preceding three levels (apparently located in the realm between the moon and the fixed stars), the atmospheric realm ("Airy earth," apparently the realm between the moon and earth's surface), and finally the earthly, corporeal realm with its own thirteen aeons presided over by the Archon creator of the sensible cosmos. Among the four treatises, it is only *Zostrianos* that traces the origin of the Matter from which the Archon shapes this corporeal realm to the downward inclination of Sophia (NHC VIII 9,2–10,20).

2.1. The Invisible Spirit

The highest being, corresponding to the Plotinian One, is the Invisible Spirit or Unknowable One, characterized by nonbeing existence, silence, and stillness. According to *Zostrianos* (64,13–66,11), the supreme deity can only be characterized negatively (the *via negativa*) and as superlative to all else (the *via eminentiae*); this passage has a nearly word-for-word parallel in Marius Victorinus's *Ar.* 1.49.9–40; clearly both authors are dependent on a common source, quite likely a Middle Platonic commentary on Plato's *Parmenides,* especially its first hypothesis, 137d–142a.[5]

---

a Nous consisting of the contemplated Ideas (νοῦς νοητός), the contemplating Mind (νοῦς νόερος or θεωρητικός or κινούμενος ἀκίνητος ὤν), and the demiurgic Mind (νοῦς διανοούμενος); cf. *Enn.* 2.9 [33].1; 9.6; 3.9 [13].1 and Numenius frg. 16 des Places).

[5] See now M. Tardieu, "Recherches sur la formation de l'Apocalypse de Zostrien et les sources de Marius Victorinus" in *Res Orientales 9* (Bures-sur-Yvette: Groupe pour l'Étude de la Civilisation du Moyen-Orient, 1996), 7–114; and my introduction and commentary to *Zostrianos* in C. Barry et al., *Zostrien (NH VIII, 1)* (BCNHT 24; Québec: Presses de l'Université Laval; Louvain-Paris: Peeters, 2000), 32–225; 481–661.

Marius Victorinus, *Adversus Arium*   *Zostrianos* VIII 64,13–66,11
                1.49.9–40

49, [9] **Before all the authentic exis-**   **64** [13] [He] was a [unity] [14] and a single
tents was the One or the Monad or [10]   one, [15] existing prior to [all those] [16]
One in itself, One before being was   that truly exist
present to it. For one must call "One" [11]
and conceive as One whatever has in
itself no appearance of [12] otherness. It
is the One alone, the simple One, the
One so-called by [13] concession. It is the
One before all existence, before [14] all   (Cf. *Allogenes* XI 61,32–39:
existentiality and absolutely before all   **XI 61** [32] Now he is [33] an entity insofar
inferiors, [15] before Being, for this One   as he exists, in that he either [34] exists
is prior to Being; he is thus [16] before   and will become, [35] or {acts} <lives> or
every entity, substance, hypostasis, and   knows, although he {lives}<acts> [36]
before [17] all realities with even more   without Mind [37] or Life or Existence [38]
potency. It is the One without exis-   or Non-existence, [39] incomprehensibly.)
tence, without substance, [18] <life>, or
intellect—for it is beyond all that—
immeasurable, [19] invisible, **absolutely**   in [an] [17] immeasurable Spirit, com-
indiscernible by anything else, by   pletely indiscernible [18] by anything else
the realities that are [20] **in it, by those**   [19] that [exists] [20] in him and [outside] [21]
that come after it, even those that   him and [remains] [22] after him. It is he
come from it; [21] **for itself alone, it is**   alone [23] who delimits himself,
distinct and **definite by its own exis-**
tence, [22] not by act, of such a sort that
its own constitution [23] and knowledge it
has of itself is not something other than
itself; absolutely **indivisible, without**   **[65]** [1] [part]less, [2] [shape]less, [quality]-
shape, [24] **without quality** or lack of   less, [3]
quality, nor qualified by absence of qual-
ity; **without** [25] **color, without species,**   [color]less, [specie]less, [4] [form]less to
without form, privated of all the forms,   them [all]. [5]
without being the form in itself by which
all things are formed.
It is the **first cause of all** the existents   [He precedes] them all: [6]
whether they are [27] universals or partic-
ulars, [28] **the principle prior to every**   [he is pre-principle of] [7] [every princi-
principle, [29] **intelligence prior to**   ple], fore[thought] [8] [of] every thought, [9]
every intelligence, the vigor of every   [strength] of every power. [10] [He is
power, [30] **more mobile than move-**   faster] <than> [his] [11] [motion], he is
ment itself, more stable than rest   more stable <than> [12] stability,
itself—for it is rest by an inexpressible
[31] movement and it is a superlative [32]
movement by an ineffable rest; **more**   he is more [compact] [13] <than> [even]
condensed than every continuity,   limitless [14] compaction [And] he is more

more exalted than every [33] **distance; more finite than every body** and greater than every [34] magnitude, **purer than every incorporeal entity, more penetrating than every intelligence** [35] **and every body; of all realities it has the most potency,** it is the potency [36] of all potencies; more universal than everything, **every genus, every species, it is in an absolutely universal way the truly** [37] **Existent, being itself the totality of the authentic existents, greater than** [38] **every totality whether corporeal or incorporeal, more particular** [39] **than every part, by a <pure> ineffable potency being <preeminently> all the authentic** [40] **existents.**

exalted than [16] any unfathomable entity, and he is [17] more [definite] than any corporeal entity, [18] he is purer than any incorporeal entity, [19] he is more penetrating than any [20] thought and any body, [21] [being] more powerful than them all, [22]

any genus or species. [23] He is their totality: **[66]** [1] [the whole of true] existence, [2] and [those who truly] exist; [3] [he is] all [these. For he is greater] [4] [than everything, corporeal] [5] [and incorporeal alike], [6] [more] particular [than] [7] [all the] parts. [8] Existing by a [pure un] [9] knowable [power, he] from whom [10] [derive] all those [11] that truly exist.

A similar characterization of the supreme deity occurs also in *Allogenes,* where the two classical epistemological approaches, the *via negativa* and *via eminentiae,* are combined. Here, the *via negativa* is implemented by negative predications followed by an adversative "but" clause: either triple negation, "it is neither X nor Y nor Z, but it is..." or double, antithetical negation, "it is neither X nor non-X, but it is..." or single negation, "it is not X but it is...." The "but" clause is always positive: "but it is something else" above, beyond, superior to the previously negated predications. Negation of all alternatives on one level of thought launches the mind upward to a new, more eminent level of insight. *Allogenes* (NHC XI 62,28–63,25) employs a series of such negative predications, part of which form a word-for-word parallel with the *Apocryphon of John* (NHC II 3,18–33), indicating some form of mutual literary dependence upon a common source, most likely a commentary on Plato's *Parmenides:*

Allogenes NHC XI, 62,28–63,25	*Ap. John* BG 8502, 24,6–25,7	*Ap. John* NHC II 3,18–33:
	24 [6] This is the Immeasurable Light, [7] pure, holy, [26] spotless, ineffable, [9] [perfect in in-]corruptibility. He is neither [10] Perfection nor [11] Blessedness nor Divinity, [12]	**3** [17] [He] is [the Immeasurable Light], [18] pure, holy, [spotless]. [19] He is ineffable, [perfect in in] corruptibility. [20] He is not in [perfection or in] [21] blessedness [or in] [22] divinity,
62 [28] He is neither Divinity [29] nor Blessedness [30] nor Perfection. Rather [31] it (this triad) is an unknowable entity of of him, [32] not what is proper to		

him. Rather [33] he is something else [34] superior to the Blessedness and [35] the Divinity and [36] Perfection. For he is not [37] perfect, but he is another thing **63** [1] that is superior. He is neither [2] boundless nor [3] is he bounded by [4] another. Rather he is something superior. [5] He is not corporeal; [6] he is not incorporeal. [7] He is not Great; [he is not] Small. [8] He is not a <quantity>; he is not a [<quality>]. [9] Nor is he something [10] that exists, that [11] one can know. Rather [12] he is something else that is superior, which [13] one cannot know. [14] He is primary revelation [15] and self-knowledge, [16] since it is he alone who knows himself. [17] Since he is not one of those things [18] that exist, but is another thing, [19] he is superior to all superlatives, [20] even in comparison what is his and [21] what is not his. He neither participates in [22] eternity nor [23] does he participate in time. [24] He does not receive anything from [25] anything else.

but rather something superior [13] to them. He is neither infinite [14] nor unlimited, [15] but rather he is something better than these. For [16] he is neither corporeal [17] nor incorporeal; he is not Great, he is not [18] Small, nor is he a quantity [19] nor a <quality>. For it is not possible for anyone to [20] intelligize him.

[but rather he is far superior]. [23]

[He is] neither corporeal [nor incorporeal], [24] he is not Great, [nor] is he Small. [There is no] [25] way to say "What is his quantity?" or "What [is his quality?"], [26] for it is not possible [for anyone to comprehend him]. [27]

He is not any of the [21] existing things, but is instead superior [22] to them. He is not anything among existing things, but rather something superior to these—not 'superior' in the comparative sense, but [25] [1] in the absolute sense. [2] Not participating in eternity, time [3] does not exist for him. For one who participates [4] in eternity, others [5] previously prepared him. [6] Time did not limit him, since he does not [7] receive from some other who limits. [8] And he has no need. There is nothing [9] at all before him.

He is not anything among [existing things, but rather he is] 28 far superior—

not 'superior' in the comparative sense, but rather in the absolute sense. [29] He [participates neither] in eternity nor [30] in time. For that which [participates in eternity] [31] was previously anticipated. He [was not divided] [32] by time, [since] he [33] receives nothing, [for it would be something received] [34] on loan. For he who precedes someone does not [lack] [35] that he may receive from [him].

2.2. The Aeon of Barbelo

The Aeon of Barbelo is the emanative product of the three-stage unfolding of the inner potency of the supreme Unknowable One or Invisible Spirit. According to *Allogenes* (XI 45,8–46,35), just as the Barbelo aeon itself becomes a substantially existing aeon who can know herself because she knows her source (the Invisible Spirit), so also each level of being within the Aeon of Barbelo comes into being by knowing both itself and its originating principle. Each successively lower being emanates from its immediate prior and achieves substantial reality by a contemplative reversion upon its suprajacent source:

> **XI 45** [8] The [9] [Mind], the guardian [I provided], [10] [for you] taught you. And it is the power that [11] [exists] in you that [extended] [12] [itself], since [it] often [13] [rejoiced in] the Triple-Powered One, the [one] [14] [of] all [those] who [truly] exist [15] with the [immeasurable] One, the [16] eternal [light of] the knowledge [17] that has [appeared], the [18] male virginal [glory], [19] [the first] aeon, the one from [20] [a] unique triple-powered [aeon], [21] [the] Triple-Powered One who [22] [truly exists]. For when it was [contracted] [23] [it expanded], and [24] [when it was separated], it became complete, [25] [and] it was empowered [with] [26] all of them by knowing [itself] [27] [in the perfect Invisible Spirit]. [28] And it [became] [29] [an] aeon who knows [herself] [30] [because] she knew that one. [31] [And] she became Kalyptos, [32] [because] she acted in those whom she [33] knows. [34] She is a perfect, [35] invisible, noetic [36] Protophanes-Harmedon. Empowering [37] the individuals, she is Triple Male, [38] since she is individually **46** [1] [...] [2] [...] [3] [...] [4] [...] [5] [...] [6] [Individual on the one hand, they are] [7] [unified] on the other, [since she] is [their] [8] [Existence], and she [sees] [9] all those who truly <exist>. [Truly] [10] [she] contains the [11] divine Autogenes. When she [knew] [12] her Existence [13] and when she stood at rest [upon] [14] this one (Autogenes), he saw them [all] [15] existing individually just as [they] [16] are. And when [they] [17] become as he is, [they shall] [18] see the divine Triple Male, [19] the power that is [higher than] [20] God. [He is the thought] [21] of all those who [are] [22] unified. If he (the Triple Male) [contemplates them], [23] he contemplates the [24] great male, [25] [perfect?], noetic [Protophanes]. As for their [26] [procession], if [he] [27] sees it, [he sees] [28] [also the truly existing ones], [29] [since it is the] procession [for those who] [30] are unified. And when [he has seen] [31] these (truly existing), he has seen Kalyptos. [32] And if he sees [33] one of the hidden ones, [he] [34] sees the Barbelo-Aeon, [the] [35] unbegotten offspring of [that One].

Just as each successively lower level of the Barbelo Aeon comes into being by knowing its immediate source, so too within the Aeon of Barbelo there is a corresponding process by which the members of each ontological level can achieve an essential relationship to the being who presides over the next higher level by an act of vision. To see the contents of the next higher level is to see at the next higher level the principle that contains them. Thus the individuals resident in the Autogenes may see Protophanes by contemplating the unified beings over which he presides. The unified beings resident in Protophanes may see the Kalyptos by contemplating those who truly exist in Kalyptos. Finally to see all the beings hidden within the Aeon of Barbelo is to see the Barbelo Aeon itself, who in turn was completed by knowing her prefigurative self in the Invisible Spirit. The chain of being is created and bound together by acts of vision and knowledge.

Within the Aeon of Barbelo, the ideal entities are alive and in agreement, separate and yet "all together" (*Zost.* VIII 115,2–13; 117,1–4). The similarity to Plotinus's description of the condition of the Ideas within the Intellect (ἐκεῖ πάντα ὁμοῦ) is obvious. Barbelo also bears characteristics echoing those of the Receptacle of Plato's *Timaeus*. According to the second stele of the *Three Steles of Seth,* Barbelo is a Hidden One (Kalyptos), a shadow from the One, who "empowers the shadows which pour from the One," probably the equivalent of Plato's images of the Forms, including principal categories (from the *Sophist* and *Parmenides*) the "equal" and "unequal," the "similar" and "dissimilar." As "begetter of multiplicity according to a division of those who really are" (the Forms), she provides "forms in [that which] exists to others," that they might become perfect individuals, dwelling in her as a cosmos of knowledge. According to *Zostrianos,* Barbelo is a "preexistence of nonbeing" (VIII 79,7–8), eternally moving from undividedness into active existence, an image that comes to be in an act of reversion ("turning"; 80,9) upon its source, making herself stable and at rest, knowing herself and the one who preexists. As such, she serves as an eternal space (χώρημα, 82,8) in order that those who indwell her, perhaps the Forms, might have a stable and limited place and that those who come forth from her, perhaps perceptible entities, might become purely simple individuals at the level of Autogenes (88,16–22; 127,7–15).

2.3. The Triple-Powered One

The most distinctive metaphysical feature of these treatises is the Triple-Powered One that mediates between the Invisible Spirit and the Aeon of Barbelo. This being is mentioned sometimes independently and sometimes in conjunction with the Invisible Spirit.[6] In *Allogenes,* by a self-

---

[6] The Invisible Spirit and the Triple-Powered One are mentioned sometimes separately (*Zost.* VIII 15,18; 17,7; 24,9–10; 93,6–9; 124,3–4; *Allogenes* XI 45,13–30; 52,19; 52,30–33; 53,30; 61,1–22; *Marsanes* X 4,13–19; 6,19; 8,11; 9,25; 14,22–23; 15,1–3); sometimes as identical with or in close conjunction with the Invisible Spirit (*Zost.* VIII 20,15–18; 24,12–13; 63,7–8; 74,3–16; 79,16–23; 80,11–20; 87,13–14; 97,2–3; 118,11–12; 123,19–20; 128,20–21; *Allogenes* XI 47,8–9, 51,8–9; 58,25;

contraction and expansion, the Invisible Spirit through his Triple-Powered One becomes the Aeon of Barbelo (XI 45,9–46,35, cited above). The corresponding account of Barbelo's emanation on pages 76–84 of *Zostrianos* reflects the same sequence of procession, reversion, and acquisition of separateness and stability; having emanated from the Invisible Spirit, her further descent and potential dispersion is halted by a contemplative reversion upon her source. She comes to stand outside him, examining him and herself, becoming separate and stable as an all-perfect (παν-τέλιος) being, the ingenerate Kalyptos:

> **VIII 76** [7] It is a [power that] [8] inhabits a [part of the] [9] ingenerateness, for it [10] always exists. It [sought] [11] after him, seeing him [there] [12] and existing as a simple [unity]. [13] Since he is [14] blessedness in [15] perfection, he [was] [16] a perfect and [blessed] unity. [17] She lacks this one's (character) [18] because she lacked his [unity], [19] since it would come later [20] with knowledge. And [21] his knowledge dwells [22] outside of him with [23] that which contemplates him [24] inwardly.... **77** [12] She was divided, [13] for she is [an] all-perfect one [14] [of] a perfection [15] existing as contemplation.... **78** [6] It is she who knows] [7] and [who foreknows] [8] herself, [truly existing] [9] as a [single] aeon [10] in act [and] [11] potency and [Existence]. [12] It is not [in] [13] time that she originated, but [she] [14] [appeared] eternally, [15] having eternally stood [16] in his presence. [17] She was overshadowed by the [18] majesty of his [majesty]. [19] She stood [20] looking at him and rejoicing. [21] Being filled with [22] kindness [she did not become separate].... **79** [5] [And she is an insubstantial Existence] [6] [and a power] that [truly exists]. [7] [She is the] first [insubstantial] [8] Existence [after] [9] that one. [10] [And from] the undivided one toward [11] existence in act [12] move the [intellectual] perfection [13] and intellectual life [14] that were [15] blessedness and [16] divinity. The [entire] Spirit, [17] perfect, simple [18] and invisible, [19] [has] become a unity [20] in existence and [21] activity, even a [22] simple Triple-[Powered] One, [23] an Invisible Spirit, an [24] image of the one that [25] truly exists.... **80** [1] [...] [2] [...] ... [...] [3] [...] able [...] [4] [...] [5] [... It is impossible to comprehend] [6] the truly [existing one] [7] [who] exists in [anything] [8] that is an image. [She began to] [9] strive, since it was [im-]possible [10] to unite with his [image]. [11] She saw the [privation of] [12] the (Triple-Powered) one who was [in the presence of] [13] the all-perfection of [14] that one, since it [15] preexists and [16] is situated over all these, [15] preexisting, being known [18] as three-powered.... **81** [6] She [was] existing [individually] [7] [as cause] of

---

66,33–34; *Steles Seth* VII 121,31–32; *Marsanes* X 7,16–17 [the "activity" of the Invisible Spirit]; 7,27–29; 8,5–7), often as "the Triple-Powered Invisible Spirit" or "the invisible spiritual Triple-Powered One"; and sometimes in conjunction with Barbelo (*Steles Seth* VII 120,21–22; 121,32–33; 123,18–30; *Marsanes* X 8,19–20; 9,7–20; 10,8–11). As the activity of the Invisible Spirit, the Triple-Powered One is perhaps identical with all three in *Marsanes* X 7,1–9,29.

[the declination]. [8] Lest she come forth anymore [9] or get further away [10] from perfection, she [11] knew herself and it (the Spirit), [12] and she stood at rest [13] and spread forth [14] [because of] it—[15] since she derived [16] [from] that which truly exists, [17] she derived from that which [18] truly exists with all [19] those—to know herself [20] and the one that preexists. [21] Having supplemented him, [22] they came into existence. {they [23] came into existence} And [24] they appear through those **82** [1] [who pre]exist. And [2] [...] through the [...] [3] [...] having appeared [4] [as a] second [5] [Mentality]. And they appeared [6] [through the one (Barbelo)] who [7] foreknows him, being [8] an eternal space, [9] having become [10] a secondary form of his knowledge, [11] even the duplication of [12] his knowledge, the ingenerate [13] Kalyptos. [They again] [14] stood at rest upon the one [15] that truly exists; [16] for she accordingly recognized him [17] in order that those following [18] her might come into being having [19] a place, and that [20] those that come forth [21] might not precede her but [22] might become holy [23] and simple. She is the [24] introspection of the god **83** [1] who pre[exists]. She] spread [2] forth .... [8] She was called [9] Barbelo by virtue of [10] thought, the [11] perfect virginal male of three [12] kinds. And her knowledge [13] originated [14] from her lest [15] [she be drawn] down and [16] come forth further [17] by the things that exist [18] in her and that follow [19] her. Rather, she is [20] simple in order that she might [21] be able to know the god [22] who preexists, since [23] she became good enough for [24] that one when she [25] [revealed her product] **83** [1] ingenerate[ly]. [2] [And she became a] third [3] [aeon].

In the *Three Steles of Seth* (VII 121,20–124,14), Barbelo is said to preexist in the preexistent Monad, a Triple-Powered One who was the first to see the preexistent One. She emerges from her source as the first shadow of light from the light of the Father, as a Hidden One (καλυπτός) who has become numerable, that is, measurable, defined Being that can be distinguished from the Monad, her source. Just as the Neopythagorean arithmological treatises consider the Triad to be the first of the defined numbers following the One and the Dyad, Barbelo is said to become threefold (as Kalyptos, Protophanes and Autogenes), while at the same time continuing to be one with her source. For example:

VII 121 [30] O nonsubstantial One [31] from an undivided, [32] triple-[powered] One, You are a threefold [33] power! You are [a] great monad [34] from [a] pure monad! **122** [1] You are a superior monad, the [2] first projected image of the holy Father, [3] light from light. [4] We bless you, [5] generator of perfection, aeon-giver! [6] You yourself have seen the [7] eternal ones, that they are from a shadow (i.e., a projected image). [8] You have become numerable. While [9] you arose and remained [10] one, yet causing multiplicity to become divided, [11] you are truly threefold. You are truly replicated [12] threefold! You are a One [13] of the One. And you are from [14] its shadow. You are a Kalyptos (i.e., hidden one), [15] you are a universe of knowledge. [16] For you know those of the One, that they [17] derive from a shadow. And these [18] are yours in thought: on account of [19] these you have empowered the eternal ones [20] with Substantiality; you have empowered [21] Divinity with Vitality; [22] you have empowered Mentality with [23] Goodness; with [24] Blessedness you have empowered the [25] shadows that flow from the One. [26] One you have empowered with Mentality; [27] another you have empowered with quality (<* ποιότης for ποιήσις = ⲧⲁⲙⲓⲟ, creation). [28] You have empowered that which is equal [29] and that which is unequal, the [30] similar and the dissimilar. [31] With generation and intelligible [32] Forms you have empowered [33] others with Being. You have flourished [34] with generation! (trans. Layton)

As will be noted below (pp. 218–21), a number of concepts in this passage and the preceding one from *Zostrianos* sound similar to what we know from the first-century Neopythagorean Moderatus: privation, projection as a shadow, the origin of defined multiplicity by intellectual limitation of indefinite enumerability, and the creation of an eternal space or receptacle to contain that multiplicity.

Marsanes (NHC X 7,4–9,20) posits an unknown silent One above the Invisible Spirit (the supreme principle of the other treatises) whose silence is actualized by the Invisible Spirit's Triple-Powered One. In this process, the first power (apparently ὑπόστασις) of the Triple-Powered One is identical with the Invisible Spirit, and its second power (apparently ἐνέργεια) is identical with its own hypostatic actuality. The Aeon of Barbelo then emerges as the third power (apparently γνῶσις) of the Triple-Powered One as it withdraws from its first two powers. It appears that these three powers, Hypostasis, Activity, and Knowledge, are *Marsanes'* equivalent for the Existence, Vitality, Mentality triad of the other three treatises:

X 7 [1] When I had inquired about these things [2] I perceived that he (the Triple-Powered One) acted [3] from silence. He exists [4] prior to those that [5] truly exist, that belong to the realm of Being. [6] He (the Triple-Powered One) is a preexistent otherness [7] belonging to the one (the Invisible Spirit) that [8] actualizes the Silent One. [9] And the silence of [that (the Triple-Powered One) which follows] [10] him (the Invisible Spirit) acts. For [so] [11] [long as] the latter (the Spirit) [acts], [12] the former (the Triple-Powered One) [acts also]. [13] The [silence which belongs to the Un] [14] begotten One (the Invisible Spirit) is among [the aeons, and from] [15] the beginning he is in-[substantial]. [16] But the activity (ἐνέργεια) of [17] that One (the Invisible Spirit) <is> the Triple-Powered One. [18] The Unbegotten One (the Invisible Spirit) is prior to [19] the Aeon, since he is in[substantial]. [20] And as for the summit of the [21] silence of the Silent One, [22] it is possible for the summit (i.e., the Invisible Spirit) [23] of the energy (ἐνέργεια) of the Triple [24] Powered One to behold it. And the One (the Invisible Spirit) who [25] exists, who is silent, [who is] [26] beyond [insubstantiality], [27] manifested [the Triple] [28] [Powered, First-] [29] Perfect One.... **8** [18] When the third [19] power (i.e., the Barbelo Aeon) of the Triple-Powered One [20] contemplated him (the Triple-Powered One), [21] it said to me, "Be silent [22] lest you should know and flee [23] and come before me. But [24] know that this One was [25] [silent], and concentrate on understanding (νόημα). [26] For [the power still] keeps [27] [guiding] me into [28] [the Aeon which] is Barbelo, [29] [the] male [Virgin]." **9** [1] For this reason the [2] Virgin became male (as νοῦς, the Aeon of Barbelo), [3] because she had separated from the male (i.e., the Invisible Spirit). The [4] Knowledge (γνῶσις) stood outside of him, [5] as if belonging to him. [6] And she who exists is she who sought. [7] She is situated just as [8] the Triple-Powered One is situated. [9] She withdrew [10] from [these] two [powers] (the first two powers of the Triple-Powered One), [11] since she exists [outside of] [12] the Great One (the Invisible Spirit), [seeing what] [13] is above [her, the Perfect One (the Triple-Powered One)] [14] who is silent, [who has] [15] this [commandment] [16] to be silent. His knowledge (γνῶσις ~ mind) [17] and his hypostasis (ὑπόστασις ~ existence) [18] and his activity (ἐνέργεια ~ life) [19] are those things that the power (δύναμις, i.e., Barbelo) [20] of the Triple-Powered One expressed.

In *Allogenes,* the Triple-Powered One is said to be the delimiter of the boundlessness subsisting in the Invisible Spirit. As an initially *unbounded* entity, the Triple-Powered One emerges from its source in the Invisible Spirit as a processing boundlessness that turns itself back to its source in an act of objectifying self-knowledge; becoming stable and bounded, it takes on form and definition as Barbelo, the self knowledge or Mind of the Invisible Spirit (XI 48,6–49,37).[7]

> **XI 48** [6] [It is not impossible for them] [7] to receive a revelation of these things [8] if they unify (in Protophanes), [9] since it is impossible that [10] the Individuals (in Autogenes) attain the All [11] [situated in the] place that is higher than perfect. [12] And they receive (the revelation) through [13] a preconception, [14] not, as it were, of mere Being—[rather] it is Being [15]

---

[7] Translating **ρεϥχιοορ** as "delimiter" (<* διαπεραίνω) rather than "traverser" (< διαπεράω). There is a certain obscurity in tracing the precise antecedents of the pronoun subjects and objects; compare the accounts in *Zost.* VIII 76,7–19; 78,10–81,20; *Steles Seth* VII 121,20–122,18 and *Marsanes* X 8,18–9,28, as well as *Ap. John* II 4,19–32: "[19] And it is he alone (the Invisible Spirit) who looks [20] at him(self) in his light which surrounds him. [21] This is the source of the Living Water [22] which supplies all the aeons. In every way (direction?) he [gazes] [23] [upon] his image which he sees [24] in the source of the [Spirit]. He invests his intention in his [25] light-[water, that is], the source of the [26] [pure] light-water [which] surrounds him. And [27] [his Ennoia became] active and she came [28] forth, namely she who had [appeared] before him [29] in [the radiance] of his light. This is [30] the first [power which was] before them all, [31] [manifested from] his thought, [32] that [is, the Pronoia of the All]."

with [the] latency (cf. Kalyptos) of Existence that he (the Triple-Powered One) provides, [16] [nourishing] [17] [it in] every way, since it is this [18] that [shall] come into being when he [19] intelligizes himself. For he is the One [20] subsisting as a [cause] [21] and source of [Being], even [an] [22] immaterial [matter and an] [23] innumerable [number and a] formless [24] [form] and a [shapeless] [25] [shape] and [a powerlessness with] [26] [power and an insubstantial substance] [27] [and a motionless] [28] [motion and an inactive] [29] [activity, but he is] [30] [a] provider of [agreement] [31] [and] a divinity [of] [32] divinity. But when [33] they receive (this kind of Being), they share [34] in the primal Vitality and [35] an indivisible activity, [36] an hypostasis (the Triple-Powered One?) of the first one, [37] of the one that [38] truly exists.

Now a second **49** [1] activity [...] [2] [...] however, is that [...] [3] [...] Male [...] [4] [...] [5] [...] he is endowed with [6] [Blessedness] and [7] Goodness, because when he (the Triple-Powered One) [8] is intelligized as the Delimiter (D) [9] of the (indeterminate) Boundlessness (B) of the [10] Invisible Spirit (IS) [that subsists] in him (D), [11] it (B) causes [him (D)] to revert to [it (IS)] [12] in order that it (B) might know what it is [13] that is within it (IS) and [14] how it (IS) exists, and [15] that he (D) might guarantee the endurance of [16] everything by being a [17] cause (of determinateness) for those who truly exist (in the Barbelo Aeon). [18] For through him (D) [19] knowledge of it (IS) became available, [20] since he (D) is the one who knows what [21] it (IS) is. But they brought forth nothing [22] [beyond] themselves, neither [23] power nor rank nor [24] glory nor aeon, [25] for they are all [26] eternal.

He is Vitality and [27] Mentality and Essentiality. [28] So then: Essentiality [29] constantly includes its [30] Vitality and Mentality, [31] and {Life has} [32] Vitality includes [33] {non-} Substantiality and [34] Mentality; Mentality includes [35] Life and Essentiality. [36] And the three are one, [37] although individually they are three.[8]

Thus the Triple-Powered One is the potency (δύναμις) of the Unknown One and/or Invisible Spirit by which he unfolds himself into the world of Being and Intellect. It is said to consist of three modalities or phases: "That-which-is" (**ΠΕΤϢΟΟΠ** or **ΠΗ ΕΤΕ ΠΑΪ ΠΕ**, perhaps translating either Essentiality [ὀντότης] or Substantiality [οὐσιότης]), Vitality, and Mentality (XI, 49,26-37).

A similar notion occurs in *Zostrianos* (NHC VIII 16,2–18; 17,20–22; and 66,14–75,11):

---

[8] Cf. Proclus *Elem. Theol.*, prop. 103 (Dodds): "For in Being [τὸ ὄν] there is Life and Intellect, and in Life there is Being [εἶναι] and Intellection [νοεῖν], and in Intellect there is Being [εἶναι] and Living [ζῆν]."

16 [2] Not only [did they dwell] [3] in thought, but he [made room for] [4] them, since he is [Becoming] in the following [5] way: he imposed a [limit] upon [6] Being, lest it become [7] endless and formless; [8] instead, it was truly delimited while it was a [9] new entity in order that [it] might become [10] something having [11] its own [dwelling], [12] Existence together with [Being], [13] standing with it, existing with it, [14] surrounding it, [and being like it] [15] on every side. [It withdrew] [16] from the [living water that it might] [17] receive the [pre] existent [18] [stability] of [...]

17 [20] And in [21] [becoming, Life] becomes [limitless] [22] [that it may receive] its [own Being].

66 [14] For they are [triple] [15] powers of his [unity]: [16] Existence, [17] Life and [18] Blessedness. In [19] Existence he exists [as] [20] a simple unity, [21] his own [rational expression] and species. [22] Whoever will find [23] him he brings into [24] existence. [And in] [25] Vitality, he is alive [and] **67** [1] [becomes; in Blessedness] [2] [he comes to] [3] [have Mentality]. ...

74 [8] And [in Existence] [9] [is] his Idea [and] [10] [Being], both [according to the] [11] activity which is [his] Life, [12] and according to the perfection [13] which [is] the luminous intellectual [14] power. [And] [15] the three stand together, [16] moving together. [17] It is everywhere and [18] nowhere that he [empowers] [19] and activates them all. [20] The ineffable, [21] unnamable one—it is [22] from himself that he [truly] exists, [23] resting himself [in] [24] in his perfection—[25] has [not] shared in [any] form, **75** [1] therefore [he is invisible to] [2] them [all. He has taken] [3] [no pattern for himself, nor] [4] [is he anything at all of] those [that] [5] [exist among the perfect ones] and [those] [6] [that are unified]. He [is] the [single] one [7] [belonging to the Entirety]. In Existence [8] [is] Being; in [Vitality] [9] <is> Life; and in [10] perfection and [11] [Mentality] is Blessedness.

The mechanism behind this metamorphosis is the Triple Power, which—as Existence, Essentiality, or Substantiality—is identical both with its source, the Invisible Spirit, and—as Mentality—is identical with its self-objectified manifestation, Barbelo. While the initial and final phases or modes of the Triple-Powered One have hypostatic instantiation as the Invisible Spirit and Barbelo, the hypostatic status of the transitional mode between the two, Vitality, is less clear. In *Zostrianos,* the Triple-Powered One mostly seems to be a faculty of the Invisible Spirit itself; in the *Three Steles of Seth,* it seems to represent the prefigurative existence of the Barbelo Aeon within the supreme preexistent One; while *Allogenes* and *Marsanes* tend to conceive it as a separate, median quasi-hypostasis between the two, as if it were the hypostatic instantiation of its median power, Vitality. In fact, the last two sometimes coalesce the first of the Triple-Powered One's three powers with the Invisible Spirit, above whom they locate an apparently even more transcendent One.

Now the closest attested parallel to this sequence of emanative phases is apparently to be found in the anonymous Turin palimpsest *Commentary on the Parmenides* first published by W. Kroll and republished and assigned to Porphyry by P. Hadot.[9] It appears that this anonymous commentator on the *Parmenides* wished to demonstrate that the "One-Being" of the second hypothesis of the *Parmenides* is paradoxically at the same time discontinuous and continuous with the absolute, unqualifiable One of the first hypothesis. The absolute, unqualified, and infinitival being (αὐτὸ τὸ εἶναι) of the first One (ἕν) somehow declines from its source and is conferred upon a second One-which-is (ἕν ὄν) that thereby acquires its determinate being by participating in the transcendent indeterminate being of the first One as its idea.

> It has not been said that Being participates in the One, but that the One participates in Being [τὸ ὄν], not because the first was Being [τὸ ὄν], but because an otherness [ἑτερότης] from the One has turned the One towards this whole One-Being [τὸ ἓν εἶναι]. For from the fact of being engendered somehow at the second level, being-One [τὸ ἓν εἶναι] is added.... the One, which is beyond substance and being [τὸ ὄν], is neither being nor substance nor act, but rather acts and is itself pure act, such that it is itself being [εἶναι] before determinate being [τὸ ὄν]. By participating this being [the εἶναι of the first One; cf. *Parmenides* 137c–142a], the One [scil. "who is," i.e., the second One of *Parmenides* 142b–144e] possesses another being [εἶναι] declined from it [the εἶναι of the Supreme One], (106) which is [what is meant by] participating in determinate being [τὸ ὄν; cf. οὐσία in *Parmenides* 142B]. Thus, being [εἶναι] is double: the one preexists determinate being [τὸ ὄν], while the other [ὄν] is derived from the One that transcends determinate being [τὸ ὄν], who is absolute being [εἶναι] and as it were the idea of determinate being [τὸ ὄν] by participation in which [the εἶναι of the first] some other One has come to be to which is linked the being [εἶναι] carried over from it. (*In Parm.* 12.16–35 Hadot)

Again, the commentator accounts for the origin of this second "One-Being" by attributing to it three modalities or phases, which he analyzed into the triad, Existence, Life, and Intellect. The term existence (ὕπαρξις), which is also used of the highest and primary phase or mode of the Triple-Powered

---

[9] The anonymous *Parmenides Commentary* (*Anon. Taurensis*), in W. Kroll, "Ein neuplatonischer Parmenides-kommentar in einem Turiner Palimpsest," *Rheinisches Museum für Philologie* 48 (1892): 599–627; here cited in the edition of P. Hadot, *Porphyre et Victorinus* (2 vols.; Paris: Études augustiniennes, 1968), 2:61–113; cf. idem, "Fragments d'un commentaire de Porphyre sur le Parménide," *Revue des études grecques* 74 (1961): 410–38.

One in *Allogenes* and *Zostrianos,* is meant to refer to the absolute infinitival being (αὐτὸ τὸ εἶναι) of the One, which is the ἰδέα of the derived determinate being (τὸ ὄν) proper to the second One now identified as the divine Intellect.

> Taken in itself as its own idea it—this power, or whatever term one might use to indicate its ineffability and inconceivability [i.e., the potential Intellect still identical with the One]—is one and simple. But with respect to existence (ὕπαρξις), life (ζωή) and thought (νόησις) it is neither one nor simple. With respect to existence (ὕπαρξις), thinking is also being thought. But when Intellect [abandons] existence for intelligizing so as to be elevated to the rank of an intelligible in order to see itself, intelligizing is life. Therefore thinking is indefinite with respect to life. And all are activities (ἐνεργείαι) such that with respect to existence, activity would be static; with respect to intelligizing, activity would be turned to itself; and with respect to life, activity would be inclining away from existence (*In Parm.* 14.15–26 Hadot).

Here Intellect unfolds from the absolute being of the One in three phases according to which each modality of the Intellect predominates at a given stage. First, *qua* ὕπαρξις, Intellect is purely potential Intellect resident in and identical with its idea, the absolute being of the One. Last, *qua* Intellect, it has become identical with the derived being (τὸ ὄν) of Intellect proper, the second hypostasis, as the hypostatic exemplification of its idea, the absolute being of the One. The transitional phase between the first and last phases of intellect in effect constitutes a median phase of Intellect in which it is "indeterminate thinking" or Intellect *qua* Life.

In *Allogenes* and *Marsanes,* the Triple-Powered One is identical with the Invisible Spirit in its first (Existence/Hypostasis) phase, discontinuous with the Invisible Spirit but identical with Barbelo in its second (Mentality/Knowledge) phase, and in its intermediate, emanative (Vitality/Activity) phase, it is simultaneously continuous—but sufficiently discontinuous to be distinguishable as a separate hypostasis—with both the Invisible Spirit and Barbelo.[10] In spite of minor differences in nomenclature, the structural and functional similarity of the triad in the *Parmenides Commentary* and in the Platonizing Sethian treatises is clear. However, the *Commentary,* like

---

[10] Its initial mode is that of Existence, a phase of rest or permanence (μονή), in which it is identical with its source, the Unknowable Invisible Spirit. In the phase of emanation (πρόοδος), it enters the mode of Vitality (also identified as "Eternal Life," XI 66,33), a boundlessness from which emanates a "shadow" or projected image. In a third phase of reversion (ἐπιστροφή) upon the Invisible Spirit as its source, this "shadow" enters the phase of Mentality and achieves substantial reality as the Barbelo-Aeon, the self-knowledge of the Invisible Spirit (XI 49,18–21).

the *Three Steles of Seth,* understands the triad as the three phases of Intellect's (Barbelo) self-deployment, while *Zostrianos* tends to conceive it as the three emanative phases of the (Triple-Powered) Invisible Spirit, and *Allogenes* and *Marsanes* tend to confer an independent hypostatic status on the triad in the figure of the Triple-Powered One interposed between the supreme Unknowable One and his separate Intellect, the Aeon of Barbelo. Hence the Triple-Powered One serves to emphasize the transcendence of the Invisible Spirit, but at the same time to prevent any ultimate gap in the chain of being.

To complicate matters further, *Allogenes* attributes directly to the Unknowable One or Invisible Spirit a similar-sounding triad of attributes, but characterizes them as acts (i.e., εἶναι, ζῆν, νοεῖν) rather than qualities (ὕπαρξις or ὀντότης or οὐσιοτης, ζωότης, νοότης) or substances (ὄν, ζωή, νοῦς): he exists, lives, and knows without mind, life, or existence (61,32–39).[11] This is a classic example of ranking by paronymns.[12]

> **61** [32] Now he is [33] an entity insofar as he exists, in that he either [34] exists and will become, [35] or {acts} <lives> or knows, although he {lives}<acts> [36] without Mind [37] or Life or Existence [38] or Nonexistence, [39] incomprehensibly.

Bearing in mind that the Aeon of Barbelo, called "an Eternal Life" in XI 66,30–34, is considered to be the "knowledge" or "first thought" of the Invisible Spirit (51,8–32), to contain the perfect Mind Protophanes, and, in its Kalyptos-level, to contain the realm of pure being (τὰ ὄντως ὄντα), one might combine the techniques of paronymy, relative predominance and mutual implication by cyclic permutation (see XI 49,26–38 and Proclus *Elem. Theol.* prop. 103 cited above, p. 193 n. 8) to arrive at an enneadic structure for the metaphysical ontology of *Allogenes.* Thus at the level of the Invisible Spirit, the Being-Life-Mind triad is present as pure infinitival indeterminacy (existing, living, thinking); on the level of the Triple-

---

[11] The Coptic requires emendation: ϥϣⲟⲟⲡ ⲇⲉ ⲛ̄ⲛⲟⲩ [33] ⲗⲁⲁⲩ ⲛ̄ⲑⲉ ⲉⲧⲉϥϣⲟⲟⲡ· ⲏ̄ ϫⲉ [34] ϥϣⲟⲟⲡ ⲁⲩⲱ ⲉϥⲛⲁϣⲱⲡⲉ [35] ⲏ̄ {ⲉϥⲣ̄ⲉⲛⲉⲣⲅⲓ} <ⲉϥⲱⲛ̄ϩ̄> ⲉϥⲉⲓⲙⲉ {ⲉϥⲟ [36] ⲛ̄ϩ̄} <ⲉϥⲣ̄ⲉⲛⲉⲣⲅⲓ> ⲉⲙⲛ̄ⲧⲁϥ ⲛ̄ⲟⲩⲛⲟⲩⲥ· [37] ⲟⲩⲧⲉ ⲟⲩⲱⲛ̄ϩ̄· ⲟⲩⲧⲉ ⲟⲩϣⲩ [38] ⲡⲁⲣ̄ⲝⲓⲥ· ⲟⲩⲧⲉ ⲡⲓⲁⲧ̄ϩ̄ⲩⲡⲁⲣ [39] ⲝⲓⲥ ϩ̄ⲛ̄ ⲟⲩⲙⲛ̄ⲧ̄ⲁⲧ̄ⲧⲁϩⲟⲥ· (cf. also 54,9–61,22).

[12] Proclus (*In Parm.* 1106.1–1108.19 Cousin) mentions a technique of paronymy in which infinitives, participles, and *nomina actionis* ontologically precede abstract denominatives in -της, which in turn ontologically precede their respective substantives, by which one may illustrate that acts precede their substantive results; an example would be this series of terms from most abstract to most substantial: νόημα, νοοῦν, νοότης, νοῦς (as though all derived from the causitive νοόω). Thus in *Allogenes,* the Unknowable One is pure act that requires no substantial entity responsible for or instantiating that act.

Powered One, it is present as a triad of abstract denominative qualities (existence, vitality, mentality), and on the level of the Barbelo Aeon, as a triad of substantival realities: being, life, and mind (Kalyptos as Being and Protophanes as Mind, although its life-component is not given a distinct identification). *Allogenes* thereby presents a dynamic three-in-one principle deploying itself in three phases in which each phase, while containing the other two, is named by the phase of the triad that predominates at each stage of its unfolding. In the accompanying diagram, the italicized term indicates the relative predominance of one of the three modalities.

Unknowable One/Invisible Spirit	*Exists*	Lives	Knows
Triple-Powered One/Eternal Life	Existence	*Vitality*	Mentality
Barbelo/First Thought	Being	(Life)	*Mind*

It is interesting to find in *Allogenes* a supreme enneadic structure of the sort that, according to P. Hadot,[13] Porphyry—on the basis of the *Chaldean Oracles*—placed at the head of his metaphysics, but is missing in the anonymous *Parmenides Commentary* where one might most expect it to appear!

3. The Position of the Platonizing Sethian Treatises in the Platonic Tradition

The precise textual interrelationships within the Platonizing Sethian treatises are difficult to determine. All four texts show no interest in the Sethite primeval history, but they continue to trade in the traditional nomenclature for the denizens of the divine world found in that part of the *Apocryphon of John* that overlaps the Barbeloite account of Irenaeus (*Haer.* 1.29) and that is also found in the *Trimorphic Protennoia* and the *Gospel of the Egyptians:* in *Allogenes* and *Marsanes,* there are the Invisible Spirit, Barbelo, and the Autogenes Son, to which the *Three Steles of Seth* adds Geradamas and Meirothea, to which *Zostrianos* adds the Four Lights, Adamas, Emmacha Seth, Sophia, the Archon, and a host of other names it shares with the *Gospel of the Egyptians.* Even more obviously, none of these texts shows any distinctive Christian influence.

As for the intertextual relationships among the four Platonizing Sethian treatises:[14]

---

[13] On the basis of Lydus *Mens.* 4.122.1–4: Θεῖος ὁ τῆς ἐννάδος ἀριθμὸς ἐκ τριῶν τριάδων πληρούμενος καὶ τὰς ἀκρότητας τῆς θεολογίας κατὰ τὴν Χαλδαϊκὴν φιλοσοφίαν ὥς φησιν ὁ Πορφύριος ἀποσώζων.

[14] See my "Typologies of the Sethian Gnostic Treatises from Nag Hammadi," in *Les textes de Nag Hammadi et le problème de leur classification: Actes du colloque tenu à Québec du 15 au 22 Septembre, 1993* (ed. L. Painchaud and A. Pasquier; Québec: Université Laval; Louvain: Peeters, 1995), 202–3, 209–10.

When one realizes that *Allogenes* and *Zostrianos* are probably to be included in the "apocalypses of Zoroaster and Zostrianos and Nicotheos and Allogenes and Messos and of other such figures" (Porphyry, *Vita Plot.* 16) whose doctrine was attacked by Plotinus and refuted at great length by Amelius and Porphyry himself in the period 244–269 CE,[15] one may provisionally date *Allogenes* and *Zostrianos* around 225–270 CE.[16] In his antignostic treatise (*Enn.* III 8; V 8; V 5 and II 9, chronologically 30–33), Plotinus surely has these tractates in view, even though his critique of gnostic thought embraces materials beyond merely these two

---

[15] Cf. Porphyry *Vit. Plot.* 16: "In his time and circle there were many different Christians, especially sectarians who drew upon [or: abandoned] the old philosophy, men of the schools of Adelphios and Aquilinos, who possessed many treatises of Alexander of Libya and Philocomos and Demostratos and Lydos [or: Demostratos of Lydia] and produced revelations by Zoroaster and Zostrianos, and Nicotheos, and Allogenes and Messos, and other people of the kind...." See C. Schmidt, *Plotins Stellung zum Gnosticismus und kirchlichen Christentum* (TUGAL 20; Leipzig: J. C. Hinrichs, 1901); C. Elsas, *Neuplatonische und gnostische Weltablehnung in der Schule Plotins* (Berlin and New York: de Gruyter, 1975), both without benefit of *Allogenes*, the *Three Steles of Seth, Zostrianos,* and *Marsanes*. More recently, see J. H. Sieber, "An Introduction to the Tractate *Zostrianos*," *NovT* 15 (1972): 233–40; idem, "Introduction" to *Zostrianos* (NHC VIII,*1*) in *Nag Hammadi Codex VIII* (ed. J. H. Sieber; NHS 31; Leiden: Brill, 1991), 19–25; M. Tardieu, "Les trois stèles de Seth," *Revue des Sciences Philosophiques et Religieuses* 57 (1973): 545–75; J. M. Robinson, "*The Three Steles of Seth* and the Gnostics of Plotinus," in *Proceedings of the International Colloquium on Gnosticism, August 20–25, 1973* (ed. G. Widengren; Stockholm: Almqvist & Wiksell, 1977), 132–42; A. H. Armstrong, "Gnosis and Greek Philosophy," in *Gnosis: Festschrift für Hans Jonas* (ed. B. Aland; Göttingen: Vandenhoeck & Ruprecht, 1978), 87–124; B. Pearson, "The Tractate *Marsanes* (NHC X) and the Platonic Tradition," in *Gnosis: Festschrift für Hans Jonas,* 373–84; idem, "Gnosticism and Platonism: With Special Reference to *Marsanes* (NHC 10,1)," *HTR* 77 (1984): 55–73 [repr. in *Gnosticism, Judaism and Egyptian Christianity* (SAC; Minneapolis: Fortress, 1990), 148–64]; idem, "Introduction" to *Marsanes* (NHC X) in *Nag Hammadi Codices IX and X* (NHS 15; Leiden: Brill, 1981), 244–50; J. D. Turner, "The Gnostic Threefold Path to Enlightenment: The Ascent of Mind and the Descent of Wisdom," *NovT* 22 (1980): 324–351; idem, "Sethian Gnosticism: A Literary History," in *Nag Hammadi, Gnosticism and Early Christianity* (ed. C. W. Hedrick and R. Hodgson; Peabody, Mass: Hendrickson, 1986), 55–86; idem, "Gnosticism and Platonism: The Platonizing Sethian Texts from Nag Hammadi in Their Relation to Later Platonic Literature," in *Neoplatonism and Gnosticism* (ed. R. T. Wallis and J. Bregman; Albany, N.Y.: SUNY Press, 1992), 424–59; idem, "Text, Translation and Notes," and A. Wire, "Introduction," to *Allogenes* in *Nag Hammadi Codices XI, XII and XIII* (ed. C. W. Hedrick; NHS 28; Leiden: Brill, 1990).

[16] Porphyry certainly recognized *Zostrianos* as a spurious and recent work; *Allogenes* is also to be included among the various Sethian works under the name of Allogenes mentioned by Epiphanius around 375 C.E. (*Pan.* 39.5.1; 40.2.2).

treatises.[17] As for the other Platonizing Sethian treatises, the date of the *Three Steles of Seth* seems indeterminate, while *Marsanes* seems to come slightly later than *Allogenes* and *Zostrianos*.[18] ... One may argue for the chronological priority of *Zostrianos* over *Allogenes* on two principal grounds: 1) It evinces traditional Sethian baptismal concerns and therefore maintains greater proximity to earlier Sethian material, and 2) the hostile reception of the Platonically-inspired content of *Allogenes* and *Zostrianos* among the members of Plotinus' seminars in early third-century Rome (Porphyry, *Vita Plotini* 16) seems more directed to *Zostrianos* than to *Allogenes*. In contrast to the other three treatises of this group, *Zostrianos* contains a number of specific features singled out for criticism and ridicule by Plotinus towards the end (*Enn.* II, 9 [33]) of his antignostic *Gross-Schrift*: the story of the "fall" of Sophia; many instances of glossalalia; frequent lists of multiple divine beings whose names may have seemed to have magical import; and various technical terms denoting levels of reality in addition to those of the Invisible Spirit, Triple-Powered One, and the tripartite Barbelo-Aeon, such as the *Antitypoi,* the *Paroikeseis,* the *Metanoiai* and the *Ge Aerodios.* Since such features were criticized by Plotinus himself, and since the late and spurious character of *Zostrianos* was pointed out by Porphyry, and since Amelius composed a 40 volume refutation of the same work, one might surmise that *Allogenes*, which lacks these features, was composed as a refinement of *Zostrianos* that would be more acceptable to the circle of Plotinus by virtue of a clearer and more accurate and technical exposition of the ontology and visionary ascent basic to Zostrianos freed from its objectionable excesses.[19]

---

[17] This is the *Großschrift* recognized by R. Harder, "Ein neue Schrift Plotins," *Hermes* 71 (1936): 1–10, repr. in *Kleine Schriften* (ed. W. Marg; Munich, 1960), 257–74. The unpublished paper of R. T. Wallis, "Plotinus and the Gnostics: The Nag Hammadi Texts" (23 pp.; summarized by me in "Gnosticism and Platonism," 455–56) gives a thorough demonstration of the relation between *Zostrianos* and the gnostics with whom Plotinus remonstrates.

[18] B. A. Pearson ("Introduction," 229–50) suggests that the name Marsanes, mentioned in the Untitled text of the Bruce Codex (235.13–23 Schmidt and MacDermot) in connection with Nicotheos (and Marsianos in Epiphanius's account of the Archontics, *Pan.* 40.7.6), reflects a Syrian background for its author, and dates *Marsanes* in the early third century. But one may also argue for dating it to the last quarter of the third century in that it posits an unknown Silent One above even the Invisible Spirit in much the same way that Iamblichus during this same period posited an ineffable One beyond even the Plotinian One that heads the noetic triad (apud Damascius *Princ.* 1.86.3–6; 101.14–15; 103.6–10 Ruelle).

[19] R. Majercik suggests a similar revision, in particular to conform with the "teachings of the great Porphyry," thereby gaining intellectual credibility in Roman intellectual circles; see below.

The fact that documents under these names were read in Plotinus's circle suggests that they were produced earlier than the refutations produced by Plotinus and others during Porphyry's six-year stay with Plotinus in Rome from 263 through 268 C.E. In the case of *Zostrianos,* so many of whose features are echoed in Plotinus's critique of the gnostics,[20] it seems nearly certain that Plotinus's circle had some earlier Greek version of this Coptic document in view during the course of his refutations of the gnostics, and that it is this treatise that Porphyry regarded as late and spurious, and against which Amelius composed a forty-book refutation. Of course, since both *Allogenes* and *Zostrianos* are extant only in Coptic translation and each bears traces of redaction and literary dependency, one cannot be certain of the precise version of these treatises available to Plotinus and his circle. Assuming Zostrianos is pre-Plotinian or at least predates his anti-gnostic *Großschrift,* then—aside from some of Plotinus's early doctrines—one would expect to find the most likely sources of *Zostrianos's* philosophical conceptuality in pre-Plotinian sources such as the Neopythagorean technical arithmetical treatises of Nicomachus and Theon, the epitome of Albinus/Alcinoos, and the theological doxographies of Moderatus, Numenius, Amelius, Cronius, and the *Chaldean Oracles,* which are equally if not more fragmentary than *Zostrianos.* And, should it turn out to be pre-Plotinian and not written by Porphyry, the anonymous *Parmenides Commentary* would also have to be considered as a very likely source.

4. The Platonizing Sethian Treatises As Post-Porphyrian: Abramowski and Majercik

In the two decades following my completion of the 1990 *editio princeps* of *Allogenes,* I have considered both *Allogenes* and *Zostrianos* to be pre-Plotinian works. However, in 1983, Luise Abramowski, and in 1990, Ruth Majercik have called this early dating into question.[21] In 1993, I attempted to address Majercik's thesis of a post-Porphyrian date for these treatises:

---

[20] Specifically, the idea that *Sophia* is derivative and alien (*Zost.* NHC VIII 9,65–11, 9; cf. *Enn.* 5.8 [31].5), or that Soul or *Sophia* declined and put on human bodies, or that *Sophia* illumined the darkness, producing an image in matter, which in turn produces an image of the image (2.9 [33].10; cf. Plotinus's own version of this in 3.9 [13].2!); the idea of a demiurge whose activity gives rise to aeonic copies (*antitypoi*), "repentances," and "sojourns" (2.9 [33].6) or an "alien earth" (2.9 [33].11; cf. the "atmospheric realm," *gē aerōdios* of NHC VIII 5,10–29; 8,9–16; 12,4–21); the unnecessary multiplication of Hypostases; and the conception of secondary knowledge of yet a higher knowledge (*Enn.* 2.9 [33].1; cf. NHC VIII 82,1–13).

[21] See L. Abramowski, "Marius Victorinus, Porphyrius und die römischen Gnostiker," *ZNW* 74 (1983): 108–28; and R. Majercik, "The Being-Life-Mind Triad in Gnosticism and Neoplatonism," *CQ* 42 (1992): 475–88.

R. Majercik has recently argued that these treatises neither predate nor are contemporaneous with Plotinus, on the grounds that: the triadic groupings used in them have an explicit and fixed form uncharacteristic of Plotinus; their technical use of the term ὕπαρξις for the first member of the Existence-Vitality-Mentality triad has no specific significance for Plotinus (who employs the nomenclature Being-Life-Mind); and the nomenclature of these triads on various levels reflects a method of paronymy and doctrine of predominance and cyclical implication likewise uncharacteristic of Plotinus. Instead, [Majercik here shares the viewpoint of L. Abramowski that] all of these features are found in Plotinus' disciple Porphyry, whose lost commentary on the *Chaldaean Oracles* (and perhaps the anonymous *Parmenides* commentary attributed to him by P. Hadot) must have been the Greek source that mediated them not only to the Sethian treatises, but also to the Christian Neoplatonists Victorinus and Synesius.[22]

In the light of such considerations, these Platonizing Sethian treatises could not have been the same texts known to Plotinus but instead are revisions of earlier works in the wake of Porphyry's and Amelius's attacks (*Vit. Plot.* 16): "the Gnostics in Rome—in light of this criticism [of the gnostic revelations mentioned in *Vit. Plot.* 16]—revised their revelations (or produced new revelations) to conform more closely to the teachings of the great Porphyry—a politic way to gain intellectual credibility in Roman philosophical circles." The gnostics depend on Porphyry, and the *terminus a quo* for the present form of *Allogenes,* the *Three Steles of Seth,* and *Zostrianos* is at least 268 C.E. (the approximate year of Plotinus's death) and, more reasonably still, since the Nag Hammadi library was probably buried in the Egyptian desert circa 350, any time during the first quarter of the fourth century. But this need not be the case, as I suggested in 1993:

> However, the principle of mutual implication and predominance is clearly present already in Plotinus (e.g., *Enn.* V.8.4.7–24), Numenius (frg. 41 des Places), and perhaps in the *Chaldaean Oracles* (frgs. 21, 27), and the dependence of Victorinus on Porphyry does not mean that Porphyry is the ultimate source of the terms τριδύναμος or ὀντότης (neither occur in Porphyry's extant works), ὕπαρξις (which occurs also in Plutarch, Philo, Alexander of Aphrodisias, as well as Porphyry), οὐσιότης (also occurring earlier in Albinus/Alcinous, *Didask.* X.3.7), ζωότης, and νοότης. The ultimate source of these ideas probably cannot be identified as a particular individual, but more than likely they stem from Middle Platonic sources referred to in the philosophical exchange within Plotinus' circle in Rome 244–269 CE, which included not only Plotinus,

---

[22] "Typologies of the Sethian Gnostic Treatises from Nag Hammadi," 205–6.

Porphyry, and Amelius, but also quite likely proponents of these self-same Platonizing Sethian treatises.[23]

5. The Platonizing Sethian Treatises Are Middle Platonic: Corrigan contra Majercik

In a much more thoroughgoing way, Kevin Corrigan's "The Anonymous Turin *Commentary on the Parmenides* and the Distinction between Essence and Existence in Middle Platonism, Plotinus's Circle, and Sethian Gnostic Texts" (herein cited as "The Anonymous Turin Commentary"; the revised version of this paper in the present volume, "Platonism and Gnosticism. The Anonymous *Commentary on the Parmenides:* Middle or Neoplatonic?" is here cited as "Platonism and Gnosticism"), argues that *Zostrianos* and *Allogenes* predate not only Porphyry, but also Plotinus: their metaphysics are Middle Platonic. In response to Majercik's thesis of a post-Porphyrian date for *Allogenes* and *Zostrianos,* Corrigan observes ("Platonism and Gnosticism," Appendix IV: "The Pre-Plotinian Character of the Gnostic Triads," 168–69; cf. 156 in the main article):

> The explicit gnostic triads are much more plausibly pre-Plotinian Platonic elaborations in the Chaldean tradition, of the type, for instance, that Amelius develops in a Neopythagorean manner. Second, all the positive evidence, as we have argued above, points to the pre-Plotinian origin of some variant of the ὕπαρξις-δύναμις-νοῦς triad. Third, the method of paronyms that seems to give rise to the ὀνότης-ζωότης-νοότης triad is surely also familiar in Middle Platonism. Αὐτότης and ἑτερότης are attested to in "Pythagorean" thought by Sextus Empiricus (*Math.* 2.248–84), and in Albinus (*Did.* 10.164) in a section on God, there occurs a triad of adjectival epithets (αὐτοτελής-αὐτοτελής-παντελής) followed by five substantial ones: divinity (θειότης), substantiality (οὐσιότης), Truth (ἀλήθεια), Symmetry (συμμετρία), Good (ἀγαθόν). Θειότης and οὐσιότης also occur in the *Corp. herm.* 12.1. So the method of paronyms is also conspicuously Middle Platonic and so too are the principles of predominance and implication, an admittedly rudimentary version of which we find in the passage immediately following in the *Didaskalikos:* the primary god is the Good because he benefits all things according to their capacities, the Beautiful insofar as he is in his own nature perfect and commensurable, and Truth because he is the origin of truth (164.32–40).[24]

---

[23] Ibid., 206.

[24] Corrigan mentions further examples of important paronyms and rudimentary versions of later triadic schemata, as well as of the principle of predominance, in

Observing that "these Gnostic writings would not have caused the obvious reaction Porphyry claims they did were they not inherently or (perhaps better) overtly philosophical in the first place (and perhaps exhibiting a tendency to become even more so, if we were able to date the Sethian Gnostic treatises in their chronological order), and did they not make the strong claim, clearly abhorrent to Plotinus, that they were interpreting Plato in some distinctive Platonist fashion" ("The Anonymous Turin Commentary," 30), Corrigan concludes:

> the texts we possess are (1) most likely to be *in nuce* what Plotinus, Amelius, and Porphyry actually read and (2) to have been dependent upon some earlier or contemporary Platonic commentary on the *Parmenides* such as was also available and read in the Plotinian school (Corrigan, "Platonism and Gnosticism," 155)

On the other hand, Corrigan agrees with Majercik that the Platonizing Sethian treatises are dependent on the anonymous *Commentary:*

> on the basis of all the positive evidence it is most plausible to suppose (1) that the *Commentary* could *not* have been written by Porphyry and that it must be earlier than Plotinus, (2) that the 'Sethian' Gnostic texts of the Nag Hammadi library, to which Porphyry appears to refer in the *Life of Plotinus* (*Vit. Plot.*) chapter 16, are dependent upon the *Commentary*, (3) that some version of these texts (and necessarily a philosophical version) was the subject of Amelius's refutation in forty volumes (as Porphyry tells us in the *Life of Plotinus)*, and (4) that Plotinus "replies" in the four works of the *Großschrift* to gnostic doctrine in general and also, probably in part, to some version of the gnostic texts. I therefore make the *Commentary* Middle Platonic (of Neopythagorean provenance), put the Sethian gnostic texts after the *Commentary*, and place the *Großschrift* and subsequent treatises in the *Enneads* as in some measure developing innovative philosophical solutions in reply to gnostic, and other, challenges and problems. (Corrigan, "Platonism and Gnosticism," 142–44)

Instead, the *Commentary* is a pre-Plotinian Middle Platonic work in the Neopythagorean tradition of interpretation "possibly from the 'school' of

---

Amelius (apud Proclus *In Tim.* 1.361.26–362.9; 1.398.15ff.), Albinus, Moderatus, Theon of Smyrna (*Exp.* 37.15–18 Hiller; Nicomachus of Gerasa (*Arith. Intro.* 2.8, p. 88, 9–10 Hoche), the *Chaldean Oracles* (frgs. 27, 26, 28, 29, 31; cf. frgs. 12, 23), Numenius, the Stoics, and especially Philo (*Abr.* 11.52–53; see Hadot, "Être, vie, pensée chez Plotin et avant Plotin," in *Les sources de Plotin* [Entretiens sur l'antiquité classique 5; Vandoeuvres-Geneva: Fondation Hardt, 1960], 126–28), "which are related—according to admittedly later testimony—to triads in and enneadic interpretations of the *Chaldean Oracles*" (Corrigan, "Platonism and Gnosticism," 169–70).

Numenius and Cronius," and the Sethian gnostic texts "in some form" pre-date the *Großschrift* and rely upon the *Commentary* (Corrigan, "Platonism and Gnosticism," 161; cf. Appendix IV: "The Pre-Plotinian Character of the Gnostic Triads").[25] By contrast with the more or less serial listing used by the *Commentary* and the Sethian treatises to describe the sequence of phases or moments in the complex generation of intellect, "Plotinus is not concerned with schemata but with the linking of the generative process and the dynamic nature of a hypostasis by means of a single thought pattern, which articulates the complexity of the hypostasis" (Corrigan, "Platonism and Gnosticism," 157).

6. *The* Parmenides Commentary *Is Anonymous and Middle Platonic: Corrigan contra Hadot*

Since 1980, all discussion of the Platonizing treatises has made reference to the occurrence of the Existence-Life-Intellect triad as it occurs in the anonymous *Parmenides Commentary,* under the assumption that Hadot had correctly assigned it to Porphyry. Now in 1995, we return to the question of the relative position of the Platonizing Sethian treatises within the spectrum of the Platonism of the first three centuries, but from a new perspective on the pivotal position of that commentary within the Platonic tradition.

Since the views of Majercik and Abramowski depend on P. Hadot's attribution to Porphyry of both the Existence-Life-Mind triad and the *Parmenides Commentary* in which it is found, Corrigan devotes the first section of his paper to an examination of the principal grounds of Hadot's thesis, namely that the *Commentary* presupposes the Plotinian doctrine of the One and Intellect and that it presupposes Plotinus's groundbreaking theological interpretation of the *Parmenides,* but in such a way as to go well beyond Plotinus's views; therefore the *Commentary* was produced between 270 C.E. and the first half of the fifth century, during which period the only likely candidate for author was Porphyry. The basic grounds for Hadot's thesis are each open to question (summarizing Corrigan, "Platonism and Gnosticism," Appendix I: "The Theses of Pierre Hadot on the Anonymous *Parmenides Commentary* and Porphyry"):

1. In response to Hadot's claim that the *Commentary* necessarily presupposes Plotinus's doctrine of the One as well as Plotinus's interpretation of the *Parmenides,* Corrigan points out that on Plotinus's own testimony his system of hypostases, including his doctrine of the One and Intellect, was shared by other Middle Platonic thinkers.

---

[25] On this whole issue, see now G. Bechtle, *The Anonymous Commentary on Plato's «Parmenides»* (Berner Reihe philosophischer Studien 22; Bern: Paul Haupt, 1999).

2. To Hadot's claim that the *Commentary* presupposes Plotinus's doctrine of intellect but goes far beyond this in deriving a second act of intellect as an unfolding out of, and original identity with, the primordial unity of the first immobile self-standing act, Corrigan argues that all of the so-called innovations in the *Commentary* are already to be found in Plotinus, and there is a remarkable affinity in thought between Plotinus, Amelius, and the anonymous commentator that stem from a still earlier tradition of commentary necessitated by the need for an intelligent reading of difficult passages in Plato's *Parmenides*. The commentator's doctrine of participation, that the Second One receives being from the idea of being that is the First One, is the sort of participation that both Syrianus and Proclus specifically deny to Porphyry but attribute to earlier pre-Plotinian Middle Platonic and Neopythagorean thinkers like Numenius, Cronius, and Amelius.

3. The two states of intellect theory in the *Commentary,* according to which in Hadot's estimation we are virtually dealing with two intellects, one that contemplates intelligible objects, and another that engages in an absolute, transcendent, objectless knowing, is much more comparable to Middle Platonic doctrine (e.g. *Chaldean Oracles,* Numenius, or even Amelius) as well as to early tendencies in Plotinus's writings to split intellect into two—a "standing" and a "moving" intellect, e.g., 3.9 [13].1.

4. The commentator's description of the dynamic process of Intellect's "autoposition" that Hadot characterizes as clearly post-Plotinian is already present in Plotinus's exploration of the ambiguities of the "traveling subject in the logic of generation" in a manner similar to the commentator, though without explicitly invoking the being-life-thought triad used by the commentator (and, I might add, by the authors of *Allogenes* and *Zostrianos*). In fact, Plotinus's (*Enn.* 6.7 [38].13.16–21) three-phase process consisting of (1) an immobile motion, (2) a moment of static identity, and (3) a moment of burgeoning duality based on motion and otherness are quite likely already formulaic in the Neopythagorean language of procession and conversion (e.g., Moderatus) and the tradition of deriving a dyad from a monad (e.g., Nicomachus, Theon).

Corrigan's conclusion is clear:

> There is, therefore, less and less reason to believe that Porphyry is necessarily the author of the anonymous *Commentary*. All the evidence indicates that the doctrines of the *Commentary* are perfectly compatible with Middle Platonist thought and also with some important passages in the *Enneads* which themselves in turn relate to earlier Middle Platonic and Neopythagorean doctrines. My preliminary conclusion here, then, is that we should take Plotinus' own word in V, 1 (10) as sufficient assurance that the vast majority of his doctrines are not original with him. What we see in Plotinus is a new way of doing philosophy (one of course very much related to the *palaia philosophia* of Plato and Aristotle), and not the sort of doxography which might permit us to establish a *terminus a quo* on

this issue. The straightforward evidence then should be given more weight: the *Commentary* is anonymous and there is nothing in it which could not be Middle Platonic. Conspicuous doctrines of the *Commentary* appear in certain Sethian Gnostic texts which appear to be (very roughly) contemporary with Plotinus. Therefore, it is more reasonable to suppose, if there is nothing to the contrary, that the Commentary is pre-Plotinian. (Corrigan, "The Anonymous Turin Commentary," 24)

7. *Plotinus's Antignostic* Großschrift *Presupposes the Platonizing Sethian Treatises*

In part 2 of his paper, Corrigan argues ("Platonism and Gnosticism," 156): (1) that the Sethian gnostic texts are, most probably, dependent upon the anonymous *Commentary* rather than vice versa; (2) that in Middle Platonism and in Amelius one of the hidden problems of *Timaeus*-interpretation, possibly prompted in part by gnostic attacks and an appropriation of Plato, was the development of a prefigurative intelligible biology within which the interpretation of Aristotelian thought in the service of Plato started to figure more prominently; (3) "that this trend evident in the *Commentary* and to a lesser extent in the existence-essence distinctions in the Sethian gnostic texts led to a new and much more developed distinction between essence and existence in Plotinus; (4) that this Plotinian distinction is to be related in the first place (i.e., chronologically) to the *Großschrift* as a whole and that it most likely presupposes (a) the more rudimentary version of the triadic distinction of the *Commentary* and (b) the more varied versions of the Sethian gnostic texts; and finally (5) that important elements in the structure of the *Großschrift* presuppose significant motifs, images, and ideas in the Sethian gnostic texts" (not necessarily, however, in precisely the form we now have them).

7.1. The Sethian Treatises Depend upon the *Anonymous Commentary*

To a large extent, Corrigan's case for the dependence of *Allogenes'* and *Zostrianos*'s "Platonic-Pythagorean" doctrine of "the emergence of a second One as an indefinite movement which by conversion knows both itself and its principle" upon the *Commentary* or its equivalent rests on the striking—thus noncoincidental—similarity between fragments 12 and 14 of the *Commentary* (cited above, p. 195) and *Allogenes* XI 48,6–49,37 and *Zost.* 66,14–75,11 (cited above, pp. 192–94). It seems to me that these parallels are clearly sufficient to establish this claim.

Michel Tardieu has also recently argued that *Zostrianos* was circulated and read in Plotinus's Roman seminar (Porphyry *Vit. Plot.* 16): "the totality of *Zostrianos*—whose content we know through the Coptic version in the Nag Hammadi Codices—was already written in 263, at the time of the arrival of the Gnostics in the School of Plotinus."[26] Moreover, it shares a word-for-word negative theological source with book 1 of Marius Victorinus's treatise *Against Arius* (VIII 64,13–66,11 = *Ar.* 1.49.9-40, cited above, pp. 184–85), which must depend upon a pre-Plotinian interpretation of the *Parmenides* similar to but not identical with the *Anonymous Commentary*. What is more, it appears that the anonymous *Parmenides* commentary that Hadot has attributed to Porphyry contains a statement[27] that depends upon both the *Chaldean Oracles*[28] and the theological source common to Victorinus[29] and *Zostrianos*;[30] thus this common negative theological source predates even the *Anonymous Commentary*.[31] Taken together, these

---

[26] M. Tardieu, "Recherches sur la formation" (pp. 7–114); and P. Hadot, "'Porphyre et Victorinus,' Questions et hypothèses" in *Res Orientales 9* (Bures-sur-Yvette: Groupe pour l'Étude de la Civilisation du Moyen-Orient, 1996), 117–25, esp. 112.

[27] *In Parm.* frg. 9.1–4: "Others, although they affirm that He has robbed himself of all that which is his, nevertheless concede that his power and intellect are co-unified in his simplicity"

[28] *Chaldean Oracles* frg. 3: "the Father snatched himself away and did not enclose his own fire in his intellectual Power" (Majercik).

[29] Esp. *Ar.* 1.50.10: "Since he is one in his simplicity, containing three powers: complete Existence, Life, and Blessedness."

[30] Esp. VIII 66,14–20: "For they are [triple] powers of his [unity: complete] Existence, Life, and Blessedness. In Existence he exists [as] a simple unity."

[31] Tardieu, "Recherches sur la formation," 100–1: "Ainsi que le note Pierre Hadot (*Porphyre et Victorinus*, II, p. 91,2), la formule *simplicitate unus qui sit tres potentias couniens* [*Ar.* 50.10] se retrouve textuellement dans le *Commentaire au Parménide*, qu'il attribue à Porphyre, IX 4: ἐν τῇ ἁπλότητι αὐτοῦ συνηνῶσθαι. Voici ce passage: «D'autres, bien qu'ils affirment qu'Il (le Père) s'est lui-même dérobé à toutes les choses qui sont à Lui, concèdent néanmoins que sa puissance et son intellect sont co-unifiés dans sa simplicité» (IX 1–4, trad. Hadot, p. 91). L'expression οἱ εἰπόντες désigne les *Oracles chaldaiques*, puisque la première partie de la tradition qui leur est attribuée, ἁρπάσαι ἑαυτόν est une citation de l'oracle 3,1: ὁ πατὴρ ἥρπασσεν ἑαυτόν. Dans la seconde partie de cette tradition, δύναμίν τε αὐτῷ διδόασι καὶ νοῦν ἐν τῇ ἁπλότητι συνηνῶσθαι, l'auteur présumé du *Commentaire*, autrement dit Porphyre, n'utilise plus la terminologie chaldaïque mais celle de l'exposé (*in simplicitate couniens*) pour interpréter le second vers du même oracle 3, connu par Psellos (= oracle 33 chez Pléthon, ed. Tambrun-Krasker, pp. 4, 18 et 147–150): οὐδ' ἐν ἑῇ δυνάμει νοερᾷ κλείσας ἴδιον πῦρ. Par conséquent, force est de constater que les témoignages cités disent tous les trois la même chose: 1) l'exposé commun à Marius Victorinus et au *Zostrien*, affirme d'abord que l'Esprit est *in semet ipso manens, solus in solo* (50,9) puis énonce le contraire, à savoir que l'Esprit co-unifie dans sa simplicité les trois puissances de l'existence, de la vie et de la béatitude (50,10–11); 2) selon le fr. 3 des *Oracles chaldaïques*, pareillement, le

factors suggest (1) that theological expositions and lemmatic commentaries on the *Parmenides* were available in the late second century, (2) that they were pre-Plotinian and Middle Platonic (Tardieu suggests Numenian authorship, while Corrigan suggests Cronius), (3) that one of these was used by the version of *Zostrianos* known to Plotinus, and (4) that the *Anonymous Commentary* need not necessarily be ascribed to Porphyry, but may be dated earlier, before Plotinus. Combined with Corrigan's argument for the pre-Plotinian origin for the anonymous *Parmenides* commentary, Tardieu's observation that the anonymous *Parmenides Commentary* may depend on both the *Chaldean Oracles* and the common source presently embedded in Victorinus and *Zostrianos* makes a strong case indeed that the *Commentary* is not by Porphyry but is a product of Middle Platonic *Parmenides* interpretation.

7.2. Middle Platonic Adaptations of Aristotle: Albinus, Numenius, Amelius, the *Chaldean Oracles,* and the Divine Intellect

Albinus, Numenius, and Amelius are three philosophers who pressed Aristotle's doctrine of God as a self-thinking intellect into the service of Middle Platonic thought concerning the relation between God, the ideas, and the demiurgic intellect in order to show how the being, life, and thought that characterize our own experience are in fact prefiguratively articulated on the transcendent plane in the form of an eternally actual intellect (see Corrigan, "Platonism and Gnosticism," Appendix IV: "The Pre-Plotinian Character of the Gnostic Triads").

The tripartition of the divine Intellect into a contemplated, a contemplating, and a demiurgic intellect in these thinkers might be compared with *Allogenes* (NHC XI 51,12–37), where Kalyptos is associated with the authentic existents, Protophanes with the reason that intelligizes (νόερος λόγος) these and acts within particulars with ἐπιστήμη and τέχνη, and Autogenes as the one that knows and acts upon the defects of nature in a particular manner; and finally the divine Triple Male is regarded as the

---

Père à la fois s'est dérobé (= reste seul) et n'enferme pas dans sa puissance le feu qui lui est propre, il ne reste donc pas seul et se déploie; 3) Porphyre, enfin, affirme, avec les *Oracles,* que l'Un se dérobe, et, avec l'exposé, que sa puissance est co-unifiée dans la simplicité. Ces trois témoignages coincident mais révèlent aussi une histoire. Dès lors, en effet, que l'auteur du *Commentaire au Parménide* réunit dans la même exégèse deux formules, l'une appartenant aux *Oracles chaldaïques,* l'autre à l'exposé, ces deux documents sont donc les sources de cet auteur, antérieures à lui et tenues par lui comme textes fondateurs. De la même façon qu'il est peu crédible qu'il y ait identité d'auteur entre 2 et 3, l'hypothèse d'une identité d'auteur entre 1 et 3 paraît, comme nous l'avons déjà vu, difficilement envisageable en raison même de la dénomination d'Esprit (Pneuma) donnée à l'Un-Père par l'exposé."

integration or preservation of these three with the Invisible Spirit, a "rational expression of deliberation" (λόγος βουλήσεως; a term also applied to Barbelo in *Steles Seth,* VII 120,28).

> **XI 51** [12] As with all [the] aeons, [13] the Barbelo-Aeon exists, [14] also endowed with the types [15] and forms of the things that truly [16] exist, the image of [17] Kalyptos. And endowed [18] with the reason cognizant of [19] these, it bears the noetic, male [20] Protophanes like [21] an image, and he acts [22] within the Individuals either with [23] craft or with skill [24] or with partial instinct. [25] It is endowed with the [26] divine Autogenes like [27] an image, and he knows [28] each one of these, [29] acting separately and [30] individually, continually rectifying [31] the defects from [32] Nature. It is endowed with [33] the divine Triple Male [34] as an integration of them all [35] with the Invisible Spirit; [36] he is a rational expression of deliberation, [37] the perfect Child.

Although the parallels are not exact, there is here a certain resemblance to the hierarchy of interlocking and interdependent functions of Amelius's three intellects (according to Proclus *In Tim.* 1.306.1–14; 1.361.26–362.4; 1.398.16–26: ὄντα-ἔχοντα-ορῶντα; βουληθείς-ὁ λογιζόμενος-ὁ παραλαβών; βουλήσει-ἐπιτάξει-μεταχειρήσει) and the three gods of Numenius among which the higher operates ἐν προσχρήσει of the lower.[32] Moreover, even the mere Sethian nomenclature for the intellectual levels of the Barbelo Aeon suggest a doctrine of successive phases in the emanation of the divine mind or thought (Barbelo) from its source in the One: at first hidden (*Kalyptos*) in its source, Barbelo/Mind then first appears (*Protophanes*) and is instantiated as a self-generated (*Autogenēs*) being. Corrigan observes further that this prefiguration of being, life and thought is present not only in Albinus, Numenius, and the anonymous *Commentary* (and perhaps even Amelius), even though a strictly derivational context occurs only in the *Commentary*. This prefigurative intelligible biology is also present in

> the *Chaldean Oracles* where the "flower of intellect" plays an archetypal role for the whole subsequent tradition (and the language of life and growth, if not the term ζωή itself, assumes a new intelligible significance (*Chaldean Oracles*, frgs. 37; 39.4; 16; 17; 33; 68 Majercik). Again, in the Hermetic and gnostic systems "life" assumes the role of a divine principle [cf. *Corp. herm.* 1.9, 12; 13.9; *De Myst.* 267.4; E. R. Dodds, *Proclus: The Elements of Theology*, 253 n. 3]. What we see by contrast in "late Middle

---

32 Proclus *In Tim.* 3.103.28–32: "The first god functions as the really existing paradigm, the second acts by πρόσχρησις as intellect [κατὰ τὸν νοῦν], and the third, again, by πρόσχρησις of the second with the third, as demiurgic and reflective [κατὰ τὸν διανοούμενον], strictly speaking."

Platonism" is a new attention to the prefigurative power of the Intelligible Universe and to its philosophical meaning. As a consequence, Aristotelian (and Stoic) thought clearly starts to assume greater significance. (Corrigan, "Platonism and Gnosticism," Appendix V: "Numenius and Amelius," 175)

7.3. Implications of the Middle Platonic Prefigurative Intelligible Biology for Plotinus: Intellect As Determinate Life

Also in part 2 of his original paper ("The Anonymous Turin Commentary," 47–52), Corrigan tried to show that the prefigurative intelligible biology based on the application of Aristotelian to Platonic thought evident in the *Commentary* and in the existence-essence distinctions in the Sethian gnostic texts leads to a new, more developed distinction between essence and existence in Plotinus. Specifically, Corrigan argues (1) that Plotinus, over the course of a long argument in 6.7 [38].18–23, 31–42, makes a highly developed and subtle distinction between what we might call essence and existence (that is, determinate being or substance, on the one hand, and unrestricted being or infinitival existence, on the other); (2) that this distinction attempts to show what thinking is and how it originates by means of a single power and activity, itself transcendent of all thought, which nonetheless constitutes the multiplicity of the intelligible world and at the same time appears to be the prefigurative model of all subsequent activities and developmental potencies; (3) that this distinction is reached by means of a highly creative use of Aristotelian thought— implicitly "entelechy" doctrine (the three moments of basic entelechy development, δύναμις-ἕξις-ἐνέργεια); (4) that this development was most likely prompted partly by Plotinus's reflection upon the more rudimentary distinction between essence and existence to be found in the *Commentary,* the *Chaldean Oracles* (according to testimony), and especially some of the more philosophical Sethian gnostic texts; (5) that the essence-existence distinction in 6.7 [38] is plausibly related to Plotinus's gnostic critique in the *Großschrift;* (6) that the sort of subtlety Plotinus's analyses demonstrate is legitimately to be explained as a reflection upon some of the major problems Gnosticism poses; and (7) that this casts significant light upon the interaction between Platonist gnostics and the Platonist Plotinian circle.

Corrigan observes that this new view in Plotinus is related (either directly or indirectly) to motifs in the Sethian gnostic texts (particularly the problem how differences arise in things, how particular properties have a transcendental source, and how diversity springs from unity; e.g., *Zost.* VIII 15–17 (cited below, pp. 222–23), *Marsanes* X 7–9 (cited above, pp. 191–92), and also to the problem of apparent intelligible individuals in intellect that are barren and generate nothing, *Allogenes* XI 49,21–25 (cited above, p. 193), and yet it goes far beyond anything we find in those texts.

In tracing out this new Aristotelian-Platonic tendency in Platonic thought, Corrigan compares the *Commentary* and some passages of the *Enneads* on the role of ζωή. In the anonymous *Commentary,* at the second moment of the intellectual triad (life), when intellect passes from existence (ὕπαρξις) to the thinking subject (εἰς τὸ νοοῦν) in order to come back up again to the intelligible object and see itself, the thinking subject is life, "which is why it is indefinite according to life" (cited above, p. 196), i.e., an indefinite duality. According to *Enn.* 2.4 [12].5.29–34, movement and otherness grew together out of the First and were indefinite (ἀόριστον) as from the First, but defined when they turn back to it. According to *Enn.* 6.7 [38].17 (cited below, n. 33), intellect's life is the trace of the giver, which shines out from the One as manifold and unbounded: "It was [ἦν] indefinite insofar as it looked to [βλέπουσα] That, but insofar as it had looked" (βλέψασα), it became limited in itself without implying any limit in the One. To distinguish phases or moments in the complex generation of intellect by careful use of verbal tense and aspect instead of the rather more simplistic serial representation found in the *Commentary* further suggests the latter's pre-Plotinian provenance.

While the triadic schemata in the *Commentary* are relatively simple and related to Middle Platonic preoccupations as evinced particularly in Albinus, the *Chaldean Oracles,* and the Neopythagoreans, the Sethian gnostic texts manifest a more complex linking of moments such as Corrigan discovers in Amelius. Moreover, the greater variety and proliferation of triads in the Sethian gnostic texts suggests to Corrigan that their innovative appropriation of Middle Platonic tradition must postdate the *Commentary* ("Platonism and Gnosticism," 157).

8. Results for the Historical Setting of the Parmenides Commentary, Zostrianos, *and* Allogenes

If Corrigan's conclusions be accepted as sound, the conceptual sphere of Middle Platonic metaphysics is larger and more varied than we once believed. The doctrine of a tripartite divine intellect containing not only the demiurgic intelligence but also the Platonic ideas as its thoughts have begun to coalesce with various Neopythagorean emanative schemes according to which the multiplicity of the sensible world is derived from an original unitary principle. The principal means of articulating this combination were various triadic schemes that attempted to identify the conceptually distinct stages of the unfolding of the divine intelligence from its unitary source. One such triadic scheme at home in the Chaldean tradition—though not explicitly in the *Oracles*—was the ὕπαρξις-δύναμις-νοῦς sequence. To avoid the notion that these entities were a succession of independent products or offspring, such conceptual devices as the principles of predominance, of mutual implication through cyclic permutation, and the method of paronymns were devised to illustrate how being or substance might derive from sheer act, or alternatively how actuality in plurality might derive from sheer unity and potential existence. The principal thinkers involved in this development were the likes of Moderatus, Nicomachus, Theon, Numenius, the author(s) of the *Chaldean Oracles,* Albinus, and Amelius.

Corrigan has argued that the emanative metaphysics and the triadic schemes of the Platonizing Sethian treatises are to be interpreted against such a background. Among these texts, *Zostrianos* and *Allogenes* are most likely to be (at least *in nuce*) what Plotinus, Amelius, and Porphyry actually read and critiqued. They in turn are dependent upon some earlier or contemporary Platonic commentary on the *Parmenides* such as was also available and read in the Plotinian school, in particular the anonymous Turin palimpsest *Commentary on the Parmenides* published by Kroll and Hadot. *Pace* Hadot and the generation of scholars (including me) that have built on his work, the *Commentary* is not likely to be by Porphyry and does not necessarily presuppose Plotinus's philosophical analysis of Plato. Rather than being post-Plotinian or even post-Porphyrian, the Sethian Platonizing texts are contemporary with or slightly prior to Plotinus, who knew their content and engaged in a critical dialogue with them and their proponents in his "antignostic" *Großschrift* and subsequent works. The Platonizing Sethian treatises are to be placed before the *Großschrift* but after the *Commentary,* whose schemata (Existence-Life-Thought/Being-Vitality-Mentality) are relatively simple Middle Platonic constructions in comparison to the greater variety and number of triads in the Sethian treatises. Moreover, the comparatively elementary distinction maintained in both the *Commentary* and the Sethian treatises between pure, unqualified existence and the realm of determined being prompt Plotinus to devote the *Großschrift* and subsequent works to the clarification and extension of various Middle Platonic attempts to explain the *Timaeus*'s picture of the relation between the intelligible and sensible realms by developing an "intelligible biology" derived from Aristotle's analysis of thinking to show how the vitality of the sensible world was already prefigured in the divine intellect.

In addition to these conclusions, with which I substantially agree, it seems to me that among the Platonizing Sethian treatises read in Plotinus's circle, the chronological priority of composition belongs to *Zostrianos* and that it is also *Zostrianos* that is the primary target of the various antignostic critiques of Plotinus and his colleagues, although they also had access at least to *Allogenes* as well. By contrast, *Allogenes* seems remarkably free of the specific objectionable features singled out by Plotinus in the concluding section of the *Großschrift* (see above, p. 196).

It may very well be that *Allogenes* was composed partly as a revision of the triadic metaphysics of *Zostrianos*. *Allogenes* eliminates all discussion of celestial aeonic levels below the Barbelo Aeon. The doctrine of the three-phase generation of the Aeon of Barbelo from the unfolding of the threefold potency of the Invisible Spirit, scattered about through *Zostrianos,* is gathered together into the initial revelations of Youel on pages 45–49. Instead of limiting the visionary ascent to the Protophanes-level of the Barbelo Aeon, *Allogenes* portrays an additional ascent through the various levels of the Triple-Powered One, which appears to have been promoted from a dynamic modalistic process inherent within the Invisible Spirit to a separately existing, quasi-hypostatic entity between a supreme Unknowable One and the Barbelo Aeon. Rather than interpreting the stages of the ascent as a sequence of baptisms administered by a plurality of revealers (Authrounios, Ephesech, and Youel), *Allogenes* structures the ascent into a set of instructions by Youel prior to the ascent through the Barbelo Aeon. By placing the "primary revelation" of the supreme unknown One in the context of Allogenes' ascent through the levels of the Triple-Powered One, *Allogenes* supplements the negative-theological revelation of the Triple-Powered Invisible Spirit in *Zostrianos* by means of a technique of learned ignorance similar to that of fragment 1 of the *Chaldean Oracles* and fragment 2 (p. 91 verso) of the *Parmenides Commentary.* In short, *Allogenes* restructures the metaphysics of *Zostrianos* into a tighter, more systematic framework, limits the metaphysical exposition to the transcendent spheres extending from the intellectual levels of the Barbelo Aeon to the supreme Invisible Spirit, more clearly articulates the process by which the Barbelo Aeon emanates from the Invisible Spirit, omits most instances of ecstatic praise and lists of divine beings, and frees the whole from a baptismal context. Omission of the role of Sophia and the Archon as well as the extensive discussion on the various types of souls entails a shift of attention away from the physical and psychological doctrine of the *Phaedo* and *Timaeus* toward the more specifically theological issues of the *Parmenides.* The result has a remarkable, if not intentional, resemblance to Diotima's initiation of Socrates into the mysteries of Eros, supplemented by the apophatic approach to the One in the *Parmenides.* The effect is to produce a work of enhanced acceptability to the critical concerns of Plotinus's circle without abandoning the essential divine beings of Sethianism and its commitment to the authority of revelation.

9. *Life: A Prefigurative Intelligible Biology and the Gnostic Contribution*

It seems that one of the major accomplishments of Middle Platonism was the recognition that the chain of the derivation of the pluriform world from an original unity demanded at some point the introduction of the principle of Life. Certainly it was a central problem for the Platonic program and for the "friends of the forms," confronted by the opposition between true being apprehensible by mind alone through reason and the realm of becoming apprehensible by body through sensation, to conceive how thought, as an activity of soul, the principle of change and motion, could have a place in the real world: were the truly real to be devoid of life and any sort of movement, thought would be impossible (*Soph.* 248e). This clearly calls for an interpretation of the process- or movement-oriented language implied by intellect and thought, as recognized also by Aristotle (in *Metaph.* 1072b13–19), to the effect that by participation in the intelligible, intellect thinks itself; becoming the intelligent recipient of substance and intelligible object, it acts in "having" them, and that act is seeing. Rather than a static state of merely containing the objects of intellection, in God the activity of thought is life; indeed God *is* that activity (See Corrigan, "Platonism and Gnosticism," Appendix V: "Numenius and Amelius").

As Corrigan notes, Amelius too (apud Proclus *In Tim.* 3.103.18–104.8) dealt similarly with the theme of transcendental intellectual movement, dividing the activity of the divine intelligence into the three phases of being, having, and seeing, on the basis of *Tim.* 39e. The same passage invited the early Plotinus (*Enn.* 3.9 [13].1) to distinguish three aspects of the divine intellect, a static, contemplated one, an active contemplating one, and a third, discursive or planning one. On the basis of this most pregnant passage, Numenius even earlier conceived his second God as a divine intellect generating itself and the sensible cosmos by a contemplative "seeing" of the first God, who thinks only insofar as he makes use of this second God (frgs. 20–22 des Places), who by preoccupation with matter gives rise to a third planning intellect.

Oddly enough, even though the supreme principle of *Tim.* 39e is "the truly living being," these Middle Platonic interpretations of the phases of the divine intellect do not seem to trade specifically in the concept of transcendental Life in quite the same way as one finds in the passages just cited from the *Sophist* and the *Metaphysics*. Yet when one turns to the Platonizing Sethian treatises, the anonymous *Parmenides Commentary,* and the later treatises of Plotinus, the term "life" and cognates assumes a central role in the generation of substantial reality, perhaps owing to the influence of those and other passages from Plato and Aristotle. But what, we might ask, was the catalyst that caused this preoccupation with life as a designation for the median phase in the movement from the apparent static transcendence of the supreme One to the manifestation of a demiurgic intellect or world soul that occupies itself with the physical world of becoming?

In his early to middle treatises Plotinus employs a three-stage deployment of defined reality from the One. For instance, in 2.4 [12].5, intellect is the end product of a movement and otherness that emerge from the First; they were indefinite (ἀόριστον) as from the First but defined when they turn back to it. Here the median term is an implicit duality "indefinite dyad," not yet fully formed that emanates from the One to form defined Being. In 5.2 [11].1.7–9, the superabundant perfection of the One overflows and makes "another" (ἄλλο), which product turns back to the One (and, as Corrigan, "Gnosticism and Platonism," 148, notes, "to *itself*" emphasis added), is "filled," and becomes Intellect by looking towards it (or itself). On the other hand, in later treatises, especially those that follow the *Großschrift,* the term ζωή begins to appear. Thus in 6.6 [34].9.39–40 there is a triadic succession of Being or unified multiplicity, movement of Intellect unraveling number into pure unities that form the content of the Living Creature or Life, which includes and unifies them all. In 6.7 [38].16.11–23, potential intellect, looking unintellectually at the One, living toward it and turning toward it, as a movement "being filled" and "filling," becomes intellect as the unified totality of all these moments. Again, in 6.7 [38].17, intellect's life is the trace of the One, which "shines out" from the One as manifold, indefinite, and unbounded (cf. the indefinite duality of 5.1 [10].6–7), but became bounded in itself without implying any limit in the One; indeed, "intellect is bounded life" (26).[33]

Clearly, this boundless life emanating from the One that we find in Plotinus's later treatises, as well as in the Sethian treatises and in the anonymous *Commentary,* play the same role as the indefinite duality inherited from Plato's unwritten doctrine and that certainly played a role in the

---

[33] In *Enn.* 6.7 [38].17.12–43: "Intellect therefore had life and had no need of a giver full of variety, and its life was a trace of that Good and not his life. So when its life was looking towards that it was unlimited, but after it had looked there it was limited, though that Good has no limit. For immediately by looking to something which is one the life is limited by it, and has in itself limit and bound and form; and the form was in that which was shaped, but the shaper was shapeless. But the boundary is not from outside, as if it was surrounded by a largeness, but it was a bounding limit of all that life which is manifold and unbounded, as a life would be which shines out from a nature of this kind ... and it was defined as many because of the multiplicity of its life, but on the other hand as one because of the defining limit. What then does 'it was defined as one' mean? Intellect: for life defined and limited is intellect. And what 'as many'? Many intellects" (trans. Armstrong). To distinguish phases of emanation, Plotinus uses a sequence of tenses (imperfect, present, and aorist) here and in 4.8 [6].1.1–11, etc., rather than the less sophisticated serial listings found in the anonymous *Commentary* and in some of the Sethian texts. The principle of Multiplicity, called "intelligible matter" in an earlier treatise (2.4) is here named "Life" (cf. also 6.5 [23].12.1–11; 2.4 [12].5.15–18). This entity, which is not hypostatized in his system, is characterized as an indefinite primary movement and otherness, a certain limitless and multiple trace of the One that, once emitted, looks back upon its source and thereby becomes defined and limited in the form of Intellect, the second hypostasis.

arithmological derivation schemes of contemporary Neopythagoreans. Thus in the anonymous *Commentary,* at the second moment of the intellectual triad (life), when intellect passes from existence (ὕπαρξις) to the thinking "it is indefinite according to life" (frg. 14.110.17–21 Hadot). This means that before the subject turns back to existence and to the One, it is an indefinite duality. As life (κατὰ τὴν ζωήν), it is "an activity moving out of existence" (ἐκ τῆς ὑπάρξεως ἐκνεύσας ἐνέργεια).

When the initial moment of Intellect as it emerges from the One is characterized in terms of indefiniteness, it is the interpretation of Plato's *Parmenides* rather than *Timaeus* that is in view. Depending upon the absence or presence of a Unity or One-which-is acting as a Limit or principle of contrast and definition, the Unlimited Multitude of hypotheses 3 (157B–158C) and 7 (164B–D) can be variously understood: in hypothesis 2 (142B–145A), (1) in the absence of Unity, as an indefinite multitude with no distinct members, or (2) in the presence of Unity, as an indefinitely numerous set of uniquely distinct members (thus generating the series of integral numbers); in hypothesis 3, as an indefiniteness arising from abstracting out the Unity (i.e., unifying factor) of a whole with individual parts; and in hypothesis 7, in the absence of Unity, as the indefiniteness of one multitude with respect to another.

From these considerations, later Platonists derived from the first hypothesis an absolutely unqualified One "beyond (determinate) being" at the summit of their hierarchy of principles, a second principle of defined being and the multiple forms, and between the two as source of defined multiplicity, an indefinite multiplicity readily identifiable with other features of Plato's teaching, e.g., the otherness (θάτερον) opposed to sameness in the *Timaeus* and *Sophist,* the limit and unlimited of the *Philebus,* and the indefinite dyad of Plato's unwritten teaching. Such speculation comes into its own in first-century Neopythagoreanism: thus according to Simplicius (*In phys.* 181.10–30 Diels) Eudorus (ca. 25 B.C.E.) posited a supreme One as the supreme God above another pair of principles, a lower One, which he calls Monad, and its opposite, the Dyad. The supreme One is the cause of Matter and all else, while the Dyad paired with the Monad beneath it he calls the Indefinite Dyad. A similar doctrine is also found in the "Pythagorean" report of Sextus Empiricus (*Math.* 10.261, 277):

> Thence moved, Pythagoras (i.e., Plato) declared that the One is the first principle of existing things by participation in which each of the existing things is said to be one. And this when conceived in self-identity [i.e. absolutely] is a Monad, but when in its otherness it is added to itself, it creates the Indefinite Dyad.

A second-century elaboration of these metaphysical constructions is offered by Moderatus, for whom the supreme principle is a first One, beyond being and all essence. According to the account of Simplicius (*In phys.* 230.34–231.26), this is followed by a second One, who is true being, intelligible (νοητόν) and is the forms (εἴδη), called the Monad or unitary Logos containing the ratios (λόγοι) of beings and the paradigms of bodies.

> It seems that this opinion concerning Matter was held first among Greeks by the Pythagoreans, and after them by Plato, as indeed Moderatus relates. For, following the Pythagoreans, [Plato] declares that the first One is above being and all essence, while the second One, the truly existent and object of intellection, he says is the Forms. The third, which is the psychic, participates in the One and the Forms, while the final nature, i.e. the sensible, does not even participate, but is ordered by reflection from those [Forms? the first and second Ones?], since Matter in the perceptible realm is a shadow of Non-being as it appears primally in quantity, and which is inferior in degree even to that. And in the second book of *On Matter* Porphyry, citing from Moderatus, has also written that the Unitary Logos, as Plato somewhere says, intending to produce from itself the origin of beings, by deprivation yielded room for [conj. Zeller, Festugière: "separated from itself"] Quantity, having deprived it of all its (the Logos') proportions and Forms. He called this Quantity shapeless, undifferentiated and formless, but receptive of shape, form, differentiation, quality etc. It is this Quantity, he says, to which Plato apparently applies various predicates, speaking of the "all receiver" and calling it "formless," even "invisible" and "least capable of participating in the intelligible" and "barely graspable by spurious reasoning" and everything similar to such predicates. This Quantity, he says, and this Form [*sic*] conceived as a privation of the Unitary Logos which contains in itself all proportions of beings, are paradigms [*sic*] of corporeal Matter which itself, he says, was called quantity by Pythagoreans and Plato, not in the sense of quantity as a Form, but in the sense of privation, paralysis, extension and disarray, and because of its deviation from that which is—which is why Matter seems to be evil, as it flees from the good. And (this Matter) is caught by it (the Logos) and not permitted to overstep its boundaries, as extension receives the proportion of ideal magnitude and is bounded by it, and as disarray is rendered eidetic by numerical distinction. So, according to this exposition, Matter is nothing else but a turning away of perceptible species from intelligible ones, as the former turn away from there and are borne downwards towards non-being.

Ontogenesis begins, not with the First One, but with the solely existing Monad or second One. By an act of self-retraction, the Monad deprives itself of its own unity, giving rise to the "first One," who then transcends it as the supreme principle and paradigm, the source of unity, limitation, and proportion.[34] In this act the Monad makes room for the "primal Quantity," the primal nonbeing that was already seminally present within it or alongside it, with its unitariness perhaps even giving rise to the First One. This incorporeal primal Quantity (ποσότης), called "all-receiver" like Plato's Receptacle of becoming—clearly Moderatus's equivalent of Plato's indefinite Dyad—is the archetype or paradigm of the corporeal quantity (ποσόν) that has been deprived of all traces of unity and form to yield the pure multiplicity and extension underlying corporeal things, which must be bounded and formed by the ideal magnitude and numerical distinction that now characterize the first One. It is as if the Monad were the One-Being (ἕν ὄν, but called here "unitary logos") of the second hypothesis of Plato's *Parmenides* that has given up its unity (ἕν) to yield the first One (who is the "simply ἕν" of the first hypothesis) and thus is now only being (ὄν) without its ἕν component, a kind of indefinite being that Moderatus calls Quantity (ποσότης).

In an alternative—non-*Parmenidean* and distinctly more Pythagorean—context, Stobaeus (*Anth.* 1.8.1–9.9) says that Moderatus conceived the Monad or second One as the formal principle that limits primal Quantity in the process of being limited (περαίνουσι ποσότης), that is, the Monad is what remains (μονή) and is stable after the subtraction of each number in turn from Multiplicity (reminiscent of Speusippus's principle of "Multiplicity," πλῆθος):

> In brief, number is a collection of monads, or a progression of multiplicity beginning from a monad, and a reversion terminating at the monad. Monads delimit Quantity, which is whatever has been deprived and is left remaining and stable when multiplicity is diminished by the subtraction of each number. For a monad does not have the power to revert beyond quantity; so that truly a monad is appropriately named from its being stable and remaining unchangeably the same, or from its being divided and being completely isolated from multiplicity.

This seems to be an adaptation of the Old Pythagorean derivation of the number One according to which the Unlimited (ἀπειρία) is drawn or breathed in and limited by Limit, except here the limiting principle draws in or contracts itself.[35] Here the function of Limit is called subtraction.

---

[34] On this and the following see G. Bechtle, *The Anonymous Commentary on Plato's «Parmenides»* (Berner Reihe philosophischer Studien 22; Bern: Paul Haupt, 1999), 107–11; 218–19.

[35] Aristotle *Metaph.* 1091a13–18: οἱ μὲν οὖν Πυθαγόρειοι πότερον οὐ ποιοῦσιν ἢ ποιοῦσι γένεσιν οὐδὲν δεῖ διστάζειν· φανερῶς γὰρ λέγουσιν ὡς τοῦ ἑνὸς συσταθέντος, εἴτ᾽ ἐξ ἐπιπέδων εἴτ᾽ ἐκ χροιᾶς εἴτ᾽ ἐκ σπέρματος εἴτ᾽ ἐξ ὧν ἀποροῦσιν εἰπεῖν, εὐθὺς τὸ ἔγγιστα τοῦ ἀπείρου ὅτι εἵλκετο καὶ ἐπεραίνετο ὑπὸ τοῦ πέρατος.

Moderatus seems to have associated this second level not only with the generation numbers but also with an elementary notion of emanation, conceiving the Monad as a permanence (μονή) from which Multiplicity (Speusippus's term for the Indefinite Dyad) generates a system of monads or ideal numbers by a progression (προποδισμός) from and a return (ἀναποδισμός) to the Monad.[36] Stobaeus also says that Moderatus distinguished between numbers as distinct but indivisible formal entities and the countable numbers of quantities and calculation[37] such that the monad, dyad, etc. are conceived ideal entities, "ideal numbers," which define pure quantity or extension by delineating it (cf. "rendering it eidetic by numerical distinction" in the Simplicius account) into groups or sets of countable objects. This quantity, however is a not-preexisting stuff, but seems to be emanated (given room) from the Monad by a self-deprivation (or subtraction from or contraction into itself) of all the proportions and forms (i.e., the multiplicity of subsequent ideal numbers, dyad, triad, etc.) of which it is the source. Thereupon, the numerical distinction of this quantity—perhaps by the first One—serves as the origin of "beings," probably the perceptible bodies of the sensible realm.[38] Thus ideal magnitude seems to have two moments, a systolic and a diastolic, the one contracting ideal multiplicity to its limit in the Monad to produce unformed quantity, and the other a generation of ideal numbers that increasingly delineate indefinite quantity into the definite mathematical objects (ratios, proportions) that will form the content of the cosmic soul.

The third One is psychical and participates in the One and the Ideas; it is the equivalent of the World Soul, which would presumably contain actual numbers and geometricals. Last comes Matter, conceived as the lower shadow cast by the primal Nonbeing, which seems to be a principle opposed to the unitary Logos, the second One, first manifested as Quantity by a privation of the eidetic power of second One.

The emergence of Barbelo from the Invisible Spirit as a projection or shadow of the One presented in *Zostrianos* (NHC VIII 78,7–83,1 cited above, pp. 189–90) and the *Three Steles of Seth* (VII 122,1–34 cited above, pp. 190–91) closely parallels Moderatus's account of the emergence of Quantity

---

[36] Cf. the Neoplatonic μονή, πρόοδος, and ἐπιστροφή and the function of the Sethian "Triple Power" discussed above.

[37] Cf. Aristotle *Phys.* 4.11.219b6.

[38] A similar notion is attested by Calcidius (*In Tim.* 293 = Numenius frg. 52 des Places): *Sed non nullo Pythagoreos vim sententiae non recte assecutos putasse dici etiam illam indeterminatam et immensam duitatem ab unica singularitate institutam recedente a natura sua singularitate et in duitatis abitum migrante—non recte, ut quae erat singularitas esse desineret, quae non erat duitas susisteret, atque ex deo silva et ex singularitate immensa et indeterminata duitas converteretur.*

from the second One: a self-privation of the unitary source results in the emergence of a receptacle of becoming that forms a place for the discrete multiplicity arising from the intellectual limitation of indefinite enumerability. Here I would claim Moderatus as an explicit source for these Sethian treatises.

However, unlike the Neopythagoreans, the Sethian treatises, the *Parmenides Commentary,* and eventually also Plotinus utilize the term "Life" to represent this indefinite otherness or boundlessness or pure quantity that proceeds from the One. What is the proximate cause of the technical use of this term for expressing the derivation of pluriform being from original unity? Among sources traditionally associated with Middle Platonism (e.g., Plutarch *Gen. Socr.* 591b; the *Corp. herm.* 1.9 and 12; 13.9), one thinks especially of the *Chaldean Oracles.*

The *Oracles* feature a feminine principle of life named Hecate, said to be a sort of diaphragm or membrane, the "center between the two Fathers" (frg. 50 Majercik), which separates the "first and second fires" (frg. 6), i.e., the Father and the immediately subjacent paternal Intellect.[39] Hecate has a dual position: On the one hand, she is the source of variegated matter, generated by the Father as the womb that receives his lightening (the ideas), "the girdling bloom of fire and the powerful breath beyond the fiery poles" (frg. 35). On the other hand, she is the life-producing fount (frgs. 30 and 32; cf. frgs. 96, 136 [ζώση δυνάμει]) from whose right side flows the World Soul (frg. 51), while her left side retains the source of virtue. Upon her back, the emblem of the moon (her traditional symbol) represents boundless Nature, and her serpentine hair represents the Father's winding noetic fire (frgs. 50–55). In her alternate designation as Rhea, she is said to be the source of the intellectuals (νόερα), whose generation she has received in her ineffable womb and upon whom she pours forth the vivifying fire (frgs. 32, 56); as ζωογόνος θεά, she is the source of life, a veritable mother of the all. Hecate is also conceived as the Womb within which all things are sown and contained, much like Plato's Receptacle,[40] and therefore seems to play a role similar to that of Plotinus's intelligible matter or trace of unbounded Life emitted from One to become bounded Intellect, not to mention the Sethian Mother Barbelo, the "Womb of the All" (*Ap. John* II 5,5; *Trim. Prot.* XIII 38,15; 45,6) who pours forth "Living Water."

---

[39] As the "center between the two Fathers," she is perhaps the triadic expression of the supreme Father's power. The terms "measuring" and "measured" (frgs. 1 and 23; in frg. 31 the νοητά are measured by the bond of a first triad "which is not the first") recall the principle of the Unlimited or of the More and Less of Plato's *Philebus,* which submits to Unity or Measure so as to produce the Forms.

[40] Frgs. 28, 30 (Majercik); cf. the "cosmic hollows" of frg. 34 (and 35), and πολλῶν πληρώματα κόλπων of frg. 96.

In addition to this quasi-philosophical source featuring a supreme principle of life or vivification, one must consider as proximate sources also the entire spectrum of Sethian gnostic treatises that feature the figure of Barbelo, where she functions not merely as the intellectual aeon, but, somewhat as the Chaldaean Hecate, even more as a merciful mother or womb[41] who grants her children enlightenment by means of baptism in the "living water" of enlightenment. The following excerpts demonstrate that Sethian authors conceived of the divine Life as pervading the various levels of the transcendent realm and is made available to the human world as a saving gift. While these texts portray a sort of intelligible biology, that "biology" is not always "prefigurative" in the sense that Corrigan claims to be the case for the Middle and Neoplatonists. In the *Apocryphon of John* (II 4,3–4; 4,19–21; 5,26; 7,6–15; 20,16–18; 23,20–25; 25,23–25), the natural availability of life is restricted to the divine realm, but since the natural realm is thought to be pervaded by death rather than life, true life can only be had as a gift from the divine Mother to the righteous seed of Seth and to those who affiliate with them. On the other hand, in the *Trimorphic Protennoia* (XIII 35,12–22; 38,30–33; 41,20–23, 46,13–20; 48,7–11), Protennoia/Barbelo, in the form of the divine Epinoia, becomes a prefigurative source of (the Water of) life at every level of the cosmos from the upper light down to material souls. Of course, true life and enlightenment remain dependent upon the receipt of the water of life in the ritual act of baptism, which alone effects the separation of the divine spirit resident in everyone from the corporeal and psychic preoccupations of fleshly existence. In the *Three Steles of Seth* (VII 123,19–21; 125,6 and 25–32), Barbelo is the source of both life and intellect, a life whose ultimate source is the supreme One, called a "living Spirit," source of Existence, Life, and Intellect. *Zostrianos* embodies this same basic conception; as in the *Trimorphic Protennoia,* the receipt of life is again especially connected with baptism of a clearly transcendental quality that enables the receipt of true being through self-knowledge, a life that is intelligibly prefigured in the triad Being-Mind-Life:

> **VIII 15** [4] It is the water of Life that [5] belongs to Vitality in which you now [6] have been baptized in the Autogenes. [7] It is the [water] of Blessedness [8] that [belongs] to Knowledge in which you [9] will be [baptized] in the Protophanes. [10] It is the water of Existence [11] [which] belongs to Divinity, that is, [12] to Kalyptos. [13] And the water of Life [14] [exists with respect to] Power, that of [15] [Blessedness] with respect to Essence, [16] and that of [Divinity] with respect to [17] [Existence].

> **VIII 17** [6] Therefore the first perfect water of [7] the Triple-Powered One, <that of> Autogenes, [8] [is] Life for the perfect souls, [9] for it is a rational

---

[41] Cf. *Ap. John* (II 5,5), and *Trim. Prot.* (XIII 38,15; 45,6).

expression of [10] the perfect god's creativity. [11] [And] that [one], [12] since he is source of [them] all, [13] is the Invisible Spirit, of whom the others— [14] they are the ones deriving [from knowledge]— [15] are likenesses. [But] he who simultaneously knows [16] [how he exists] and what [17] [the] living [water is], [18] [such a one] lives within [19] [knowledge. That which belongs to knowledge] is the [20] [water of] Vital[ity]. And in [21] [generation, Life] becomes [limitless] [22] [that it may receive] its [own Being].

In contrast to the Middle Platonists and Plotinus, this transcendent life, rather than being freely available in the natural realm, must be made available there by divine initiative or else experienced in the course of a transcendental vision.

One must ask, could it be that the gnostics themselves were the catalyst that precipitated the Middle and Neoplatonic focus upon life and vitality as a designation for the median phase in the movement from an original static unity to the manifestation of a demiurgic intellect or world soul that administers the physical world of becoming? Could certain gnostic speculations on Life have urged Plotinus and his immediate predecessors to concentrate on developing a prefigurative intelligible biology out of the thought of Aristotle and Plato? Certainly these gnostics, in their quest for saving enlightenment, stressed the central role of an eternal life made available by a divine mother in the context of a baptismal ritual. In the case of the Sethians, the doctrine of the divine Mother Barbelo was inspired by the biblical figure of the divine Wisdom, who was believed to be not merely the artificer of the physical cosmos (e.g., Prov 8) but also the source of living water, the true bread, source of life and light, who sought a permanent resting place among receptive humans.[42] Surely this figure, combining aspects of both life and intelligence, presented a much more vital image for the unfolding of the multiple world of becoming from its origin in a supreme One than did the more Neopythagorean and Old Academic notion of a dyadic principle of indefiniteness. In the gnostic estimation, a

---

[42] In the Jewish wisdom tradition, the exalted Sophia is the fountain or spring (cf. Sir 15:3; 24:30; Philo *Fug.* 195) from which flows the Word like a river (Philo *Somn.* 2.242; cf. *Fug.* 97). She is also equated with the living water of which God is the source (cf. Prov 16:22; 14:27; Cant 4:15; and Bar 3:12 with Jer 2:13; 17:13 [LXX], John 4:10; 7:38; and *Odes Sol.* 11:5–9; 30:1–6). She is the Mother of the Word through whom the universe came to be (Philo *Fug.* 109), indeed mother of all creatures (Philo *Det.* 115–16). To be baptized in her water is to receive true Gnosis. Her Voice is the revelation of the truth. The same sort of myth of descent applied to Barbelo or the First Thought in the Sethian treatises figures also in the story of Sophia in *1 En.* 42 and other sources such as the Johannine prologue, where Wisdom (or the Logos) descends to find a place to dwell among humans, but meeting with initial failure, reascends or tries again.

feminine principle of Life could be found at most every level of reality, from the divine First Thought, through the errant Sophia, down to the primordial appearance of the spiritual Eve as the "mother of the living." As a mediating term, Life could be considered as both substance and process, as both a potentiality and an actuality, mysteriously present in yet also prior to soul as the source of all animation, the hidden potentiality of every seed to achieve full actuality as a living being, a feminine principle of potential indefiniteness containing the power to generate real beings.

Iamblichus, the Sethians, and *Marsanes*

John F. Finamore
University of Iowa

The purpose of this paper is to continue the investigation of this seminar into the question of a hypothesized interchange of ideas between gnostics and Neoplatonic philosophers. In particular, I will consider the metaphysical system of the Sethian gnostic text, *Marsanes* (NHC X, *1*), and compare its system to that of the Neoplatonic philosopher, Iamblichus (ca. 250–325 C.E.) in order to see whether *Marsanes* shows the influence of Iamblichean ideas. First, however, in order to understand the Sethian background of *Marsanes,* I will examine three other Sethian treatises (*Allogenes, Zostrianos,* and the *Three Steles of Seth*) in order to uncover their underlying metaphysical systems and to see how *Marsanes* is similar to and/or different from them.

Let me begin with the dating of *Marsanes*. The general trend among gnostic specialists has been to date *Marsanes* late. Although Pearson first believed that Marsanes should be included among the gnostic treatises known to Plotinus (*Vit. Plot.* 16), he later changed his mind and now accepts a later date at the end of the third century C.E.[1] Turner says that it belongs "to the last quarter of the third century since it indeed posits an Unknown Silent One above even the Invisible Spirit, in much the same way as Iamblichus during the same period posited an 'Ineffable' beyond

---

[1] For the earlier date, see B. A. Pearson, "The Tractate Marsanes (*NHC* X) and the Platonic Tradition" in *Gnosis: Festschrift für Hans Jonas* (ed. B. Aland; Göttingen: Vandenhoeck & Ruprecht, 1978), 375; his introduction to the *Marsanes* in *Nag Hammadi Codices IX and X* (ed. B. A. Pearson; Leiden: Brill, 1981), 250; and *Gnosticism, Judaism, and Egyptian Christianity* (Minneapolis: Fortress, 1990), 152–53. I will refer to these three texts throughout by the author's name and "Tractate," "*Marsanes*," and "*Gnosticism*," respectively. More recently, in *The Nag Hammadi Library in English* (ed. J. M. Robinson; 3d ed.; San Francisco: Harper-Collins, 1988), 461, he has said that "*Marsanes* represents a kind of Platonism which coheres well with … Iamblichus." In his response to my paper, Pearson indicated that he could now accept a date as late as the last quarter of the third century, agreeing with Turner (see next note). He denies that *Marsanes* is specifically Iamblichean, however.

even the One of Plotinus."[2] Majercik also sees *Marsanes* as "a reflection perhaps of Iamblichus's metaphysics, who postulated a similar doctrine of two transcendent 'Ones' uncoordinated with any lower principles."[3]

The consensus of modern scholars is therefore that *Marsanes* is relatively late and may be Iamblichean in metaphysics because it posits a separate "Silent One" higher than the first principle of the other Sethian texts. Pearson has noted other tenets of *Marsanes* that are compatible with Iamblichus's philosophy: a distinction between the intelligible and sensible realms, the positing of a realm beyond being, a predilection for triadic structure, and a belief that the soul is spherical and that embodiment is detrimental to the soul.[4] All of these, however, are also compatible with other Neoplatonic and Middle Platonic systems. The concept of a higher, completely ineffable One would certainly be good evidence for Iamblichean influence, since no other Neoplatonic philosopher that we know of except Damascius accepted this concept. Before we investigate that line of thought, however, we should investigate the metaphysical systems of earlier Sethian texts to see if and how *Marsanes* adapts and alters them, perhaps to bring its own system more into line with that of Iamblichus.[5]

---

[2] J. D. Turner, "Sethian Gnosticism: A Literary History," in *Nag Hammadi, Gnosticism, and Early Christianity* (ed. C. W. Hedrick and R. Hodgson; Peabody, Mass: Hendrickson, 1986), 84. I will refer to this work by Turner's name and "History" throughout.

[3] R. Majercik, "The Existence-Life-Intellect Triad in Gnosticism and Neoplatonism," *CQ* 42 (1992): 479. I will refer to this work by Majercik's name and "Triad" throughout.

[4] Pearson, *Marsanes,* 244–47.

[5] Although there is some question about the exact dates, it is agreed that *Zostrianos, Three Steles of Seth,* and *Allogenes* predate *Marsanes.* J. D. Turner, "History," 82, dates *Allogenes* to "around 200 C.E.," *Zostrianos* to "around 225 C.E.," and the *Three Steles of Seth* to the same time period; however, in "The Setting of the Platonizing Sethian Texts in Middle Platonism: The Theses of Kevin Corrigan," a paper written for the 1995 SBL seminar, Turner places *Zostrianos* before *Allogenes* (p. 19) and says that the date of the *Three Steles* is "indeterminate" (p. 17). A. C. Wire in her introduction to the *Allogenes* in *Nag Hammadi Codices XI, XII, and XIII* (ed. C. W. Hedrick; Leiden: Brill, 1990), 191, "would locate *Allogenes* at latest by the mid-third century C.E. in Rome where Plotinus was writing against the Gnostics, possibly already in Alexandria at the time of Plotinus' studies with Ammonius from 232–243 C.E." J. E. Goehring in his introduction to the *Three Steles of Seth* in *Nag Hammadi Codex VII* (ed. B. A. Pearson; Leiden: Brill, 1996), 384, dates this treatise to "the first half of the third century." J. H. Sieber, in his introduction to *Zostrianos* in *Nag Hammadi Codex VIII* (ed. J. H. Sieber; Leiden: Brill, 1991), 23–25, argues that *Zostrianos* reflects a Middle Platonic worldview and therefore "must have been written either in the last half of the second century C.E. or quite early in the third

1. *The System of Iamblichus*

Iamblichus revamped the old four-level Plotinian system.[6] He added a fifth ontological level,[7] the Intellectual realm between the Intelligible and Psychic realms, and expanded each of the realms. His methodology involved use of a means of triadization such that the highest member of each realm is the unparticipated essence of that realm (ἀμέθεκτος), the next lower member is that essence capable of being participated by a lower entity (μετεχόμενος). The lowest member is the essence existing in lower entities (κατὰ μέθεξιν). This will be seen most clearly when we reach the realm of the Intellect. Also, further to separate (yet connect) the different realms, the lowest member of one realm was also considered the highest member of the next realm, but the entity *qua* member of the higher realm was somehow also differentiated from it *qua* member of the lower.

Our evidence for Iamblichus's conception of the realm of the One comes from Damascius.[8] He posited a "completely ineffable" One (παν-τελῶς ἄρρητον), followed by "the simply One" (ὁ ἁπλῶς ἕν), followed by the Indefinite Dyad of the Limit and the Unlimited (πέρας, τὸ ἄπειρον), and

---

century" (25). R. Majercik, "Triad," 488, thinks that the earliest date for *Allogenes, Zostrianos,* and the *Three Steles of Seth* is 268 C.E. It would help us to date these Sethian texts if we could finally establish their relationship to the gnostic texts known to Plotinus (mentioned by Porphyry in *Vit. Plot.* 16). If the "revelations by Zoroaster, Zostrianos, Nikotheos, Allogenes, Messos" and others are those included in the Nag Hammadi Sethian texts, then they would have had to have been written before 266 C.E. If however the Nag Hammadi texts are revisions of the earlier works, a later date must be assigned. I myself agree with Majercik that *Allogenes, Zostrianos,* and the *Three Steles of Seth* postdate Plotinus's writings. I make no claims about the priority of any one of these to one another, although Turner's conclusion (reiterated in his response to my paper) that *Zostrianos* predates both of the others is plausible.

[6] I have laid out the metaphysical systems of Iamblichus and the Sethian texts in a chart attached to the end of this paper (pp. 256–57). I am indebted throughout this section to J. M. Dillon, ed. and trans., *Iamblichi Chalcidensis in Platonis Dialogos Commentariorum Fragmenta* (Leiden: Brill, 1973), 26–53.

[7] Proclus (*In Tim.* 1.308.18ff.) alludes to a work, "Concerning the Speech of Zeus in the *Timaeus,*" in which Iamblichus adds an "Intelligible and Intellectual" realm between the Intelligible realm and the Intellectual realm. This is a later development, dependent on Iamblichus's study of the *Chaldean Oracles.* See Dillon, *Iamblichi Chalcidensis,* 417–19.

[8] *Princ.* chs. 43, 50, and 51 (2.1.1–13; 2.25.1–17; and 2.28.1–6 in the edition of Westerink and Combès). Damascius says this information was contained in Iamblichus's (lost) commentary on the *Chaldean Oracles.* Iamblichus *Myst.* 8.2, however, contains information about the two lowest of the three Ones (see below).

finally "The One Existent" (τὸ ἓν ὄν). We have then a triad of Ones along with a principle of multiplicity.

The Intelligible realm was presided over by "the One Existent" seen as the first member of the triad Being-Life-Mind (ὄν-ζωή-νοῦς). This is Iamblichus's interpretation of *Soph.* 248e, whereby Being is unparticipated Existence, Life is participated Existence, and Intellect is the result of participation in Existence. (There cannot be Mind without Being and Life.) The Demiurge exists at the level of Intellect, as do the Forms themselves. (These would be the differentiated Forms. They come into existence throughout the realm, existing in an undifferentiated manner as "Monads of the Forms" in Being.)[9]

The Intellectual realm also consists of three moments: the unparticipated Intellect, the participated Intellect, and the Intellect-in-participation. This last member is also the highest member of the next realm, viz. the Hypercosmic Soul (Unparticipated Soul) in the Psychic realm. This soul in turn divides into the World Soul (Participated Soul) and individual souls (Souls-in-participation). Beneath these is the realm of Nature. Notice that Iamblichus stresses the individual soul's inferiority to Intellect by its removal to a lower hypostasis.

2. The System of Allogenes

Allogenes presents a description of the ascent from this world to the highest level of the Invisible Spirit. It is given by Allogenes, a savior figure, who has been given divine instruction by Youel, the luminaries of Barbelo, and finally by the Invisible Spirit itself. Turner has studied *Allogenes* carefully over the years, and I will be following him closely in what follows.[10]

The following is an overview of the work's metaphysical schema. Through Allogenes' ascent, the reader is introduced to a fourfold Platonic universe of One-Intellect-Soul-Nature.[11] The highest being is the Invisible

---

9 Iamblichus *In Phil.* frg. 4 Dillon.

10 See J. D. Turner, "The Gnostic Threefold Path to Enlightenment," *NovT* 22 (1980): 334–38; idem, "Ritual in Gnosticism," in *SBL Seminar Papers, 1994* (SBLSP 33; Atlanta: Scholars Press, 1994), 172–79 [included in the present volume]; and his translation of and notes to *Allogenes* in *Nag Hammadi Codices XI, XII, and XIII* (ed. C. W. Hedrick; Leiden: Brill, 1990), 192–267. I will refer to these three texts throughout by the author's name and "Threefold Path," "Ritual," and "*Allogenes,*" respectively. I have also gained valuable insight from K. L. King's edition and translation, *Revelation of the Unknowable God with Text, Translation, and Notes to NHC XI,3 Allogenes* (Santa Rosa, Calif.: Polebridge, 1995). Translations of *Allogenes* are by Turner.

11 Turner hesitates over whether to call the system three- or four-tiered. In the end he seems to opt for the four Platonic levels but thinks that the level of Soul is not fully articulated. See Turner, "Threefold Path," 332; "Ritual," 172.

Spirit, who is said to dwell in silence and stillness beyond existence (XI 62,20–27). He exists beyond both eternity and time (63,21–23 and 65,22–23). His placement, therefore, is that of the Neoplatonic One. Beneath him is the second hypostasis Barbelo. *Allogenes* says little about the next two realms of Soul and Nature.[12] Between the levels of the Invisible One and Barbelo is an intermediary level of the Triple-Powered One.[13] It is this level with which we will be most concerned.

Allogenes begins his ascent through the Barbelo aeon by means of the revelations of Youel. Barbelo is called an entity separate from the Triple-Powered One, an "incorporeal [eternal] knowledge [γνῶσις]," and an aeon containing "the types [τύπος] and forms [εἶδος] of those who truly [ὄντως] exist" (51,7–16). Barbelo is an Intellect-figure. Her separate existence from the Triple-Powered One places her in a lower realm, and the reference to her as γνῶσις shows that she is intellectual. The "types and forms" she contains are clearly the Forms of Platonism.[14] All of this is Platonic and in keeping with what we saw in the Iamblichean universe.

Barbelo is subdivided into four parts (45,13–46,16; 51,16–37; and 58,12–22), not into a triad.[15] Allogenes himself, after a hundred years of

---

[12] See Turner "Threefold Path," 334; "Ritual," 172–73. Souls begin to exist at the level of Autogenes, the third emanation from Barbelo.

[13] See Turner, "Threefold Path," 334–35; "Ritual," 173–74; also K. King, *Revelation,* 19–20.

[14] See Turner, *Allogenes,* 245 and 254. Cf. 45,16–17 with Turner's note, 244.

[15] On the problem of the Triple Male and whether it is a true fourth hypostasis or rather "perhaps an aspect or syzygy of Protophanes," see Turner, *Allogenes,* 245–47. I cannot agree with Turner that the system of *Allogenes* displays a triadic structure throughout. The preponderance of the evidence is that the Barbelo system is tetradic. The movement toward triadization, a movement that we will see evidenced in *Zostrianos,* can probably best be seen as caused by the influence of Platonism. Cf. Turner, *Allogenes,* 246–47. Pearson in his response to my paper cites the evidence of King, *Revelation,* 83–84, that the term "Triple Male" in the *Allogenes* refers not to a part or aeon of Barbelo but rather to the whole Barbelo aeon. Although it is certainly true that the term "Triple Male" is used in other Sethian texts to refer to the whole Barbelo aeon, the matter is different both here in *Allogenes* and in *Zostrianos.* See especially, *Zost.* 24,1–10, where the ascending initiate can see each of the four members of the Barbelo aeon (Autogenes, Triple Male, Protophanes, and Kalyptos) with a different organ of perception (soul, mind, πνεῦμα, and the powers of the πνεῦμα arising from the revelation from the Invisible Spirit, respectively). The Invisible Spirit is known by a fifth, more pure means, viz., thought or ἔννοια. This kind of hierarchy, which includes the Triple Male as a part, seems to me to be precisely what we find in the *Allogenes.*

Turner in his reply to my paper takes another tack. He states (correctly) that *Allogenes* associates three phases of soul/Forms with the triad Kalyptos-Protophanes-

preparation, sees the entire Barbelo aeon, from bottom to top, in this order: Autogenes, Triple Male, Protophanes-Harmedon, and Kalyptos (58,12–19).

Barbelo first unfolds (downward) into Kalyptos, who contains "those whom she [i.e., Barbelo] knows" (45,32–33). Turner identifies these entities with "the 'hidden ones, whom to see is to see the Aeon of Barbelo (46,32–34)."[16] The "hidden ones" in Kalyptos are further unfolded through the aeons that follow and eventually, it seems, become individuated souls.[17] Kalyptos contains the Forms and Protophanes (the next lowest level) paradigmatically, i.e., what exists in further differentiation below ("iconically," κατὰ εἰκόνα) exists as a unity and paradigm in Kalyptos (51,12–21).[18] Although Kalyptos seems unitary and unmoving from a lower perspective, from above he appears as the activity of Barbelo: Barbelo "became Kalyptos [who] acted [ἐνεργεῖν] in those whom she knows" (45,31–33). The relationship between Kalyptos and Barbelo, then, mirrors that between Barbelo and the Triple-Powered One.

Autogenes: "authentic existents" (paradigmatic souls/Forms) are in Kalyptos, "those who are unified" (undifferentiated souls/Forms) in Protophanes, and "individuals" (differentiated souls/Forms) in Autogenes. The Triple Male, Turner says, does not contain any such "specific ontological content" and hence is not a separate level within Barbelo but is rather "a sort of transitional or transformational figure who mediates between the aeons of Protophanes and Autogenes." This is ingenious but still does not (I believe) commit the author of *Allogenes* to a triad. A mediator within a triad is unusual, to say the least. Triads are mediators. Each phase (as Turner and I agree) represents an unfolding of Barbelo. The Triple Male plays a role. It is not a large role. It is not even a role with a named subclass of souls/Forms. But it is a role. It will help, I think, to imagine a soul becoming more soul-like in its descent. In Kalyptos, it is more monad than soul; in Protophanes, more a plurality in undifferentiated unity; in Triple Male, less undifferentiated, less unified, but not yet individual; in Protophanes more individuated yet (but still not completely differentiated as souls—souls preexisting in Intellect); and finally in their own realm souls become fully individual. This is a five-step process, but four of the levels are in Barbelo. I would be willing to say that there is a kind of tension in *Allogenes* (as there is in *Zostrianos*) and that each text is striving toward a triad in its own way. Nonetheless, neither text completely succeeds.

[16] Turner, *Allogenes,* 247.

[17] On the distinction between "perfect individuals," i.e., individuated souls and Forms found in the lowest level of Barbelo (Autogenes) and "those who are together," i.e., these souls and Forms that exist at a higher plane in Protophanes, see Turner, *Allogenes,* 243–44. The "hidden ones" should be seen as their proto-type in Kalyptos.

[18] See Proclus *Elem. Theol.* 65 and *In Tim.* 1.8.13–29, cited by Turner, *Allogenes,* 254.

The next lower level is that of Protophanes-Harmedon, the "perfect Intellect" (τέλειος νοῦς, 58,17–18).[19] As Turner explains,[20] Protophanes "is the domain of those who are together," i.e., of Forms and souls before they are differentiated (46,26–30). At 51,12–24, Protophanes seems to be the middle point between the Forms and souls that exist paradigmatically in Kalyptos and the Forms and souls that exist individually below Protophanes. He is the active principle (ἐνεργεῖν, 51,21) of Kalyptos working on the individuals existing beneath the Protophanic level.

The third level is that of the Triple Male.[21] This entity is closely related to the "individuals" (45,36–37), that is, individual Forms and souls that actually reside in the Autogenes aeon. He is also placed beneath "those who exist together," that is the undifferentiated Forms and souls that reside in Protophanes: "[He is] the [Thought (ἔννοια)] of all those who [exist] together" (46,20–22).[22] Further, just as to see any of the "hidden ones" in Kalyptos is to see Barbelo (46,32–34), so too to see the Triple Male is to see Protophanes (46,22–25). Thus, he occupies the ontological level just below Protophanes and acts to bring the undifferentiated beings there into differentiated existence in the level of Autogenes. And, conversely, he helps the differentiated souls in Autogenes to ascend to the higher realms. Thus, at 58,13–15 he is called a savior.

The lowest of the four aeons is Autogenes. Whereas the Triple Male acts on the "individuals" from above, Autogenes is directly involved with them. He "saw them [all] existing individually [-κατά] as [he] is" (46,14–16).

---

[19] See also 45,34–35, τέλεος … νοῦς, and 51,20.

[20] Turner, *Allogenes,* 248–49.

[21] On one occasion (51,32–37)—as Turner, *Allogenes,* 246 points out—the Triple Male is mentioned fourth, after Autogenes: "He [i.e., Autogenes] is endowed with the divine Triple Male" (32–33). Turner, *Allogenes,* 254, prefers that the unnamed "he" refer to Barbelo, but the whole passage (12–35) clearly runs in order from the highest aeon, Kalyptos, to the lowest, the Triple Male, with each higher aeon containing the next lower: Kalyptos-Protophanes-Autogenes-Triple Male. There is no reasonable way to "explain away" this anomalous passage. It probably represents an alternate, perhaps earlier, Sethian ontology that has not been harmonized with the rest of *Allogenes.* The Triple Male is placed between Protophanes and Autogenes at 45,28–46,11; 46,11–34; and 58,12–22.

[22] Cf. 58,15–17, where Protophanes is the "goodness" of the Triple Male. Protophanes is then the originating cause of the Triple Male as well as the source of his divine qualities. See also 56,13–14, where it is said that the "self-begotten ones" are in the Triple Male. On the self-begotten ones, see both Turner, *Allogenes,* 247, who, citing *Marsanes* 3,18–21, identifies them with "individual souls in Platonism," and *Steles Seth* 126,26–30, where the unbegotten ones appear to be the souls in Autogenes. In *Marsanes,* it is the self-begotten ones who are the individual souls in their highest stage (3,18–25; see my discussion below).

Yet there is a distinction in kind between Autogenes and the individuals, for they must become like him in order to see the Triple Male (46,16–18). Thus, in the ascent of the individual soul, the soul must arrive at the Autogenes level before proceeding to the Triple Male. Autogenes, then, must be set at a higher plane than the individuals, and this too is in keeping with Platonism, where the Intellect (νοῦς) is the hypostasis before soul. Autogenes' role is to act as Intellect that can descend to the realm of soul and nature: "He acts [ἐνεργεῖν] separately [κατὰ μέρος] and individually [-κατά], continuing to rectify the failures from nature [φύσις]" (51,28–32).[23] Unlike Protophanes and the Triple Male, Autogenes is individuated and able to work directly upon the lower realms.

Thus, in Platonic terms, *Allogenes* has divided the realm of Intellect into four parts. Kalyptos is static and undifferentiated, containing "the hidden ones," Forms and Souls-in-Unity, completely undifferentiated. They are like the monads of the Forms in Iamblichus's system (*In Phil.* frg. 4). Protophanes-Harmedon is an image of Kalyptos. He is undifferentiated, yet Forms and souls exist in him "all together," i.e., with a plurality not existing in Kalyptos but without complete differentiation found in Autogenes. He is best seen as a median between pure unity and individuation into parts. The Triple Male acts as mediary between the lack of differentiation in Protophanes and the individualization of Autogenes. He has no parallel in the Iamblichean system. In Autogenes we reach the level of individual Forms and souls. In this aspect he is

---

[23] Turner, *Allogenes,* 254, says that "Autogenes may play here the role of the νέοι θεοί in Plato *Tim.* 41–42." This is incorrect. The Neoplatonists interpreted the younger gods as the visible gods, i.e., the stars and planets, who are made of intellect, soul, and ethereal body (or "vehicle"). They are above the realm of nature but control it. They exist "individually" in the sense that they are differentiated by their ethereal bodies, but they remain above and have no direct contact with the realm of nature. Autogenes, on the other hand, is said to engage with nature to the extent that he "rectifies" it. King (above, n. 10), 113–14, interprets the Coptic term as implying that Autogenes is a member of the transcendent sphere who is in contact with nature and who "rectifies" the "instability" introduced by the lower realm. Thus, Autogenes is an Intellect-in-participation, the active power of Protophanes at work in the lower realms. He would therefore precede the visible gods (being an Intellect) but act within their sphere and even beneath it, playing a role similar to that of Attis in Julian's *Hymn to the Mother of the Gods* 171a. See my *Iamblichus and the Theory of the Vehicle of the Soul* (Chico, Calif.: Scholars Press, 1985), 140–44. For Julian, however, Attis descends no further than the moon (i.e., he stops just short of nature). Autogenes acts immediately on the realm of nature. He would be a holdover of the gnostic descending Demiurge figure but without the overtones of it being evil or ignorant, more like a saving Sophia. Autogenes, as an Intellect figure that descends into nature, is not possible in a fully Platonic universe.

like the Intellect in Iamblichus's system. Unlike Iamblichus's Intellect, however, Autogenes also interacts directly with nature. The rationale behind the entire Barbelo system mirrors that of Iamblichus: it provides greater distance between the highest level (Invisible Spirit, the One) and nature, while at the same time allowing for step-by-step means of reascent to the higher principles.

If the Barbelo aeon represents the Platonic realm of Intellect with some added connections from it to the realm of nature, the Triple-Powered One is a purely Sethian concept. It represents the means by which the Invisible Spirit (the static, unitary One of the Platonists) may produce the Barbelo aeon without any activity of its own. The procession is the activity of the Triple-Powered One, not of the Invisible Spirit. Thus, the Triple-Powered One can best be seen as the activity of the Invisible Spirit. The Triple-Powered One therefore takes the place of the Indefinite Dyad in Platonic systems. The Triple-Powered One unfolds itself from the Invisible Spirit in Platonic fashion by a procession from, a contemplation of, and a knowledge of the Invisible Spirit (45,22–27).[24] The Triple-Powered One then becomes the aeon of Barbelo (45,28–30).[25]

The Triple-Powered One is a unity in diversity and has three aspects (49,26–37):[26]

> He is Vitality and Mentality and That-Which-Is. For [γάρ] then [τότε] That-Which-Is constantly possesses its Vitality and Mentality [νοήτης], and Vitality possesses Being [-οὐσία] and Mentality. Mentality [νοήτης] possesses Life and That-Which-Is. And the three are one, although individually [-κατά] they are three.

We have then the triad Being-Life-Intellect of Platonism (derived from *Soph.* 248e), but in the realm between the highest god and the Intellect rather than in the realm of Intellect itself.

---

[24] See 49,5–14, where the Triple-Powered One is called the "traverser of the boundlessness of the Invisible Spirit." On the Platonism of this, see Turner, *Allogenes,* 251–52.

[25] See 47,7–36, where the Triple-Powered One contains the whole Barbelo aeon in itself (11–14), permeates it (16–18), and is its source (26–27).

[26] On the triad and the passage, see Turner, "Threefold Path," 334–36; "Ritual," 173; and *Allogenes,* 252–53; King, *Revelation,* 20–29. It is odd that the passage gives the triad first in the (ascending) order Vitality-Mentality-Being, instead of the Iamblichean Mentality-Vitality-Being. The following lines, however, give the Iamblichean descending order. There is some hesitancy in the ordering of the triad in Sethian texts. When we turn to *Zostrianos,* we will see the two orderings again, and so we shall discuss them there.

The relationship between the Triple-Powered One and Barbelo is further described when Allogenes, after his hundred-year preparation, ascends to its Mentality phase (58,7–59,3). Allogenes sees Autogenes, the Triple Male, Protophanes-Harmedon

> and the blessedness [-μακάριος] of the Kalyptos; and the primary origin [ἀρχή] of the blessedness [-μακάριος], the Aeon of Barbelo, full of divinity; and the primary origin [ἀρχή] of the one without origin [-ἀρχή], the spiritual [πνεῦμα], invisible [ἀόρατον] Triple-Powered One, the Universal One that is higher than perfect [τέλειος]. (58,18–26)

It is possible that the term "blessedness" is used as a synonym for "Mentality" in Sethian texts.[27] If it is used so here, the "blessedness of Kalyptos" is the Mentality phase of the Triple-Powered One immanent in the aeon of Barbelo, which is itself the origin of the blessedness. That is to say, Barbelo is herself the fully actualized Mentality phase of the Triple-Powered One; the Mentality then emanates from her directly to Kalyptos. As such, Mentality or Intellect pervades the entire Barbelo aeon, as we have already seen. This gradual unfolding of one realm into another is a feature of the anonymous commentary on the *Parmenides* and especially of Iamblichus and the later Neoplatonists. It is the Mentality phase of the Triple-Powered One that *Allogenes* sees (58,23–26).[28] Later (58,34–59,3), Allogenes is taken into the Mentality level and has the knowledge of Barbelo.[29]

Ascent through the Triple-Powered One is first described by the luminaries of Barbelo (59,9–60,12) and then narrated by Allogenes himself (60,13–61,22). Allogenes has already attained the level of Blessedness (59,10 and 60,16–18). He moves through Vitality (59,14–18 and 60,19–24) to Existence (59,18–26 and 60,28–37). At this point, Allogenes has attained the highest level within the Triple-Powered One. He has moved from knowledge and activity to pure inactivity, and he becomes like the Triple-Powered One in his lack of mental activity. In this, Allogenes is a likeness of the Triple-Powered One (59,22) and has the inactivity of the Invisible

---

[27] See Turner, *Allogenes,* 259 and 263. For problems in the *Three Steles of Seth,* see n. 54 below.

[28] As Turner, *Allogenes,* 259 says, the "one without origin" is Barbelo.

[29] Turner, *Allogenes,* 259 and 261, in the phrase "the knowledge [γνῶσις] [of] the Universals, the Aeon of Barbelo" (59,2–4) interprets the Universals as Platonic forms. This seems correct. However in "Ritual," 175, he says that the knowledge of the Universals is that "of the Triple-Powered One and the Invisible Spirit." This seems unlikely not only because the word "Barbelo" appears in lines 3–4 but also because Allogenes has not yet received the two revelations from the luminaries of Barbelo about the Triple-Powered One and the Invisible Spirit.

One in him (60,7–8) Indeed the realm of Existence is itself "like [κατά] an image [εἰκών]" of the inactivity in Allogenes that he received from the Triple-Powered One and the Invisible Spirit (60,30–37).[30]

There is therefore a continuation of the gradual ontological hierarchy that we have been observing throughout the *Allogenes*. The movement from Mentality to the Triple-Powered One as a whole is one of increasing stillness and inactivity. The summit of the entire system, the Invisible Spirit itself, is revealed only through a negative theology (61,25–67,38), the intent of which is to show the complete inactivity of the first principle. Any activity on Allogenes' part will result in detachment from it. The Invisible Spirit is beyond both time (which comes into being in the Psychic realm in Neoplatonism) and eternity (which comes into being in the realm of Intellect) (63,21–23; 65,22–23), is characterized by nonbeing existence (62,23; 65,32)[31] and by silence and stillness (61,21; 62,24–25; 65,19), and is completely unknowable (61,22; 63,9–11; 63,28–32; 64,10–12; 64,14–23; 66,23).

Before concluding our examination of the *Allogenes,* we should consider Turner's claim to have found an "enneadic structure" in it, whereby the triad of being-life-mind is located at three levels: Invisible Spirit, Triple-Powered One, and Barbelo.[32] According to this theory, which is based in

---

[30] The text reads: "by a revelation of the Indivisible One and the One who is at rest" (60,35–37). Although Turner, *Allogenes,* 261, thinks that the two terms are "hendiadys for the Triple-Powered One," it makes more sense to see the two terms describing two entities, the Invisible Spirit and Triple-Powered One, respectively. (See 67,25–32, where the term "Unknowable One" is substituted for "Indivisible One.") For the two mentioned together, see 61,5–6, where "the One who exists in me" is the Invisible Spirit, 61,8–14, and 53,29–31 (where Turner again argues for hendiadys, *Allogenes,* 256). At 61,14–22, the Mediator of the Triple-Powered One is the Invisible Spirit. But see Turner, *Allogenes,* 261. In his response to Corrigan, p. 37, Turner goes so far as to say that the Mediator might be Allogenes himself. The term is problematic (how can the highest principle be a mean?) but probably means no more than that the power in the Invisible Spirit is channeled through the activity of the Triple-Powered One to Barbelo. The Invisible Spirit is a Mediator *qua* its potentiality, which is mediated. [The text "mediator of the Triple Powered One" must be emended to read: "mediator (i.e., the Triple Powered One) of the Unknowable One." JDT]

[31] At XI 53,31, the Existence level of the Triple-Powered One is itself called "the non-substantial [-οὐσία] Existence [ὕπαρξις]." Lines 23–31 describe, partly in metaphorical language, Barbelo, Protophanes (both in terms of Mentality), the Invisible Spirit, the Triple-Powered One, and Existence. It is odd that Vitality is omitted here. It appears in a mutilated passage of Youel's praise of the Triple-Powered One on the next page (54,8).

[32] See Turner, "Threefold Path," 336; "Ritual," 173–74; his reply to Corrigan, 14–16. [The previous paper in this volume, "The Setting of the Platonizing Sethian Treatises in Middle Platonism," is a revised version of this reply. JDT]

part on the schema found in the anonymous commentary on the *Parmenides, Allogenes* presents the triad in three varying ways at the three main ontological levels. At the level of the Invisible Spirit the triad is found represented by infinitives (εἶναι, ζῆν, νοεῖν) and considered as acts; at the level of the Triple-Powered One represented by abstract nouns (ὕπαρξις or ὀντότης or οὐσιότης, ζωότης, νοότης) and considered as qualities; and at the level of the Barbelo aeon represented by nouns or, in one case, a substantive (τὸ ὄν, ζωή, νοῦς) and considered as substances. We thus have a triad in each level. Next, Turner says, since each level is actually just a phase in the unfolding of the Invisible Spirit into Barbelo, each level can be considered as the term of the triad that predominates at that level. In other words, at the level of the Invisible Spirit existence predominates, at the level of the Triple-Powered One life, and at the level of Barbelo intellect. Thus the Triple-Powered One (in its Life phase) is discontinuous with both the Invisible Spirit (in its Being phase) and Barbelo (in its Intellect phase).

Turner provides the following chart in explanation:[33]

Unknowable One/Invisible Spirit	*Exists*	Lives	Knows
Triple-Powered One/Eternal Life	Existence	*Vitality*	Mentality
Barbelo/First Thought	Being	(Life)	*Mind*

This is intriguing, but there are problems here. First, as I have stated above, the Barbelo aeon is tetradic not triadic. Moreover, the terms Being-Life-and Mind are not applied to it in quite the way that Turner wishes. For the term Mind is applied to Kalyptos (the highest phase) and Protophanes (the middle phase), not to Autogenes (the lowest). Indeed, this is crucial because Kalyptos as Blessedness (= Mentality) is at once the highest phase of Barbelo (who is herself Blessedness) and the lowest phase of the Triple-Powered One. It is again the gradual unfolding from top to bottom that is being stressed. Finally, as Turner admits, the term "Life" is never applied to Protophanes. Indeed, there is no evidence of the triad being applied to the Barbelo tetrad.

What about the triad at the level of the Invisible Spirit? At first glance, there does seem to be support in the text. At the beginning of their second revelation, the luminaries of Barbelo say (61,32–39):

> Now [δέ] he is something insofar as he exists in that he either [ἤ] exists and will become, or [ἤ] acts [ἐνεργεῖν] or [ἤ] knows, although he lives without Mind [νοῦς] or [οὔτε] Life or [οὔτε] Existence [ὕπαρξις] or [οὔτε] Non-Existence [-ὕπαρξις], incomprehensibly.

---

[33] Turner, "Ritual," 174; and his reply to Corrigan, 16.

As it stands the triad is not applied to the Invisible Spirit but is rather denied of him. Turner, however, edits the text to yield the following:[34]

> Now he is something (in the most general sense) in that he exists, seeing that he either exists or <lives> or knows, <acting> without mind or life or existence or non-existence in an incomprehensible way.

Turner argues that the phrase "'exists and will become' . . . is awkward" and that "will become" is the "translator's equivalent to ὑπάρχειν." Further, he thinks that the word "acts" must be moved, that "lives" should be inserted, and that "Non-Existence" "seems gratuitous."[35] Turner's reasoning is straightforward. With the proposed changes, we have a better parallel between the triad of verbs and triad of nouns. But this may not be what the author of *Allogenes* intended.

One attribute of the Invisible Spirit that continually arises is that he is without being (62,22; 63,9–10; 63,17–18; 65,28–30; 65,32–33; 66,25–28). Nonetheless, he is something, "another thing" (63,18). Thus, although he is strictly beyond existence, he nonetheless has a kind of existence. This is the meaning of his having "nonbeing existence." It is, if you will, a preexisting existence, for Existence will devolve from him. The Existence is in him paradigmatically.[36] This, then, is the meaning in our passage as well. He "exists" (in the technical sense just explained) so he "will become," i.e., will unfold into Existence at a lower stage, just as he will "act" and "know" at lower levels. (His activity is the Triple-Powered One; his knowledge Barbelo.) And he does all of this without Mind, Life, or Existence, which will not properly exist until the level of the Triple-Powered One. This is further explained at 62,18–27, where we are told that he does not need Mind or Life or anything. "He is superior to the Universals" (i.e., the Forms), is "nonbeing existence" and is not "diminished by those who are not diminished." Thus, we have the Platonic concept of undiminished giving from a power that transcends the qualities that he causes to exist at the lower level. In sum, although the triad is of course preexistent in the Invisible Spirit, it would be incorrect to see the full triad operating at his level. On the

---

[34] Turner, *Allogenes,* 261. Cf. his reply to Corrigan, 15. See also the translation of King, *Revelation,* 155–57 and her notes on this sentence, which she deems "extremely well-balanced stylistically," 157–59. Her translation nicely brings out the negative nature of the sentence with regard to the Invisible Spirit.

[35] Turner, *Allogenes,* 261.

[36] Cf. 62,28–63,1, where the Invisible Spirit is not the triad divinity-blessedness-perfection, but rather the triad is "an unknowable entity of him" (62,31). He is "superior to" them (32–36) and is "another thing" (37). See also 63,33–64,4 and Turner's notes, *Allogenes,* 263–64.

contrary, it would be appropriate to say that it does not. Rather, the Existence of the Invisible Spirit is stressed over the others, but in a way that makes clear that he surpasses both it and its opposite "incomprehensibly."[37]

In the end, then, the system of *Allogenes* is only partly Platonic. It is Platonic in its positing of a higher principle "beyond being," of an emanation or "undiminished giving" from it to the lower realms, of the separation of Intellect into its own hypostasis, and of the emanation of soul and nature from there. It is unplatonic in its conception of the Triple-Powered One as a separate hypostasis, its placement of the Being-Life-Intellect triad in that hypostasis instead of in Intellect, and its division of Intellect into a tetrad.

3. The System of Zostrianos

Zostrianos presents the most complete worldview of all four Sethian texts, since it actually discusses how the upper realms unfold themselves into the material world. In *Zostrianos,* we are presented with a savior figure (Zostrianos) who with the aid of four divinities (Authrounios, Ephesech, Youel, and Salamex) ascends from the lowest strata of matter to the highest sphere of the Invisible Spirit and then descends again to bring the message of salvation to the seed of Seth.

The system follows the fourfold Platonic system: the realms of the One, of the Intellect, of the Soul, and of Nature. Let us concentrate first on the two highest realms. The highest god is the Invisible Spirit. Immediately below this god is the aeon of Barbelo, which is subdivided further into three aeons: Kalyptos, Protophanes, and Autogenes.[38] As in *Allogenes,* the

---

[37] What is most intriguing about the system of *Allogenes* is its proximity to Iamblichus's concerning the devolving of strata. This is true not only in the multiplication of levels within hypostases but also in the way the gradual unfolding takes place. Existence is the highest level of the Triple-Powered One, yet it preexists in another form in the next highest entity, the Invisible Spirit. Mentality comes into full existence in Barbelo, yet preexists in the lowest level of the Triple-Powered One. This raises the question of which writings are prior and may help confirm Majercik's thesis for a late dating of *Allogenes.*

[38] The three are mentioned together at VIII 20,4–15; 58,12–16; and 129,2–26, with no mention of the Triple Male. At times this fourth aeon is added between Protophanes and Autogenes. See 24,1–10; 44,23–31; and 56,15–19. Sieber, however, in the notes to his translation in *Nag Hammadi Codex VIII* (ed. J. H. Sieber; NHS 31; Leiden: Brill, 1991), 129, identifies the Triple Male with the Protophanes aeon in the last mentioned passage. This is possible, since at 61,15–22 the Triple Male seems to form part of the Protophanes aeon. This additional entity suggests that other Sethian materials (like those in *Allogenes*) were not fully integrated into the metaphysical scheme of *Zostrianos.*

aeon of Barbelo proceeds naturally from the first god. The role of the Triple-Powered, however, is different. For the Invisible Spirit itself is identified with the Triple-Powered One (24,12–13; 63,6–8; 87,13–14; 97,1–3; 118,9–13; 128,20-22), but it does not become another separate triadic hypostasis. Instead, its triple-power overflows into and immediately becomes Barbelo and her triad.

This occurs, it would seem, in Platonic fashion. Barbelo emanates or divides from the Invisible Spirit (77,12–15; 83,19–24; 87,10–14), then turns to contemplate him and thereby becomes a separate hypostasis (78,6–80,18; 81,6–20; 87,14–16). Further, since the Barbelo aeon becomes the triad of Kalyptos, Protophanes, and Autogenes, these three are also potentially in the Invisible Spirit, waiting to become unfolded from him (75,12–14).[39]

It is in the aeon of Barbelo that the Existence-Life-Mind triad comes into being, but not however in this order. The triad is first mentioned in Ephesech's revelation to Zostrianos and involves the triad emanating from Barbelo herself (14,1–14). The triad—existence (ὕπαρξις), blessedness (μακάριος, i.e., mind or intellect), and life—is termed a first principle (ἀρχή) that comes from a single first principle. The text is problematic here, but the single first principle seems to be Barbelo herself. This triad is integrated with the Barbelo Aeon's three members through the imagery of baptismal waters (15,4–17), where "the water of life" and Vitality are associated with Autogenes, the lowest of the three Barbelo aeons; the water of blessedness with Protophanes, the middle aeon; the water of existence with Kalyptos, the highest aeon. Thus, the triad is organized in non-Iamblichean order. Later (66,7–66,18), the triad—this time in the Iamblichean order, existence, life, blessedness—derives from "the [truly] existent Spirit, the sole One."[40] Since the Invisible Spirit is the highest cause, he is the cause of Barbelo as well as of the Barbelo aeons. Thus, the Barbelo aeons can be said to emanate from either the Invisible Spirit or Barbelo. This is more clearly expressed at 79,9–25, where Barbelo herself is termed the "first [insubstantial] existence" after the Invisible Spirit. She emanates from the undivided Spirit to the level of Existence. Unlike the Spirit she is an activity (ἐνέργεια), and at the level of Existence she becomes a Triple-Powered One, i.e., "an image of the one that truly exists."[41] Thus, Barbelo is the moving image and activity of the Invisible Spirit and as such is called

---

[39] "All [these] were [in the] indivisibility of [the] Spirit." Translations from *Zostrianos* are from *Nag Hammadi Codex VIII* (ed. J. H. Sieber; NHS 31; Leiden: Brill, 1991) unless otherwise noted. I have also benefited from Turner's translations of sections of *Zostrianos* in his response to Corrigan. For the referent of "all [these]," see Sieber's note (152).

[40] The translation is from Turner's reply to Corrigan, 29.

[41] The translation of 79,9–25 is from Turner's reply to Corrigan, 29.

"Triple-Power" herself. This "Triple Power" is actualized in the triad of Kalyptos (Existence), Protophanes (Blessedness), and Autogenes (Life).[42] In this way, then, the Invisible Spirit is "Three Powered" only potentially. The actual triadization occurs through Barbelo.

It is worth noticing that there are two occasions in *Zostrianos* when the triad may be given in Iamblichean order. Once, in the lines immediately following 66,7–66,18, discussed just above, where the triad was given in the order Existence-Blessedness-Life, the author may reverse himself and give the triad in Iamblichean order:

> In Existence he (i.e., the Invisible Spirit) exists [as] a simple unity, his own [rational expression] and species. Whoever will find him he brings into existence. [And in] Vitality, he is alive.... [43]

The triad also appears along with the Barbelo triad at 20,22–24 in this order, but the text is again badly damaged. If these two passages do represent a change in the order of the triad (and their mutilated condition makes this only a hypothesis), then we have evidence of a tension within Gnosticism itself as to the order of the triad. If anything, however, the position of *Zostrianos* certainly favors the non-Iamblichean formulation. Thus, in *Zostrianos,* we do not find the second, non-Platonic triad between the first and second principles (the Invisible Spirit and the Barbelo aeons) that we found in *Allogenes,* and there is a tendency toward non-Iamblichean ordering of the triad.

Before we leave *Zostrianos,* we should look also at the psychic realm, for it shares vocabulary with *Marsanes. Zostrianos* 27,9–28,30 divides disembodied immortal souls into three classes: "the ones who have taken root among the Sojourn" (παροίκησις), "those that stand [upon the] Repentance" (μετάνοια), and "the souls of the Self-generated ones" (αὐτογενιόν).[44] The term μετάνοια occurs in *Marsanes* 3,15; παροίκησις may represent the verb for "dwell" in 3,17.[45] Both terms are associated with the fifth seal, which (as we shall see) is the appropriate place for disembodied souls. *Marsanes'*

---

[42] The triad is given in this order also at 3,8–11.

[43] The translation is from Turner's reply to Corrigan, 29. In brackets, he finishes the sentence thus: "and enters into blessedness and comes to have Mentality." The text is corrupted, but it is fairly certain that the triad occurs in this form. [While precise details of the reconstruction are open to question, the traces of the letters for ϩⲩⲡⲁⲣⲝⲓⲥ, ⲱⲛϩ, and ⲙⲁⲕⲁⲣⲓⲟⲥ are such as to render these words in that order extremely likely (85–90 percent). JDT]

[44] The translation is from Turner's reply to Corrigan, 48. See also there his discussion of these souls and their relation to Plato's *Phaedo.*

[45] See Pearson, *Marsanes,* 256.

sixth seal concerns "the self-begotten ones" (αὐτογέννητος). We shall return to this point below.

4. *The System of the* Three Steles of Seth

The *Three Steles of Seth* presents a liturgy intended to be repeated by a group of Sethians in imitation of or perhaps coincident with an ascent ritual through the three main figures of Sethianism. According to the introduction (118,10–23), Dositheos saw the three steles and preserved what was written upon them. The first stele is to Autogenes, the second to Barbelo, and the third to the Unbegotten.[46]

Autogenes is presented as belonging to a higher realm but as revealing the entities in the higher realm to the Sethians below (119,15–120,6). Like Autogenes in the *Allogenes,* he is the intermediary between higher and lower realms, and he is active in the lower realms (121,10–11). He is a savior figure (121,11–12). He, not Protophanes, is identified with the Triple Male (120,29; 121,8–9). The Triple Male, therefore, does not exist in a level separate from him.

Barbelo is delineated as the intermediary between the Unbegotten One above and Autogenes below. She is, on the one hand, "the first glory of the invisible Father" (121,22–23), a monad from a monad (121,33–34), "the first [shadow] of the holy Father" (122,2–3; 124,3–5), "one ... of the One" (122,12–13).[47] On the other hand, just as Barbelo unfolds as a shadow from the Unbegotten, so the other eternal ones are from her (122,6–12; 123,11–14).

Although the usual Sethian triad of Kalyptos-Protophanes-Autogenes is not explicitly drawn, the names of Kalyptos and Protophanes do appear as extensions of her. She is said to be Kalyptos[48] (122,14; 123,1) and to become the νοῦς Protophanes (123,4–5). Her relationship to Autogenes is clear enough from the fact that the stele dedicated to her is between those dedicated to him and the Unbegotten. Thus, there is sufficient reason to see the triad of aeons existing in Barbelo.[49]

---

[46] [For the view that these are three separate entities, see B. Layton, *The Gnostic Scriptures* (New York: Doubleday, 1987), 152–53. For the identification of Autogenes with both Geradamas and the Triple Male, see Goehring, *Nag Hammadi Codex VII,* 376–77 (see n. 47 below) JDT].

[47] Translations are by J. M. Robinson and J. E. Goehring in *Nag Hammadi Codex VII* (ed. B. A. Pearson; NHMS 30; Leiden: Brill, 1996). For 122,1–34, see also Turner's translation in his reply to Corrigan, 9–10.

[48] For the use of "the *nomen sacrum* for Kalyptos," see Goehring's note in *Nag Hammadi Codex VII,* 401.

[49] She can therefore be called "aeon of aeons" at VII 123,25–26 and 124,8–9.

Whether the triad Existence-Life-Intellect is also in Barbelo is harder to say. The text reads (122,18–25):

> For their sake you have empowered the eternal ones in being; you have empowered divinity in living; you have empowered knowledge in goodness; in blessedness you have empowered the shadows which pour forth from the one.

Goehring (402) says that the "influence of the ... triad is evident here. While Barbelo is the empowering force behind the attributes, the Father 'is' the attributes." The first half of this statement is correct.[50] It is Barbelo, as the monad in which each member of the triad preexists, who brings the triad into existence in the aeons beneath her (presumably Kalyptos, Protophanes, and Autogenes). There are problems, however. Whereas Barbelo is said to empower the aeons *in being* and *in living,* this parallelism breaks down when it is said that she empowers knowledge *in goodness*. Further, it is in the fourth clause where Barbelo empowers the aeons *in blessedness* (μακάριος). Now, as we have seen, blessedness may be used as another term for "Intellect." The text seems to give a tetrad (being, life, goodness, blessedness). It is difficult to explain why, but the reason may again have to do with alternate Sethian arrangements of the Barbelo aeon.[51] The point to note for now is that the three terms of the usual triad (given in the Iamblichean order) are preexistent in Barbelo.[52]

Proof for the triad itself in the *Three Steles* can be found in two passages from the third stele, which is dedicated to the Unbegotten. One passage (125,28–32) gives the triad straightforwardly as caused by the Unbegotten:

> For you are the existence [ὕπαρξις] of them all. You are the life of them all. You are the mind [νοῦς] of them all.

Here the Unbegotten is the source of being, life, and mind in the entities below him. The second passage (124,26–33) is more difficult. It calls the Unbegotten "the non-being [-οὐσία], existence [ὕπαρξις] which is before

---

[50] As we shall see, it cannot be the case that the Father *is* Being, Life, and Mind. He must preexist them.

[51] See below for further discussion.

[52] The passage at 123,18–22, where Barbelo is the source of life and mind for lower entities is helpful but not definitive. At 123,23, however, she is called a triple power, which is at least suggestive of the triad, although the term may refer rather to the triad of Kalyptos, Protophanes, and Autogenes, since she is immediately called an "aeon of aeons" (123,25–26).

existences" (ὕπαρξις) (124,26–27). As in *Allogenes,* the first principle is beyond being yet the cause of being in the entities below.[53] He is (124,28–33):

> the first being [οὐσία] which is before beings [οὐσία], Father of divinity and life, creator of mind [νοῦς], giver of good [ἀγαθόν], giver of blessedness [-μακάριος].

Here we have the three members of the triad (being, life, and mind) coupled, it seems, with two others (goodness and blessedness).[54] Leaving the problem of the extra elements aside, it seems clear enough that if the Unbegotten is the source of Being, Life, and Mind, then the triad would come into existence in the aeon of Barbelo.

5. *Comparison of the Sethian Systems*

The three Sethian texts provide systems that are similar in certain features but that are also divergent in crucial ways. Although it is true that all three systems contain realms roughly equivalent to the Platonic realms of the One, Intellect, Soul, or Nature, that all three present a single first cause that is beyond being, and that all three contain some formulation of the Being-Life-Mind triad, nonetheless the differences are more impressive than these similarities.

First, there is the question of the Triple Power. In *Allogenes* it is conceived as distinct from the Invisible Spirit; in *Zostrianos* it is combined with it as the "Invisible Three-Powered Spirit"; in *Three Steles of Seth* the term is used of both the Unbegotten and Barbelo but is not used for an entity or realm distinct from them.[55]

---

[53] The Unbegotten is "the really [ὄντως] preexistent one" who "really [ὄντως] exists" (124,18–21). Cf. 121,25–27, where Barbelo sees that "the one who truly [ὄντως] preexists is non-being [-οὐσία]."

[54] For goodness and blessedness, see 122,18–25, cited above. All five elements are in both passages, although knowledge and goodness are combined at 122,22–23. Also, at 124,31–33, mind and blessedness are separated. Indeed, 122,18–25 seems to exhibit a tetradic structure: being, life, goodness, and blessedness; while 124,28–33 exhibits a pentadic one: being, life, mind, goodness, and blessedness. (Note that "mind" and "blessedness" are listed separately, suggesting that, at least for the *Three Steles,* the two are not equivalent.) The two texts suggest that the triad was at one time submerged in a larger set of elements and that attempts were under way to extricate or highlight the triad. On the face of it, this set of circumstances suggests that the triad preexists gnostic literature and indeed moved the gnostics to form the triad in their own metaphysics. If so, this presents further evidence for Platonism as the likely source of the triad.

[55] See Goehring's note in *Nag Hammadi Codex VII,* 399.

Second, there is the placement and arrangement of the Being-Life-Mind triad. *Allogenes* places the triad (given in Iamblichean order) in the Triple-Powered One, making it a separate hypostasis between the Invisible Spirit and Barbelo. *Zostrianos* associates each element of the triad with a member of the Barbelo aeon: Existence with Kalyptos, Blessedness (= Intellect) with Protophanes, and Vitality with Autogenes. The triad is therefore given in non-Iamblichean order. The *Three Steles of Seth* places the three elements of the triad in the Barbelo aeon but associates these three elements with others so that it is doubtful that we are dealing with a triad.

Third, there is the problem of the Triple Male. The *Three Steles of Seth* associates this Sethian divinity with Autogenes.[56] *Zostrianos* usually associates him with Protophanes but sometimes makes him a separate level in the aeon of Barbelo. *Allogenes* consistently presents the Triple Male as a fourth level of the Barbelo aeon, usually between Protophanes and Autogenes.

These three differences highlight three areas of flux within Sethian Gnosticism. Sethian writers are concerned with the inclusion and placement of divine entities or powers within a system that has already taken on a Middle Platonic or Plotinian slant. What I mean by this is that the metaphysical system is already four-tiered: One-Intellect-Soul-Nature. What the Sethians seem to be arguing over (or, at least, considering individually) is the placement within the Platonic universe of certain Sethian entities. Now, in this they are doing for Sethianism what Iamblichus is doing for paganism. For Iamblichus is likewise fitting various religious entities into his universe. Thus, it seems to me that we have, as it were, a religious enlarging and repopulating of the Plotinian universe. This is how a religious believer inserts his or her own gods, demigods, divine powers, and the like into a streamlined universe. If this view is correct, then the Sethians are doing what Iamblichus and presumably other Platonists after Plotinus are doing. The Iamblichean universe is more developed, of course, which proves that Iamblichus's writings postdate these three Sethian texts. It is time to see how the *Marsanes* fits into this scheme.

6. The System of Marsanes

The treatise *Marsanes,* like *Allogenes* and *Zostrianos,* presents the reader with the exposition of a savior figure about his ascent and subsequent descent through the universe. The savior here is Marsanes himself, and his tale is intended for a knowledgeable audience of Sethians.[57] The text of *Marsanes* is riddled with lacunae; especially after the first ten pages,

---

[56] [See note 46. JDT]

[57] *Marsanes* has been studied and translated by B. A. Pearson. See the works cited in note 1, above.

whole pages are unreadable or even missing. Nonetheless, enough remains for us to examine its metaphysical structure and to make some decisions about its place in the history of Gnosticism and Platonism.

The treatise begins with Marsanes reassuring the Sethians that the "Father" (one of the supreme gods) is benevolent, protects his followers, and cares for them (1,11–27). After a lacuna, Marsanes describes what he refers to as thirteen "seals." Each seal refers to a step on the metaphysical ladder.[58] These are presented from the bottom up, but only after Marsanes has assured his readers that he has "established" (2,13–14) the highest seal, i.e., that he has made the mystical journey through the various levels to the highest one and has returned safely himself.

The thirteen seals are presented at 2,16–4,23. Pearson has shown that they form a hierarchy that is consistent with the four-level metaphysics of Platonists.[59] At the bottom of the hierarchy are the first three seals representing "the worldly [κοσμικός] and the material [ὑλικός]" realms (2,16–26). These correlate with the Platonic realm of Nature. It should be noted that *Marsanes* adds that "in every respect [πάντως] the sense-perceptible [αἰσθητός] world [κόσμος] is [worthy] of being saved entirely" (5,24–26). This is a palpable move away from the pessimism of the gnostics toward the optimism of the Platonists.[60]

---

[58] On the seals, see Pearson, *Marsanes,* 235 and 249; "Tractate," 377–78; and *Gnosticism,* 153–54 (where discussion of the seventh seal seems to have dropped out). Since *Zostrianos* marks each successful attempt to move up the ladder with a "baptism" and since the term "seal" is often associated with baptism in Sethian texts, it may seem tempting to see some connection between *Marsanes'* use of the term "seal" and a baptismal rite. See Turner, "Ritual," 171–72. As Turner says, however, there is no mention of baptism in *Marsanes,* and so the author's use of the term remains mysterious. Pearson, in his article "Theurgic Tendencies in Gnosticism and Iamblichus' Conception of Theurgy," in *Neoplatonism and Gnosticism* (ed. R. T. Wallis and J. Bregman; Albany: SUNY Press, 1992), 264–65, associates the thirteen seals with "ritual praxis" and says that "the various 'seals' are to be understood as equivalent to what Iamblichus calls the synthemata."

[59] Pearson, *Gnosticism,* 155–56.

[60] See Pearson, *Gnosticism,* 162–64. He believes that this passage, together with 41,30–42,6 about the one who gazes at the planets being "blessed," shows Platonic influence. (Cf. Pearson, *Marsanes,* 247–48.) In *Gnosticism,* 163, Pearson cites as evidence for this Platonic optimism Taurus's view that souls descend "for the completion of the universe," i.e., the descent is voluntary on the soul's part and positive (for the good of the universe) and not caused by τόλμα. The Taurus quotation comes from Iamblichus's *De Anima,* in a passage in which Iamblichus is discussing the issue of the soul's descent. Iamblichus adopts Taurus's view, arguing (against Plotinus and others) that the descent is necessary and that pure souls descend willingly, impure souls unwillingly for punishment for the conduct of their past lives.

Seals four through six (2,26–3,25) are equivalent to the psychic realm of the Platonists. The text contains many lacunae, but the general meaning is clear enough. As the first three seals were characterized by what is perceptible (αἰσθητή, 2,22), these next three are characterized by what is incorporeal (ἀσώματον, 3,19; cf. 3,9). Although it is true, as Pearson says,[61] that Platonists use this term of the intelligible, here its domain is lower. For the soul too is incorporeal. This is further verified by the use of the term "partially" (κατὰ μέρος, 3,21), for souls are parts of the Hypercosmic Soul and are often termed "partial natures," whereas intelligible objects are not.

The fourth seal is the next highest after nature (φύσις, 3,1–2).[62] It "is incorporeal" (-σῶμα) (3,9). Although the precise entities of the fourth seal are lost in a lacuna, the description of the fifth and sixth seals will allow us to make a good guess as to what they were.

The fifth seal concerns "conversion [μετάνοια] [of] those that are within me" and includes "those who dwell in that place" (3,15–17). The human souls are conceived as existing inside Marsanes. This must mean, as Pearson thinks,[63] that these are the souls of the true believers in the Sethian fold. Pearson couples the verb for "dwell" with the Greek term παροικεῖν, notes that both terms are given by Plotinus (2.9.6.1–3) as examples of gnostic terminology associated with the soul, and points out that μετάνοια "is apparently to be understood as the first step in the return of the gnostic soul to its place of origin."[64] The two terms also appear in *Zostrianos,* as Pearson also says.[65]

Before examining the relevant passages in *Zostrianos,* let's turn to *Marsanes'* sixth seal:

> concerning the self-begotten ones [αὐτογέννητος], concerning the incorporeal [ἀσώματον] being [οὐσία] which exists partially [κατὰ μέρος], together with those who exist in the truth of the All [...] for understanding [ἐπιστήμη] and assurance.

See Finamore, *Iamblichus and the Theory of the Vehicle of the Soul* (Chico, Calif.: Scholars Press, 1985), 96–101.

[61] *Marsanes,* 256.

[62] The text is marred. Pearson, *Marsanes,* 255, would read, "He exists after the [ ] and the [divine] nature [φύσις]." The reading "divine" is highly conjectural. It seems better, therefore, to take the subject "he" as some being in the fourth realm or seal who exists (as the seal itself does) directly above the third: "He exists after the [world? (κόσμος)] and nature."

[63] *Marsanes,* 256.

[64] Pearson, *Marsanes,* 256 and 247; cf. *Gnosticism,* 153 n. 24.

[65] *Nag Hammadi Codices IX and X,* ad loc.

The term "self-begotten" recalls Autogenes, who will appear in the next seal in *Marsanes*. These are the highest "partial," i.e., individual souls, and probably are to be identified with purified human souls as well as divine souls. Hence, they gain insight into the true conception of the universe and thereby attain knowledge, unsullied as they are by material accretions.

Thus, *Marsanes* presents a triad within the realm of the soul. *Zostrianos* presents a similar threefold division of souls, which will allow us to understand better the triad in *Marsanes*. After Zostrianos leaves the realm of nature in his ascent and passes through the sphere of the seven planets (5,17–22), he ascends first to the παροίκησις (5,24), then to μετάνοια (5,27), then to a third place (the name is lost in a lacuna) where he sees the "self-begotten [αὐτογενής] root" of truth (6,5); he is thereupon baptized in Autogenes. Later, after discussing embodied souls (26,19–27,9), Zostrianos differentiates three kinds of immortal souls (27,9–28,30).[66] There are "the ones that have taken root upon the exile [παροίκησις]" (27,14–15), "those that stand [upon the] repentance [μετάνοια]" (27,21–22), and "the souls [ψυχή] of the self-begotten ones [αὐτογενιόν]" (28,11–12). Finally, in a third passage (42,10–44,22), *Zostrianos* identifies two sorts of embodied souls (called "dead" at 42,13, 16, and 20): those who completely identify themselves with the body and the material world and those who raise themselves higher but not to the level of the gods. It then differentiates these from three types of immortal souls. The first type are "in exile [παροίκησις]." This kind of soul, when it "discovers the truth" is classed higher than the other, embodied souls (43,13–18). The second type are those that repent (μετάνοια). When this soul turns itself from the things of the body (here called "dead things") and toward true existence, it attains its proper place in the universe (43,19–30). The highest type are the souls "that can be saved." These seek and find their intellect and themselves, know things as they really are, withdraw into themselves, and become divine (44,1–22).

Both *Zostrianos* and *Marsanes* present a threefold division of souls. Whereas *Zostrianos* presents souls in exile at a level lower than that of souls that repent, *Marsanes* places them at the same level but has "repentance" precede (i.e., be lower than) "dwelling" in the fifth seal. First comes the soul's change, then it can come to dwell in a higher place.[67] What then of the lowest seal? Marsanes assures his readers that the entities of this seal are incorporeal (3,9). These are probably, then, souls either still embodied or newly disembodied that are still in the process of learning the ways of

---

[66] For discussion of this and the next passage in *Zostrianos,* see both Sieber's notes in *Nag Hammadi Codex VIII* and Turner, in his reply to Corrigan, 47–48.

[67] The "place" of *Marsanes* 3,17 is almost certainly the ὑπερουράνιος τόπος of *Phaedr.* 247c3. Cf. *Marsanes* 5,20, where the Greek word is τόπος.

Gnosticism. This represents a step intermediate between *Zostrianos*'s higher kind of "dead" soul and the soul in exile. The "self-begotten" souls of the sixth seal are equivalent to those in *Zostrianos*.[68] The three parts of the Psychic realm in *Marsanes* show a soul becoming more pure. It should be noted, however, that the Soul-triad in *Marsanes* is not equivalent to Iamblichus's triad of Hypercosmic, World, and Individual souls.

The remaining seals concern the two highest Platonic realms. Seals seven through ten take us into the realm of the Intellect and reintroduce us to familiar characters. The seventh seal concerns "the self-begotten [αὐτογενής] power [δύναμις]," i.e., Autogenes (3,25–26); the eighth "the Mind [νοῦς] which is [male, which] appeared [in the beginning]," i.e., Protophanes (4,2–7);[69] the ninth, marred by a lacuna, Kalyptos;[70] and the tenth Barbelo. The realm of the One, as we know it from *Allogenes, Zostrianos,* and *Three Steles of Seth,* is given in seals eleven and twelve (4,13–19):

> the Invisible One [ἀόρατος] who possesses three powers [δύναμις] and the Spirit [πνεῦμα] which does not have being [οὐσία], belonging to the first Unbegotten (fem.).

Finally, the thirteenth seal concerns the Silent One "who was not [known]" (4,19–22).

If we compare these two highest realms to the highest realms of the other three Sethian texts, we can discern certain important differences in *Marsanes*. Working from the top down, the first obvious difference is the addition of the Silent One. Second, *Marsanes* agrees with *Allogenes* against the other two texts in dividing the next highest being into two: an invisible three-powered One and a Spirit. Third, it does not add a third

---

[68] Souls are discussed later in *Marsanes*. At 25,17–20, there seems to be a "division" that takes place from a soul at its higher ("self-begotten?") phase to lower (embodied state). See Pearson's note in *Nag Hammadi Codices IX and X,* ad loc. Later at 25,26–26,6 the text distinguishes the soul "that came into existence" from "the self-begotten soul." This again seems to indicate a fall from a higher to lower (embodied) phase. "Come into existence" would mean "come into bodily existence." Corresponding to the fall is a loss of the soul's power, represented by sets of vowels. See Pearson's note in *Nag Hammadi Codices IX and X,* ad loc. Finally, at 41,16–22, there is a distinction between embodied souls "that are upon the earth" and "those outside of the body [σῶμα], those in heaven." The latter class are "more than the angels," which Pearson assumes means that there are more human than angelic souls. Rather, the idea may be that pure human souls in heaven are more divine ("more" = "higher"?). Compare *Chald. Or.* frg. 138, where souls of theurgists exist "in the angelic space."

[69] On the identification, see Pearson, *Gnosticism,* 154.

[70] See Pearson's note in *Nag Hammadi Codices IX and X,* ad loc.

hypostatic realm between the One and the Intellect, as *Allogenes* does. Fourth, it divides the realm of the Intellect into three members, not four, as *Allogenes* and (sometimes) *Zostrianos* does. Fifth, it does not mention the Being-Life-Mind triad. We must now address the question of whether these changes reflect an Iamblichean stance.

7. *Iamblichus and* Marsanes

Although *Marsanes* posits a Silent One over and above the Invisible Spirit/Unbegotten One of the other Sethian texts, the Silent One is not equivalent to Iamblichus's Completely Ineffable. The defining characteristic of the Ineffable is that it completely transcends the realms beneath it. The Ineffable "is not therefore participated [μετέχεται], nor does anything have a share [μεταδίδωσι] of it" (Damascius *Princ.* 1.25.21–22).[71] *Marsanes'* Silent One communicates with lower levels of being through the Triple-Powered One, which is its agent (7,12–15). Indeed, we are told (6,5–8):

That one who exists before all of them reaches [to the divine] Self-engendered One [αὐτογέννητος].

If the Silent One reaches to the lowest level of the Barbelo aeon, it cannot be Iamblichus's Completely Ineffable One.

Some have thought that Iamblichus's *Myst.* 8.2 also presents evidence for the Completely Ineffable.[72] There Iamblichus distinguishes two Ones (261.9–262.8):

Before truly existing beings and universal principles is the One God, prior even to the First God and King. It remains unmoving in the oneness of its unity. Neither the intelligible nor anything else is interwoven with it. It is situated as a paradigm of the self-produced, self-engendered god who is the only Father of the true Good, for he [the One God] is something greater and prior, a source of all things and base of the intelligible primary forms that really exist. And from this One the independent god manifests itself, for which reason he [the first God and King] is both a

---

[71] Cf. *Princ.* 1.21.11–14 and the texts cited by A. Linguiti, "Giamblico, Proclo, e Damascio Sul Principio Anteriore All'Uno," *Elenchos* (1988): 101 n. 23.

[72] H. D. Saffrey and L. G. Westerink, eds. *Proclus: Théologie Platonicienne* (6 vols.; Collection des universités de France; Paris: Les Belles Lettres, 1968), 3:xxx–xxxiii, followed by Linguiti, "Giamblico, Proclo, e Damascio," 95 n. 2. P. Hadot, *Porphyre et Victorinus* (2 vols.; Paris: Études augustiniennes, 1968), 1:97 n. 1, correctly sees that the higher One of the *De mysteriis* passage is the second One discussed by Damascius. For a comparison of *Myst.* 1.5 with 8.2, see Finamore, *Iamblichus,* 40–42.

principle and father to himself because he is a principle and god of gods, a monad from the One, pre-existent and a principle of Being. From him [the first God and King] is substantiality and essence, for which reason he is called the Father of Essence. He [the first God and King] is pre-existent Being, the principle of intelligibles, for which reason he is named Ruler of the Intelligible.

Saffrey and Westerink[73] mistakenly associate the "One God" of this passage with the Ineffable and the "First God and King" (ὁ πρῶτος θεὸς καὶ βασιλεύς) with the "Monad uncoordinated with the triad" (οὔτε ... νοητὸν αὐτῷ ἐπιπλέκεται). Iamblichus, however, is clear that this entity is, rather, the One God (θεὸς εἷς). The subject of the first sentence (261.9–11) is this One God, and the pronoun (αὐτῷ, 261.12) in the next sentence must therefore refer to him. Thus the highest of the Ones mentioned by Iamblichus in this passage is described in terms similar to that of the second of his three Ones in Damascius *Princ.* 2.1.4–8:

After this we must examine whether there are two first principles before the first intelligible triad, the completely ineffable and the one unconnected with the triad [ἡ ἀσυντάκτος πρὸς τὴν τριάδα], as the great Iamblichus says in the 28th book of his most perfect *Chaldaean Theology.*

Furthermore, Iamblichus in *Myst.* 8.2 is expounding the Hermetic doctrine on the first cause (τό πρῶτον αἴτιον, 8.1.260.4). Thus whichever Ones Iamblichus discusses in 8.2 will be *causal* Ones, not a Completely Ineffable One. We must conclude, therefore, that the *De Mysteriis* passage concerns not the highest two (of three) Ones, but the lowest two. The highest One of *Myst.* 8.2 does, therefore, bear a resemblance to the Silent One of *Marsanes,* but neither is equivalent to the Completely Ineffable, which exists apart from and has no causal effect upon the rest of the universe.

In Iamblichus's realm of the One there were not only three Ones, but also a principle of diversity, the Indefinite Dyad. *Marsanes* differs not only from Iamblichus's system but also from that of other Sethian treatises. *Marsanes* preserves three ones (none of which is completely ineffable) but maintains the Sethian "Triple Power" as the cause of multiplication in the lower realms. In *Allogenes,* there were two first-principles, the Invisible Spirit and Triple-Powered One. The Triple-Powered One, however, became Mind (Barbelo) through the emanation of the Being-Life-Mind triad inherent in the Triple-Powered One. In other words, the Triple-Powered One truly had three "powers" or levels through which the multiplicity of the aeon of Barbelo could be said to be produced. *Marsanes*

73 *Proclus: Théologie Platonicienne,* 3:xxxii–xxxiii.

presents no such triad. Instead, the power of multiplication comes from the Triple-Powered One as a median between the Silent One and Spirit Without Being, above, and Barbelo and her aeon, below. Thus, the Triple-Powered One is called the activity (ἐνέργεια) of the Silent One (7,16–19)[74] and is also the source of the knowledge that Barbelo becomes (9,1–8). This active One is "triple" in the sense that it is the active nature of the Silent One, exists after the Silent One but before Barbelo, and is the knowledge that Barbelo becomes.

If this is correct (and we will deal with an alternate view momentarily), then the *Marsanes* again differs from Iamblichus's system in lacking both an Indefinite Dyad and the Being-Life-Mind triad.

Turner has recently attempted to introduce the Being-Life-Mind triad into the Triple-Powered One in *Marsanes*.[75] There are two passages to consider. In the first (8,18–29) there is an ambiguity in the clause "the third power of the Three-Powered, when it had perceived [νοεῖν] him,[76] said to me." Pearson takes the third power as referring to Autogenes and the pronoun "me" to Marsanes; Turner thinks the former refers to Mentality and the latter to Barbelo. Now if *Marsanes* were assuming a Being-Life-Mind triad in the Triple-Powered One, then the third power would be Mentality, if *Marsanes* adopted the Iamblichean order. On the other hand, if *Marsanes* were assuming that the Triple-Powered One is the immediate source of the Barbelo aeon (as it is in *Zostrianos*), then the third power would be Autogenes. As Pearson points out,[77] Autogenes is called a "power" (δύναμις) that is "third [perfect (τέλειος)]."[78] Further, it is unprecedented

---

[74] The text does not name him. It reads: "But the energy [ἐνέργεια] of that One <is> the Three-Powered One, the One unbegotten [before] the Aeon [αἰών], not having [being (οὐσία)]." Turner, in his reply to Corrigan (10), thinks that the words "that One" refer not to the Triple-Powered One but to the Invisible One, which exists between the Silent One and the Triple-Powered One. [The text should read: "But the activity of that One (the Invisible Spirit) <is> the Triple Powered) One. The Unbegotten One (i.e., the Invisible Spirit) is prior to the Aeon, since he is in-[substantial]." JDT]. (There is a similar ambiguity at 7,12.) Turner's interpretation is, of course, possible, and it provides a role for the Invisible Spirit, about which *Marsanes* says little otherwise. Nonetheless, elsewhere the words ἐνέργεια/ἐν-εργεῖν are used of the Triple-Powered One in its role as the activity of the Silent One (6,22; 7,1–3; 7,23–24).

[75] Turner in his reply to Corrigan, 10–11.

[76] Or perhaps "me," see Pearson, *Marsanes,* 272–73.

[77] Pearson, *Marsanes,* 258 and 265.

[78] Interestingly, the Triple-Powered One is called "the first perfect One" at 7,27–29 and 8,4–7. This suggests that it is not Autogenes' position in the aeon of Barbelo that gains him this epithet, but rather his position as Son in the old Sethian

for an abstract concept like "Mentality" to address the Sethian elect, whereas Autogenes, as a descending savior figure, would naturally address them. The preponderance of the evidence is on Pearson's side.

The second problematic passage (9,1–28) concerns Barbelo, who divides herself from the Triple-Powered One and stands apart as Knowledge (γνῶσις) of him. After Barbelo is hypostatized outside of the Triple-Powered One, the text continues (9,9–14):[79]

> She withdrew [ἀναχωρεῖν] from [these] two [powers], since she exists [outside of] the Great One, [seeing what] is above [her, the Perfect One] who is silent.

Pearson[80] remarks that "it is not clear from this passage exactly what Barbelo is withdrawing from." Turner believes that the two powers in question are Existence and Vitality. The only two beings discussed in the twenty-eight-line passage (besides Barbelo herself), however, are the Silent One and the Triple-Powered One. Furthermore, the clause immediately following the phrase "these two powers" refers to these two beings. The phrase "the Great One" is the Triple-Powered One, from which Barbelo emanated and outside of which she now stands. The "Perfect One who is silent" is clearly the Silent One, who is above her and the Triple-Powered One, who "is situated as she is situated" (9,7–8).[81] It is in Barbelo's separation from these higher beings that she begins the process of the creation of her complete aeon.[82]

---

triad of Father-Mother-Son. This would make Barbelo the second perfect One. See Pearson, *Marsanes,* 258.

[79] The translation is Turner's in his reply to Corrigan, 10.

[80] *Marsanes,* 275.

[81] The translation is Turner's in his reply to Corrigan, 10.

[82] This is, of course, a different meaning of "power" than that of 8,19, where the three powers seemed to be Father-Mother-Son. It is worth noting that, in *Marsanes'* description of the twelfth seal (4,11–19), the Invisible Spirit is described as "belonging to the first Unbegotten [fem.]." This must be a reference to the Silent One, but the use of the feminine is puzzling. It is possible that the feminine noun to be understood is "power," from "three powers" that the Triple-Powered One possesses (4,15–16). If so, then the first power of the Triple-Powered One is the phase in which it is unified with the Silent One (and this is equivalent to the Invisible Spirit), the third power is Barbelo, the phase at which there is complete differentiation between knower and object, and the middle phase will be the Triple-Powered One itself, existing separately from the Silent One but not yet differentiated from the lower realm. If this were correct, then we may be able to make sense of the triad knowledge/γνῶσις–hypostasis/ὑπόστασις–activity/ἐνέργεια belonging to the Silent One in 9,16–18. His knowledge is Barbelo, his activity is the Triple-Powered One, and his hypostasis, then, would be what he is in himself *qua*

In the end, one cannot prove with absolute certainty that the author of *Marsanes* is not alluding to the Being-Life-Mind triad. One can only say that there is no overt mention of the triad here, that there is no need to summon up the triad to explain the text, and that the burden of proof rests on those who attempt to find allusions to the triad.

Iamblichus had placed the Being-Life-Mind triad in the realm of the Intellect. *Marsanes* does not, although it does establish a triad in the Barbelo aeon: Kalyptos-Protophanes-Autogenes. Indeed, *Marsanes* shows a triadic structure within all of its levels, as we have seen. Iamblichus also created such triadic structures in his hypostatic realms, but there are important differences in *Marsanes* (viz., no use of the structure Unparticipated-Participated-In Participation, no Being-Life-Mind triad, no separate Intellectual realm).

This brings us to a final difference with Iamblichus, the role of Autogenes. We have seen from the other Sethian texts that Autogenes is a character who does not fit well into the Platonic system because his movements are unrestricted from the highest realms to the lowest. The same is true in *Marsanes*. Autogenes ("self-begotten") descends from the "Unbegotten One, who does not have being [οὐσία], who is the Spirit [πνεῦμα]" (6,3–5). "That one who exists before all of them reaches [to the divine] Self-engendered One (αὐτογέννητος)," i.e., to Autogenes (6,5–7).[83] Autogenes is called a savior,[84] who descended to our realm to save humanity. Just as in *Allogenes,* Autogenes is an Intellect figure that can descend into the realm of matter. A descending Intellect is not possible in Platonism and is specifically denied by Iamblichus himself.[85]

Pearson is wrong therefore when he claims that "Autogenes here plays the same role as 'the demiurgic intellect' in Iamblichus' discussion of Egyptian theology."[86] At issue between us is the interpretation of *Myst.* 8.3.

---

supreme being. The use of "power" in this instance then is in reference to the three powers of the Triple-Powered One. If the same conception were used at 8,18–29, then the "third power" would be Barbelo, not Autogenes. Even on this interpretation there is still no compelling reason to see the Being-Life-Mind triad at work in either passage. [See discussion and translation of *Marsanes* 7,1–9,20 in the previous paper in this volume, "The Setting of the Platonizing Sethian Treatises in Middle Platonism." JDT]

[83] For the identification, see Pearson, *Marsanes,* 265–66. Whether "the one who exists before them all" is the Silent One, as Pearson says, or the Invisible Spirit is inconsequential to the point that Autogenes' source is higher than the realm of Intellect.

[84] 6,15–16: "as it is manifest that he saved a multitude." See Pearson, *Marsanes,* 235.

[85] *Myst.* 1.12. See also above, note 23.

[86] Pearson, *Marsanes,* 264.

254 *John F. Finamore*

I will summarize this important chapter and explain why I do not think it entails a descending Demiurge.

Iamblichus begins by delineating an Egyptian system consisting of a transcendent One (Eikton), an Intellect (Emeph), and various celestial gods (262.14–263.9). He then discusses the demiurgic intellect under various names (Amoun, Phtha, Osiris) (263.9–264.4). This intellect "descends to generation and leads the invisible power of the hidden reason-principles into light" (ἐρχόμενος μὲν ἐπὶ γένεσιν, καὶ τὴν ἀφανῆ τῶν κεκρυμένων λόγων δύναμιν εἰς φῶς ἄγων, 263.9–10). The reason principles are, as it were, enmattered forms that produce in nature what the gods have planned out beforehand and separately from nature. The Intellect does not mix with matter but illuminates the reason principles, which thereby produce order in the material realm. Iamblichus goes on to explain that the Egyptians assign one set of rulers in the sun over the celestial bodies and another set in the moon over material ones, and so on (264.5–14). These and not the Demiurge/Intellect mix with matter. Thus, Iamblichus concludes (in the passage that Pearson translates) that the Egyptians adopt a single system from the One to matter. The One produced[87] matter from the essentiality of divided materiality; the Demiurge created (ἐδημιούργησε, 265.9) the impassive spheres (of the planets); he distributed (διεκόσμησεν, 265.10) the lowest form of matter among mortal bodies. The point is that the Demiurge/Intellect does not descend into and mix with matter.

In summary, then, *Marsanes* differs in significant ways from the writings of Iamblichus. In the realm of the One, *Marsanes'* Silent One is not like Iamblichus's Completely Ineffable and *Marsanes* does not make use of the Indefinite Dyad. *Marsanes* does not mention the Being-Life-Mind triad. The role of Autogenes is unlike that of Iamblichus's Intellect. There is no use of Iamblichus's metaphysical triad of Unparticipated-Participated-In Participation and no separate Intellectual realm between the Intelligible and Psychic realms. The Iamblichean Psychic triad of Hypercosmic Soul, World Soul, and Individual Souls is not equivalent to the triad in *Marsanes*.

8. Conclusion

I began this paper with an examination of the metaphysical systems of Iamblichus and the three Sethian texts *Allogenes, Zostrianos,* and the *Three Steles of Seth.* I tried to show that the three Sethian texts while

---

[87] παρήγαγεν, 265.6; it is a technical term. See Proclus *Elem. Theol.* 7 ("Every productive cause [τὸ παρακτικόν] is greater than any nature it produces [παραγομένου]." See also the note of E. R. Dodds, *Proclus: The Elements of Theology* (2d ed.; Oxford: Clarendon Press, 1963), 194.

exhibiting a core Sethian system nonetheless differ from each other in significant ways. The dissimilarities show their various ways of dealing with Sethian tenets (such as the Triple-Powered One, the placement and order of the Being-Life-Mind triad, the number of entities in the Barbelo aeon, and the role of Autogenes) and with the Platonic system. *Marsanes* fits well with these three texts. It shares with them the Sethian divinities and Platonic structure. It exhibits differences too, such as the lack of the Being-Life-Mind triad and of the Triple Male, but it clearly belongs with the other three Sethian texts.

The dating of *Marsanes* remains problematic. Since it bears no marked similarity to Iamblichean Neoplatonism, it may easily be dated to the same time period as the other three Sethian treatises. Although its use of a higher "Silent One" does not necessarily mark it as a work later than the others, its thoroughgoing use of triadic structure may suggest (but no more than that) the influence of the kind of Neoplatonism existing in the time of Porphyry.[88] If my earlier conjecture is correct that the other three Sethian treatises are to be placed in this same time period, then we have four Sethian texts each using different methods of adapting Sethianism to Platonism during a time when Porphyry is publishing the writings of Plotinus (including those against the gnostics) and (presumably) his own anti-gnostic works.

Although Iamblichus composed his works after *Marsanes* was written, there is no decisive evidence that he knew either it or any similar Sethian treatise. In Iamblichus's only recorded reference to the gnostics (*DA* 375.9), he states that they claim that the reason for the soul's descent is παράνοια and παρέκβασις. These two words are not found in *Marsanes* or any other gnostic text.[89] His use of the terms certainly does not convey any direct knowledge of *Marsanes*.

Thus, *Marsanes,* like the other Sethian treatises discussed above, seems to belong to a pre-Iamblichean time. Iamblichus, in his turn, seems unaware of its existence. There is no compelling reason to see any connection between the Neoplatonic philosopher and this Sethian treatise. It seems (again, if my chronology is accepted) that Plotinus and Porphyry settled once and for all the Neoplatonic arguments against the gnostics. Thereafter the Sethians presented no threat to later Platonic philosophers such as Iamblichus.

---

[88] The triadization exists throughout the system, even in the psychic and material realms. The desire to establish triads in each hypostasis may explain the addition of the Silent One to the realm of the One, for otherwise the Silent One seems to add very little to *Marsanes'* system or to the Invisible Spirit/Unbegotten One in the other three Sethian texts.

[89] See Pearson, *Marsanes,* 267 and 275 n. 80.

Metaphysical Schemata

Plotinus	Iamblichus	*Marsanes*
The One	Completely Ineffable One (παντελῶς ἄρρητον) Simply One (ὁ ἁπλῶς ἕν)	The Silent One Spirit without Being
	Limit (πέρας)—The Unlimited (τὸ ἄπειρον) The One Existent (τὸ ἓν ὄν)	Invisible One with Three Powers
Intellect	Being (ὄν) Life (ζωή) Mind (νοῦς) Unparticipated Intellect Participated Intellect Intellect-in-Participation	Barbelo: Kalyptos Protophanes Autogenes
Soul	Hypercosmic (Unparticipated Soul) World (Participated Soul) Individual Souls (in Participation) Nature and Matter	Self-begotten ones Repentant Souls Lower incorporeal soul κοσμικός and ὑλικος realms

Allogenes	*Zostrianos*	*Three Steles of Seth*
The Invisible Spirit	The Invisible Spirit	Unbegotten One

Triple-Powered One:
   That Which Is
   Vitality
   Mentality		

Barbelo Aeon:
Kalyptos
   The hidden ones
   paradigmatic Forms
	Barbelo (Triple Power)
	Kalyptos-Existence
		Barbelo
		Kalyptos

Protophanes-Harmedon
   Those who are toge-
   ther (undifferentiated
   Forms and souls)
	Protophanes-Blessedness	Protophanes

Triple Male
   The thought of those
   who are together
	Triple Male	

Autogenes
   The individuals
   (individual Forms
   and souls)
	Autogenes-Vitality	Autogenes (= Triple
		   Male)

	Soul: Self-begotten ones Those in repentance Those in exile Two kinds of "dead" (i.e., embodied) soul	

ANCIENT APOPHATIC THEOLOGY

John Peter Kenney
Saint Michael's College (Vermont)

Ideas are malleable things, creatures of context and hostages to historical use. Formed in original clusters, they may migrate into distant domains, where they can lose much of their natural shape and be drawn to novel ends. Few ideas in religious history are more difficult to track than apophatic theology, the paradoxical claim that the ultimate deity exceeds the bounds of human discourse. It is a complex notion, relying upon a nexus of concepts in order to be intelligible. Its meaning is thus systematic and abstract, nesting in a host of related ideas and providing a second-order commentary upon them. Hence the project of its assessment by historians and philosophers of religion is itself difficult and fraught with peril.

This paper is but a brief effort at that task, undertaken at the close of our seminar's inquiry into the relationship between "Gnosticism" and later Platonism. Both are traditions that are reputed to emphasize apophatic theology; both do indeed evince such thinking in varying degrees. The intention of our session this year is to reflect on these trajectories, which are often depicted as the twin sources of negative theology in Western religious thought. My efforts will be directed primarily towards the Neoplatonic side of the discussion, using Plotinus as my principal informant, but I will refer to "Gnosticism" throughout. I have also tried to connect my analysis to Michael Williams's paper[1] in order to focus our seminar discussion and to make the connection to the Nag Hammadi corpus more firmly. Separate sections of the paper will address aspects of the apophatic tradition that seem particularly salient.

In scholarship, as in life, idiosyncrasies should never be discarded lightly. They add vividness to our intellectual passing and may be what is most memorable about our work. For some time I have been framing a thesis regarding the emergence of philosophical monotheism in late antiquity. That thesis cannot be presented in any detail here, although its ramifications are sketched out in reference to our present topic. More details may be found in my earlier works, to which references are made. Because

---

[1] [See the paper of M. A. Williams, "Negative Theologies and Demiurgical Myths in Late Antiquity," in this volume]

we are now attempting to analyze "gnostic" and later Platonic theology, I have concentrated on theory, rather than on adducing and compiling texts. We seem to be at that stage in our collective inquiry when we are attempting to achieve some theoretical grasp of the materials we have been considering. Indeed, we have also been engaged in reviewing and, in many cases, moving beyond some earlier, well-established theories. This paper is meant to push on with that effort by collecting a series of different points that may be of use in this project of reappraisal. Finally, I have written this piece as a seminar paper, inviting response on the points articulated below. Hence it is framed in a less conclusive fashion than is perhaps customary, and it offers a number of explicit questions that are intended to direct our discussion. My goal is to connect up with the very fruitful exchange that we enjoyed at our 1996 meetings in New Orleans.

1. Apophasis and Transcendence

We might begin with the most technical aspect of the apophatic tradition, its role in the articulation of divine transcendence. Ancient metaphysics found the topic irresistible. The denial of predicative ascription to the first principle was part of a strategy for presenting the ontological status of such an entity. It is an approach whose roots go back at least as far as Parmenides. It is worth remembering that in the background of Parmenides' thought lay the early mathematical realism of the Pythagoreans, whose numerology was a first step towards an articulation of a class of divine entities removed from the spatio-temporal world. This is an initial, historical clue to the nature of classical apophatic theology, its critical association with some form of realism.

But realism itself was constitutive of the effort to reconceptualize the divine world, to offer an alternative to the pantheon, and to discover a different mode of articulating the "place" of the divine. We find in Plato a formal and abstract account of a transcendent world, a level of existence not just invisible or hidden, but also nonspatial and atemporal. The forms were separate from the sensible world because they were predicatively stable, unlike the transients of the visible world. Moreover, forms occupied a level of reality superior to the things of this world, so that the noetic cosmos was understood to be divine and perfect in contrast to the ontological squalor of becoming.

Two points should be noted: transcendence in Plato was initially understood in reference to predication, to the perfect predication that defined the nature and status of the εἴδη. The constituents of "being" were supremely knowable because they were perfect paradigms of the qualities that they defined. The intelligible world transcended the sensible realm precisely because of its apodictic character. This meant that separation from change, time, and space was tied conceptually to the perfection and qualitative stability of the forms. There was, therefore, nothing murky about transcendence. An additional upshot of this approach was its non-anthropomorphism. The forms were primarily conceived as being properties, and, although there was considerable discussion about the scope of being in the Academy, there remained a preponderant emphasis on what might be called the predicative foundations of transcendence. The other natural source for a theory of transcendence, psyche, was relegated to a subordinate status. Accounts of the immortality of psyche in the *Phaedo* and of its origins in the *Timaeus* associate animacy with the higher world of the intelligibles. Hence the roots of the Platonic tradition's understanding of transcendence rested upon a particular, abstract theory about universals, predicates, qualities, and properties.

So too did the origins of apophatic ontology. It is with the difficulties that Plato identified in his own theory of forms that the impetus for apophatic discourse can be found. However the *Parmenides* might be read, it was a preeminent source for apophatic discourse in subsequent classical thought. There Plato confronted the conundrum of his realism: its potentially recessive character, exhibited in the infamous "third-man" argument. Plato may very well have been experimenting with conceptions of unity that avoid the problems that the *Parmenides* identified as endemic to the theory of self-predicable forms. In that case, such unities might have served as replacements for forms, as a new class of intelligibles. But the evidence of Speusippus and the Old Academy indicates that this thinking was applied to a final unity beyond the intelligibles. What matters for our purposes is this: the transcendence of the forms and the further transcendence of a final One were conceptually linked from the beginning within the Platonic tradition.

Realist ontology was vital, then, to the notion of the apophatic One. As a seminar we need to come to terms with this. The doctrine of the One as the transcendent "ground of being" was postulated as an extension of Platonic ontology. As Aubenque suggested, it represented "un dépassement de l'ontologie grecque classique."[2] This is true of the thought of Plotinus as well as that of earlier—if poorly attested—figures such as Moderatus. The apophatic theology of these authors in the Pythagorean-Platonic trajectory rested on a degree of reality metaphysics. The One stood in a complex but superior relation to the constituents of "being," which themselves are preeminent in reference to their ontological clients. The ὄντα were thus conceptually pivotal: they were the standards that lower entities only approximated, while they were also the level of finite perfection that the One exceeded.

---

[2] Cited in J. P. Kenney, *Mystical Monotheism: A Study in Ancient Platonic Theology* (Hanover and London: Brown University Press, 1991), 135.

Apophatic theology might thus be said to have been part of a "double" transcendence theory. The first level of transcendence was the postulation of the intelligibles, which stood outside space, time, qualitative alteration, etc. A second, higher notion of transcendence was then employed in reference to the One, which was understood to exceed even the perfection of the ὄντα. As has been suggested, the One's transcendence of being may have been required to staunch the explanatory regress identified by the "third-man" argument. If one postulates a hierarchy of perfect unities upon which lower entities depend ontologically and by which they are defined, then a problem arises regarding the source and foundation of these unities. A host of related philosophical issues are involved with this line of reflection, prominent among which are the principle of sufficient reason and the paradoxes of self-reference. None can be explored here, but they should be registered in order to underscore one central point: the apophatic One was not a theological notion independent of some very precise claims in metaphysics upon which its conceptual character depended.

One critical question now emerges for our consideration of "Gnosticism": do the various sorts of "gnostic" theology indicate a commitment to realist ontology? If so, then we have before us distinct but conceptually related theologies. If not, then we are faced with at least a partial impasse. There is no doubt that some of the same discourse, the language of classical apophatic theology, was transferred into some "gnostic" theologies. But are the ontological foundations of both trajectories similar? I attempted to address these questions in a paper on the *Tripartite Tractate* for the great Oklahoma Gnostic "Roundup" of 1984.[3] But I remain uncertain whether the same ontology underlies, for example, both the Platonic intelligible world and the Valentinian pleroma, despite some obvious thematic similarities. What follows from this is agnosticism regarding the exact commensurability of apophatic theology in Platonic and Valentinian thought. This worry could, of course, be generalized further. Notice in particular that the Platonic tradition had quite exact reasons for its "double transcendence" thesis and a precise account of the perfect predication that it forswore in reference to the One. Apophatic theology did not serve as a "first-order" articulation of divine transcendence. Rather, it constituted a higher-order support for the transcendent nature of the εἴδη, and it articulated by projection the general notion of a final divine unity.

The point might be put somewhat differently by asking two related sets of questions. First, what was the "metaphysical location" of those entities in the "gnostic" texts that seem analogous to "being" and the forms? Were the pleroma, the aeons, the Triple-Powered One, Barbelo, etc. separate from

---

3 J. P. Kenney, "The Platonism of the *Tripartite Tractate* (NHC I,5)," in *Neoplatonism and Gnosticism* (ed. R. T. Wallis and J. Bregman; Albany: SUNY Press, 1992).

the spatio-temporal cosmos in the same way as the intelligibles were? We are all aware how vexed the question of transcendence was in antiquity and how difficult was the Platonic notion of metaphysical separation. Do the various "gnostic" texts tell a story about intracosmic entities, about powers within this cosmos? Or do we have the Platonic two-world theory—a story about distinct levels of reality—clearly involved? The same question applies, as we know, to patristic texts, with the relevant contrast existing between Stoicizing Christians such as Tertullian and Platonizing authors such as Clement of Alexandria and Origen. And we might further recall that this very issue—the nature of transcendence—was central to Augustine's anti-Manichean polemic in the middle books of the *Confessions*. Are we certain that this same Augustinian contrast, between a strong or Platonic theory of divine transcendence and a much weaker one, is not also to be found between the two traditions that we are analyzing?

Here a brief parenthetical remark might be apposite. I take it that we are now quite uncomfortable with the universal attribution of anticosmism to the "gnostics." Perhaps we might begin to wonder whether we fell into that mistaken mode of analysis because we also have tended to interpolate a tacit Platonic ontology into these texts. Have we been culturally disposed to supply a "degree of reality" metaphysics where there was no such sharply articulated understanding of transcendence? Perhaps we have been disposed to represent the structure of reality along lines subtly different from those that were original to the "gnostic" texts and to see negative evaluations of the visible cosmos as far more sweeping than the texts portray. To denigrate part of an interconnected cosmos is, after all, different from rejecting a separate level of reality. It might then be asked whether an earlier misreading of the inherent anticosmism of many "gnostic" texts was itself not founded on another misreading, the tendency of several generations of scholars to use Platonic "degree of reality" ontology as a foundation for interpreting "gnostic" ontologies?

These queries lead to a second set of concerns about the strategy of *apophasis* in "Gnosticism." Does apophatic theology function in "gnostic" texts to establish a further ontological level beyond the threshold of transcendence? Or do these accounts articulate the hidden presence of an entity that is vastly greater and more exalted than those that can be described, but that is not clearly understood as marking off or occupying a status "beyond" the transcendent character of the intelligibles? We know, for example, that *Marsanes* postulates a silent and unknown One beyond the Invisible Spirit, itself above the Triple-Powered One, from which emanates the Aeon of Barbelo. Is the ontological status of this Invisible Spirit, or of the Triple-Powered One, or the "summit" of the silent One's silence (*Marsanes* 7,20–21), analogous to the sharply separate character of the Plotinian One? The question is not whether there might not be a general similarity based on a transference of ideas, but whether we can find the same foundational ontology involved. If not, then we would need to differentiate separate schools of negative theology with distinctive meanings, though similarity through mutual interaction would be an open historical question. I take it that the work of this seminar has advanced this latter question toward the affirmative. But the former issue remains—in my judgment—still open.

I hasten to add that I agree with the suggestion of Michael Williams that we can certainly see the transference of Platonic apophatic language into "gnostic" texts.[4] John Turner's papers for this group have also been convincing regarding the transfer of discourse between these trajectories of thought. The *Apocryphon of John,* the *Tripartite Tractate, Marsanes,* and *Allogenes* are obvious examples. But that discourse needs to be understood differently, for it has been embedded into another theological grammar and has lost its original ontological foundations. Our task, then, as historians of theology is to recover that new context and its adjusted meaning, and perhaps to understand the purpose behind these instances of borrowing.

2. Apophatic and Kataphatic Theology

All apophatic theology requires a first-order religious discourse to which it takes exception. As A. H. Armstrong put it in one of his later papers: "a negative theology needs a positive theology to wrestle with and transcend."[5] This observation might allow us to expand upon the point made in the first section: apophatic theology in the Platonic tradition turned on classical realism; perhaps that much might be granted. But an initial, broader question emerges: Are there some guiding reasons for the effort to correct, extend, or reject this initial level of theological discourse? And we might further inquire whether those reasons are articulated. To approach these questions I will make a few observations regarding the Platonic tradition and invite parallel suggestions regarding the "gnostic" trajectory.

The "critical value" of negative theology has been discussed for some time.[6] This reading of the ancient Platonic texts suggests that the ascension of the spiritual intellect—which apophatic theology seems meant to

---

[4] M. A. Williams, "Negative Theologies and Demiurgical Myths in Late Antiquity," *SBL Seminar Papers, 1997* (SBLSP 36; Atlanta: Scholars Press, 1997), 20–46. [See the following paper in this volume.]

[5] A. H. Armstrong, "On Not Knowing Too Much about God," in *Hellenic and Christian Studies* (Aldershot, Hampshire, Great Britain: Variorum; Brookfield, Vt.: Gower, 1990), 131.

[6] Cf. J. P. Kenney, "The Critical Value of Negative Theology," *HTR* 86 (1993): 439–53.

initiate among Platonists—could not have begun without a fairly well-grounded conception of the divine world. Otherwise, there would have been nothing to negate, nothing for the contemplative soul to exceed and surpass. An established theology would seem, then, to have been a precondition of Platonic *apophasis*. The critical value of negative theology should thus be seen as the result of this exception to a fixed set of theological claims. For Platonists, that meant correcting their metaphysical account of the intelligible world. The great apophatic ascension texts of the Platonic tradition derive their spiritual drama from the soul's forced movement beyond what was otherwise understood to be perfection as such. Thus "being," "life," "mind," "divinity," "rest," "beauty," "goodness," and the like all must be rejected and surpassed by the soul seeking the One. The energy of the *via negativa* is directly proportional to the degree to which these epithets had been previously understood as descriptive of divinity. There was, within the Platonic tradition, an intricate process by which a normative metaphysical language was first established in regard to the intelligible world and then excerpted to a higher, contemplative end. Apophatic theology among Platonists derived its critical value and its contemplative efficacy from the shock of *aphairesis,* of conceptual stripping away from accepted accounts of "being" and the intelligibles.

But there was no escaping *kataphasis*. This was true in several ways. As Michael Williams noted in reference to "gnostic" texts, apophatic theology was usually connected up with kataphatic claims.[7] This—we might now see—is a conceptual necessity, for they are interrelated. *Apophasis* without *kataphasis* would be empty. Moreover, even the most intensely apophatic theology is guided by a tacit conception of its divine or ultimate principle. Otherwise, its process of negation would be nothing but an exercise in skepticism. Yet it is clear that the Platonists of late antiquity took the reality of the One very seriously and were guided both by their kataphatic accounts of intelligible "being" and by their tacit understanding of the One.

This last point is an important opening for our comparative inquiry. It invites us to look for a moment at this subtle, Platonic conception of the One and the grounds for its articulation. We might, on that basis, have grounds to compare it to "gnostic" conceptions. Despite the strenuousness of Plotinian *aphairesis,* there is a cluster of notions that lurk behind Plotinus's discussion, wrapped in his characteristic οἶον phrases. Even Plotinus uses some privileged language, terms such as "One," "Good," "first," "source," etc. And it is also clear that, while the One resists conceptual specification, some concepts fit better than others.

---

[7] M. A. Williams, "Negative Theologies and Demiurgical Myths in Late Antiquity," in the present volume, esp. 283–84, 290–92.

Thus to call it "evil," or "limited," or "corporeal" would be a greater violation than to call it by any of the licit "pointer" terms, like "unlimited" or "good." This suggests that beneath the apophaticism of Plotinus, beneath his general proscription of predication, there lay a general understanding of ultimate divinity. Here we need to take particular care with this sensitive—indeed neuralgic—point for Plotinus, given his constant and insistent proscriptions against kataphatic description of the One. This vague notion of what was, and was not, acceptable in reference to the One was based in part on those philosophical scruples we have already discussed. But it was also founded upon a theological reflection, of what was understood culturally to be proper to the ultimate divinity, of what was θεοπρεπής. To say that the One was "good" was to rely on some theological representation, however qualified by *apophasis*. It is admittedly difficult to know quite how to represent this spiritual understanding. While Plotinus would not allow it to be presented as conceptual or intellective, it was nevertheless either a vector for the contemplative soul or perhaps a preconceptual grasp of at least some aspect of the One. This suggests that there was a proper way towards the One, despite the soul's fears of contemplative ascent (e.g., *Enn.* 5.1.9.3). Or alternatively, it suggests that there was a preconceptual, approximate sense of the One available to the soul, according to Plotinus. Either construal (and they are not exclusive) indicates that Plotinus was trading upon some general representation of divinity, despite his commitment to *apophasis*.

The story may be more interesting even than this, and we shall return to explore the connection of Hellenic theology and *apophasis* in the next section. But we need now to recognize that apophatic theology trades upon kataphatic theology in a variety of ways. These patterns of semantic interrelation are determinative of the meaning of any given theological tradition. This binary relationship between kataphatic and apophatic components established the special character of Neoplatonic theology, with (as we have seen) its particular notion of the intelligibles and its cluster of "pointer terms" that it diffidently employed in reference to the One. These formed the normative theological foreground against which *apophasis* was employed.

This suggests both a general and a specific observation. If kataphatic theology is understood to be central to *apophasis,* then—as a rule—negative theologies differ in their meaning depending on the theological tradition upon which they are based. While formally related as modes of negative discourse, they each establish a different form of theological portraiture. In the case of Plotinus, this contextualist thesis indicates that his negative theology requires a reading that keeps that foreground present. We might turn now to an exploration of that issue.

3. Hellenic Theology

If negative theologies are not all alike, but only formally similar, then kataphatic traditions emerge again as highly significant to the study of apophatic theology. The kataphatic foundations of the various sorts of "gnostic" thought would be an interesting inquiry, one that might threaten to plunge its investigators back into the quest for the origins of "Gnosticism," or at least into the specification of some theological context for each "gnostic" text. But I assume—perhaps wrongly—that the kataphatic foreground of the Sethian or Valentinian texts was quite different from that of Plotinus and the Platonic school. This is another question that might warrant further discussion. Nonetheless, the background of Plotinian thought is itself quite clearly Greco-Roman, and it might be useful now to bring that to bear on our subject.

We might consider the religious roots of Neoplatonic *apophasis*. The thesis that I have argued elsewhere is that negative theology was a constitutive development within Greco-Roman religious thought, a result of efforts to refine and elaborate the archaic account of sacred reality.[8] On this view, the ancient pantheon of sacrificial polytheism underwent various strategies of revision in the classical period, among which was the gradual elaboration of a type of Greco-Roman monotheism. Were I a comparativist, it would be tempting to connect this pattern of polytheistic revision with similar changes in the Vedic pantheon, to which Greco-Roman theology was remotely related historically, and to which it bears considerable resemblance. The willingness to countenance various theological appraisals of a sacrificially based polytheism is a feature, common to both Hindu and Hellenic thought, worth underscoring as we continue our reflections.

What remains to be said about this thesis is perhaps already obvious: the employment of negative theology was an indigenous part of the emergence of Greco-Roman monotheism out of archaic polytheism. This transition was a prolonged and complex development. Its basis was the religious structure of classical polytheism, which tended to see the gods, including the Olympians, as focal manifestations of the more obscure power of divinity itself. The gods were the anthropomorphic foreground of the divine, but behind them was a deeper, primordial reservoir of power. There was also a pronounced effort in the classical period, exemplified by Aeschylus, to collect these anthropomorphic forces into a single power and to associate this principle with primordial divinity itself. This "Zeus monotheism" was

---

[8] J. P. Kenney, *Mystical Monotheism,* 32–42, 150ff.; and "Monotheistic and Polytheistic Elements in Classical Mediterranean Spirituality," in *Classical Mediterranean Spirituality* (ed. A. H. Armstrong; New York: Crossroad, 1986), 269–92.

one response to the need to clarify the theology of ancient polytheism. Related to it was the gradual emergence of the divine mind as a distinct theological principle separate from the gods. Xenophanes and Empedocles were examples of this, so too are Aristotle and Xenocrates. The Middle Platonic conception of a supreme mind at the level of transcendent being was the direct result of this line of theological development.

The theological character of Middle Platonism had several aspects that warrant our attention. First is the exaltation of a supreme and transcendent *nous,* whose primordial status was achieved by emphasizing its remoteness and indifference to the cosmos. An abstraction from earlier "Zeus theism," this theology presented the divine mind as distant and removed. As a result, compensatory focus was placed upon secondary or intermediary powers, whose spiritual accessibility was greater and whose cosmological influence was more immediate. Chief among these was the second mind, or demiurge, the fashioner of the cosmos. The theologies of Numenius and Alcinous both evince this pattern.[9] This "demotion of the demiurge" suggests a determined effort to clarify the character of the first god such that it is wholly removed from materiality. Implicit in this model, of course, is a tacit dualism from which Middle Platonism was never free. The details of this model varied, but it was common for active agency to be located in a secondary or even tertiary power. Lesser gods, astral powers, and other traditional deities had a place as well.

This hierarchical theology, with its ranks of powers culminating in the first *nous,* seems a natural one, consistent as it surely was with the conventions of classical piety and with Platonic "degree of reality" ontology. But there remained one problem. To identify the first principle as a divine mind at the head of a chain of powers ran the risk of collapsing that divine entity into the rest of that series. By locating the supreme mind within the hierarchy of being, Middle Platonic theism tended to assimilate it to the overall systems of reality and to obscure its supremacy.[10]

It was in this context that negative theology came to the fore. It is possible to trace its history, even if our evidence is meager.[11] We can find it employed in authors such as Alcinous to help refine the nature of the first *nous.* In the well-known *Did.* 10 passage, Alcinous attempted to remove the first *nous* from epithets that would associate it with lower levels of reality, while also endorsing its self-sufficiency, perfection, goodness, and paternity. Here negative theology is used as one strategy of divine portraiture. Yet it was also true that others were articulating a somewhat

[9] J. P. Kenney, *Mystical Monotheism,* ch. 2.

[10] Ibid., 88–90.

[11] Ibid., ch. 1.

different, more abstract conception of a first principle through the use of negative theology. As we are all aware, it is difficult to achieve much historical precision on this subject. Yet I do think it likely that a more sweeping theological use of negative theology was employed prior to Plotinus by monotheistic Neopythagoreans such as Eudorus and Moderatus. This suggests that apophatic thought was particularly central to the development of another type of Greco-Roman theism, the theology of the divine One, a power beyond both *nous* and being.

The pre-Plotinian history of this theology matters for us only to the extent that it furnishes a context for Plotinian *apophasis*. In Plotinus this alternative form of Greco-Roman monotheism begins to come very clearly into focus, largely through his relentless use of negative theology. His was a theology of divine simplicity. Negative theology was systematically deployed to prevent the One's assimilation to all other sorts of reality, which were treated as its consequents. The One was the final divine unity, the ultimate source of reality. As such it was necessary to delineate the One from all finite beings subsequent to it by removing it from the logic of predicative ascription. Apophatic discourse allowed Plotinus to reject resolutely any conception that might have allowed the One to be drawn back into the structure of reality, whether that reality was transcendent of the spatio-temporal world or contained within the cosmos. As noted earlier, this "double transcendent" thesis was a hallmark of Plotinian theology and marked a critical advance in monotheistic theory. What Plotinus achieved, therefore, was the codification, through innovation, of Greco-Roman monotheism.[12]

Negative theology was, on this account, part of the theological grammar of Hellenic theism. Its limited use among pre-Plotinian thinkers, such as Alcinous or Numenius, was nonetheless important to their representation of the first deity. In Plotinus, apophatic discourse became a preeminent tool for philosophical theology, the chief method for clarifying the character of the first principle. In each of these cases, negative theology was deeply interwoven into the tradition, an aspect consistent with Hellenic religious thought and piety. Through its use, a long-standing element of that tradition, its latent theism, came to new conceptual clarity. In this respect, negative theology should be seen as a specific strategy within the Greco-Roman tradition, rather than merely a conceptual or philosophical device that was—in its formal character—largely "portable." Negative theology might thus be said to have had its own particular history, tied in with the emergence of monotheism within Greco-Roman religion.

This reading of classical negative theology raises, then, the question of the relation between Greco-Roman *apophasis* and "gnostic" versions. Here

---

[12] Ibid., ch. 3.

is a fertile source for renewed discussion. If this reading is generally correct, then Neoplatonic theology was endemically apophatic. Moreover, this "negative theism" was a natural outgrowth of Hellenic spirituality, the result of the gradual effort to explore the divine unity behind the surface tale of polytheism. Several issues then emerge: Can we discover a similar account to explain "gnostic" *apophasis?* In the past I have tended to contrast Hellenic theism, and its indigenous negative theology, to Abrahamic monotheism, which was centered on a single, personalized divine being.[13] Free from the burden of grounding a pantheon in an ultimate divine unity, Abrahamic monotheism went about the project of articulating its more sharply exclusive sort of theism in a different way. Hellenic apophatic theology was an importation into that tradition; Philo or Clement of Alexandria are examples. But these remained two separate traditions of ancient monotheism.

Can "gnostic" *apophasis* be given a local habitation and a fairly specific reason for its emergence? Was it similarly central to any given form of "gnostic" theology? I take it from Michael Williams's paper that we have in the past overemphasized the apophatic component in "gnostic" thought. Again, this may be due to the tendency, noted earlier, to import Platonism into our hermeneutic of "Gnosticism." But if we have placed too much weight on "gnostic" *apophasis,* then we need to adjust and consider anew its proper value in any given "gnostic" text or school of thought. To do so we need to decide what conceptual role apophatic theology played in each case, and whether this represented only a marginal role—perhaps as a culturally based instance of borrowing—or a more significant function, though not an essential one. In this regard I would ask in particular whether those who study "Gnosticism" might regard it as perhaps an effort to re-envision elements of the Abrahamic tradition using the resources of Hellenic theism, including apophatic discourse. This has been a question that has lingered in my own mind over the past few years as we traced the lines of interaction between later Platonism and "Gnosticism." If that is plausible, at least in some instances, then we would need to reflect on the reasons for that effort to translate and revise a mode of religious thought held by a minority group into the discourse of the culturally dominant pagan world. The present task, then, is to work through specific apophatic texts within the "gnostic" pleroma and to sort out the theological context from which such theology departed. If "gnostic" *apophasis* follows patterns that are rational, then recovery of these kataphatic foundations and the implicit rules of their negation should be specifiable.

A final note on demiurgic theology and *apophasis:* Michael Williams has suggested that we might use the category "demiurgical myth" to collect

---

13 See J. P. Kenney, "Monotheistic and Polytheistic Elements in Classical Mediterranean Spirituality," 269–92.

some of the theologies we have been considering. The operative distinction would be between a first god and that entity to which active cosmological agency was attributed. This is an interesting approach and suggests a further point that follows from the thesis iterated here. The concept of an active demiurge, subordinated to first god, would be—on my analysis—a fundamental feature of Hellenic theism. Emphasis upon a demiurgic second power was part of the project of moving away from the lingering anthropomorphism of earlier accounts of a divine mind. This was, in part, the impetus for thinkers like Numenius and Alcinous. It is interesting that more dualistic philosophers such as Plutarch or Atticus were inclined to retain a first principle that acts directly as a demiurge.[14] As noted, the demotion of the demiurge, which was increasingly pronounced in the later Middle Platonic period, was a development driven by the need to secure a clear claim to ultimacy of a first principle. There was a compelling logic to this move within the Hellenic theological tradition.

We might then consider whether we can offer a similar conclusion regarding "Gnosticism." There are several alternative ways to get its demiurgic character. One would be to identify a similar, indigenous reason for the postulation of a demiurge. Another would be to discover a basis for the adoption of this demiurgic model within any form of "Gnosticism." This would be to assume a Hellenic origin for this theology and would focus attention on the basis for its transfer into a different mode of theology. The latter analysis would suggest once again that Greco-Roman theism was drawn upon by "gnosticizing" thinkers intent upon revising an antecedent system of theology. These two approaches clearly have implications regarding the sources of "Gnosticism," or at least of any given "gnostic" text.

Perhaps I might conclude this section with an incautious observation. The real work for future comparative analysis between Greco-Roman and "gnostic" theology lies here, in the study of the complex development of Hellenic theism in late antiquity and the stimulation that this afforded to other religious schools, especially some forms of Judaism and Christianity. Just as we have been conditioned to think about "Gnosticism" through the lens of Platonic transcendentalism, so too have we been inclined, by habit and disposition, to treat the theology of the majority tradition of the pre-Theodosian Empire as if it were a minor sideshow, unlikely to have had the merit to have influenced anyone, except in details. I do not wish to sound crypto-Harnackian, but we will continue to make progress in our comparative work only if we could treat the wide band of later Hellenic theism (i.e., the Neopythagoreans, the Middle Platonists, Hermetica,

---

[14] J. P. Kenney, *Mystical Monotheism,* 57–84 on Numenius and Alcinous; ibid., 43–53 on Plutarch.

Chaldean Oracles, Plotinian and Iamblichean Neoplatonism, etc.) as a
powerful theological tradition, prestigious and authoritative as it was.
Then we will begin to imagine better why others might have wished to
adopt its ideas and why its closely connected conceptions of an apophatic One and a demiurge were adapted by other schools and traditions.
If we can make this shift in our dispositions, then we can describe the
connections of "Gnosticism" and Platonism in different, more comprehensive terms.

4. Soteriology and Sacred Hierarchy

Mention has been made in our recent sessions of the "locative"
dimension of both "gnostic" and later Platonic theology. I would like to
get at this aspect briefly, but without being drawn into terminology based
on agendas from outside our domain. Perhaps we might use the notion
of "hierarchy," that is, the idea that there are levels of divinity and reality.
There is an inevitable spatial component to such thinking, one that is difficult to remove. Apophatic theology was related to this hierarchical
aspect of later antique religious thought in ways that invite reflection. One
dominant theme throughout Greco-Roman theism is the idea that the cosmos is an ordered whole that mirrors the transcendent order. Gregory
Shaw has done a fine job of articulating this aspect of later Platonism in
his recent book on Iamblichus.[15] Following J. Z. Smith,[16] he suggests that
Iamblichus was the great restorer of the "locative" religious model,
whereby the soul's salvation is understood to derive from its congruence
with the cosmos, from its inhabitation of its proper place in a fundamentally ordered and good universe. On this account, Iamblichus rejected the
more pessimistic Numenian-Plotinian line of thought, which culminated in
Plotinus's innovative view "that the soul did not descend entire." This doctrine of the undescended soul suggested that the lower reaches of the
cosmos were evil, so that the soul's descent brought it into polluted contact with matter. Why else would the soul's connection with the transcendental world be so assiduously retained, by insisting on its continued
ontological association with the noetic realm, if its embodiment were not
an act of evil defilement?

The central contrast would be between Plotinus and the "gnostics" on
the one hand, over against the school of Iamblichus on the other. To
quote Shaw:[17]

---

[15] G. Shaw, *Theurgy and the Soul: The Neoplatonism of Iamblichus* (University
Park: Pennsylvania State University Press, 1995), 1–17.

[16] J. Z. Smith, *Map Is Not Territory* (Leiden: Brill, 1978), 88–103.

[17] G. Shaw, *Theurgy and the Soul,* 10.

> The pervasive acosmic mood of late antiquity effected a change in this locative orientation, and its influence was felt even in Platonic circles where it reversed the tradition of locative taxonomy....
>
> Iamblichus' position developed in the context of this cosmic pessimism: he was the inheritor of a Plotinian Platonism where the soul never descended into a body; it remained in the heavens, above the flesh and the physical world. Plotinus' ... view of the soul, which may have been influenced by Gnostic dualists, was unorthodox from a Platonic perspective.

Iamblichus emerges on this account as a neoconservative Platonist. The burden of his efforts was to restore the classical valuation of the physical universe. He did so through his restoration of the "locative" aspect of Platonism, its commitment to the principle of hierarchy, and his adoption of theurgy, the practice of Hellenic ritual. It is the former that is apposite to our topic.

We might now consider apophatic theology in reference to this contrast within the Platonic tradition. Let's set aside the question of late antique pessimism and its attribution to "Gnosticism" or to Plotinus. What is interesting about the contrast between Plotinus and Iamblichus is their common commitment to apophatic theology and to Hellenic theism. What divides them is their separate understanding of the hierarchy of reality and the soul's place within it. Their dispute centers on soteriology. To quote Shaw again:[18]

> In theurgy, Iamblichus provided a soteriology that theoretically could touch any soul, from the most material to the most spiritual, while preserving their communal affiliations. With a more consistent metaphysics Iamblichus succeeded in restructuring Plato's teachings in a way that preserved the mystical elements of Plotinus' soteriology without losing contact with the physical cosmos or society.

Plotinus and his school are thus committed to what might be called an "autosoteriology." As Porphyry put it in *De Abstinentia* (2.49.1): "In every respect the philosopher is the savior of himself."

This analysis suggests that apophatic theology could support two distinctive types of theism within Neoplatonism: an Iamblichean theology in which the idea of the hidden One reinforced the idea of levels of reality, and a Plotinian theology in which the notion of an ineffable One was conducive of greater permeability among these levels. Hierarchy and the "locative" aspect of classical theology would be undercut by the Plotinian model, both by the doctrine of the undescended soul and by his under-

---

[18] Ibid., 14.

standing of the omnipresence of the One. Thus Plotinian soteriology would track the special character of his ontology.

But it might also be argued that Plotinian apophatic theology does not undercut the locative dimension of later Platonism. By its predicative resistance, the One can be said to be omnipresent to all its consequents in ways consistent with their nature, for it has no fixed nature of its own to enforce separation. For Plotinus, that then means that θεωρία can reveal the soul's place in the structure of reality and its underlying ontological connection to the One. It is the latter feature that appears to the contemplative soul as its undescended aspect. To admit this is not to deny hierarchy or to reject the locative, only to press out the implications of ontological omnipresence. Indeed, a proper reading of Plotinian contemplation would be grounded in an enlightened recognition of the soul's rootedness in all levels of reality and in the One.[19] The late antique Platonic debate over soteriology may well be the product of Porphyry's own approach to his master Plotinus, with his emphasis on the model of psychic flight, and of Iamblichus's reaction to that approach. Even so, the dispute indicates that Platonic negative theology was open to a range of variations.

That point raises a final series of comparative questions. Is it possible to find similar approaches to hierarchy within the various "gnostic" texts? Can these be seen to track along the same lines of ontological representation, and is there any connection of these different ontologies to divergent soteriologies? Do instances of "gnostic" *apophasis* underscore or subvert the "locative" aspect of such theology? All of these seem to be natural points of comparison.

5. Noetic Postscript

Fear of revisionism is the beginning of scholarly wisdom. This seminar paper was intended in that spirit, in recognition of our place in what is surely the initial phase in the study of "Gnosticism" and its relation to late antique Platonic theology. We are still, I believe, at the stage of reconnaissance, as we survey the texts and try out different theories to explain their features. There are several modest suggestions embedded in this paper that I should like now to collect in lieu of a conclusion. They are designed to help make the future task of debunking our contributions more difficult.

As has been suggested, I have come to think that importation of Platonic transcendentalism into the study of "Gnosticism" may be a source of confusion. This has been the "*tolmeric*" basis of my concerns, voiced in

---

[19] This is argued at some length in my paper, "Mysticism and Contemplation in the Enneads," *American Catholic Philosophical Quarterly* 71.3 (Summer 1997) 1–23.

earlier years, about commensurability. I worry that this may be yet another item that found its way uncritically into the study of "Gnosticism," a result of the training of most students in the field. Using Platonism as a template may have led to a more radical reading of the hierarchical character of "Gnosticism," to a more rarefied understanding of its notion of transcendence, and perhaps to a heightened sense of its acosmism. Again, allow me to reiterate that this is not meant as a wholesale criticism of the comparative work that many scholars have done. Rather, it is a plea for continued refinement of the basis of those comparison. Perhaps we have done the "gnostics" a disservice by too often reading them as mythologically inclined Platonists.

The other concern beneath the surface in this paper is our continuing need—indeed, scholarly obligation—to recover the authentic tradition of pagan Hellenic theology. It is necessary that we come to understand seriously and sympathetically the metaphysics and theology of what was, for much of the period we study, the most prestigious and culturally authoritative tradition, and the one subscribed to, at various levels, by the majority in the Roman world. Only then will its persuasive force be clear to us and its powerful presence be more certainly recognized within "gnostic," Jewish, and Christian thought. This is now a great opportunity for progress in comparative study, one to which many of our members have made distinguished contributions. This is surely one of the great desiderata in the study of Western religious thought, the need for recovery of the late classical tradition. In this respect, our short-lived seminar has been quite singular, even exemplary. And, nested as it has been in the Society of Biblical Literature, who would dare to think that the irony of its presence has failed to excite delight in Elysium?

Negative Theologies and Demiurgical Myths in Late Antiquity

Michael A. Williams
University of Washington (Seattle)

1. Introduction

Among the most famous examples of negative theological speculation from late antiquity are some of those sources customarily assigned to the category "Gnosticism." In an insightful article surveying various ancient forms of negative theology and their emphases on the unknowability of the highest God or suprasensible reality, the late Richard Wallis suggested that "it is in Gnosticism ... that we find the strongest pre-Neoplatonic affirmations of divine unknowability." And yet Wallis also observed that in spite of our greatly expanded information about such myths, due to the availability in the latter part of this century of new sources such as those from Nag Hammadi Coptic codices or the related Berlin Codex 8502, "the significance of Gnostic negative theology remains as controversial as ever."[1]

Drawing on certain pertinent results and implications of scholarly research on Nag Hammadi and related sources over the past several years, I would like in this paper to offer for consideration a set of four propositions: (1) Although "negative theology," or at least an insistence on the unknowability of the highest God, is often assumed to be one of the essential features of "gnostic" myth, this feature is in fact not ubiquitous among the myths normally viewed as "gnostic." And the number of such sources in which one encounters any significant amount of negative theological discourse is relatively limited. (2) In those sources in which we do find extended passages with negative theological discourse we also tend to find this language formulated with discernible patterns and structures that imply some interest in the usefulness of rational argument. Thus, contrary to the notion that "gnostic" revelation typically entailed a despair and abandonment of rationality and that negative theology was the ultimate

---

[1] R. T. Wallis, "The Spiritual Importance of Not Knowing," in *Classical Mediterranean Spirituality: Egyptian, Greek, Roman* (ed. A. H. Armstrong; New York: Crossroad, 1986), 468 and 461.

expression of this, it seems to be precisely in the sources where negative theology is most exploited that we can make the best case for the adaptation of philosophical argument. (3) In the analysis of the role of negative theology in these mythic sources, it is necessary not to restrict the focus too narrowly on the negation itself, the insistence on the absolute unknowability of God. Paradoxically, the exercise of negation is an important part, but only one part, of what is often a much larger more multifaceted experience of "knowing God" that is attested in these myths. (4) In particular, narrow emphasis on formulas of negation in such myths has frequently been one of the key building blocks in the characterization of an alleged "gnostic" worldview as so "anticosmic" that it could find no help from the visible cosmos in the quest for knowledge of the divine. By contrast, I will argue that exactly the sources with the most prominent examples of negative theology turn out also to provide some of the best evidence for appeals to forms of cosmological argument.

Recently I have argued at some length that the very category "Gnosticism" is no longer serving us well as a tool for analysis.[2] In most of its constructions, it tends to suffer from a vagueness that has prevented real consensus about its meaning and application (i.e., there are too many cases where we seem not to be able to reach agreement about whether a source is to be classified in this category). And in any event, the category tends to be constructed out of clichés that too often turn out to be misrepresenting many of the supposedly "gnostic" sources. "Anticosmism" is one of the most common of such clichés, and, I have become more and more certain, it is one of the least enlightening and most problematic. I hope to have included in what follows some further illustration of why this verdict is justified.

The title of this paper self-consciously avoids the category "Gnosticism" and mentions instead a general classification, "demiurgical myths." I use the term "demiurgical myth" to mean simply a myth in which a distinction is made between the highest God or ultimate principle and the entity or entities to whom are ascribed the initiative and responsibility for the fashioning of the material cosmos. As a matter of fact, this definition would include most of the myths conventionally classified under "Gnosticism." But there are also other writers or traditions, such as philosophers like Numenius or Alcinous, who present at least "demiurgical" *doctrines,* even if they are not always framed in the form of more elaborate mythic narratives.[3]

---

[2] M. A. Williams, *Rethinking "Gnosticism":An Argument for Dismantling a Dubious Category* (Princeton, N. J.: Princeton University Press, 1994).

[3] See J. M. Dillon, *The Middle Platonists: 80 B.C. to A.D. 220* (Ithaca, N.Y.: Cornell University Press, 1977); J. Whittaker and L. Pierre, eds. and trans., *Alcinoos: Enseignement des doctrines de Platon* (Paris: Les Belles Lettres, 1990); J. M. Dillon,

The classification "demiurgical myth" is intended here as a category that is more neutral and less freighted than "Gnosticism." I employ it as a heuristic category, hoping to "find out" things that such myths might and might not convey or imply. "Demiurgical myth" is not being used here as a label for a single religion or religious tradition, and I do not assume that I will find exactly the same results in every such myth. What do we find out about demiurgical myths and negative theology?

2. Absence/Presence of Negative Theological Discourse

The first thing we note is that not all demiurgical myths seem to have a negative theology. A writing such as the Nag Hammadi *Apocalypse of Adam,* for example, contains a demiurgical myth in which Adam and Eve are created by a lesser god,[4] and the author speaks fairly matter-of-factly about the higher, "eternal" or "living God," or "God of truth." While knowledge of the latter was lost by Adam and Eve (*Apoc. Adam* 65,10–11), it is restored by means of later revelations all down through history. In this text, the true God is not wrapped in alpha privatives, and the myth is not about God's unknowability or incomprehensibility. To the contrary, the writing speaks straightforwardly of the importance of having true knowledge of this God.[5]

I mention an example such as this because precisely in discussions of the theme of divine transcendence or negative theology in late antique sources one can encounter generalizations such as: "The doctrine of the unknowability of God represents also a fundamental feature of the theology of Gnosticism."[6] These days, the demiurgical myth in the *Apocalypse of Adam* is always counted as an important representative of this category "Gnosticism," and yet it hardly supports the assertion just quoted. Indeed, it would be fairly easy to produce a relatively long list of sources from Nag Hammadi and heresiological accounts of sectarian mythologies in which there is no, or relatively little, actual use of negative theological labels or discourse. Admittedly, this absence in many instances may be a misleading silence, more a factor of an author's specific purposes at the moment than an indication of no interest at all in such discourse. But it is worth keeping in mind the fact that there is actually a rather limited number of

---

trans., *Alcinous: The Handbook of Platonism* (Oxford: Clarendon Press; New York: Oxford University Press, 1993).

[4] *Apoc. Adam* 64,17–19, etc.; called "God almighty" (e.g., 69,4), or "Sakla" (e.g., 74,3), or "God of the powers" (e.g., 77,4–5).

[5] *Apoc. Adam* 64,13; 65,10–11; 72,14; 82,21–23; 83,11–21; 84,10; 85,15.

[6] S. Lilla, *Clement of Alexandria: A Study in Christian Platonism and Gnosticism* (London: Oxford University Press, 1971), 219.

cases where we *do* encounter explicit formulations of negative theological language in these myths.

A long-standing favorite illustration of radically negative theology is the account given by Hippolytus of Rome about the doctrines of the early second-century C.E. Christian teacher Basilides. This source alleges Basilides to have taught a supreme God who was absolutely beyond any name or description whatsoever, a "non-existent God" prior to being itself (Hippolytus, *Ref.* 7.20.2–21.4). In his summaries of teachings of Valentinian Christians, Irenaeus of Lyons refers to their use of negative theological language (e.g., *Haer.* 1.1.1), though certainly not a usage with the panache encountered in the doctrine ascribed to Basilides.

The discoveries of sources such as the Berlin Codex 8502 and the Nag Hammadi codices have provided a few important new examples of negative theology among demiurgical myths. The texts containing the most elaborate articulations of negative theology are: the *Apocryphon of John;* the *Letter of Eugnostos* (and a text that is likely dependent on it, the *Sophia of Jesus Christ*); *Allogenes,* and probably also the tractate *Zostrianos* (though the relevant passages in the latter are quite fragmentary); and the *Tripartite Tractate.* There are significant instances of negative theological jargon in other tractates as well, though the works just mentioned stand out by their inclusion of extended sections devoted to this topic. As Roelof van den Broek has commented, some of them contain "descriptions of the ineffable God which in length and elaborateness surpass all those known from Platonic or orthodox-Christian sources."[7]

3. Negative Theologies: Patterns

Among the demiurgical myths that do contain negative theological discourse in significant quantity, research has now demonstrated that we should be cautious not to mistake these instances as merely a kind of haphazard potluck of mystical-sounding or "numinous" jargon. Though there is increasing awareness of this among scholars, it is an important fact that has not always been appreciated: In an article several years ago, William Schoedel presented a convincing and important argument about monistic implications underlying the use in certain "gnostic" sources of a specific formula of "topological" theology—God as "containing" while being "uncontained." In developing his argument, Schoedel at one point justifiably contrasted the formula as strictly defined with other uses of the label "uncontained" (ἀχώρητος), where it appears without the other half of the formula ("containing"), as one term in a list of negative theological

---

[7] R. van den Broek, *Studies in Gnosticism and Alexandrian Christianity* (NHMS 39; Leiden: Brill, 1996), 43–44.

attributes. Then as an aside he added: "The language of negative theology in a Gnostic setting is 'numinous' language. The wonder of God's being is magnified without specific reference to precise theological formulation."[8] Now although this generalization probably does express what has been a widely held impression, it can no longer be defended. For contrary to the implication of such an assertion, we will see that some of the most extensive examples of negative theology among these sources actually seem to display some care in their employment of negations.

I quote one further example illustrating how this has not always been understood, this time from comments by the late Hans Jonas on the very important instance of negative theology in the opening sections of the *Apocryphon of John:*

> Like all gnostic speculation, the revelation of the Apocryphon (the reve-
> latory stage first having been set) starts with a dissertation on the ultra-
> transcendent First Principle; and here we meet with the kind of emphatic
> and pathetic verbosity which the "ineffable" seems to have incited in
> many of its professors: the over four pages of effusive description devoted
> to the very indescribability of the divine Absolute—expatiating on the
> theme of His purity, boundlessness, perfection, etc., being beyond meas-
> ure, quality, quantity, and time; beyond comprehension, description,
> name, distinction; beyond life, beatitude, divinity, and even existence—
> are a typical example of the rising "negative theology," whose spokesmen
> did not tire for centuries of the self-defeating nature of their task. Justly
> more reticent, the Valentinians contented themselves on this point with a
> few telling symbols (as "Abyss", "Silence").[9]

Now in a section of his forthcoming book on the *Apocryphon of John,* Michael Waldstein has forcefully demonstrated how inadequate is such a characterization of the negative theological discourse in the *Apocryphon of John* as mere "pathetic verbosity" and "effusive description."[10] Rather, Waldstein contends that the long passage about the Invisible Spirit in *Ap. John* II 2,26–4,18 (= BG 22,17–26,14) is "a disciplined piece of writing which develops not only

---

[8] W. R. Schoedel, "'Topological' Theology and Some Monistic Tendencies in Gnosticism," in *Essays on the Nag Hammadi Texts in Honour of Alexander Böhlig* (ed. Martin Krause; NHS 3; Leiden: Brill, 1972), 91.

[9] H. Jonas, *The Gnostic Religion* (2d ed.; Boston: Beacon, 1963), 199; and the corresponding German version in idem, *Gnosis und spätantiker Geist,* part 1 (3d ed.; FRLANT 51 Göttingen: Vandenhoeck & Ruprecht, 1964), 393. Certainly the last comment about the parsimony of Valentinians in this regard is no longer tenable in light of such works as the *Tripartite Tractate* from Nag Hammadi Codex I (see below).

[10] I am grateful to Michael Waldstein for allowing me the opportunity of reading a 1995 draft of part of his book, and my citations here refer to pages in that draft.

an account of the first principle, but, at the same time, an account of the different forms of argument and language by which it can be approached."[11] He shows that this portion of the *Apocryphon of John* may be analyzed into discrete sections with recognizable organization and development, and manifesting continuity in both form and content with similar material from Middle Platonic school tradition, especially Alcinous and the Christian apologist Aristides. I give here only outlines of some of Waldstein's analysis:[12]

After a brief opening list of attributes of the Invisible Spirit (BG 22,17–23,3 = II 2,26–32) there is a first series of assertions, each followed by a supporting clause introduced by γάρ, "for" (BG 23,3–14 = II 2,33–3,7):

> It is not right to think of him as God...
>> for he is more than God,
> (He is) a principality [ἀρχή] over which nothing rules [ἄρχει],
>> for there is nothing prior to him;
> Nor does he need them: he does not need life,
>> for he is eternal;
> He does not need anything,
>> for he cannot be completed as if he were lacking so as to be completed,
>> but rather he is always entirely complete.

After this is a series of seven negations (II 3,7–15 par.), all but one supported by a clause introduced, not by γάρ, but by the Coptic **ЄΒΟΛ ϪЄ** or **ϪЄ**, "since" (= Greek ὅτι?). Rather than a full translation, I provide a somewhat more skeletal rendering that brings into relief the structure:

Illimitable	since no one prior to him to limit him
Unexaminable	since no one prior to him to examine him
Immeasurable	since no one prior to him to measure him
Invisible	since no one has seen him
Eternal	existing forever
Ineffable	since no one comprehended him to speak about him
Unnamable	since no one prior to him to name him

Waldstein points out that a *via negationis* argument with a similar structure and "rhythmical application of negation" is found in Aristides.[13] The next

---

[11] M. Waldstein, *The Apocryphon of John: A Curious Eddy in the Stream of Hellenistic Judaism* (draft version), 110.

[12] Cf. M. Tardieu, *Écrits gnostiques: Codex de Berlin* (Sources Gnostiques et Manichéenes 1; Paris: Cerf, 1984), 248–53.

[13] Waldstein, *Apocryphon of John*, 98; Aristides *Apology* 1 (J. R. Harris, ed. and trans., *The Apology of Aristides* [2d ed.; TS 1.1; Cambridge: Cambridge University Press, 1893], 35–36).

major section of the negative theology in the Apocryphon of John (II 3,20–28 par.) is structured in still another way, with a *via eminentiae* pattern: "He is neither A nor B (nor C nor D), but *something better* than these." As is well known, this section of the *Apocryphon of John* is closely paralleled by the text of *Allogenes* 62,27–63,14, indicating a literary relationship of some sort, perhaps a matter of a dependence on a common source. And finally, still a further clear pattern is found in II 4,3–10 par., where several positive attributes are applied to the Invisible Spirit, but in such a way as to underscore that the Invisible Spirit is *source* of all such things (once again, in a more skeletal rendering):

Eternal	the one who supplies eternity
Light	the one who supplies light
Life	the one who supplies life
Blessed	the one who supplies blessedness
Knowledge	the one who supplies knowledge
Good	the one who supplies good
Mercy	the one who supplies mercy
Grace	the one who supplies grace

The famous section of negative theology in Alcinous *Did.* 10.3–4 contains the same kind of argument about attributes of the "First God." The latter can be said to be the Good (ἀγαθόν) since "he is the source [αἴτιος] of all good"; he is Truth (ἀλήθεια) since he is the origin (ἀρχή) of every truth (10.3).

I have outlined only a few key elements of Waldstein's analysis here, but his discussion presents a splendid case for treating the account of the Invisible Spirit in the *Apocryphon of John* as something much more than merely "numinous" language without any very precise theological formulation. What might seem at first glance to the reader to be a rambling stream of "pathetic verbosity" actually does have a structure and a certain level of precision in argumentation.

Perhaps part of the reason underlying dismissive characterizations such as that quoted from Jonas is that earlier generations of scholarship had been more inclined to view even some of the corresponding passages from more "professional" Middle Platonic figures, like that in Alcinous *Did.* 10, as theologically incoherent. For on the one hand, God is described by disallowing the validity of any predication whatsoever, while in virtually the next breath positive attributes are applied. Jaap Mansfeld has addressed this problem of how *via negationis, via eminentiae,* and *via analogiae* argumentation can seemingly coexist in a kind of "peaceful jumble."[14] He argues

---

14 J. Mansfeld, "Compatible Alternatives: Middle Platonist Theology and the Xenophanes Reception," in *Knowledge of God in the Graeco-Roman World* (ed. R. van den Broek, T. Baarda and J. Mansfeld; EPRO 112; Leiden: Brill, 1988), 92.

that such writers viewed these as "alternative modes of cognition, compatible albeit of unequal value." Alcinous, observes Mansfeld, "is most conscientious in informing us about the three modes of cognition; other surviving Middle Platonist authors seem to take them for granted and provide us with a clutter of epithets without being very clear about the justification for their procedure, although hints are occasionally provided."[15] And it is perhaps just such hints that we find through a close analysis of the structure of the description of the Invisible Spirit in the *Apocryphon of John*.

Both *Eugnostos* and the *Tripartite Tractate* also manifest in their sections that describe the highest God features that indicate some amount of care in the structure of the argument (*Eugnostos* III 71,13–73,3; *Tri. Trac.* 51,8–55,26).[16] Roelof van den Broek[17] has pointed out that much of the relevant section in *Eugnostos* may be analyzed as a series of four arguments, each with three parts. *Eugnostos* III 71,18–72,13:

He is immortal, eternal,
(1) Having *no birth,*
    (2) for everyone who has birth will perish;
      (3) he is unbegotten;
(1) Having no *beginning* [ἀρχή],
    (2) for everyone who has a beginning has an end;
      (3) nothing rules [ἄρχει] over him.[18]
(1) Having *no name,*
    (2) for whoever has a name is the creature of another;
      (3) he is unnamable;
(1) He has *no human form,*
    (2) for whoever has human form is the creation of another;
      (3) he has his own form, not like the form that we have received or seen, but a strange form that surpasses all things and is better than the totalities. It looks to every side and sees itself from itself.

---

[15] Mansfeld, "Compatible Alternatives," 110–11.

[16] On the negative theological discourse in *Eugnostos* in general, see the very informative treatment by D. Trakatellis, *The Transcendent God of Eugnostos* (trans. C. Sarelis; Brookline, Mass.: Holy Cross Orthodox Press, 1991), especially 35–65, who provides extensive discussion of parallels, though he does not comment on the patterns identified by van den Broek.

[17] R. van den Broek, "Eugnostos and Aristides on the Ineffable God," in *Knowledge of God in the Graeco-Roman World* (ed. R. van den Broek, T. Baarda and J. Mansfeld; EPRO 112; Leiden: Brill, 1988), 207.

[18] Van den Broek, "Eugnostos and Aristides," 207, suggests that the Coptic here was a mistranslation of the Greek *anarchos estin,* "he was without beginning." This may be, though there may also be simply a play on the multiple connotations of *archein.* See *Ap. John* BG 23,6–7 = II 2,36–3,1, and my discussion below.

Moreover, van den Broek has noted the unquestionable parallel between the order of the four negations here and the same sequence in the same four negations in both Aristides and in the *Tripartite Tractate*. The section in the *Tripartite Tractate* is admittedly longer and more complex, but it cannot be accidental that the description of the Father in that text includes a sequence of sections treating the following themes:[19]

> *Not begotten* (and not created)—51,28–52,6
> *No beginning* (and no end)—52,6–53,5
> Completeness (no defect)—53,5–54,1
> *No name*—54,2–27
> *No face or form*—54,27–55,14

One can see that the sequence of themes exactly matches that in the passage from *Eugnostos* cited above, with the exception of the inclusion in *Tripartite Tractate* 53,5–54,1 of a section on perfection/lack of defect. But van den Broek has noted that the same series of themes, including a section on perfection/lack of defect, is also found in the description of God in the Syriac version of the apology of Aristides:[20]

> Not begotten, not made;
> A constant nature, without beginning and without end;
> Immortal, complete, and incomprehensible: and in saying that he is
> > complete I mean this: that there is no deficiency in him. . . .
> He has no name, for everything that has a name is associated with
> > the created;
> He has no likeness, nor composition of members; for he who possesses
> > this is associated with things fashioned. . . .

Van den Broek suggests that all three authors have made use of some common source.[21]

---

[19] Cf. the extensive analysis of this section of the *Tripartite Tractate* in E. Thomassen and L. Painchaud, eds. and trans., *Le Traité Tripartite (NH I, 5)* (BCNHT 19; Quebec: Les Presses de l'Université Laval, 1989), 264–76. Thomassen subdivides the section in much the same way (though without the comparison to *Eugnostos* and Aristides), and provides important citation of parallels for individual elements from philosophical literature. On parallels for individual elements, see also H. W. Attridge, ed., *Nag Hammadi Codex I (The Jung Codex): Introductions, Texts, Translations, Indices* (2 vol.; NHS 22–23; Leiden: Brill, 1985), 2:221–33.

[20] Van den Broek, "Eugnostos and Aristides," 217–18. Translation here from J. R. Harris, ed. and trans., *The Apology of Aristides*, 35.

[21] Van den Broek, "Eugnostos and Aristides," 205.

Actually, it is possible to extend the comparison even further by noting that at least part of the above pattern of thematic progression might be isolated also in the *Apocryphon of John:*

> (He is) a principality [ἀρχή] over which nothing rules [ἄρχει], for there is nothing prior to him;
>
> Nor does he need them: he does not need life, for he is eternal; He does not need anything, for he *cannot be completed* as if he were lacking so as to be completed, but rather he is always entirely complete.... (BG 23,6–14)
>
> the *unnamable* One, since there is no one prior to him to name him.... (BG 24,4–6)
>
> For he is not corporeal; he is *not incorporeal;* he is not large; he is not small; he is not a quantity; for he is not a creature.... (BG 24,15–19).

The fourth item here is not precisely parallel to the theme of form/likeness in the lists from *Eugnostos,* Aristides, and the *Tripartite Tractate,* though the connection with createdness[22] in all four is striking. And "unnameability" is one member of a long list of attributes at that point in *Apocryphon of John,* so perhaps it is merely accidental that its position comes at a point after a discussion of ἀρχή and "completeness" as in the other three sources. Nevertheless, there may be some amount of relationship in thematic order, rather than mere randomness.

In any event, it is clear from the above discussion that at least several of the most important examples of negative theological discourse from the Nag Hammadi codices (or from anywhere in so-called "gnostic" literature)—the *Apocryphon of John, Eugnostos* (and the *Sophia of Jesus Christ*), and the *Tripartite Tractate*—manifest intentional structures in the presentation of their arguments, rather than being merely a stream of alpha privatives.[23]

---

[22] At least in the shorter recension of *Apocryphon of John.* This element is absent in the longer recension.

[23] K. King, *Revelation of the Unknowable God with Text, Translation and Notes to NHC XI,3: Allogenes* (Santa Rosa, Calif.: Polebridge, 1995), 154–57, has shown how the important apophatic theology in *Allogenes* is also patterned in accordance with conventional and identifiable structures and formulas. That some of these structures involved interpretation of Plato's *Parmenides* has been recognized for some time (see, e.g., J. D. Turner, "Gnosticism and Platonism: The Platonizing Sethian Texts from Nag Hammadi and Their Relation to Later Platonic Literature," in *Neoplatonism and Gnosticism* [ed. R.T. Wallis and J. Bregman; Studies in Neoplatonism: Ancient and Modern 6, Albany: SUNY Press, 1992], 449–50).

4. Negative Theologies and Knowledge of God

I mentioned above that the demiurgical myth in the *Apocalypse of Adam* lacks any negative theological discourse and contains straightforward references to the possibility of having knowledge of the God of Truth. But even the presence of significant negative theology does not always rule out a strong emphasis on seeking after knowledge of the Unknowable.

Some of the most striking examples of this are to be found in forms of Valentinian Christian myth. There is first of all the classic account that Irenaeus provides of the mythology of the Valentinian teacher Ptolemy (Irenaeus *Haer.* 1.1.1–8.5). In this myth, the aeon Wisdom longs to comprehend the incomprehensible Father. This is referred to as "an impossible effort" (1.2.2), and of course the passion produced in this futile attempt resulted in the series of events leading to the material creation. However, even though it might be true to say that according to this myth, "[e]vil originates in the desire of Sophia (Wisdom) to comprehend the Father,"[24] that is not quite the same as saying that the desire to know the Father is evil.

Indeed, in Ptolemy's myth a wish to know the Father seems to be shared by *all* of the aeons in the realm of Perfection (1.2.1), not just Wisdom. Among the aeons, Only-Begotten Mind (Nous) alone was actually able to behold and know the Father, yet even Mind *wished* to share knowledge with all the rest of the aeons. Interestingly, the knowledge that Mind wished to share with the others is described as essentially negative knowledge: that the Father is without beginning, incomprehensible, and invisible. But by the Father's will, Mind was constrained by Silence from conveying any knowledge about the Father, and this left the remaining aeons still wishing for such (1.2.1). In other words, the highest God may be incomprehensible and ineffable, but *seeking after* knowledge of God is portrayed here as the most prominent and "natural" instinct among the aeons in the realm of divine Perfection.

Moreover, the course of Ptolemy's myth as a whole conveys the message that the Unknowable *wishes* to be known, though only through a knowledge mediated by Only-Begotten Mind (1.2.1; 1.2.5). The very restraint of Mind by Silence seems to lead to Wisdom's attempt at comprehension. The latter does eventually have as part of its "fallout" the evils of the material realm. However, the process as a whole results, by divine providence, in the fullest possible distribution and attainment of knowledge of God.

The *Tripartite Tractate* is an example of a form of Valentinian myth that contains a very elaborate development of negative theological discourse,

---

[24] Wallis, "Spiritual Importance," 468.

and yet somewhat paradoxically stresses that the unknowable Father wants very much to be known. Immediately following the lengthy negative theological discourse on the Father (*Tri. Trac.* 51,28–55,14) that I have mentioned above, we find the comment: "Now if this (Father) who is unknowable in his nature, and who possesses all of the majestic attributes that I have mentioned, wishes to provide knowledge so that they might know him, from the abundance of his sweetness, then he is able to do this" (55,27–34). And the remainder of the myth in this text reveals that this is precisely the Father's will. But this revelation is a gradual process, since the Father is so great that a sudden revelation would have overloaded the circuits, so to speak (64,28–37). The revelation is also not direct but mediated, through the Son, who is the "trace" (ἴχνος) of the Father (66,3) and is all of the Father's names,[25]

> the form of the formless,
> the body of the incorporeal,
> the face of the invisible,
> the expression of the ineffable,
> the mind of the inconceivable.... (66,13–17)

This self-revelation, we are told, is intended to inspire a constant searching after the Father, even though the Father's primordial essence is unsearchable (71,15–20).[26] Thus, it is by the will of the Father that the Father is known, because he breathes a spirit into all things that creates in them the idea of seeking after the Unknowable, so that they are drawn to him as if by a sweet aroma (71,35–73,8).

The Wisdom figure in the *Tripartite Tractate* is the Logos, and like Wisdom in Ptolemy's myth, the Logos here attempts in vain to comprehend the incomprehensibility of the Father (75,17–19). But once again what I want to emphasize here is that the myth portrays this *quest* for knowledge as something good or well-intentioned (76,2–4), even though the futility of the Logos's attempt leads to defects and consequences that must be brought under control through the creation of the cosmos. But even all of these consequences, according to the author, happened completely in accordance with the will of the Father (76,13–77,11). The Logos's initial effort is a kind of necessary, programmed failure.

Not only is there a paradoxical relationship here between an elaborate negative theology that insists that the Father is completely beyond

---

[25] On this, see Thomassen and Painchaud, *Le Traité Tripartite,* 307–10.

[26] The passage possibly assumes a "distinction between knowledge of the Father's existence and knowledge of his essence" (Attridge, *Nag Hammadi Codex I,* 2:285).

imagining and a message of revelation that declares that the Father wants all things to seek after knowledge of him. It is also the case that this paradoxical tension appears to be quite integral to the theology here, and more specifically, it is integral to the theodicy. For the dynamics of the myth in this form of Valentinian speculation render precisely the highest values, love for and knowledge of God, as the unintentional sources of evil. The very aspiration that triggers the problem is at the same time a quest for that which is most highly valued. To appreciate the unique dynamic here, we might contrast this with a myth such as that offered by Origen of Alexandria. In Origen's theology, the source of evil is traced to the gradual turning away of rational souls from concentration on God, a version of the Platonic notion of evil-as-absence. Now the *Tripartite Tractate* (and Ptolemy, according to Irenaeus) handled the same basic Platonic notion in a different way. The Logos (or Wisdom) does not really turn *away* from God, but *toward* God—in an intense but futile reaching after God. The "absence" that becomes evil here is the failure of a well-intentioned effort, unlike Origen's "sinning" souls, who cannot be said to have been well intentioned.

Now the particular dynamic I have just mentioned, where the origins of evil are, ironically, linked as intimately as possible to laudable aspirations for divine knowledge, is certainly not present in all demiurgical myths, and in fact, it may have been limited to certain forms of Valentinian speculation.[27] A somewhat analogous motif is found in the myth that Hippolytus ascribes to Justin "the pseudo-gnostic," though this myth as narrative is entirely different from the myth in the *Tripartite Tractate* or Ptolemy. Justin's myth has evil originate when the creator, Elohim, aspires to discovery of realities more transcendent than himself and in so doing ascends to "the Good," at the same time abandoning his previously contracted marriage relationship to Eden (Hippolytus *Ref.* 5.26.21). Elohim's actions become paradigmatic for the human initiate, but his ascent is both the highest good and the cause of evil. Once again, while searching after knowledge of the highest God is the central value, it is also offered up as the solution to problems of theodicy. However, Justin's myth contains nothing like the elaborate negative theology found in the *Tripartite Tractate,* and therefore knowledge of "the Good" is not portrayed in the same way as epistemologically problematic or paradoxical.

Even though sources such as the *Apocryphon of John* or *Eugnostos* or *Allogenes* do not seem to capitalize on this theodicy-related potential in the paradoxical relationship between elaborate negative theological assertions and the search for knowledge of God, their myths do in other ways embody tensions entailed in placing a premium on seeking knowledge of

---

[27] Cf. Thomassen and Painchaud, *Le Traité Tripartite,* 329.

the Unknowable. One dimension of this involves sharply paradoxical formulations concerned with the mystical, "peak" experience. Many others
have commented on the way the author of the tractate *Allogenes,* for example, distills the ultimate experience of knowledge of the Unknowable in
the terminology of "*not*-knowing knowledge" or an "ignorance that sees"
(e.g., *Allogenes* 59,28–32; 60,8–12; 61,1–2; 64,10–14), and the author may
have been among the earliest experimenters with this kind of formulation
in the history of Western mysticism.[28]

However, there is another type of tension that I am more interested in
exploring here, and that is the larger and somewhat more implicit one
between, on the one hand, the assertion of divine unknowability and, on
the other, the assumption that knowledge about the divine can be gained
from the visible cosmos.

5. Negative Theologies and Sensibility about the Cosmos

The classic study by A.-J. Festugière, *La révélation d'Hermès Trismégiste,* distinguished two broad currents among religious and philosophical traditions in late antiquity, according to how the supreme Being was
imagined: a type in which God's nature could be known in some measure
through observation and contemplation of the visible cosmos, and a type
in which God was understood to be hyper-cosmic, beyond any analogy in
the visible world—i.e., the sort of God described in the more enthusiasti-
cally negative theologies. As Festugière put it, in the latter case knowledge
of God is not aided by the visible world, "because it is a matter of reaching a Principle of which nothing here below offers an image, since It is, in
essence, different from everything else."[29] Thus, the only way for such a
God to be known is by means of revelation.

Now it has become commonplace that one of the ways in which "gnostic" negative theology is distinguished from "nongnostic" Jewish, Christian,
or Platonist negative theologies in antiquity is by asserting that for "gnostics" the description-by-negation somehow went hand in hand with a complete absence of any faith in rational paths to knowledge or any sensibility
for the material cosmic realm as revelatory of divine truth. As van den Broek
has put it recently, in an introductory chapter to a collection of his essays:

> At first sight, the gnostic and hermetic doctrines of God have much in
> common, since both start from a theological concept which was wide-

---

[28] See Turner, "Gnosticism and Platonism," 448; King, *Revelation,* 19, 148–52,
169; Wallis, "Spiritual Importance," 470.

[29] Festugière, *La révélation d'Hermès Trismégiste* (4 vols.; Paris: Librairie Lecoffre, 1949–1954), 4:59.

spread in the classical world. It is the idea that God is so transcendent that he can only be described in the terms of what we call "negative theology:" he is ineffable, invisible, incomprehensible, unbegotten, without beginning and without end, incorruptible, immeasurable, invariable, unnamable, etc. This view is found among pagan philosophers, Christian theologians, gnostics and hermetists. There is a difference, however, for the philosophers, and some early Christian theologians as well, said that, though it may be true that God is unknowable in his essence, he can nevertheless be comprehended by the human mind (*nous*), through philosophical reasoning and through contemplation of the cosmic order. This emphasis on the human *nous* as a useful, though imperfect, instrument for the knowledge of God is also found in the hermetic texts, but never in those of the gnostics: in their view, the supreme God was inaccessible to the human mind. However, like the platonic philosophers of their time, the gnostics felt no difficulty in combining this negative theology with positive qualifications of the ineffable God.[30]

Werner Foerster's introductory comments in his anthology of "gnostic" texts contain another good illustration of this common perception of the implications of negative theology in these myths. He notes that God in these traditions is "the unknown Father" and that frequently there is the attempt "to describe this unknown God with an array of negative expressions," or with the prefix "fore-" (Fore-Father, etc.), so that "all that can be said is simply this, that it lies before all that is visible and conceivable." "So," continues Foester, "God and the world stand apart and in opposition."[31] Similarly, in his general treatment of *Gnosis: The Nature and History of Gnosticism*, Kurt Rudolph includes a section on "the unknown God," in which he covers, among others, the negative theologies of Basilides, the *Apocryphon of John, Eugnostos,* and the *Tripartite Tractate.* Rudolph then concludes:

> These examples, which could be extended without difficulty ... show that the gnostic conception of God is dictated by a contrast to all previously existing conceptions and so has a thoroughly revolutionary character. Certainly the terminology is indebted to contemporary philosophy; also it is possible to note certain agreements in cosmology (Plotinus knew that very well), but the underlying world-denying tone cannot be mistaken.[32]

---

[30] Van den Broek, *Studies,* 10.

[31] W. Foerster, ed., *Gnosis: A Selection of Gnostic Texts* (trans. R. McL. Wilson; 2 vols. Oxford: Clarendon Press, 1972–1974), 1:4–5.

[32] K. Rudolph, *Gnosis: The Nature and History of Gnosticism* (trans. R. McL. Wilson; San Francisco: Harper & Row, 1983), 64–65.

What I would like to argue here is that this widespread tendency to single out negative theology in "gnostic" texts as symptomatic of things like a peculiarly virulent anticosmism, or a rejection of any usefulness in human intellection or contemplation of cosmic order, runs up against the following embarrassments: (1) As we have seen, developed negative theological discourse is *not* ubiquitous among these demiurgical myths and is in fact limited to a handful of them. (2) On the other hand, we have also observed that in most of the sources that do contain extensive negative theological discourse such language is not being employed haphazardly, but in patterns that may be understood as forms of rational argumentation. In other words, even though the invocation of *via negationis* or *via eminentiae* arguments in these demiurgical myths comes in the medium of a revelation, it seems fair to ask why the possibility of an openness to a role also for human intellection should be dismissed in *these* cases, any more than when such arguments are invoked in authors like, say, Gregory of Nazianzus.[33] (3) And finally, it is noteworthy that just those "gnostic" sources that contain the most remarkable instances of extended negative theological discourse happen also to be among the very sources where arguably the most positive— *not* most negative—relationship is depicted between true divinity and the material cosmos. This is exactly opposite from the general impression sometimes conveyed by treatments of "Gnosticism," to the effect that "gnostic" negative theology is simply the ultimate expression of "gnostic" world-denial. I need to elaborate on this latter point.

For example, it has long been recognized that the *Tripartite Tractate* is among the examples of Christian demiurgical myth with the least evidence for animosity toward the demiurge or the material cosmos. The archon who is assigned the role of "beautifying"[34] and "working on" the things below is used "as a hand" by the Logos, to effect the divine purposes (*Tri. Trac.* 100,30–36). Because the creative activity of this lower demiurge is being guided, without his awareness, by inspiration from the divine spirit, the things that come into being from this agent are in the

---

[33] Gregory can speak at great length of the deep mystery of God's essence that is impossible for human reason to comprehend and within the same oration also discourse on theological implications humans should see in the marvels of the visible cosmos (*Theological Oration* 2 [*Orat.* 28]).

[34] I follow Attridge (*Nag Hammadi Codex I,* 1:275) in using this translation of the Coptic ⲦⲤⲀⲈⲒⲰ, which could be a translation of some form of the Greek κοσμεῖν, which of course has connotations both of ordering and adornment, with order being a form of beauty. Thomassen and Painchaud (*Le Traité Tripartite,* 171) render ⲦⲤⲀⲈⲒⲰ with "façonner." The English translation "beautify" provides an explicit and legitimate reminder that producers and readers of writings such as the *Tripartite Tractate* did indeed see beauty in the cosmos.

image of the spiritual realities (100,36–101,9). This notion that the lower demiurge is unwittingly operating under divine guidance from above is not unique to this tractate but is found elsewhere in Valentinian myth.[35] I wish to underscore its presence because the obvious implication is that the physical creation is understood in such traditions as containing images and signs of divine realities.

Indeed, Irenaeus does apparently indicate that in support of their views his Valentinian Christian opponents would often appeal to this correspondence between patterns in the pleromatic realm and patterns in the visible cosmos. He says at one point (*Haer.* 2.15.3) that when he engaged them in conversation they would question him as though he knew nothing about the creation. But when he, in turn, pressed them about details concerning *their* notions about the transcendent realm, or Pleroma, they would rely either on metaphors involving human emotions or on language pertaining only to "that harmony that can be observed in creation." Irenaeus thinks he has them cornered here, since they must resort to discussions of patterns in secondary realities in order to explain their theories about the Pleroma. But for our purposes, the passage is enormously revealing, for what it tells us is that Valentinian Christians appealed to cosmological arguments in support of their transcendental theology.

The writing *Eugnostos* is another familiar example of a myth in which any anticosmism is less obvious.[36] I have mentioned earlier some of Roelof van den Broek's insightful analyses of patterns in the negative theology in *Eugnostos*. However, the way in which he frames those insights with respect to the "gnostic" character of *Eugnostos* illustrates how that category has become encumbered with presuppositions that may often obscure what is actually in the text. In the opening section of *Eugnostos* the author states that:

> Everyone born since the foundation of the world turns to dust. Though they seek after God—who he is and what he is like—they have not found him. Many of the wise among them have made likenesses of the truth

---

[35] E.g., Irenaeus *Haer.* 1.5.1; and see the numerous parallels cited in the commentary sections in Attridge, *Nag Hammadi Codex I,* and Thomassen and Painchaud, *Le Traité Tripartite.*

[36] So much so that there has been debate as to whether the work should be classified as "gnostic." See, e.g., D. M. Parrott, "Eugnostos and 'All the Philosophers,'" in *Religion im Erbe Ägyptens: Beiträge zur spätantiken Religionsgeschichte zur Ehren von Alexander Böhlig* (ed. M. Görg; Ägypten und Altes Testament 14; Wiesbaden: Otto Haarassowitz, 1988), 153–67, and the summary of views in J. L. Sumney, "The Letter of Eugnostos and the Origins of Gnosticism," *NovT* 31 (1989): 172–81.

based on the management [διοίκησις] of the cosmos, but the likeness has
not attained to the truth. For the management is described in three ways
by all the philosophers, so that the three accounts are in conflict.... (III
70,3–16)

The author then summarizes and rejects the three different theories: that
the cosmos simply operates under its own direction, that it is guided by
providence, or that it is ruled by fate (III 70,16–71,5). In the remainder of
the work the author claims to be presenting the reader with the truth about
God. Now based on the parallels in their negative theological discourse
that I mentioned earlier, van den Broek suggests that both *Eugnostos* and
the Christian apologist Aristides

> made use of a source which, in the traditional way, inferred from the
> orderly government of the universe that its Maker and Mover must be
> God, but at the same time asserted that, though we can see God's works
> it is impossible to know his nature, and then went on to develop an
> explicitly negative theology based on the opposition between the unbe-
> gotten and the begotten. Their dependence on a common source explains
> the correspondences between Eugnostos and Aristides. The differences
> between them can be explained by Eugnostos' gnostic world-view, which
> forced him to reject the cosmological proof of God's existence with argu-
> ments developed in the Sceptical tradition.[37]

Commenting specifically on the reference to argument from διοίκησις that
I quoted above, van den Broek asserts that

> Eugnostos starts his argument by referring to and then firmly rejecting the
> idea that God's existence and nature can be known from the *dioikēsis* of
> the cosmos. Though he does not explicitly say so, we may assume that
> he had to reject this view because, as a gnostic, he ascribed the origin of
> the world to a lower, most probably evil demiurge.[38]

Now the problem here is twofold: First, we really do *not* know precisely
the shape of *Eugnostos*'s teaching about the demiurge. I would agree with
van den Broek that the overall nature of the myth in this writing does make
it probable that the author "ascribed the origin of the world to a lower ...
demiurge" and that therefore we likely have a demiurgical myth. But there
is no justification for assuming that this demiurge is "most probably evil."
Secondly, it is not in fact clear that the author of *Eugnostos* is rejecting the
proposition that the διοίκησις of the cosmos has relevance for discerning

---

[37] Van den Broek, "Eugnostos and Aristides," 211.

[38] Ibid., 209.

the nature of God. What are rejected are three conflicting philosophical positions *derived* from such analogical argumentation. And in fact, later in the work the author seems to appeal precisely to cosmological argument in support of the truth of the assertions in the myth. After the negative theology in III 71,13–73,3 that I have discussed earlier, the author emphasizes the importance of understanding the distinction between the invisible and the visible, the imperishable and the perishable (III 73,3–74,7). Then the author says that if anyone wishes to trust the information set forth in the myth, that person should "search from what is hidden to the completion of what is visible, and this thought [ἔννοια] will teach him how belief in invisible things has been discovered from what is visible. It [= the belief] is a source of knowledge" (III 74,14–20). The remainder of *Eugnostos* does just this. Beginning with the highest God who had been described in the negative theological discourse, the author traces the various levels of emanation down just to the point of the appearance of the visible cosmos. Thus this author, like the Valentinian traditions discussed above, assumes a congruence between the ordering of the visible cosmos and the supernal, invisible realities.[39] The author probably does reject the sufficiency of human reasoning alone in attaining the truth, and the author certainly asserts that the true nature of the highest divine source is beyond the grasp of human intellect. However, that does not rule out any role at all for intellection, as is indicated by the author's appeal to ἔννοια, "thought."[40] Nor in particular does revelation exclude a place for cosmological argument in gaining assurance concerning the truth about the

---

[39] See also J. Dillon, "*Pleroma* and Noetic Cosmos: A Comparative Study," in *Neoplatonism and Gnosticism* (ed. R. T. Wallis and J. Bregman; Studies in Neoplatonism: Ancient and Modern 6; Albany: SUNY Press, 1992), 107, who notes that *Eugnostos* "envisages quite an extensive parallelism between the noetic and physical worlds," although Dillon wonders "how coherent a theory of archetypes the Gnostic writers had." But, just as with any other writers from antiquity, that question should be considered on a case-by-case basis. P. Perkins, "Beauty, Number, and Loss of Order in the Gnostic Cosmos," in ibid., 285, rightly notes that *Eugnostos* "apparently proposes some form of contemplation of heavenly order as a key to the knowledge of the divine received by the Gnostics."

[40] Parrott, "Eugnostos," 161–62, feels compelled to take this "thought" as a reference to an aspect of the highest God who functions essentially as a revelatory being, "communicating with those who are open to it," rather than as a contemplative exercise in thought invited by the author. But I see nothing that requires such a reading of *ennoia* as a hypostasized being here. Trakatellis, *The Transcendent God,* 37, makes a similar mistake, in my view, in emphasizing that the prologue to *Eugnostos* "constitutes a radical rejection of the possibility to gain even a partial knowledge of God, either through the thinking processes or through research."

divine realm. In fact, the author seems to view as fundamentally important that the reader think through the implications of correspondences
between visible and invisible realms.

Now the *Apocryphon of John* unquestionably presents a much more
negative portrait of the creator, Ialdabaoth. However, even in this work we
find evidence that the material cosmos itself is not understood to be a
repulsively grotesque and chaotic environment completely alien to, and
unrevealing of, the nature of true divinity. For with respect to the creation
of the earth and all the various heavens, the author says that Ialdabaoth

> put everything in order, in the likeness of the first aeons that had come
> into being, so as to create them in an incorruptible pattern—not that he
> himself had actually seen the incorruptible things; rather, it was the power
> within him (that did so), which he had received from his Mother, since
> she had begotten within him the likeness of the cosmos. (II 12,34–13,5)

The short recension does not mention the role of the Mother here, but
it does state that the arrangement of the various firmaments, heavens,
and aeons in the created realm corresponds to the image and pattern
(τύπος) of the transcendent, incorruptible aeons (BG 44,5–9).[41] There
must be a sensibility here to a level of order in the visible world that
results from a corresponding beauty and order in the transcendent
divine realm. Something about the structure of divinity can be observed
in the visible cosmos, though a full understanding of the nature of the
relationship depends on further revelation—as it did for many Jewish
and Christian authors.[42]

---

[41] Waldstein has noted this passage (*Apocryphon of John,* 169) and rightly
stresses the presence in *Apocryphon of John* of what can be called a form of "cosmic piety" (165–68).

[42] In comparing Platonic notions of an intelligible, paradigmatic realm with
"gnostic" notions of the Pleroma, Dillon has commented that "there are elements
in the Pleroma, in both Valentinian and Sethian systems ... which do seem to serve
as paradigms" ("*Pleroma* and Noetic Cosmos," 106). However, the similarities
should probably be pushed even further than Dillon mentions. For he suggests that
one might object that: "the Pleroma is not really a model on which the physical
world is based. The physical world is an error and an abortion for the Gnostics,
and the Demiurge receives little or no guidance from above in creating it, nor has
he access to the Pleroma as a model to work with" (106). Dillon cites the teachings of Marcus (Irenaeus *Haer.* 1.17.2) as an exception to this general rule (109 n.
15). Yet certainly the *Apocryphon of John,* the *Tripartite Tractate,* and Ptolemy are
other examples, and it may well be that this sense of a correspondence between
order and beauty in the material cosmos and order and beauty in the aeonic realm
was not uncommon among other demiurgical traditions.

Finally, we may comment about this matter with respect to texts such as *Allogenes* and *Zostrianos* and the opponents of Plotinus whom the latter criticizes in *Enn.* 2.9. As I have mentioned, *Allogenes* contains some very striking negative theology, culminating in the affirmation that the Unknowable is so transcendent that it can actually only be "known" through a form of "unknowing." On the other hand, it is harder to say much about the nature of the relation between negative theology and cosmology in this case, since the writing (at least what survives of it) contains so little direct mention of the material realm. But the few passages that do seem to be pertinent indicate a less dualistic worldview than is often assumed for "Gnosticism."[43] The Unknowable is the "source" (πηγή) for everything else, being related to things like matter, number, form, and shape only as immaterial matter, numberless number, shapeless shape, etc. (*Allogenes* 48,21–32).[44] The related tractate *Zostrianos,* though also frustratingly fragmentary, contains more direct allusions to the relation between the transcendent realms and the material cosmos. Several passages seem to refer to the presence in certain levels of the transcendent realm of archetypal patterns for realities in the visible world—not only of people, but of the elements earth, water, air, and fire, and also of animals, trees, fruit, even weeds![45] As John Dillon has commented, "What we seem to have portrayed here is a comprehensive archetype of the physical world, right down to the tares among the wheat."[46]

The acquaintances whom Plotinus criticizes in *Enn.* 2.9 seem to have used writings such as *Allogenes* and *Zostrianos,* and we may thus assume that they had some fondness for the negative theological discourse in such texts. The controversy between Plotinus and these opponents is often imagined to have involved sharply different positions about the role of cosmic piety in contemplation of the intelligible and supraintelligible, and certainly it is true that Plotinus himself understood the difference partly in these terms.

---

[43] See Schoedel, "'Topological' Theology," 108; King, *Revelation,* 11, 105; B. Pearson, *Gnosticism, Judaism, and Egyptian Christianity* (SAC 5; Minneapolis: Fortress, 1990), 163.

[44] See King, *Revelation,* 97. K. Corrigan, "The Anonymous Turin Commentary on the *Parmenides,*" 57 (seminar paper that appears in this volume in revised form as: "Platonism and Gnosticism. The Anonymous *Commentary* on the *Parmenides:* Middle or Neoplatonic?") has suggested that both *Allogenes* and the *Tripartite Tractate* represent a "Speusippan-Stoic view of the origin of life (although in an ambiguous and probably much mitigated form)," so that the "embryonic *dynamis* of all future creation indwells primordially in the depth" of the first principle.

[45] *Zost.* 48,2–29; 55,15–25; 113,1–117,15.

[46] Dillon, "*Pleroma* and Noetic Cosmos," 104; cf. Corrigan, "Anonymous," 72–73 (see n. 44).

In *Enn.* 2.9.17.28 Plotinus says that these people "despise the beauty that is here." He implies that they speak of "another cosmos better than this one" (2.9.8.26–28; cf. 2.9.5.25), and we have seen evidence from texts such as *Zostrianos* for notions of a transcendent intelligible cosmos. But though there clearly were differences between Plotinus and his opponents about the relation between the material cosmic order and supramaterial reality, we should be careful not to conclude too quickly that it was merely a matter of some blunt "gnostic" hatred of all matter and a lack of interest in, and even an inability to see any beauty in, the material realm. In fact, Plotinus himself seems to admit that his opponents do not deny the beauty in the cosmos; they just refuse to grant it the kind of interpretation and importance that he deems appropriate. He says that their arrogant sense of superiority is based precisely on their claim to have disdain for something they call "beautiful"— i.e., it would not have been so special to claim to despise something "ugly" (2.9.17.30–33). Thus it was not really an argument over whether there was visible beauty and order in the cosmos, but rather over the question of divinity in that beauty and order of the heavens and stars. Plotinus says that these people assert their own souls to be immortal and divine but reject the notion that the heavens and stars share that divinity, and they do so even though on the one hand they see the order and beautiful form and arrangement in the heavens, while on the other they especially complain about the disorder here on earth (2.9.5.8–14). Such an argument would not be so effective if it were the case that these acquaintances of Plotinus somehow were denying any beauty or order in the heavens.

As a matter of fact, we do find what appears to be a positive exhortation to the contemplation of cosmic order in at least one tractate from Nag Hammadi, *Marsanes,* which also happens to be closely related to works such as *Allogenes* and *Zostrianos.* Birger Pearson has pointed out how *Marsanes* speaks of the salvation of the sense-perceptible world (*Marsanes* 5,17–26), and Pearson notes that a positive evaluation is given to cosmic contemplation on the fragmentary pages 41–42 of *Marsanes:* "Blessed is ... whether he is gazing at the two (sun and moon) or is gazing at the seven planets or at the twelve signs of the Zodiac or the thirty-six Decans...."[47] Now Pearson is inclined to view such a passage as a deviation from "the usual gnostic attitude toward the heavenly bodies," and he explains this as the result of influence on *Marsanes* from Platonism. The presence of Platonic influence is clear, though that is the case, at some level, with a great many "gnostic" sources. I would simply suggest that there may be no need to be labeling instances of openness to contemplation of the implications of cosmic order as exceptions or deviations from the "usual attitude" in these demiurgical myths.

---

[47] See Pearson, *Gnosticism,* 163.

The remark by Plotinus (*Enn.* 2.9.5.8–14) that I mentioned above, about his opponents complaining about disorder here on earth, is actually a clue to the real issue regarding disorder here. The focus of his opponents' criticism was not on ugliness in the structure of the heavens or what we would call the natural world, but rather on ugliness in the moral and social realm, the realm of motivations, attitudes, and relationships, and the field of human fortunes. When Plotinus is most explicit about the complaints that these opponents have about the world, it is not about the ugliness of the heavens, but rather about social inequities such as wealth and poverty, the injustices that befall individuals in the great sports arena of life where there are winners and losers (2.9.9.1–28). Why is everyone not good and perfect; why is there evil (2.9.13.22–33)? They were concerned about disease, but in this area they evidently did not merely complain about human misfortune. They actually cured diseases through exorcisms—experiencing them not merely as "natural" calamities but as the work of demons with intentions (2.9.14.14–18). We can also see this concern with the issue of motivations in the fact that, according to Plotinus, they said that the demiurge created the cosmos out of a desire to be honored (2.9.4.14; 2.9.11.22).

In *Enn.* 2.9.6.30–33, Plotinus remarks that by their introduction of plurality (multitude of names, etc.) into the intelligible order, his opponents bring the intelligible nature into likeness with the perceptible and inferior realm. He naturally sees this as a flaw in their argument, since in his view this amounts to dragging supernal realities down to the level of inferior models. However, what for him is a flawed approach may be read by us as another confirmation that these opponents were using a form of cosmological argument, extrapolating the nature of the wonderful levels of the transcendent realm partly from features in the visible cosmos. Of course, if we take texts such as *Allogenes* or *Zostrianos* as windows on some of their views, their negative theology exalted the ultimate Source of all things beyond the reach of such analogy. But the very nature of ascent visions such as those in *Allogenes* or *Zostrianos* seems to be that the "peak" experience of proximity to the Unknowable is only a fragile moment in the larger blissful experience of knowing divinity.

6. Summary and Conclusions

I have argued here that much of the attention that has been given to the presence of negative theology in demiurgical myths such as those found among Nag Hammadi and related sources has frequently misread the timbres, implications, and functions of such language. Most often this misreading has been a function of larger assumptions about the values and worldviews expressed in such traditions—assumptions that, it seems to me, are becoming ever more difficult for us to entertain in light of the last few decades of scholarship on such materials. While relationships have long been recognized between negative theology encountered in such demiurgical myths and forms of negative theological discourse in other ancient sources such as Platonic philosophical literature or Christian theologians, these parallels tend to be routinely qualified in such a way that a peculiarly "gnostic" strain of negative theology is successfully isolated. "Gnosticism" has often been imagined as a form of piety that entails radical negative theology virtually by definition. Moreover, "gnostic" negative theology has been regarded as a key symptom of a general abandonment of any confidence in rationality, as the unsystematic heaping up of numinous attributes. The rather steep elevation in negative theological discourse in some of these sources has typically been understood as an expression of a singularly fierce sense of opposition between God and the cosmos, alleged to have been a defining characteristic of "Gnosticism." There has often been the assumption that in "gnostic" sources negative theology and cosmological argument must stand in inverse proportion, so that there can hardly have been room left here for any positive sensibility about seeing images of the divine in the beauty and order of the cosmos.

I have argued that an analysis of negative theological discourse among the demiurgical myths conventionally classified as "gnostic" suggests that most all of the above assumptions are false. Significant use of negative theological discourse is limited to a certain selection of these sources. Where it is found, in writings such as the *Apocryphon of John, Eugnostos,* the *Tripartite Tractate,* or *Allogenes,* its employment is far from being completely unsystematic, and in fact we find patterns and structures that reflect attempts to develop organized argument and presentation of theological position. And, ironically, contrary to the notion that negative theology is the quintessential expression of anticosmism, it would seem that the sources in which are found the most significant instances of negative theology are also among those where it is easiest to demonstrate more positive sensibilities with respect to the material cosmos, and even the employment of forms of cosmological argument.

In a paper on "Negative Theology in Gnosticism and Neoplatonism," Curtis Hancock primarily underscored the similarities between Plotinus and "gnostics" in the deployment of negative theological discourse. But he suggested that a notable difference was that "gnostics" often applied negation somewhat "farther down the hierarchy of realities," whereas Plotinus limited it to the One.[48] There may be some validity in this contrast,[49] but in

---

[48] C. Hancock, "Negative Theology in Gnosticism and Neoplatonism," in *Neoplatonism and Gnosticism* (ed. R. T. Wallis and J. Bregman; Studies in Neoplatonism: Ancient and Modern 6; Albany: SUNY Press, 1992), 176, 180.

[49] Though this contrast would not work if we move beyond Plotinus to other Neoplatonists. Wallis notes, for example, that also in Iamblichus's view, ineffability

my view much more interesting than locating some precise "cut off" mark in the application of negation is the recognition that in these demiurgical myths, as in most other instances of negative theology, a radical emphasis on the ultimate unknowability of God is paradoxically only one dimension of the larger experience of knowing God.

In his brilliant study of vision and imagination in medieval Jewish mysticism, Elliot Wolfson[50] has distinguished between two types of contemplative vision in the Western mysticism: (a) the "introvertive" type, influenced primarily by Neoplatonic notions of the transcendent One, where the goal is to strip away image and form through a *via negativa* and achieve an "imageless" vision "beyond differentiation and distinction" and where logically the approach "should culminate in an apophatic theology that assumes that statements about what God is not have more truth value than statements about what God is"; and (b) the "cognitive" type that "affirms that supernatural or spiritual knowledge comes by way of revelation, intuition or illumination."[51]

Wolfson notes that proponents of the first type often "will, in the end, insist that things invisible must be pursued through visible reality, through the agency of imagination." However, there is still the claim in this type that seeing God is something beyond image. "Imagelessness thus overcomes image in the *visio mystica,* yielding the paradoxical situation that sensible or imaginative seeing is spiritual blindness."[52] But Wolfson's central concern is to argue that the second, cognitive type has been misunderstood in previous study, since scholars have traditionally explained the use of images in this second kind of mystical literature as "the translation of ineffable experience into communicable form" and have not always realized that "recourse to sensible images and symbols is part of the mystical experience itself."[53] In general contrast with the more "purely Neoplatonic vision," contemplative vision in Jewish, Christian, and Islamic traditions is "not entirely free of concrete and sensible images":

> Seeing God—like seeing anything—is seeing God as something, that is, under certain aspects that are informed by some prior interpretative framework. The imaging of the divine, therefore, does not simply result

---

"extended much further down the metaphysical scale," and Proclus imagines degrees of unknowability in the hierarchy of the transcendent (Wallis, "Spiritual Importance," 475–76).

[50] E. R. Wolfson, *Through a Speculum That Shines: Vision and Imagination in Medieval Jewish Mysticism* (Princeton, N.J.: Princeton University Press, 1994), 58–67.

[51] Ibid., 58–60.

[52] Ibid., 58, 59.

[53] Ibid., 60.

from the mystic's desire to translate the ineffable experience into a communicable form, but is an intrinsic part of the experience itself.[54]

With some adaptation of these important insights, I would like to make a similar point about material I have discussed in this study. But rather than focusing on the twofold typology that Wolfson has sketched out, I am more interested in how elements of his discussion may help bring into relief the relation in some of these demiurgical traditions between negative theology and knowing God. It is a fundamental mistake, in Wolfson's view, to think of the "real" mystical visionary experience as being some ineffable moment, with all the imagery encountered in descriptions of it being relegated to the status of nonessential and replaceable commentary. He insists that we pay more attention to how integral the agency of imagination can be even in the experience of what is often claimed by mystics to be unimaginable.

In a similar vein, I would argue that it is a mistake in the case of the sources I have discussed here to place narrow emphasis on negations stressing the ultimate unknowability of God or to focus only on a sharp polar tension between the abstract affirmation of the true God's absolute incomprehensibility and a consequent total dependence on some critical moment of divine revelation. It seems to me that an inclination toward this kind of reading of the significance of negative theology has been especially characteristic when it comes to negative theology in demiurgical myths such as those in the examples from Nag Hammadi. What needs to be seen is the far more protracted, more complex experience of knowing God that seems often implied in these myths—an experience stretched out over important and informative stages, levels, and media (e.g., the structure of the material cosmos) that are as integral to the total experience of knowing as is the realization of God's unknowability.

---

[54] Ibid., 66.

Aseity and Connectedness in the Plotinian Philosophy of Providence

Frederic M. Schroeder
Queen's University, Kingston

1. Introduction

We may imagine, proceeding from some texts in Plotinus *Enn.* 6.7 and Plato's *Timaeus,* the following anachronistic dialogue between Plato and Plotinus:

> PLATO: The Demiurge and his children ordered all things in the cosmos according to a rational plan. Thus you can see that the ox has horns in order to defend itself.
>
> PLOTINUS: Now, my revered Plato, in addition to particular things that we behold with our senses, do you not also claim that there are Forms or Ideas, known alone to the eye of intellect? And such Forms ground the characters of things that we perceive with our senses?
>
> PLATO: Indeed I do, Plotinus, as I have said on many occasions.
>
> PLOTINUS: Just now, my dear Plato, you were speaking of oxen, were you not?
>
> PLATO: Indeed I was, Plotinus.
>
> PLOTINUS: Now you were saying that the ox has horns in order to defend itself. Yet you would have another reason for its possession of horns. Would you not then say, Plato, that in addition to the sensible ox there is also an intelligible Ox, a Form of Ox? And would you not say that the sensible ox has horns through participation in or imitation of the Form of Ox?
>
> PLATO: Indeed I would, Plotinus.
>
> PLOTINUS: Now the sensible ox has horns in order to defend itself against other oxen, or other animals. Is this correct?
>
> PLATO: To be sure, Plotinus. But it also has horns by participation in or imitation of the Form of Ox.
>
> PLOTINUS: But this Form of Ox, oh divine one, does it have horns in order to defend itself against other Forms, e.g., the Form of Wolf, or the Form of Man?
>
> PLATO: Such a result would be absurd, oh creature of a day!
>
> PLOTINUS: Then the Form of Ox, apart from the particular ox, why does it have horns?
>
> PLATO: Why, to be an ox, of course.

Our imagined dialogue establishes that the sensible ox has two dimensions, one horizontal (it has horns in order to defend itself against other creatures on the same plane of existence) and another vertical (it has horns by participation in or imitation of the Form of Ox). The Form of Ox, however, seems not to have the horizontal relationship yielded by the theme of self-defense. In the universe of discourse that surrounds the ox *qua* ox, the ox has horns in order to be an ox. The Form of Ox is an expression of aseity.

By "aseity" I mean the state or condition of ontological independence. "Aseity" means *a se*. As such, it could be taken to mean "dependent upon itself," a phrase that might introduce an unwanted duality. I take it rather as *a se explicandum,* i.e., to be understood from within a universe of discourse belonging to itself. I do not mean "self-dependent," but "independent," i.e., not depending for its existence on other entities. An objection that may properly be made to my use of the term "aseity" is that the sensible world is dependent upon and explained with reference to the Soul, the Soul bears this relationship to Intellect, and Intellect to the One for its being. Thus Soul and Intellect, as dependent, could not have aseity. For the purposes of my discussion, however, I bracket the question of Intellect's dependence upon the One when I discuss the relationship, for example, between the sensible world and the intelligible world. From the horizon of the relationship between the intelligible and sensible worlds, the intelligible world possesses aseity in contrast to the sensible world. Now, further enquiry will reveal that the intelligible world is dependent upon the One for its existence, but that is another question.

To return to our example, in the particular ox, the quality of having horns may share in that aseity through participation. Yet the attribute "having horns" belongs to its connectedness with other particulars. We may say the same of "having eyes." The ox has eyes in order not to bump into things or to find food. On another plane of discourse, the ox has eyes in order to be itself.

Plotinus teaches that there is also connectedness in the World of Forms. In Intellect, each Form contains all of the others in an internal relationship. To think one is to think all the others at once. Thus to noetic intuition, the Form of Ox is in some way all the other Forms as well. In Intellect, there is no contradiction between aseity and connectedness, and Intellect is the perfect realization of providence and its eternal model. In the sensible world, however, the principles of aseity and connectedness come apart. Thus the sensible ox will be viewed as having horns only from the horizon of its connectedness with other things, i.e., its need to defend itself. Yet this connectedness is a vulgar connectedness. As the sensible world, not particular by particular, but as a whole approaches the unity of Intellect, a deeper connectedness is revealed that preserves the aseity of each thing.

We may examine some texts that will support the Platonic-Plotinian dialogue we have constructed. In the *Tim.* 45de Plato describes how the mortal body is equipped with vision for the sake of preservation (σωτηρία, d7). Following this text, Plotinus says that humans and other animals are equipped with sense for preservation (ὡς οὕτως ἂν σῴζοιτο, 6.7.1.1–5).

Aristotle, in the *An. post.* 2.8.93a17–21 argues that we must know the "that" or existence of a thing (τὸ ὅτι) before we know its reason for existence (τὸ διότι). However, he argues further (*An post.* 2.8.93a39–b8) that it is possible to know a thing's existence and its reason for existence by the same act: thus the definition of and the reason for an eclipse admit of the same account: the occultation of the sun by the moon. Plotinus asks, concerning the intelligible world, "How then can the alone and the one and the simple contain explicitly the 'this that there should not be that,' and 'there had to be this if not that' and 'this appeared useful and this preservative [σωτήριον] when it came to be'?" (6.7.1.39–42).[1] Plotinus argues further that both the human being and human sight exist in the intelligible world in such a way that "that" (τὸ ὅτι) and "why" (τὸ διότι) coalesce. He offers as an illustration of that coalescence Aristotle's example of the eclipse (6.7.2.1–12). Intellect is everything that it contains so that "that" and "why" are embraced by that unity (6.7.2.10–11). He asks further how horns in the intelligible world could exist for the sake of defense? Surely it is only for completeness (πρὸς τὸ αὐταρκές τοῦ ζῴου καὶ τὸ τέλεον, 6.7.10.1–2).[2]

From the above discussion, we may see that there are two different kinds of salvation or preservation (σωτηρία). In the first, shared by both Plato and Plotinus, something has a characteristic in order to preserve itself against perils in the sensible world. In the second, in which Plotinus covertly disagrees with a Platonic statement, while undertaking a legitimate extension of Plato's views of Form, it has that characteristic, not because

---

[1] The translations shall be taken from A. H. Armstrong, ed. and trans., *Plotinus: Enneads. English and Greek* (7 vols.; LCL; Cambridge: Harvard University Press; London: W. Heinemann, 1966–1988); the line numbering follows the *editio minor* of P. Henry and H.-R. Schwyzer, *Plotini Opera* (3 vols.; Scriptorum classicorum bibliotheca Oxoniensis; Oxford: Oxford University Press, 1964–1982).

[2] Cf. F. M. Schroeder, *Form and Transformation: A Study in the Philosophy of Plotinus* (Montreal: McGill-Queen's, 1992), 17–19; P. P. Matter, *Zum Einfluss des Platonischen "Timaeus" auf das Denken Plotins* (Winterthur: Keller, 1964), 115–16. In 2.9.8.1, Plotinus blames the gnostics for asking why (διὰ τί) Soul made the universe: the question arises on the part of those who think the universe had a beginning in time and was made by a being who turned from one thing to another; cf. C. Parma, *Pronoia und Providentia: Der Vorsehungsbegriff Plotins und Augustins* (Leiden: Brill, 1971), 31. The absorption of "why" into "that" in Plotinus may belong to the ambit of his antignostic polemic.

of its connectedness to other things, but in order to be itself: the characteristic belongs to its aseity and completeness. We shall see from our ensu-
ing discussion that it has that characteristic, not only to be complete in
itself, but also because its possession of that characteristic, observing the
creature's own aseity, contributes to the perfection of the cosmos as an
organic whole.

2. Hierarchy and Connectedness

The Greek word that we translate as "providence," πρόνοια, is derived
from προ-, "before," and νοεῖν, "to think." From this etymology we are
tempted to see providence as a taking thought beforehand, so that God
deliberates like a craftsman when designing the creation. Plotinus warns
against this interpretation:

> And further, [consider it] also like this: we affirm that each and every thing
> in the All, and this All here itself, is as it would have been if the free
> choice [προαίρεσις] of its maker had willed it, and its state is as if this
> maker proceeding regularly in his calculations [προϊέμενος] with foresight
> [προϊδῶν] had made it according to his providence [πρόνοιαν]. But since
> things here are always like this and always come to be like this, so their
> rational principles also always rest among the things which exist all
> together, standing still in a better order; so that the things here transcend
> providence and transcend free choice, and all the things which are in real
> being stand in intellectual stillness. So that if someone calls this disposi-
> tion of things providence, he must understand it in this way, that Intellect
> is there standing still before this All [πρὸ τοῦδε νοῦς τοῦ παντὸς ἑστώς],
> and this All here is from and according to Intellect. (6.8.17.1–12)

Plotinus loves to play with language: we may notice the semantic field of
words or phrases beginning with the prefix προ- ("before"): προαίρεσις,
προϊέμενος, προϊδῶν, πρόνοια, πρὸ τοῦδε. The beforeness or priority of
providence then does not belong to foresight as we would understand it,
but to the beforeness, firstness, or priority of Intellect.[3] Now the priority of

---

[3] On the etymology of πρόνοια in this passage see Parma, *Pronoia und Providentia,* 23 who compares 3.2.1.21–23: τὴν πρόνοιαν ὀρθῶς ἄν καὶ ἀκολούθως λέ-
γοιμεν τῷ παντὶ εἶναι τὸ κατὰ τὸν νοῦν εἶναι καὶ νοῦν πρὸ αὐτοῦ (sc. τοῦδε τοῦ
παντός). We may see a similar etymology in 5.3.6.18–22 where Plotinus derives
διάνοια from διὰ νοῦ; ultimately discursive thought is parasitic on the thought of
Intellect; cf. W. Beierwaltes, *Selbsterkenntnis und Erfahrung der Einheit: Plotins
Enneade V.3. Text, Übersetzung, Interpretation, Erläuterungen* (Frankfurt am Main:
Klostermann, 1991), 113, and my review of Beierwaltes in *Ancient Philosophy* 14
(1994):, 474–75. V. Schubert, *Pronoia und Logos: Die Rechtfertigung der Weltordnung
bei Plotin* (Munich: Anton Pustet, 1968), 30–31, sees πρόνοια as having a mediating

Intellect is not like the priority of a series, e.g., of numbers, for it is not merely one member of the series.

The person who complains about the imperfection of the cosmos is objectively finding fault that plants have no sense perception, a quality that belongs to a higher order, viz., animals, or the one who blames human deficiencies wants a human being to be a god (3.3.3). Yet such aspersions are not merely a failure to observe hierarchy. They are also a refusal to allow each thing to be what it is in its aseity, i.e., as sufficient unto itself in the absence of hierarchical reference:

> For one ought not to enquire whether one thing is less than another but whether it is, as itself, sufficient [ὡς αὐτὸ αὐτάρκως]; for all things ought not to have been equal. Is this then so, because the creator measured them out with the deliberate intention that all things ought not to be equal? Not at all; but it was so according to nature for things to come about so. For the rational forming principle of this universe follows upon another soul, and this soul follows upon Intellect, and Intellect is not some one of the things here but all things. (3.3.3.17–22)

Here Intellect, which initiates a hierarchy, is not what it is by membership in that hierarchy.

The Plotinian Form, apart from its uses in explanation, ontological, epistemological, or ethical, retains aseity and a value independent of its functions as cause. The Form reveals its aseity to those who are open to receive it, not simply as an explanation, but as an intrinsically valuable object of intellective vision. The Form is also, in the hypostasis of Intellect,

---

position between the intelligible and the sensible world: it does not belong to the intelligible world which is "beyond providence" (ἐπέκεινα προνοίας, 6.8.17.7). However, the providence transcended in 6.8.17 is the vulgar providence of foresight; as we have seen, in a higher sense providence is founded in the priority of Intelligence, that νοῦς is πρό. Schubert generally sees providence as a mediation between intelligible and sensible reality. He sees the following hierarchy (53): Intellect is the origin, the Soul the place, Nature the vehicle, Logos the content, providence the result, and matter the object of formation. Schubert's treatment neglects what I am calling "aseity." He is properly critical of Harder's translation of Logos as "Weltplan" on the grounds that it implies rational planning and an exercise of discursive thought (115). However, he falls into the trap himself (109): "Plotin geht von der Voraussetzung aus, dass die Welt dem Nous gemäss, also vernünfitg geordnet ist; diesen Sachverhalt drückt bei ihm der Pronoiabegriff aus." Yet Intellect is not the locus of discursive thought. Thus that the world imitates Intellect or unfolds its content in such a way that it would appear orderly to the discursive mind does not mean that it imitates Intellect and *hence* is orderly. Schubert's censure (124) of Plotinus as a dogmatist follows from Schubert's misunderstanding of hierarchy in Plotinus.

poised in a unity of mutual implication with other Forms. Each Form, in being what it is, is also and contemplates also the other Forms.

It is only in the sensible world that aseity and connectedness are brought into conflict. To say that something's existence is justified only by its contribution to the whole is to deny its aseity. On the other hand, to say that something might exist unto itself, without reference to the whole, is to affirm aseity at the cost of connectedness. The most basic problem in Plotinian providence and theodicy is how to reconcile aseity and connectedness in the sensible world.

If the prefix προ- ("before") belongs to aseity, then the prefix συν- ("with") describes connectedness. We may see a semantic field involving this prefix at work in *On Providence 2*, where Plotinus argues that apparently chance events are embraced by the universal connectedness of the cosmos. The semantic field sharing the prefix συν- ("with") is in this passage complemented by a semantic field initiated by the prefix προ- ("before"). The connection of these two semantic fields suggests that aseity and connectedness are brought into a dialectical relationship with each other:

> Chance circumstances [συντυχίαι] are not responsible for the good life, but they, too, follow harmoniously [συμφώνω] on the causes before them, and proceed woven into the chain of causation by so following. The ruling principle weaves all things together [συμπλέκει], while individual things co-operate [συμφερομένων] on one side or the other according to their nature, as in military commands the general gives the lead and his subordinates work in unity with him [συμπνεόντων δὲ τῶν συντεταγμένων]. The universe is ordered by the generalship of providence [προνοία στρατηγικῇ] which sees the actions and experiences and what must be ready to hand, food and drink, and all weapons and devices as well; everything which results from the interweaving is foreseen [ὅσα ἐξ αὐτῶν συμπλεκομένων προεώραται], in order that this result [τὸ ... συμβαῖνον] may have room to be well placed, and all things come in a well-planned way from the general—though what his enemies planned to do is out of his control. But if it was possible for him to command the enemy force as well, if he was really "the greater leader" to whom all things are subject, what would be unordered [ἀσύντακτον], what would not be fitted into [συνηρμοσμένον] his plan? (3.3.2)

Plotinus begins with the word συντυχία, "chance circumstance," a compound noun consisting of the prefix συν-, "with, together with" and τύχη, "fortune." One event happens to occur with another: it is a *co*-incidence. Now he dwells upon the prefix συν- ("with"), showing how an apparent coincidence is really embraced in the universal synchronicity of the cosmos. The substantive translated as "result" above, τὸ συμβαῖνον, would normally mean just "something that happened." But we are now prepared to see how its prefix συν- is involved in the providential skein, in that everything that results from the interweaving, literally "with-weaving" or "together-weaving," of events (συμπλεκομένων) is *fore*seen (προεώραται).[4]

These same semantic fields initiated by the prefixes συν- ("with") and προ- ("before") are also brought together in the discussion of providence in 6.7.1–2. Plotinus argues against the view that the world was created by planning and deliberation:

> Therefore neither forethought [πρόνοια] for a living thing nor forethought for this universe in general derived from a plan; since there is no planning there at all, but it is called planning to show that all things there are as they would be as a result of planning at a later stage, and foresight [προόρασις] because it is as a wise man would foresee [προίδοιτο] it. For in things which did not come to be before planning [πρὸ λογισμοῦ], planning is useful because of the lack of the power before planning, and foresight, because the one who foresees did not have the power by which there would be no need for foresight. (6.7.1.28–35)

In 6.7.2, a passage that we examined above, Plotinus is showing how "that" (τὸ ὅτι) and "why" (τὸ διότι) coalesce in Intellect. To understand this, we are to comprehend how the whole transcends the parts. If our perspective is simply how one part relates to another (linear causation) we shall never see how everything is embraced in a transcendent wholeness. Indulging an *amplificatio*, Plotinus illustrates the connectedness of Intellect from the lesser connectedness of the sensible cosmos. Notice here the semantic field initiated by the prefix συν- ("with"):

> And truly, just as in this All here below, which is composed of many things [ἐν τῷδε τῷ πάντι ἐκ πολλῶν συνεστηκότι], all of them are linked

---

[4] This passage is dependent upon the image of the general and his army in Aristotle *Metaph.* Λ 10.1075a14–16. Observe the uses of συντέτακται 1057a16 and 19. Compare Plotinus 3.3.2.5–6: συντεταγμένων. Plotinus proceeds from his use of Aristotle's verb to other words initiated by σύν but introduces the complementary use of vocabulary initated by πρό toward his own purposes. R. Harder, R. Beutler and W. Theiler, *Plotins Schriften* (5 vols.; Hamburg: Felix Meiner, 1959–1960), ad loc., prefer a reference to *Mot. an.* 10.703a29–34, but P. Boot, *Over Voorzienigheid (Enneade III.2–3 [47–48])* (Amsterdam: VU Uitgeverij, 1984), 280, is doubtless correct in preferring the reference to the *Metaphysics.* Porphyry *Vit. Plot.* 14.5–7 emphasizes Plotinus's acquaintance with that work. The linguistic parallels also seem closer. We may also see the influence of Plato, *Phaedr.* 246e4 and *Laws* 905e and 906e on the martial imagery (Boot, ibid.); on the reference to the *Laws* see R. Ferwerda, *La Signification des Images et des Métaphores dans la Pensée de Plotin* (Groningen: J. B. Wolters, 1965), 165. Note the occurrence of συντεταγμένοις at *Laws* 906e5–6.

[συνείρεται] to each other, and each individual reason why is contained
in their being all—just as in each individual the part is seen relating to
the whole—it is not that this comes to be, and then this comes after that,
but they jointly establish [συνιστάντων] cause and caused together in
relation to each other, so much more there in the intelligible must all
things be each of them related to the whole and each to itself. If therefore there is a joint existence [συνυπόστασις] of all things together, of all
things with nothing random about it, and there must be no separation,
then the things caused would have their causes in themselves, and each
would be of such a kind as to possess its cause causelessly. If then the
intelligibles have no cause of their being but are self-sufficient and independent of cause, they would be in possession of their cause in themselves and with themselves. For again, if nothing there is purposeless,
and there are many things in each, you could say that all the things
which each individual has are each individual reason why. So there in
the intelligible the reason why was before [προῆν] and with the things
[συνῆν] and was not a "why", but a "that": but rather both are one.
(6.7.2.30–46).

In the concluding sentence we may see that, in Intellect, just as "why" and
"that" coalesce, so do "before" (προ-) and "with" (συν-). We have seen that
"before" belongs to aseity: the intelligible cause is not in its own nature a
cause nor is it "before" as in "antecedent cause." "With" belongs to connectedness, but not of a kind that may be understood in terms of linear
causation, of one thing causing another. All is embraced in a universal connectedness. Intellect models providence, while, strictly speaking, it is not
itself *prov*idential, i.e., there is no προ- or "before" in it. Its connectedness
is organic: the function or contribution of any part may be understood, not
with reference to some other part or parts, but always in relation to organic
wholeness and connectedness. The sensible cosmos imperfectly imitates
Intellect, so that here for the first time "before" and "with," "why" and
"that" come apart.

The connectedness then of the intelligible world is undone in the sensible world as the descended Form is sundered by its relationships to other
things. Thus aseity is challenged by the kind of connectedness that prevails
in the horizontal dimension of the sensible cosmos. Yet there is also a challenge to aseity in hierarchical connectedness. If we see any link in the
hierarchical chain as confined to the role of mediating between the phase
above and the phase below itself we deny its aseity. That there is a hierarchy and that mediation occurs within it is clear. Yet it is Plotinus's task
to preserve the aseity of each entity in his universe. The hierarchy is established, not by some external Demiurge, or by the thought of any philosopher, but by each entity within it being itself and realizing the horizontal
connectedness appropriate to itself.

3. Providence and Human Salvation

In our previous discussion of σωτηρία, "salvation" or "preservation," we saw that the term applied both to the sensible and the intelligible dimensions. On the sensible plane, something has a characteristic or safeguard for the sake of preservation against perils that it confronts on that plane. It should, however, be stipulated that a safeguard of something in the sensible world is grounded in the thing's intelligible essence.[5] On the intelligible plane, a creature has a characteristic both for the sake of its completeness and for the sake of the integrity of the whole cosmos. We may expect that these distinctions are relevant to Plotinian anthropology.

Ἀδράστεια is the cosmic law by which the sins or good deeds of past lives are respectively punished or rewarded in future lives.[6] Thus bad masters in this life are made slaves in the next, intemperate rich men made poor, etc. (3.2.13). On the horizontal plane of salvation, even unjust suffering in this life will eventually be remedied in the next. This *karma,* as it were, that redresses the wrongs of past lives is deployed in the sensible world (certainly it is founded ultimately in the intelligible realm). The operation of this cosmic law, while it may not, as the safeguard of substance in the sensible world, afford us immediate preservation or salvation from perils, works long range in favor of the just upon that plane.

The second sense of salvation is realized in the sage's indifference to fate and his contemplative deliverance from concern with this world. If we are plundered of our identity by the parasitic division of our attributes as they are deployed in the sensible cosmos, our transcendence of our relationships with the sensible world secures our aseity. That transcendence in turn introduces us to the community and perfect connectedness of the intelligible cosmos.[7]

Plotinus enjoins indifference to the hazards of this world. We should observe murders and the sackings of cities as if they were events on a stage (3.2.15.43–47). Our ability to escape the evils of the world depends upon a fundamental principle: it is not matter that diminishes us or drags us down: the struggle is between the higher and the lower self (3.3.4.27–

---

[5] 6.7.3.15–22.

[6] The principle of ἀδράστεια is borrowed from Plato, *Phaedr.* 248c2; cf. Plotinus 3.2.13.16.

[7] V. Schubert, *Pronoia und Logos,* 92–93 (cf. 126), complains that in 3.2.16 Plotinus tries to establish the same sort of benign opposition between good and evil as is embraced by the opposites such as high and low, white and black, hot and cold. It depends surely upon one's eschatology. Plotinus sees the sensible cosmos as an imperfect imitation of the intelligible world. On this model, there can be no final victory of good over evil: they can only be counterpoised in a cosmic balance.

34).[8] The human soul may escape the cycle of birth and rebirth and stand with the Soul outside becoming (ἔξω γενέσεως, 3.2.4.6–11).

In a previous article, I have argued that Plotinus makes an abundant use of the ontological term initiated by the συν- ("with") prefix, συνουσία, and other epistemological vocabulary initiated by the same prefix (σύνεσις and συναίσθησις).[9] The word συνουσία bears the senses of coherence of an entity with itself, presence of one superior entity to a lower entity, and dependence of a lower entity upon a higher one. Plotinus prefers συνουσία to παρουσία as a term to describe presence because, where παρουσία describes only the presence of a higher entity to a lower one, συνουσία and related words initiated by the συν- prefix offer an elaborate and elastic inventory of presence and dependence.

The uses of the συν- prefix in our present context of providence offer a familiar elasticity. Such words describe the coherence (connectedness) of both the sensible and intelligible worlds. The connectedness of the sensible world is founded in the greater connectedness of the intelligible world. Συνουσία may properly describe both instances of connectedness. Yet the συνουσία of the sensible world has both horizontal and vertical dimensions. It is founded in the priority of Intellect as providence. Yet that providence is before by being with, i.e., with itself, in the greatest sense of connectedness. So the withness of the sensible world, as it is intensified, enters progressively into the prior connectedness of the intelligible world, so that the "before" of providence becomes "with" for us and we "with" it.

Apart from the question of transcendence, there abides the question of free choice in this world and whether it is compromised by the determinations of providence. We have seen how in 6.8.17.3 προαίρεσις as deliberated choice is excluded from the act of creating the sensible world. It is eliminated together with other words initiated by the προ- prefix, including providence as a kind of foresight or taking thought beforehand. We have also seen how "before" is, in Intellect, absorbed into "with." This scheme is mapped onto Plotinus's account of free will:

> Suppose you say: "I have power to choose this or that"? But the things that you will choose [αἰρήσει] are included in [συντέτακται] the universal order, because your part is not a mere causal interlude in the All but you are counted in as the person you are. (3.3.3.1–3)

---

[8] Cf. Armstrong's note, which refers us to 1.1.10; 2.9.2; 4.4.18; 6.4.14–15. The same point is made in 3.6.5.

[9] F. M. Schroeder, "Presence and Dependence in the Plotinian Philosophy of Consciousness: *Sunousia, Sunaisthêsis* and *Sunesis*," *ANRW* 2.36.1:677–99.

The verb translated as "include" (συντάττειν) is initiated by the συν- ("with") prefix. Here what we see as priorities and choices are already enmeshed in a universal connectedness. Notice how this connectedness does not negate the aseity of the human person. The human being is not simply the object, but the subject of providence, insofar as he or she is a microcosm: "we are each one of us an intelligible universe" (ἐσμὲν ἕκαστος κόσμος νοητός, 3.4.3.22).[10] The bad man is responsible for his evildoing: "For he is not only what he was made but has another free principle, which is not outside providence or the rational principle of the whole" (3.3.4.6–8). One could say that his error consists in electing his own and partial providence, not looking to the whole and its beneficent order.[11] In the organic All, the part is saved by the whole (ἕκαστον τῷ ὅλῳ σώζε- ται, 4.4.32.33). Salvation lies in integrity.[12]

That principle of aseity is admirably expressed in the lapidary sentence: "Providence ought not to exist in such a way as to make us nothing" (Οὐ γὰρ δὴ οὕτω τὴν πρόνοιαν εἶναι δεῖ, ὥστε μηδὲν ἡμᾶς εἶναι, 3.2.9.1–2). Nothing in the Plotinian universe is ever merely an instrument. It is also the case that human beings, while they may be determined, are also determinants in universal providence: "men, too, are principles" (ἀρ- χαὶ δὲ καὶ ἄνθρωποι, 3.2.10.18).

When a seer looks into the future, he does not see the causes that lead to the things he foresees, e.g., he would see visions of war and carnage, but he would not see the causes that led to the Second World War. He would see "that" and not "why." In 3.3.6, the ordinary person is unable to distinguish between providence and the body of cause and effects on which it works. Providence is the form, the network of cause and effect the matter. When the diviner sees a person in the future, he does not work out the network of causes that produced that person. He sees the end toward which providence has been working. He sees the "that" (τὸ ὅτι), not the "why" (τὸ δίοτι). The end of providence is suchness, not the "reason why." The poet and contemplative Angelus Silesius says: "Die Rose ist ohne warum; Sie blühet, weil sie blühet"[13] ("The rose has no 'why': it blooms because it blooms"). That sense of suchness and aseity is at the heart of the Plotinian doctrine of providence.[14]

---

[10] Cf. Parma, *Pronoia und Providentia,* 102; cf. 106.

[11] Cf. Ibid., 135–36.

[12] Cf. Ibid., 67.

[13] Angelus Silesius, *Sämtliche Poetische Werke* (ed. H. L. Held; 3 vols.; Munich: Carl Hansen, 1949), 1:209.

[14] V. Schubert, *Pronoia und Logos,* 124, who faults Plotinus's attempt to derive the moral from the cosmic order, sees in this passage merely an example of the

The human being in the sensible world mirrors the connectedness of the intelligible cosmos. Plotinus argues (3.2.14) that, while in Intellect each is all, in this world "man" is a part and an individual, not all. Yet he continues:

> But there would certainly not be any grudging by the whole if the part did gain in beauty and order so as to make it of greater worth; for it makes the whole more beautiful when it has become of greater value by its gain in beauty and order. For it becomes of this kind by being made like the whole and, so to speak, being allowed to be like this and given such a place that in the region of man, too, something may shine in him as the stars shine in the heaven of the gods; a place from which there may be a perception of something like a great and beautiful image of a god—whether a living one or one made by the art of Hephaestus—in which there are stars flashing on the face, and in the breast others, and a setting of stars placed where it will be clearly seen. (3.2.14.20–30)

We are reminded of an astronomical illustration of the unity of Intellect (5.8.4):

> Each there has everything in itself and sees all things in every other, so that all are everywhere and each and every one is all and the glory is unbounded; for each of them is great, because even the small is great: the sun there is all the stars, and each star is the sun and all the others. (5.8.4.6–10).

In 3.2.14, Plotinus makes clear that the sensible world can never achieve the identity of each and all that is to be discovered in Intellect. Yet at times that completeness may be approximated, as in the present image of the starry face of the contemplative in which the illumination manifests the wholeness of Intellect. Even as there the stars are all the sun and the sun is all the stars, so this countenance participates in that heavenly noetic unity. At the same time, the human being who achieves that participation is at the greatest level of individual perfection and is most human. Thus the aseity of human perfection is at one with the interconnectedness of all things.[15]

---

human inability to sort out what is caused by providence and what is caused by matter. In this he fails to see the positive character of divining the "that," as opposed to discovering the "why" of things.

[15] R. Turcan, *The Cults of the Roman Empire* (trans. A. Nevill; Oxford and Cambridge, Mass.: Blackwell, 1996), 152, sees in this passage a reference to an idol of Zeus Heliopolitanus. The god of Baalbek's statue is distinguished by the fact "that his idol combines the cuirass with a celestial garment. The compartments of his garment are occupied by busts or symbols of the planetary gods." (See plate 18 in the

4. Some Thoughts about Plotinian Providence and Gnosis

In Sethian texts the descent of Sophia results in a further emanation of a Demiurge who fashions the sensible cosmos. The gnostic resists the creation of the Demiurge in seeking deliverance from the evil world that he has made. In his treatise *Against the Gnostics,* 2.9.10–12 Plotinus attacks those who present a similar view. His assault upon the gnostic Demiurge is well prepared by his deconstruction of the Platonic Demiurge. Certainly Plotinus takes the view that the Demiurge of the *Timaeus* is a device to demonstrate the relationship of imitation that exists between the intelligible and sensible worlds, i.e., the story is to be interpreted, not literally, but figuratively. What is more, divine making is not to be considered as an exercise in deliberative thought. Now the Demiurge is a mediator who mediates between the intelligible and the sensible reality. Plotinus's insistence on aseity does not dispute a hierarchical ordering of the All in which the One stands first, Intellect second, Soul third, and the sensible cosmos last. Yet "first" is not "first" in the sense that it exists either to initiate a series or to mediate between one level of reality and another. Hierarchy is an article of suchness rather than a tool of mediation.[16] Intellect is the content of the sensible world.[17] If we ask, what does the sensible world mean, the answer is: Intellect. The *approfondissement* of sensible connectedness *is* Intellect.

---

same volume). Turcan, however, sees 3.2.14 as referring only to the sky and not to a human figure. That it does refer to a human or somewhat anthropomorphic figure only enhances Turcan's argument that this passage refers to the sculpture in question. We may think of Plotinus's view that the sculptor Pheidias, while employing a sensible model, portrayed Zeus as he would appear if he chose to appear among us (5.8.1.38–40). In 2.9.18.30–35, Plotinus, censuring the gnostics for their despising of the cosmos, urges that we imitate the soul of the All and of the stars. Perhaps this material influences Porphyry to write in the *Vit. Plot.* 13.5–7 that "when he [Plotinus] was speaking his intellect visibly lit up his face."

[16] Cf. Parma, *Pronoia und Providentia,* 59–60, 72. For an example of the other view, see E. Früchtel, *Weltentwurf und Logos: Zur Metaphysik Plotins* (Frankfurt am Main: Klostermann, 1970), 41: "Die dritte Hypostase, die Seele, hat die Aufgabe, zwischen dem mundus intelligibilis und dem mundus sensibilis zu vermitteln." In Plotinus, "such" (τοιοῦτον) refers both to what kind of thing something is and also to something substantial: "I mean 'of this kind' [τὸ τοιοῦτον] having together with their substance also the cause of their existence [τὸ σὺν αὐτῶν τῇ οὐσίᾳ ἔχειν καὶ τῆς ὑποστάσεως τὴν οὐσίαν], so that the observer afterwards can say why each of its inherent parts is there, for instance why there is an eye and why the feet of these particular beings are as they are and the cause which brings into existence together each part of each thing and brings them into existence on account of each other" (6.8.14.20–25). Surely the use of τοιοῦτον here expresses what I am calling "aseity" very nicely.

[17] Cf. Parma, *Pronoia und Providentia,* 42ff.

For Plotinus, the gnostics err in thinking that a hierarchy implies an unredeemed diminution. This is because they misunderstand the very nature of the true hierarchy that preserves the aseity of each phase. For the gnostics "before" destroys "with" and without "with" there is no meaning. Human salvation, in its first and most important sense, depends, not upon the mediation of a savior figure, but upon an autonomous and codetermining role in the cosmos and the deepening of that connectedness until it debouches upon the noetic unity and connectedness of Intellect.[18]

Finally, Plotinus insists against the gnostics that if, after every argument, one persists in blaming the order of the cosmos, there is no need to act as a citizen of it (πολιτεύεσθαι, 2.9.9.17).[19] We are altogether too accustomed to construe the final words of the *Enneads* in Porphyry's arrangement, the "flight of the alone to the alone" (6.9.11.51), as a statement of contemplative individualism at the cost of community. As Gurtler has shown, a sense of community informs all of Plotinus's thinking.[20] We may feel entitled to see in 2.9.9 an ethical rejection of what Plotinus perceives as gnostic exclusivity. In Intellect, where the relationship between part and whole is as it should be, all is friendship (πᾶν αὐτῷ φίλον, 3.2.1.32). In the sensible cosmos, the parts are at war and there is no longer only friendship (φιλία). One part is at variance with another part at whose cost it is saved (σῴζεται, 3.2.2.1–7). Note that we have here a negative version of salvation. Aristotle observes that the good ruler will promote civic friendship because it produces justice more effectively than constitutional articles.[21] As friendship

---

[18] Thus Plotinus excludes the efficacy of petitionary prayer: 3.2.8.36–42.

[19] Cf. the reference to the cosmos as polis at 2.9.9.19.

[20] G. M. Gurtler, "Human Consciousness and Its Intersubjective Dimension in Plotinus" (Ph.D. diss., Fordham University, 1978); and idem, *Plotinus: The Experience of Unity* (New York: Peter Lang, 1988); cf. F. Schroeder, *Form and Transformation,* 91–113; see K. Corrigan, "'Solitary' Mysticism in Plotinus, Proclus, Gregory of Nyssa and Pseudo-Dionysius," *JR* 76 (1996): 28–42, for an excellent discussion of how the formula "alone to the alone" is neither narcissistic nor autoerotic. As Corrigan points out (35), in the same chapter that describes the "flight of the alone to the alone," Plotinus says, "This is the life of gods and godlike and blessed men" (6.9.11.49–51). This statement suggests a sense of community.

[21] Cf. *Eth. nic.* 8.1.1155a22–28 and F. M. Schroeder, "Friendship in Aristotle and Some Peripatetic Philosophers," in *Greco-Roman Perceptions on Friendship* (ed. John Fitzgerald; Atlanta: Scholars Press, 1997), 40. For further exploration of friendship in Plotinus, see Schroeder, *Form and Transformation,* 91–113. I wish to thank Kevin Corrigan for his helpful critique of my paper on the occasion when it was presented at the Gnosticism and Later Platonism Seminar at the Annual Meeting of the Society of Biblical Literature in Orlando, Florida, on November 21, 1998. I have benefited greatly from his remarks in preparing this final version. Of course, any remaining defects are entirely my own responsibility.

transcends and fulfills law, so does providence and its friendship transcend the cosmic law of fate. The connectedness of Intellect is the model to which the righteous will look for the realization of justice in the city of the sensible cosmos.

BIBLIOGRAPHY

Abramowski, L. "Marius Victorinus, Porphyrius und die römischen Gnostiker." *ZNW* 74 (1983): 108–28.

Aland, B., ed. *Gnosis: Festschrift für Hans Jonas.* Göttingen: Vandenhoeck & Ruprecht, 1978.

Armstrong, A. H. "The Apprehension of Divinity in the Self and the Cosmos in Plotinus." Pages 187–98 in *The Significance of Neoplatonism.* Edited by R. B. Harris. Norfolk, Va.: International Society for Neoplatonic Studies, 1976.

————. "Dualism: Platonic, Gnostic, and Christian." Pages 29–52 in *Plotinus amid Gnostics and Christians: Papers Presented at the Plotinus Symposium Held at the Free University, Amsterdam, on 25 January 1984.* Edited by D. T. Runia. Amsterdam: VU Uitgeverij/Free University Press, 1984. Repr., pages 33–54 in *Neoplatonism and Gnosticism.* Edited by R. T. Wallis and J. Bregman. Studies in Neoplatonism: Ancient and Modern 6. Albany: SUNY Press, 1992.

————. "Gnosis and Greek Philosophy." Pages 87–124 in *Gnosis: Festschrift für Hans Jonas.* Edited by B. Aland. Göttingen: Vandenhoeck & Ruprecht, 1978.

————. *Hellenic and Christian Studies.* Aldershot, Hampshire, Great Britain: Variorum; Brookfield, Vt: Gower, 1990.

————. "On Not Knowing Too Much about God." Pages 129–45 in *Hellenic and Christian Studies.* Aldershot, Hampshire, Great Britain: Variorum; Brookfield, Vt: Gower, 1990.

————, ed. *The Cambridge History of Later Greek and Early Medieval Philosophy.* Cambridge: Cambridge University Press, 1967.

————. *Classical Mediterranean Spirituality: Egyptian, Greek, Roman.* World Spirituality 15. New York: Crossroad, 1986.

————, ed. and trans. *Plotinus: Enneads. English and Greek.* 7 vols. LCL. Cambridge: Harvard University Press; London: W. Heinemann, 1966–1988.

Athanassiadi, P. "Dreams, Theurgy and Freelance Divination: The Testimony of Iamblichus." *JRS* 83 (1993): 123–29.

Atkinson, M. *Ennead V.1: On the Three Principal Hypostases: A Commentary with Translation.* Oxford and New York: Oxford University Press, 1983.

Attridge, H. W., ed. *Nag Hammadi Codex I (The Jung Codex): Introductions, Texts, Translations, Indices.* 2 vols. NHS 22–23. Leiden: Brill, 1985.

Baladi, N. *La pensée de Plotin.* Initiation philosophique 92. Paris: Les Presses des Universités de France, 1970.

Barry, C., et al. *Zostrien (NH VIII, 1).* BCNHT 24. Québec: Presses de l'Université Laval; Louvain-Paris: Peeters, 2000.

Bechtle, G. *The Anonymous Commentary on Plato's «Parmenides».* Berner Reihe philosophischer Studien 22. Bern: Paul Haupt, 1999.

Beierwaltes, W. *Selbsterkenntnis und Erfahrung der Einheit: Plotins Enneade V.3. Text, Übersetzung, Interpretation, Erläuterungen.* Frankfurt am Main: Klostermann, 1991.

Bergmeier, R. "Quellen vorchristlicher Gnosis." Pages 200–20 in *Tradition und Glaube.* Edited by G. Jeremias et al. Göttingen: Vandenhoeck & Ruprecht, 1971.

Beutler, R. "Plutarchos von Athens." PW 21:974–75.

Beyschlag, K. "Zur Simon-Magus-Frage." *ZTK* 68 (1971): 395–426

Boese, H. *Procli Opuscula: De providentia, libertate, malo. Latine Guilelmo de Moerbeka vertente et Graeci ex Isaacii Sebastocratoris.* Berlin: de Gruyter, 1960.

Boot, P. *Over Voorzienigheid (Enneade III.2–3 [47–48]).* Amsterdam: VU Uitgeverij, 1984.

Bos, A. P. "World-views in Collision: Plotinus, Gnostics, and Christians." Pages 11–28 in *Plotinus amid Gnostics and Christians: Papers Presented at the Plotinus Symposium Held at the Free University, Amsterdam, on 25 January 1984.* Edited by D. T. Runia. Amsterdam: VU Uitgeverij/Free University Press, 1984.

Bossier, F. and C. Steel. "Priscianus Lydus en de 'In de Anima' van Pseudo(?)-Simplicius." *Tijdschrift voor Filosofia* 34 (1972): 761–882.

Bouffartigue, J., and M. Patillon, eds. and trans. *Porphyre: De l'abstinence.* 3 vols. Paris: Les Belles Lettres, 1977–1995.

Bradshaw, P. F., ed. *Essays in Early Eastern Initiation.* Alcuin/GROW Liturgical Study 8: Nottingham: Grove, 1988.

Bregman, J. "Synesius, the Hermetica and Gnosis." Pages 85–98 in *Neoplatonism and Gnosticism.* Edited by R. T. Wallis and J. Bregman. Studies in Neoplatonism: Ancient and Modern 6. Albany: SUNY Press, 1992.

Bréhier, É. *Les Ennéades de Plotin: Texte établi et traduit par Émile Bréhier.* 6 vols. Collection des universités de France. Paris: Les Belles Lettres, 1924–1938.

Brisson, L. "Amélius: Sa vie, son oeuvre, sa doctrine, son style," *ANRW* 2.36.2:793–860.

Brisson, L., et al. *Porphyre: La Vie de Plotin.* Vol. 1: *Travaux préliminaires et index complet.* Histoire des doctrines de l'antiquité classique 6. Paris: J. Vrin, 1982.

———. *Porphyre. La Vie de Plotin.* Vol. 2: *Études d'introduction, texte grec et traduction française, commentaire, notes complémentaires, bibliographie.* Histoire des doctrines de l'antiquité classique 16. Paris: J. Vrin, 1992.

Burkert, W. *Greek Religion.* Translated by J. Raffan. Cambridge: Harvard University Press, 1985.

Burnet, J. *The [Nicomachean] Ethics of Aristotle.* London: Methuen, 1900.

Bussanich, J. R. *The One and Its Relation to Intellect in Plotinus.* Leiden: Brill, 1988.

Cilento, V. *Plotino. Paideia antignostica: Ricostruzione d'un unico scritto da Enneadi III 8, V 8, V 5, II, 9.* Firenze: F. Le Monnier, 1971.

Claude, P. *Les trois stèles de Seth.* BCNHT 8. Québec: Presses de l'Université Laval; Louvain-Paris: Peeters, 1983.

Corrigan, K. "Amelius, Plotinus and Porphyry on Being, Intellect and the One." *ANRW* 2.36.2:975–93.

———. "The Anonymous Turin *Commentary on the Parmenides* and the Distinction between Essence and Existence in Middle Platonism, the Plotinian Circle, and Sethian Gnostic Texts." Paper presented at the SBL Gnosticism and Later Platonism Seminar, 1995 AAR/SBL Annual Meeting, Philadelphia. Manuscript. [See "Platonism and Gnosticism. The *Anonymous Commentary* on the *Parmenides:* Middle or Neoplatonic?" in this volume.]

————. "Essence and Existence in the *Enneads*." Pages 103–29 in *The Cambridge Companion to Plotinus*. Edited by L. P. Gerson. Cambridge and New York: Cambridge University Press, 1996.

————. "Is There More Than One Generation of Matter in the *Enneads*?" *Phronesis* 31.2 (1986): 167–81.

————. "Light and Metaphor in Plotinus and St. Thomas Aquinas." *The Thomist* 57 (1993): 187–99.

————. "A Philosophical Precursor to the Theory of Essence and Existence in St. Thomas Aquinas." *The Thomist* 48 (1984): 219–40.

————. "Plotinus, *Enneads* 5, 4 (7) 2 and Related Passages. A New Interpretation of the Status of the Intelligible Object." *Hermes* 114.2 (1986): 195–203.

————. *Plotinus' Theory of Matter-Evil and the Question of Substance: Plato, Aristotle, and Alexander of Aphrodisias.* Recherches de théologie ancienne et médiévale, Supplementa 3. Louvain: Peeters, 1996.

————. "'Solitary' Mysticism in Plotinus, Proclus, Gregory of Nyssa, and Pseudo-Dionysius." *JR* 76 (1996): 28–42.

Corrigan, K., and P. O'Cleirigh. "The Course of Plotinian Scholarship from 1971 to 1986." *ANRW* 2.36.1:571–623.

Deck, J. *Nature, Contemplation, and the One: A Study in the Philosophy of Plotinus.* Toronto: University of Toronto Press, 1967.

Desjardins, M. R. *Sin in Valentinianism.* SBLDS 108. Atlanta: Scholars Press, 1990.

Des Places, É. *Jamblique: Les mystères d'Égypte.* Paris: Les Belles Lettres, 1966.

————. *Numénius: Fragments.* Collection des Universités de France. Paris: Les Belles Lettres, 1973.

————. "Les Oracles Chaldaïques." *ANRW* 2.17.4:2300–35.

————. *Oracles Chaldaïques, avec un choix de commentaires anciens.* Collection des Universités de France. Paris: Les Belle Lettres, 1971.

Dieterich, A. "ABC-Denkmäler." *Rheinisches Museum für Philologie* 56 (1901): 77–105.

Dillon, J. M. "The Descent of the Soul in Middle Platonic and Gnostic Theory." Pages 357–64 in *The Rediscovery of Gnosticism: Proceedings of the International Conference on Gnosticism at Yale, New Haven,*

Connecticut, March 28–31, 1978. Vol. 1: *The School of Valentinus.* Edited by B. Layton. SHR 41. Leiden: Brill, 1980.

———. "The Knowledge of God in Origen." Pages 219–28 in *Knowledge of God in the Graeco-Roman World.* Edited by R. van den Broek, T. Baarda and J. Mansfeld. EPRO 112. Leiden: Brill, 1988.

———. *The Middle Platonists, 80 B.C. to A.D. 220.* London: Duckworth; Ithaca, N.Y.: Cornell University Press, 1977. Rev. ed. with a new afterword, Ithaca, N.Y.: Cornell University Press, 1996.

———. "Plêrôma and Noetic Cosmos: A Comparative Study." Pages 99–110 in *Neoplatonism and Gnosticism.* Edited by R. T. Wallis and J. Bregman. Studies in Neoplatonism: Ancient and Modern 6. Albany: SUNY Press, 1992.

———. "Plotinus and the Chaldean Oracles." Pages 131–40 in *Platonism in Late Antiquity.* Edited by S. Gersh and C. Kannengeisser. Notre Dame, Ind.: University of Notre Dame Press, 1992.

———, ed. and trans. *Iamblichi Chalcidensis: In Platonis Dialogos Commentariorum Fragmenta. Edited with Translation and Commentary.* Philosophia Antiqua 23. Leiden: Brill, 1973.

———, trans. *Alcinous: The Handbook of Platonism. Translation, Introduction and Commentary.* Oxford: Clarendon Press; New York: Oxford University Press, 1993.

———, *Proclus: Commentary on Plato's Parmenides.* Princeton, N.J.: Princeton University Press, 1987.

Dodds, E. R. *The Greeks and the Irrational.* Berkeley and Los Angeles: University of California Press, 1951.

———. "New Light on the Chaldaean Oracles." Pages 693–701 in H. Lewy, *Chaldean Oracles and Theurgy: Mysticism, Magic, and Platonism in the Later Roman Empire.* Recherches d'archéologie et de philosophe et d'histoire 13. Cairo: Institut français d'archéologie orientale, 1956. New edition edited by M. Tardieu; Paris: Études Augustiniennes, 1978.

———. "Numenius and Ammonius." Pages 3–61 in *Les sources de Plotin.* Entretiens sur l'antiquité classique 5. Geneva: Fondation Hardt, 1960.

———. *Pagan and Christian in an Age of Anxiety.* Cambridge: Cambridge University Press, 1965.

———. "The *Parmenides* of Plato and the Origin of the Neoplatonic 'One.'" *CQ* 22 (1928): 129–42.

————, ed. and trans. *Proclus: The Elements of Theology*. Oxford: Clarendon Press, 1963.

Dornseiff, F. *Das Alphabet in Mystik und Magie*. 2d ed. Berlin: Teubner, 1925.

Edwards, M. J. "Porphyry and the Intelligible Triad." *JHS* 110 (1990): 14–25.

Elsas, C. *Neuplatonische und Gnostische Weltablehnung in der Schule Plotins*. Religionschichtliche Versuche und Vorarbeiten 34. Berlin and New York: de Gruyter, 1975.

Evrard, E. "Le maître de Plutarque d'Athènes et les origines du néoplatonisme athénien." *L'Antiquité classique* 29 (1960): 391–406.

Ferwerda, R. *La signification des images et des métaphores dan la pensée de Plotin*. Groningen: J. B. Wolters, 1965.

Festugière, A.-J. *La révélation d'Hermès Trismégiste*. Vol. 1: *L'astrologie et les sciences occultes*. Vol. 2: *Le Dieu cosmique*. Vol. 3: *Les doctrines de l'âme*. Vol. 4: *Le Dieu inconnu et la gnose*. Études bibliques. Paris: J. Gabalda/Librairie Lecoffre, 1949–1954.

Finamore, J. *Iamblichus and the Theory of the Vehicle of the Soul*. Chico, Calif.: Scholars Press, 1985.

Finn, T. F. *The Liturgy of Baptism in the Baptismal Instructions of St. John Chrysostom*. CUA: SCA 15. Washington, D.C.: Catholic University of America Press, 1967.

Foester, W., ed. *Gnosis: A Selection of Gnostic Texts*. Translated by R. McL. Wilson. 2 vols. Oxford: Clarendon Press, 1972–1974.

Frede, M. "Numenius." *ANRW* 2.36.2:1034–75.

Früchtel, E. *Weltentwurf und Logos: Zur Metaphysik Plotins*. Frankfurt am Main: Klostermann, 1970.

Funk, W.-P., P.-H. Poirier and J. D. Turner. *Marsanès (NH X,1)*. BCNHT 25. Québec: Presses de l'Université Laval; Louvain-Paris: Peeters, 2000.

Gaffron, H.-G. "Studien zum koptischen Philippusevangelium unter besonderer Berücksichtigung der Sakramente." Th.D. diss. Friedrich-Wilhelms-Universität, Bonn, 1969.

Gandillac, M. de. "Plotin et la Métaphysique d'Aristote." Pages 247–59 in *Études sur la Métaphysique d'Aristote: Actes du VIe Symposium Aristotelicum*. Edited by P. Aubenque. Paris: J. Vrin, 1979.

García Bazán, F. *Plotino y la gnosis*. Buenos Aires: Fundación para la Educación, la Ciencia y la Cultura, 1981.

Gauthier, R. A., and J. Y. Jolif. *L'Ethique à Nicomaque: Introduction, traduction et commentaire.* 2d ed. Louvain-Paris: Publications universitaires, 1970.

Gero, S. "With Walter Bauer on the Tigris: Encratite Orthodoxy and Libertine Heresy in Syro-Mesopotamian Christianity." Pages 287–307 in *Nag Hammadi, Gnosticism, and Early Christianity.* Edited by C. W. Hedrick and R. Hodgson. Peabody, Mass: Hendrickson, 1986.

Goulet-Cazé, M.-O. "L'arrière-plan scholaire de La Vie de Plotin." Pages 231–327 in *Porphyre: La Vie de Plotin.* Vol. 1. Edited by L. Brisson et al. Histoire des doctrines de l'antiquité classique 6. Paris: J. Vrin, 1982.

Grant, R. M. "The Mystery of Marriage in the Gospel of Philip." *VC* 15 (1961): 129–40.

Green, H. "Ritual in Valentinian Gnosticism." *JRH* 12 (1982): 109–24.

Gurtler, G. M. "Human Consciousness and Its Intersubjective Dimension in Plotinus." Ph.D. diss. Fordham University, 1978.

———. *Plotinus: The Experience of Unity.* New York: Peter Lang, 1988.

Guthrie, W. K. C. *A History of Greek Philosophy.* 6 vols. London: Cambridge University Press, 1962–1981.

Hadot, P. "La distinction de l'être et de l'étant dans le *de Hebdomadibus* de Boèce." Pages 147–53 in *Die Metaphysik im Mittelalter, ihr Ursprung und ihre Bedeutung: Vorträge des II. Internationalen Kongresses für Mittelalterliche Philosophie, Köln, 31. August 6–September 1961.* Edited by P. Wilpert and W. P. Eckert. Im Auftrage der Société internationale pour l'étude de la philosophie médiévale. Miscellanea mediaevalia 2. Berlin: de Gruyter, 1963.

———. "Être, vie, pensée chez Plotin et avant Plotin." Pages 107–41 in *Les sources de Plotin.* Entretiens sur l'antiquité classique 5. Vandoeuvres-Genéve: Fondation Hardt, 1960.

———. "L'être et l'étant dans le Néoplatonisme." *RTP* 2 (1973): 101–13.

———. "*Forma essendi:* Interprétation philologique et interprétation philosophique d'une formule de Boèce." *Les études classiques* 38 (1970): 143–56.

———. "Fragments d'un commentaire de Porphyre sur le Parménide." *REG* 74 (1961): 410–438.

———. "L'harmonie des philosophies de Plotin et d'Aristote selon Porphyre." Pages 31–47 in *Atti del Covegno internazionale sul tema*

Plotino e il neoplatonismo in Oriente e in Occidente (Roma, 5–9 otto-bre 1970). Problemi attuali di scienza e di cultura quaderno 198. Rome: Accademia nazionale dei Lincei, 1974.

―――. *Marius Victorinus: Traités théologiques sur la trinité.* Vol. 1, Texte établi par Paul Henry; introduction, traduction et notes par Pierre Hadot. Vol. 2, Commentaire par Pierre Hadot. SC 68–69. Paris: Cerf, 1960.

―――. "La métaphysique de Porphyre." Pages 127–57 in *Porphyre.* Entretiens sur l'antiquité classique 12. Vandoeuvres-Genéve: Fondation Hardt, 1965.

―――. "Ouranos, Kronos, and Zeus in Plotinus' Treatise *Against the Gnostics.*" Pages 124–37 in *Neoplatonism and Early Christian Thought.* Edited by H. J. Blumenthal and R. A. Markus. London: Variorum, 1981.

―――. *Plotin: Traité 38. VI. 7.* Paris: Cerf, 1988.

―――. *Porphyre et Victorinus.* 2 vols. Paris: Études augustiniennes, 1968.

―――. "'Porphyre et Victorinus.' Questions et hypothèses." Pages 117–25 in *Res Orientales 9.* Bures-sur-Yvette: Groupe pour l'Étude de la Civilisation du Moyen-Orient, 1996.

Haenchen, E. "Gab es eine vorchristliche Gnosis?" *ZTK* 49 (1952): 316–49. Repr., pages 265–98 in *Gott und Mensch: Gesammelte Aufsätze.* Tübingen: Mohr Siebeck, 1965.

Hancock, C. "Negative Theology in Gnosticism and Neoplatonism." Pages 167–86 in *Neoplatonism and Gnosticism.* Edited by R. T. Wallis and J. Bregman. Studies in Neoplatonism: Ancient and Modern 6. Albany: SUNY Press, 1992.

Harder, R. "Ein neue Schrift Plotins." *Hermes* 71 (1936): 1–10.

Harder, R., R. Beutler and W. Theiler, eds. *Plotins Schriften.* 5 vols. Hamburg: Felix Meiner, 1959–1960.

Harris, J. R., ed. and trans., *The Apology of Aristides.* 2d ed. TS 1.1. Cambridge: Cambridge University Press, 1893.

Hedrick, C. W. ed., *Nag Hammadi Codices XI, XII, and XIII.* NHS 28. Leiden: Brill, 1990.

Heinemann, F. *Plotin: Forschungen über die plotinische Frage Plotinsentwicklung und sein System.* Leipzig: F. Meiner, 1921.

Henry, P. *Études plotiniennes.* Vol. 1: *Les états du texte de Plotin.* Paris: Desclée de Brouwer; Brussels: L'Édition universelle, 1938.

——. *Études plotiniennes.* Vol. 2: *Les manuscrits des Ennéades.* Paris: Desclée de Brouwer; Brussels: l'Édition universelle, 1941; 2d ed. 1948.

Henry, P., and H.-R. Schwyzer, eds. *Plotini Opera.* 3 vols. Scriptorum classicorum bibliotheca Oxoniensis. Oxford: Clarendon Press, 1964–1982.

Horn, C. "Der Platonische *Parmenides* und die Möglichkeit seiner prinzipientheoretischen Interpretation." *Antike und Abendland* 41 (1995): 95–114.

Horst, P. W. van der, and J. Mansfeld. *An Alexandrian Platonist against Dualism.* Leiden: Brill, 1974.

Igal, J. "Aristoteles y la evolución de la antropología de Plotino." *Pensiamento* 35 (1979): 315–16.

——. "The Gnostics and 'The Ancient Philosophy' in Plotinus." Pages 138–52 in *Neoplatonism and Early Christian Thought: Essays in Honour of A. H. Armstrong.* Edited by H. J. Blumenthal and R. A. Markus. London: Variorum, 1981.

Janus, C., ed., *Musici Scriptores Graeci.* Leipzig: Teubner, 1895. Repr., Hildesheim: Olms, 1962.

Jervell, J. *Imago Dei: Gen 1, 26 f. im Spätjudentum, in der Gnosis und in den paulinischen Briefen.* FRLANT NS 58. Göttingen: Vandenhoeck & Ruprecht, 1960.

Joachim, H. H. *The Nicomachean Ethics: A Commentary.* Edited by D. A. Rees. Oxford: Clarendon Press, 1951.

Jonas, H. *Gnosis und spätantiker Geist.* Vol. 1: *Die mythologische Gnosis.* 3d ed. FRLANT NS 33. Göttingen: Vandenhoeck & Ruprecht, 1934. Repr., 1966.

——. *The Gnostic Religion.* 2d ed. Boston: Beacon, 1963.

Kahn, C. H. "On the Terminology for Copula and Existence." Pages 151–58 in *Islamic Philosophy and the Classical Tradition: Essays Presented By His Friends and Pupils to Richard Walzer on His Seventieth Birthday.* Edited by S. M. Stern, A. Hourani and V. Brown. Columbia, S.C.: University of South Carolina Press, 1972.

Kenney, J. P. "The Critical Value of Negative Theology." *HTR* 86 (1993): 439–53.

——. "Monotheistic and Polytheistic Elements in Classical Mediterranean Spirituality." Pages 269–92 in *Classical Mediterranean Spirituality.* Edited by A. H. Armstrong. New York: Crossroad, 1986.

——. *Mystical Monotheism: A Study in Ancient Platonic Theology.* Hanover and London: Brown University Press, 1991.

————. "Mysticism and Contemplation in the Enneads." *American Catholic Philosophical Quarterly* 71 (1997): 315–37.

————. "The Platonism of the *Tripartite Tractate* (NHC I, 5)." Pages 187–206 in *Neoplatonism and Gnosticism*. Edited by R. T. Wallis and J. Bregman. Studies in Neoplatonism: Ancient and Modern 6. Albany: SUNY Press, 1992.

King, K. *Revelation of the Unknowable God with Text, Translation, and Notes to NHC XI,3 Allogenes*. Santa Rosa, Calif: Polebridge, 1995.

Klibansky R., and C. Labowsky, eds. *Corpus Platonicum Medii Aevi: Plato Latinus*. Vol. 3. London: Warburg Institute, 1953.

Klijn, A. F. J. "An Early Christian Baptismal Liturgy." Pages 216–28 in *Charis kai Sophia: Festchrift Karl Rengstorf*. Edited by U. Luck. Leiden: Brill, 1964.

Krämer, H. J. *Der Ursprung der Geistmetaphysik: Untersuchungen zur Geschichte des Platonismus Zwischen Platon und Plotin*. 2d ed. Amsterdam: B. R. Grüner, 1967.

Kroll, W. "Ein neuplatonischer Parmenides-kommentar in einem Turiner Palimsest." *Rheinisches Museum für Philosophie* 48 (1892): 599–627.

Lampe, G. W. H. *A Patristic Greek Lexicon*. Oxford: Oxford University Press, 1961.

Layton, B. *The Gnostic Scriptures*. New York: Doubleday, 1987.

————, ed. *The Rediscovery of Gnosticism: Proceedings of the International Conference on Gnosticism at Yale, New Haven, Connecticut, March 28–31, 1978*. Vol. 1: *The School of Valentinus*. Vol. 2: *Sethian Gnosticism*. SHR 41. Leiden: Brill, 1980–1981.

Lear, J. *Aristotle: The Desire to Understand*. Cambridge: Cambridge University Press, 1988.

Lewy, H. *Chaldean Oracles and Theurgy: Mysticism, Magic, and Platonism in the Later Roman Empire*. Recherches d'archéologie et de philosophe et d'histoire 13. Cairo, 1956. New edition edited by M. Tardieu. Paris: Études augustiniennes, 1978.

Lilla, S. R. C. *Clement of Alexandria: A Study in Christian Platonism and Gnosticism*. London: Oxford University Press, 1971.

Linguiti, A. "Commentarium in Platonis «Parmenidem»." Pages 63–202 in *Corpus dei Papiri Filosofici Greci e Latini*. Part 3: *Commentari*. Firenze: L. S. Olschki, 1995.

————. "Giamblico, Proclo, e Damascio Sul Principio Anteriore All'Uno." *Elenchos* 9 (1988): 95–106.

Lloyd, A. C. *The Anatomy of Neoplatonism*. Oxford: Oxford University Press, 1990.

————. "Plotinus on the Genesis of Thought and Existence." Pages 155–86 in *Oxford Studies in Ancient Philosophy*. Edited by Julia Annas. Oxford: Clarendon Press, 1987.

Lowry, J. N. P. *The Logical Principles of Proclus' STOICHEIÔSIS THEO- LOGIKÊ As Systematic Ground of the Cosmos*. Amsterdam: Rodopi, 1980.

Majercik, R. *The Chaldean Oracles: Text, Translation, and Commentary*. Studies in Greek and Roman Religion 5. Leiden: Brill, 1989.

————. "The Existence-Life-Intellect Triad in Gnosticism and Neoplatonism." *CQ* 42 (1992): 475–88.

Mansfeld, J. "Compatible Alternatives: Middle Platonist Theology and the Xenophanes Reception." Pages 92–117 in *Knowledge of God in the Graeco-Roman World*. Edited by R. van den Broek, T. Baarda and J. Mansfeld. EPRO 112. Leiden: Brill, 1988.

Markus, R. A., and H. J. Blumenthal, eds. *Neoplatonism and Early Christian Thought: Essays in Honour of A. H. Armstrong*. London: Variorum, 1981.

Massagli, M. "Amelio Neoplatonico e la Metafisica del Nous." *Rivista di filosofia neo-scolastica* 74 (1982): 225–43.

Matter, P. P. *Zum Einfluss des Platonischen "Timaeus" auf das Denken Plotins*. Winterthur: Keller, 1964.

Meeks, W. "The Image of the Androgyne: Some Uses of a Symbol in Earliest Christianity." *HR* 13 (1974): 165–211.

Meijer, P. A. *Plotinus on the Good or the One (Ennead VI, 9): An Analytical Commentary*. Amsterdam classical monographs 1. Amsterdam: J. C. Gieben, 1992.

Merlan, P. *Monopsychism Mysticism Metaconsciousness*. The Hague: Martinus Nijhoff, 1963.

Miller, J. *Measures of Wisdom: The Cosmic Dance in Classical and Christian Antiquity*. Toronto: University of Toronto Press, 1986.

Miller, P. C. "In Praise of Nonsense." Pages 481–505 in *Classical Mediterranean Spirituality: Egyptian, Greek, Roman*. Edited by A. H. Armstrong. New York: Crossroad, 1986.

Müller, K. "Beiträge zum Verständnis der valentinianischen Gnosis." Pages 179–242 in *Nachrichten von der Königlichen: Gesellschaft der Wissenschaften zu Göttingen*. Philologisch-historische Klasse. Göttingen: Dieterichschen Buchhandlung, 1920.

Nussbaum, M. *Aristotle's De Motu Animalium*. Princeton, N. J.: Princeton University Press, 1978.

O'Brien, D. "Plotinus and the Gnostics on the Generation of Matter." Pages 108–23 in *Neoplatonism and Early Christian Thought: Essays in Honour of A. H. Armstrong*. Edited by H. J. Blumenthal and R. A. Markus. London: Variorum, 1981.

———. "Plotinus on Evil: A Study of Matter and the Soul in Plotinus' Conception of Human Evil." Pages 114–46 in *Le Néoplatonisme: Colloque international sur le néoplatonisme, Royaumont, 9–13 juin 1969*. Paris: Éditions du CNRS, sciences humaines, 1971.

———. *Plotinus on the Origin of Matter. An Exercise in the Interpretation of the Enneads*. Napoli: Bibliopolis, 1991.

———. *Théodicée plotinienne, théodicée gnostique*. Leiden: Brill, 1993.

O'Brien, E. *The Essential Plotinus*. New York: Mentor Books, 1964.

O'Meara, D. J. "Gnosticism and the Making of the World in Plotinus." Pages 364–78 in *The Rediscovery of Gnosticism: Proceedings of the International Conference on Gnosticism at Yale, New Haven, Connecticut, March 28–31, 1978*. Vol. 1: *The School of Valentinus*. Edited by B. Layton. SHR 41. Leiden: Brill, 1980.

———. *Plotinus: An Introduction to the Enneads*. Oxford: Clarendon Press, 1993.

———, ed. *Neoplatonism and Christian Thought*. Albany: SUNY Press, 1982.

Parma, C. *Pronoia und Providentia: Der Vorsehungsbegriff Plotins und Augustins*. Leiden: Brill, 1971.

Parrott, D. M. "Eugnostos and 'All the Philosophers.'" Pages 153–67 in *Religion im Erbe Ägyptens: Beiträge zur spätantiken Religionsgeschichte zur Ehren von Alexander Böhlig*. Edited by Manfred Görg. Ägypten und Altes Testament 14. Wiesbaden: Otto Haarassowitz, 1988.

Pearson, B. A. "The Figure of Norea in Gnostic Literature." Pages 143–52 in *Proceedings of the International Colloquium on Gnosticism, Stockholm, August 20–25, 1973*. Edited by G. Widengren. Kungl. Vitterhets historie och antikvitets akademiens handlingar. Filologisk-filosofiska serien 17. Stockholm: Almqvist & Wiksell, 1977.

———. "Gnosticism and Platonism: With Special Reference to *Marsanes* (NHC 10,1)." *HTR* 77 (1984): 55–73. Repr. as "Gnosticism As Platonism." Pages 52–83 in *Gnosticism, Judaism, and Egyptian Christianity*. SAC 5. Minneapolis: Fortress, 1990.

———. *Gnosticism, Judaism, and Egyptian Christianity*. SAC 5. Minneapolis: Fortress, 1990.

———. "Introduction" to *Marsanes* (NHC X). Pages 229–50 in *Nag Hammadi Codices IX and X*. Edited by B. A. Pearson. NHS 15. Leiden: Brill, 1981.

———. "Theurgic Tendencies in Gnosticism and Iamblichus' Conception of Theurgy." Pages 253–76 in *Neoplatonism and Gnosticism*. Edited by R. T. Wallis and J. Bregman. Studies in Neoplatonism: Ancient and Modern 6. Albany: SUNY Press, 1992.

———. "The Tractate Marsanes (NHC X) and the Platonic Tradition." Pages 373–84 in *Gnosis: Festschrift für Hans Jonas*. Edited by B. Aland. Göttingen: Vandenhoeck & Ruprecht, 1978.

———, ed. *Nag Hammadi Codex VII*. Nag Hammadi and Manichaean Studies 30. Leiden: Brill, 1996.

———. *Nag Hammadi Codices IX and X*. NHS 15. Leiden: Brill, 1981.

Pépin, J. "Eléments pour une histoire de la relation entre l'intelligence et l'intelligible chez Platon et dans le néoplatonisme." *Revue de philosophie* 146 (1956): 39–64.

———. "Plotin et les mythes." *Rivista di filosofia e di lettere* 53 (1955): 5–27.

Perkins, P. "Beauty, Number, and Loss of Order in the Gnostic Cosmos." Pages 277–96 in *Neoplatonism and Gnosticism*. Edited by R. T. Wallis and J. Bregman. Studies in Neoplatonism: Ancient and Modern 6. Albany: SUNY Press.

Peters, F. E. *Greek Philosophical Terms*. New York: New York University Press, 1967.

Peterson, E. "Einige Bemerkungen zum Hamburger Papyrus-Fragment der Acta Pauli." Pages 194–96 in *Frühkirche, Judentum und Gnosis: Studien und Untersuchungen*. Rome: Freiburg; Vienna: Herder, 1959.

Peyron, B. "Notizia d'un antico evangeliario bobbiese che in alcuni fogli palimpsesti contiene frammenti d'un greco tratato di filosofia." *Rivista di filologia e di istruzione classica* 1 (1873): 53–71.

Poduval, R. *Kathākil and the Diagram of Hand Poses*. Trivandrum: Department of Archaeology, Travancore State, 1930.

Priscianus Lydus [Ps. Simplicius]. *In Aristotelis libros de anima commentaria.* Pages 1–329 in *Simplicii in libros Aristotelis de anima commentaria.* Edited by M. Hayduck. Commentaria in Aristotelem Graeca 11. Berlin: Reimer, 1882.

Puech, H.-C. "Plotin et les gnostiques." Pages 161–74 (discussion, 175–90) in *Les sources de Plotin.* Entretiens sur l'antiquité 5. Vandoeuvres-Genève: Fondation Hardt, 1960.

Rist, J. M. "Monism: Plotinus and Some Predecessors." *HSCP* 69 (1965): 329–44.

Robinson, J. M. "On the *Gattung* of Mark (and John)." In *Jesus and Man's Hope: 175th Anniversary Festival on the Gospels at Pittsburgh Theological Seminary. Perspective* 11.2 (1970): 99–129.

———. "*The Three Steles of Seth* and the Gnostics of Plotinus." Pages 132–42 in *Proceedinqs of the International Colloquium on Gnosticism, Stockholm, August 20–25, 1973.* Edited by G. Widengren. Kungl. Vitterhets Historie ock Antikvitets Akademiens Handlingar, Filologisk-filosofiska serien 17. Stockholm: Almqvist & Wiksell; Leiden: Brill, 1977.

Robinson, J. M., and R. Smith, eds. *The Nag Hammadi Library in English.* 3d rev. ed. Leiden: Brill; San Francisco: Harper & Row, 1988.

Rudolph, K. *Gnosis: The Nature and History of Gnosticism.* Translated by R. McL. Wilson. San Francisco: Harper & Row, 1983.

———. *Die Mandäer.* Vol 2: *Der Kult.* FRLANT NS 57. Göttingen: Vandenhoeck & Ruprecht, 1961.

Runia, D. T., ed. *Plotinus amid Gnostics and Christians: Papers Presented at the Plotinus Symposium Held at the Free University, Amsterdam, on 25 January 1984.* Amsterdam: VU Uitgeverij/Free University Press, 1984.

Rutten, C. *Les catégories du monde sensible dans les Ennéades de Plotin.* Paris: Les Belles Lettres, 1961.

Saffrey, H. D., and L. G. Westerink, eds. *Proclus: Théologie platonicienne.* 6 vols. Collection des universités de France. Paris: Les Belles Lettres, 1968–1997.

Schenke, H.-M. "Das Evangelium nach Philippus." *TLZ* 84 (1959): 1–26.

———. "The Phenomenon and Significance of Gnostic Sethianism." Pages 588–616 in *The Rediscovery of Gnosticism: Proceedings of the International Conference on Gnosticism at Yale, New Haven,*

Connecticut, March 28–31, 1978. Vol. 2: *Sethian Gnosticism.* Edited by B. Layton. SHR 41. Leiden: Brill, 1980.

Schenke, H.-M., and J. Leipoldt. "Koptisch-gnostiche Schriften aus den Papyrus-Codices von Nag-Hammadi." *TF* 20 (1960): 35–38.

Schmidt, C. *Plotins Stellung zum Gnosticismus und Kirchlichen Christentum.* TUGAL 20. Leipzig: J. C. Hinrichs, 1901.

Schoedel, W. R. "'Topological' Theology and Some Monistic Tendencies in Gnosticism." Pages 88–108 in *Essays on the Nag Hammadi Texts in Honour of Alexander Böhlig.* Edited by M. Krause. NHS, 3. Leiden: Brill, 1972.

Schroeder, F. M. "Ammonius Saccas." *ANRW* 2.36.1:493–526.

———. "Conversion and Consciousness in Plotinus. *Enneads* 5, 1 (10) 7." *Hermes* 114 (1986): 186–95.

———. *Form and Transformation: A Study in the Philosophy of Plotinus.* Montreal: McGill-Queen's, 1992.

———. "Friendship in Aristotle and Some Peripatetic Philosophers." Pages 35–57 in *Greco-Roman Perceptions on Friendship.* Edited by J. Fitzgerald. Atlanta: Scholars Press, 1997.

———. "Presence and Dependence in the Plotinian Philosophy of Consciousness: *Sunousia, Sunaisthêsis* and *Sunesis.*" *ANRW* 2.36.1:677–99.

———. Review of W. Beierwaltes, *Selbsterkenntnis und Erfahrung der Einheit. Plotins Enneade V.3. Text, Übersetzung, Interpretation, Erläuterungen. Ancient Philosophy* 14 (1994): 469–75.

Schubert, V. *Pronoia und Logos: Die Rechtfertigung der Weltordnung bei Plotin.* Munich: Anton Pustet, 1968.

Schwyzer, H.-R. "Zu Plotins Deutung der sogenannten Platonischen Materie." Pages 266–80 in *Zetesis: Album amicorum door vrienden en collega's aangeboden aan Prof. Dr. E. de Strycker ter gelegenheid van zijn 65e verjaardag.* Antwerp: De Nederlandsche Boekhandel, 1973.

Segelberg, E. "The Baptismal Rite according to the Coptic-Gnostic Texts of Nag Hammadi." Pages 117–28 in *Studia Patristica.* V. Edited by F. L. Cross. TU 80. Berlin: Akademie, 1962.

———. "The Coptic-Gnostic Gospel according to Philip and Its Sacramental System." *Numen* 7 (1960): 189–200.

———. "The Gospel of Philip and the New Testament." Pages 204–12 in *The New Testament and Gnosis: Essays in Honour of Robert McL.*

Wilson. Edited by A. H. B. Logan and A. J. M. Wedderburn. Edinburgh: T&T Clark, 1983.

———. *Masbuta: Studies in the Ritual of Mandaean Baptism.* Uppsala: Almqvist & Wiksells, 1958.

———. "Prayer among the Gnostics? The Evidence of Some Nag Hammadi Documents." Pages 55–69 in *Gnosis and Gnosticism: Papers Read at the Seventh International Conference on Patristic Studies (Oxford, September 8th–13th, 1975).* Edited by M. Krause. NHS 7. Leiden: Brill, 1977.

Sevrin, J.-M. *Le dossier baptismal Séthien: Études sur la sacramentaire gnostique.* BCNHE 2. Québec: Presses de l'Université Laval, 1986.

———. "Les noces spirituelles dans l'Evangile selon Philippe." *Muséon* 87 (1974): 143–93.

———. "Practique et doctrine des sacraments dans l'Evagile selon Philippe." Th.D. diss. Catholic University of Louvain, 1972.

Shaw, G. *Theurgy and the Soul: The Neoplatonism of Iamblichus.* University Park: Pennsylvania State University Press, 1995.

Sieber, J. H. "An Introduction to the Tractate *Zostrianos* from Nag Hammadi." *NovT* 15 (1973): 233–40.

———. "Introduction" to *Zostrianos* (NHC VIII, *1*). In *Nag Hammadi Codex VIII.* Edited by J. H. Sieber. NHS 31. Leiden: Brill, 1991.

———, ed. *Nag Hammadi Codex VIII.* NHS 31. Leiden: Brill, 1991.

Silesius, A. *Sämtliche Poetische Werke.* Edited by H. L. Held. 3 vols. Munich: Carl Hansen, 1949.

Simon, J. *Histoire d l'école d'Alexandrie.* 2 vols. Paris: Joubert, 1843–1845.

Sinige, Th. G. "Gnostic Influences in the Early Works of Plotinus and Augustine." Pages 73–97 in *Plotinus amid Gnostics and Christians: Papers Presented at the Plotinus Symposium Held at the Free University, Amsterdam, on 25 January 1984.* Edited by D. T. Runia. Amsterdam: VU Uitgeverij/Free University Press, 1984.

Smith, A. "Porphyrian Studies since 1913." *ANRW* 2.36.2:717–73.

———. *Porphyrii philosophi fragmenta.* Leipzig: Teubner, 1993.

———. *Porphyry's Place in the Neoplatonic Tradition: A Study in Post-Plotinian Neoplatonism.* The Hague: M. Nijhoff, 1974.

Smith, J. Z. "The Garments of Shame." *HR* 5 (1965): 217–38.

————. *Map Is Not Territory: Studies in the History of Religions.* SJLA 23. Leiden: Brill, 1978.

Solmsen, F. "Aristotle's Word for Matter." Pages 393–408 in *Didascaliae: Studies in Honour of A. M. Albareda, Prefect of the Vatican Library.* Edited by S. Prete. New York: B. M. Rosenthal, 1961.

Spoerri, W. *Spräthellenistische Berichte über Welt, Kultur und Götter.* Schweitzerische Beiträge zur Altertumswissenschaft 9. Basel: F. Reinhardt, 1959.

Stead, G. C. "The Valentinian Myth of Sophia." *JTS* NS 20 (1969): 75–104.

Steel, C. *The Changing Self: A Study on the Soul in Later Neoplatonism: Iamblichus, Damascius and Priscianus.* Verhandelingen van de Koninklijke Academie voor Wetenschappen, Letteren en Schone Kunsten van België, Klasse der Letteren 40.85. Brussel: Palais der Academien, 1978.

Stewart, J. A. *Notes on The Nicomachean Ethics.* New York: Arno, 1973. Repr. of 1892 ed., Oxford: Clarendon Press.

Strange, S. "Plotinus' Treatise 'On the Genera of Being.'" Ph.D. diss. University of Texas at Austin, 1981.

Sumney, J. L. "The Letter of Eugnostos and the Origins of Gnosticism." *NovT* 31 (1989): 172–81.

Szlezák, T. *Platon und Aristoteles in der Nuslehre Plotins.* Basel: Schwabe, 1979.

————. "Speusipp und die metaphysische Deutung von Platons 'Parmenides.'" Pages 339–73 in *En kai Plêthos: Festschrift für Karl Bormann zum 65. Geburtstag.* Edited by L. Hagemann. Würzburg: Echter, 1993.

Taormina, D. P. *Plutarco di Atene. l'Uno, l'anima, le forme: saggio introduttivo, fonti, traduzione e commento.* Catania: Università di Catanio; Rome: L'Erma di Bretschneider. Centro di studi sull'antico Cristianésimo, Università di Catania, 1989.

Tardieu, M. *Écrits gnostiques: Codex de Berlin.* Sources Gnostiques et Manichéennes 1. Paris: Cerf, 1984.

————. "Recherches sur la formation de l'Apocalypse de Zostrien et les sources de Marius Victorinus." Pages 7–114 in *Res Orientales 9.* Bures-sur-Yvette: Groupe pour l'Étude de la Civilisation du Moyen-Orient, 1996.

————. "Les trois stèles Seth." *RSPT* 57 (1973): 545–75.

Thedinga, F. "Plotin oder Numenius." *Hermes* 54 (1919): 249–78.

Thomassen, E. "The Philosophical Dimension in Gnosticism: the Valentinian System." Pages 69–79 in *Understanding and History in Arts and Sciences*. Edited by R. Skarsten et al. Acta Humaniora Universitatis Bergensis 1. Oslo: Solum, 1991.

Thomassen, E., and L. Painchaud. *Le Traité Tripartite (NH I, 5)*. BCNHT 19. Québec: Les Presses de l'Université Laval, 1989.

Thomson, J. A. K. *The Ethics of Aristotle*. New York: Penguin, 1955.

Trakatellis, D. *The Transcendent God of Eugnostos*. Translated by C. Sarelis. Brookline, Mass.: Holy Cross Orthodox Press, 1991.

Trautmann, C. "Organization communautaire et pratiques rituelles." *Histoire et archéologie* 70 (1983): 44–51.

Tripp, D. H. "The 'Sacramental System' of the Gospel of Philip." Pages 251–60 in vol. 1 of *Studia Patristica XVII in Three Parts*. Edited by E. A. Livingstone. Oxford: Pergamon , 1982.

Trouillard, J. *La purification plotinienne*. Paris: Presses Universitaires de France, 1955.

Turcan, R. *The Cults of the Roman Empire*. Translated by A. Nevill. Oxford and Cambridge, Mass: Blackwell, 1996.

Turner, J. D. "Allogenes: Coptic Text, English Translation, and Notes." Pages 192–267 in *Nag Hammadi Codices XI, XI, XIII*. Edited by C. W. Hedrick. NHS 18. Leiden: Brill, 1990.

———. "The Gnostic Threefold Path to Enlightenment." *NovT* 22 (1980): 324–51.

———. "Gnosticism and Platonism: The Platonizing Sethian Texts from Nag Hammadi in Their Relation to Later Platonic Literature." Pages 425–59 in *Neoplatonism and Gnosticism*. Edited by R. T. Wallis and J. Bregman. Studies in Neoplatonism: Ancient and Modern 6. Albany: SUNY Press, 1992.

———. Introduction to *Trimorphic Protennoia (XIII, 1)*. Pages 511–13 in *The Nag Hammadi Library in English*. Edited by J. M. Robinson and R. Smith. 3d rev. ed. Leiden: Brill; San Francisco: Harper & Row, 1988.

———. "Ritual in Gnosticism." Pages 136–81 in *SBL Seminar Papers, 1994*. SBLSP 33. Atlanta: Scholars Press, 1994. [Revised version in this volume.]

————. "Sethian Gnosticism: A Literary History." Pages 55–86 in *Nag Hammadi, Gnosticism, and Early Christianity*. Edited by C. W. Hedrick and R. Hodgson. Peabody, Mass: Hendrickson, 1986.

————. "Typologies of the Sethian Gnostic Treaties from Nag Hammadi." Pages 169–217 in *Les textes de Nag Hammadi et le problème de leur classification: Actes du Colloque tenu à Québec du 15 au 22 Septembre, 1992*. Edited by L. Painchaud and A. Pasquier. Québec: Les Presses de l'Université Laval; Louvain: Peeters, 1995.

Turner, V. W. "Betwixt and Between: The Liminal Period in Rites of Passage." In *The Forest of Symbols: Aspects of Ndembu Ritual*. Ithaca, N.Y.: Cornell University Press, 1967.

Unnik, W. C. van. "Die Gotteslehre bei Aristides und in gnostischen Schriften." *TZ* 17 (1961): 166–74.

Vacherot, E. *Histoire critique de l'école d'Alexandrie*. 3 vols. Paris: Lagrange, 1846–1851. Repr., Amsterdam: Adolf M. Hakkerty, 1965.

Van den Broek, R. "Eugnostos and Aristides on the Ineffable God." Pages 202–18 in *Knowledge of God in the Graeco-Roman World*. Edited by R. Van den Broek, T. Baarda and J. Mansfeld. EPRO 112. Leiden: Brill, 1988.

————. *Studies in Gnosticism and Alexandrian Christianity*. NHMS 39. Leiden: Brill, 1996.

Van den Broek, R., T. Baarda and J. Mansfeld, eds. *Knowledge of God in the Graeco-Roman World*. EPRO 112. Leiden: Brill, 1988.

Van Winden, J. C. M. *Calcidius on Matter: His Doctrine and Sources*. Philosophia Antiqua 9. Leiden: Brill, 1959.

Vigne, D. "Enquête sur Basilide." Pages 285–313 in *Recherches et Tradition: Mélanges patristiques offerts à Henri Crouzel, S.J., professeur honoraire à la Faculté de théologie de l'Institut catholique de Toulouse*. Edited by A. Dupleix. ThH 88. Paris: Beauchesne, 1992.

Wachsmuth, C., and O. Hense, eds. *Stobaeus Anthologium*. Berlin: Weidmanns, 1884–1912. Repr., 1958.

Waldstein, M. *The Apocryphon of John: A Curious Eddy in the Stream of Hellenistic Judaism*. Draft version.

Wallis, R. T. *Neoplatonism*. London: Duckworth, 1972.

Wallis, R. T. "The Spiritual Importance of Not Knowing." Pages 460–80 in *Classical Mediterranean Spirituality: Egyptian, Greek, Roman*. Edited by A. H. Armstrong. World Spirituality 15. New York: Crossroad, 1986.

Wallis, R. T., and J. Bregman, eds. *Neoplatonism and Gnosticism*. Studies in Neoplatonism: Ancient and Modern 6. Albany: SUNY Press, 1992.

Westerink, L. G. *The Greek Commentaries on Plato's Phaedo I*. Amsterdam: North-Holland Publishing, 1976.

Whitaker, E. C. *Documents of the Baptismal Liturgy*. London: SPCK, 1970.

Whittaker, J., and P. Louis, eds. and trans. *Alcinoos: Enseignement des doctrines de Platon*. Paris: Les Belles Lettres, 1990.

Williams, M. A. "Negative Theologies and Demiurgical Myths in Late Antiquity." Pages 20–46 in *SBL Seminar Papers, 1997*. SBLSP 36. Atlanta: Scholars Press, 1994. [Reprinted in this volume.]

————. *Rethinking "Gnosticism": An Argument for Dismantling a Dubious Category*. Princeton, N. J.: Princeton University Press, 1996.

Wilson, R. McL. *The Gospel of Philip: Translated from the Coptic text, with an Introduction and Commentary*. New York: Harper & Row, 1962.

Wire, A. "Introduction," to *Allogenes* in *Nag Hammadi Codices XI, XII and XIII*. Edited by C. W. Hedrick. NHS 28; Leiden: Brill, 1990.

Wolfson, E. R., *Through a Speculum That Shines: Vision and Imagination in Medieval Jewish Mysticism*. Princeton, N. J.: Princeton University Press, 1994.

Wundt, M. "Platons Parmenides." *Tübinger Beiträge zur Altertumswissenschaft* 25 (1935): 24–26.

Wurm, K. *Substanz und Qualität: Ein Beitrage zur Interpretation der plotinischen Traktate VI 1, 2 und 3*. Quellen und Studien zur Philosophie 5. Berlin and New York: de Gruyter, 1973.

Ysebaert, J. *Greek Baptismal Terminology: Its Origins and Early Development*. Graecitus Christianorum Primeva 1. Nijmegen: Dekker & Van de Vegt, 1962.

Zandee, J. *The Terminology of Plotinus and of Some Gnostic Writings, Mainly The Fourth Treatise of the Jung Codex*. Uitgaven van het Nederlands Historisch-Archaeologisch Instituut te istanbul 11. Istanbul: Nederlands Historisch-Archaeologisch Insituut in het Nabije Oosten, 1961.

Zeller, E. *Die Philosophie der Griechen in ihrer geschichtlichen Entwick-lung*. Vol. 3, ii (5). Revised by E. Wellmann. Leipzig: O. R. Reisland, 1923.

Zintzen, C. *Damascius, Vitae Isidori Reliquiae*. Bibliotheca Graeca et Latina suppletoria 1. Hildesheim: G. Olms, 1967.